INTERNATIONAL SERIES OF MONOGRAPHS IN
PURE AND APPLIED MATHEMATICS
GENERAL EDITORS: I. N. SNEDDON AND M. STARK
EXECUTIVE EDITORS: J. P. KAHANE, A. P. ROBERTSON AND S. ULAM

VOLUME 100

THEORY OF AUTOMATA

THEORY OF
AUTOMATA

ARTO SALOMAA
Professor of Mathematics,
University of Turku, Finland

THE QUEEN'S AWARD
TO INDUSTRY 1966

PERGAMON PRESS
OXFORD · LONDON · EDINBURGH · NEW YORK
TORONTO · SYDNEY · PARIS · BRAUNSCHWEIG

Pergamon Press Ltd., Headington Hill Hall, Oxford
4 & 5 Fitzroy Square, London W.1
Pergamon Press (Scotland) Ltd., 2 & 3 Teviot Place, Edinburgh 1
Pergamon Press Inc., Maxwell House, Fairview Park, Elmsford, New York 10523
Pergamon of Canada Ltd., 207 Queen's Quay West, Toronto 1
Pergamon Press (Aust.) Pty. Ltd., 19a Boundary Street, Rushcutters Bay,
N.S.W. 2011, Australia
Pergamon Press S.A.R.L., 24 rue des Écoles, Paris 5e
Vieweg & Sohn GmbH, Burgplatz 1, Braunschweig

© 1969 A. Salomaa

First edition 1969

Library of Congress Catalog Card No. 71-76796

Printed in Hungary
08 013376 2

ERRATA
Theory of Automata by Arto Salomaa

p. xi, last line: *add* date November 1967

p. 2, 1. 17: *for* $x_1^2)^i$ *read* $(x_1^2)^i$

p. 4, 1.–8: *for* $((\alpha\beta) + (\beta\gamma))$ *read* $((\alpha\gamma) + (\beta\gamma))$

p. 63, 1. 13: *for* 2201^2 *read* $201^2 2$

p. 82, lines –9 and –10: *add* index j to p′

p.118, 1. 5: *for* γ_μ *read* $|\gamma_\mu|$

p. 140, 1. 10: *add* + in front of a_{n-1}

p. 179, 1.–3: *for* Xj *read* X_j

p. 179, last line: *for* L^ϕ *read* L_ϕ

p. 183, 1.–10: *for* L *read* L_2

p. 183, 1.–9: *for* b *read* be

p. 210, 1.–5: *for* $^B X$ *read* $^B x$

p. 256, 2nd column, 1. 10: *for* 214 *read* 213

To my wife
and children Kai and Kirsti

CONTENTS

PREFACE

THE past ten years have witnessed the vigorous growth of mathematical disciplines concerning models for information-processing. In addition to the classical theory of mechanically executable processes (or Turing machines, algorithms or recursive functions), attention has been focused on more restricted models such as finite deterministic automata which were investigated originally in connection with sequential switching circuits. The results are so numerous and diverse that, although one would limit the choice to material independent of technological developments, one could still write several books entitled "Theory of Automata" with no or very little common material. Even for the same material, the approach can vary from an engineering oriented one to a highly abstracted mathematical treatment.

In selecting material for this book, I have had two principles in mind. In the first place, I have considered the finite deterministic automaton as the basic model. All other models, such as finite non-deterministic and probabilistic automata as well as pushdown and linear bounded automata, are treated as generalizations of this basic model. Secondly, the formalism chosen to describe finite deterministic automata is that of regular expressions. To give a detailed exposition regarding this formalism, I have included a separate chapter on the algebra of regular expressions.

This book deals with mathematical aspects of automata theory, rather than applications. However, I have tried to avoid unnecessary abstractions because no advanced mathematical background is assumed on the part of the reader. The reader is supposed to be familiar with the very basic notions in set theory, algebra and probability theory. One of the reasons for the choice of the formalism of regular expressions (rather than predicate calculus or more algebraic formalisms) was that it can be developed very briefly *ab ovo*.

This book is self-contained. All results stated as theorems are proven (except for minor details and proofs analogous to earlier proofs which are sometimes left as exercises). Some results are mentioned without-proofs in Sections 3, 4 and 7 of Chapter IV. The level of presentation corresponds to that of beginning graduate or advanced undergraduate work. An attempt has been made to cover also the most recent developments.

Exercises form an important part of the book. They are theoretical rather than "numerical". Many of them contain material which could equally well be treated in the text. However, the text is independent of the exercises (except for some minor points in the proofs). Because some exercises are very difficult, the reader is encouraged to consult the given reference works. In addition to the exercises, there are also "problems" at the end of some sections. The problems are topics suggested for research.

Both of the Chapters III and IV can be studied also independently, provided they are supplemented with a few definitions. A reader who wants only the basic facts concerning various types of automata may read only Sections 1, 2 and 4 of Chapter I, 1 and 2 of Chapter II and 1–8 of Chapter IV. These sections form a self-contained "short course". Thereby, some of the more difficult proofs in Chapter IV may be omitted.

ACKNOWLEDGEMENTS

THIS book has been written during my stay with the Computer Science Department of the University of Western Ontario. I want to thank the Head of the Department, Dr. J. F. Hart, for providing me the opportunity to work within such a stimulating atmosphere. Special thanks are due to Dr. Neil Jones whose sophistication in formal languages has been of an invaluable help in the preparation of many sections in the book. Of the other members of the Department, I want to thank especially Mr. Andrew Szilard for many fruitful discussions and critical suggestions. Of my colleagues at the University of Turku, I express my gratitude to Professor K. Inkeri for much encouragement and help during many years. I want to thank also Professor Lauri Pimiä for planning and drawing the figures and Messrs. Magnus Steinby and Paavo Turakainen for reading the manuscript and making many useful comments.

ARTO SALOMAA

London, Ontario

NOTE TO THE READER

REFERENCES to theorems, equations, etc., without a roman numeral mean the item in the chapter where the reference is made. References to other chapters are indicated by roman numerals. Thus, (I.2.1) means the equation (2.1) in Chapter I and Problem III.6.1 means Problem 6.1 in Chapter III.

We use customary set theoretic notations. In particular, $A \times B$ denotes the Cartesian product of the sets A and B, and

$$\{x \,|\, P_1, \ldots, P_k\}$$

denotes the set of all elements x which possess each of the properties $P_1, \ldots, P_k$.

The symbol $\square$ is used to mark the end of the proof of a theorem. Throughout the book, the expression "if and only if" is abbreviated as "iff".

CHAPTER I

FINITE DETERMINISTIC AUTOMATA

AUTOMATA are mathematical models of devices which process information by giving responses to inputs. Models for discrete deterministic computing devices possessing a finite memory will be our concern in this chapter. Their behavior at a particular time instant depends not only on the latest input but on the entire sequence of past inputs. They are capable of only a finite number of inputs, internal states and outputs and are, furthermore, deterministic in the sense that an input sequence uniquely determines the output behavior.

§ 1. Regular languages

By an *alphabet* we mean a non-empty set. The elements of an alphabet I are called *letters*. In most cases, we shall consider only finite alphabets. Sometimes a subscript is used to indicate the number of letters. Thus, I_r is an alphabet with r letters.

A *word* over an alphabet I is a finite string consisting of zero or more letters of I, whereby the same letter may occur several times. The string consisting of zero letters is called the *empty word*, written λ. Thus

$$\lambda, \quad x_1, \quad x_1x_2x_2, \quad x_1x_1x_1x_1x_1, \quad x_2x_2x_1x_2$$

are words over the alphabet $I_2 = \{x_1, x_2\}$. The set of all words over an alphabet I is denoted by $W(I)$. Clearly, $W(I)$ is infinite.

If P and Q are words over an alphabet I, then their *catenation PQ* is also a word over I. Clearly, catenation is an associative operation and the empty word λ is an identity with respect to catenation: $P\lambda = \lambda P = P$, for any word P. For a word P and a natural number i, the notation P^i means the word obtained by catenating i copies of the word P. P^0 denotes the empty word λ.

By the *length* of a word P, in symbols $\lg(P)$, is meant the number of letters in P when each letter is counted as many times as it occurs. By definition, $\lg(\lambda) = 0$. The length function possesses some of the formal properties of logarithm:

$$\lg(PQ) = \lg(P) + \lg(Q),$$
$$\lg(P^i) = i\,\lg(P), \quad \text{for } i \geqq 0.$$

A word P is a *subword* of a word Q iff there are words P_1 and P_2, possibly empty, such that $Q = P_1 P P_2$. If $P_1 = \lambda$ ($P_2 = \lambda$), then P is termed an *initial* (a *final*) subword of Q. If P is a subword of Q, then clearly $\lg(P) \leqq \lg(Q)$.

Subsets of $W(I)$ are referred to as *languages* over the alphabet I. For instance, the following sets are languages over the alphabet $I_2 = \{x_1, x_2\}$:

$$L_1 = \{x_1 x_2 x_2, x_1 x_2 x_1, \ x_1 x_2 x_1 x_2\},$$
$$L_2 = \{\lambda, \ x_1, \ x_2, \ x_1 x_1, \ x_1 x_2, \ x_2 x_1, \ x_2 x_2\},$$
$$L_3 = \{x_1^p \,|\, p \text{ prime}\},$$
$$L_4 = \{(x_1^2)^i \,|\, i \text{ natural number}\},$$
$$L_5 = \{x_1^i x_2^i \,|\, i \text{ natural number}\}.$$

The languages L_1 and L_2 are *finite*, i.e. contain only a finite number of words, whereas the languages L_3–L_5 are infinite. The language L_2 consists of all words over the alphabet $\{x_1, x_2\}$ with length less than or equal to 2.

We consider also the *empty language* L_ϕ, i.e. the language containing no words. Note that L_ϕ is not the same as the language L_λ or $\{\lambda\}$ consisting of the empty word λ. Sometimes we identify an element and its unit set to simplify notation: we may denote simply by P the language $\{P\}$ consisting of the word P. In such cases, the meaning of the notation will be clear from the context.

We shall now introduce some operations for the family of languages over a fixed alphabet I. Because languages are sets, we may consider the *Boolean operations*. The *sum* or *union* of two languages L_1 and L_2 is denoted by $L_1 + L_2$, their *intersection* by $L_1 \cap L_2$, and the *complement* of a language L with respect to the set $W(I)$ by $\sim L$. We use also the notation

$$L_1 - L_2 = L_1 \cap (\sim L_2).$$

The *catenation* (or *product*) of two languages L_1 and L_2, in symbols L_1L_2, is defined to be the language

$$L_1L_2 = \{PQ \mid P \in L_1, \ Q \in L_2\}.$$

Catenation of languages is associative because catenation of words is associative. Thus, the notation L^i, $i \geq 1$, is meaningful for a language L. Furthermore, we define L^0 to be the language L_λ consisting of the empty word. Note that the languages L_ϕ and L_λ are zero and identity elements with respect to catenation of languages: for any language L, $LL_\phi = L_\phi L = L_\phi$ and $LL_\lambda = L_\lambda L = L$.

The *catenation closure* (or *iteration*) of a language L, in symbols L^*, is defined to be the sum of all powers of L:

$$L^* = \sum_{i=0}^{\infty} L^i.$$

Later on, we shall define some further operations for the family of languages.

We shall now introduce the notion of a *regular expression* which will be one of the basic notions in our subsequent discussions. Consider the auxiliary alphabet

$$I' = \{+, \ ^*, \ \phi, \ (,)\}$$

and any alphabet I such that I and I' are disjoint. A *regular expression* over the alphabet I is any word over the union of the alphabets I and I' which satisfies the condition formulated in the following

DEFINITION. (i) Each letter belonging to the alphabet I is a regular expression over I, and so is the letter ϕ.

(ii) If α and β are regular expressions over I, then so are also $(\alpha+\beta)$, $(\alpha\beta)$ and α^*.

(iii) Nothing is a regular expression over I, unless its being so follows from a finite number of applications of (i) and (ii).

Thus, for instance,

$$\phi, \ \phi^*, \ x_1, \ (x_1+x_2), \ ((x_1+x_1)(x_1+x_2))^* \tag{1.1}$$

are regular expressions over the alphabet $I_2 = \{x_1, x_2\}$.

DEFINITION. Each regular expression γ over an alphabet I denotes a language $|\gamma|$ over I according to the following conventions:

(i) $|\phi| = L_{\phi}$.

(ii) For all letters x belonging to I, $|x| = \{x\}$.

(iii) For all regular expressions α and β over I,

$$|(\alpha+\beta)| = |\alpha|+|\beta|, \quad |(\alpha\beta)| = |\alpha| \, |\beta|, \quad |\alpha^*| = |\alpha|^*.$$

A language L is *regular* iff there is a regular expression α such that $L = |\alpha|$.

For example, the regular languages denoted by the regular expressions (1.1) contain zero, one, one, two and an infinite number of words. (Note that it follows from convention (iii) of the preceding definition and from the definition of catenation closure that $|\phi^*| = L_\lambda$.) Below are listed some of the words contained in the infinite regular language denoted by the last of the regular expressions (1.1):

$$\lambda, x_1x_1, \; x_1x_2, \; x_1x_1x_1x_1, \; x_1x_2x_1x_1x_1x_2x_1x_2.$$

Clearly, if a language L is regular, then there is a finite alphabet I such that L is a language over I.

It may happen that two different regular expressions α and β denote the same regular language. For instance, both of the regular expressions $(x+x)^*$ and x^{**} denote the language consisting of the words x^i, $i = 0, 1, \ldots$, i.e. of all words over the alphabet $\{x\}$. Similarly, both $(x+y)^*$ and $(x^*y^*)^*$ denote the language consisting of all words over the alphabet $\{x, y\}$. If α and β denote the same language, i.e. $|\alpha| = |\beta|$, then we write simply $\alpha = \beta$ and refer to this equation between the regular expressions α and β as a *valid* equation. Simple examples of valid equations are the following associative, commutative, distributive and idempotence laws:

$$(\alpha+(\beta+\gamma)) = ((\alpha+\beta)+\gamma), \quad (\alpha(\beta\gamma)) = ((\alpha\beta)\gamma), \quad (\alpha+\beta) = (\beta+\alpha),$$
$$(\alpha(\beta+\gamma)) = ((\alpha\beta)+(\alpha\gamma)), \quad ((\alpha+\beta)\gamma) = ((\alpha\beta)+(\beta\gamma)), \quad (\alpha+\alpha) = \alpha,$$

where α, β and γ are arbitrary regular expressions. By forming compositions of the three operations sum, catenation and catenation closure, we may construct very complicated valid equations whose validity is not easy to recognize. In Chapter III we shall characterize the set of valid equations axiomatically.

For convenience, unnecessary parentheses will sometimes be omitted from regular expressions. We shall make the following conventions concerning the order of strength of the three operations: catenation is performed before sum, and catenation closure before both sum and catenation. (In fact, the latter convention is due to point (ii) of the definition of a regular expression.) Thus, instead of the regular expression $(x_1+(x_2x_3))$, we may write simply $x_1+x_2x_3$. Because of the associativity, parentheses are not needed in grouping terms in sums with more than two terms and factors in catenations with more than two factors. Thus, we may write $x_1+x_2+x_3+x_4$, $x_1x_2x_2$ and x_1^5. We may also use the customary $\sum$-notation for sums, as well as the notation $(\alpha)^k$, where α is a regular expression and $k \geqq 1$. As far as the denoted languages are concerned, no confusion will arise because of these notational simplifications and we may always replace these simplified regular expressions by ones formed exactly according to the definition.

Below are listed some examples of regular languages.

EXAMPLE 1. The regular expression $(x_2+x_1x_2)^*$ denotes the language over the alphabet $\{x_1, x_2\}$ consisting of all words P such that x_2 is the last letter of P and x_1x_1 is not a subword of P and, in addition, of the empty word λ.

In the following examples, we consider the alphabet

$$I_r = \{x_1, \ldots, x_r\}$$

and an arbitrary word P over I_r.

EXAMPLE 2. $|(x_1+\ldots+x_r)^*| = W(I_r)$.

EXAMPLE 3. $(x_1+\ldots+x_r)^*P$ denotes the language consisting of words which possess P as a final subword.

EXAMPLE 4. $P(x_1+\ldots+x_r)^*$ denotes the language consisting of words which possess P as an initial subword.

EXAMPLE 5. $(x_1+\ldots+x_r)^*P(x_1+\ldots+x_r)^*$ denotes the language consisting of words which possess P as a subword.

EXAMPLE 6. $x_1+\ldots+x_r$ denotes the language consisting of all words of length 1.

EXAMPLE 7. For $k \geqq 2$, $(x_1+\ldots+x_r)^k$ denotes the language consisting of all words of length k.

EXAMPLE 8. For $k \geqq 1$, $((x_1+\ldots+x_r)^k)^*$ denotes the language consisting of all words whose length is a multiple of k.

The languages in these examples are infinite, except the languages given in Examples 6 and 7. Any language denoted by a regular expression without the star (*) is finite. Conversely, any finite language is denoted by a regular expression and, hence, is regular. (Cf. Exercise 1.1.)

EXERCISE 1.1. Show that finite languages are regular. Give examples of regular expressions involving the star (*) which denote finite languages.

EXERCISE 1.2. By the *mirror image* mi (P) of a word $P = x_1x_2 \ldots x_k$ we mean the word $x_k \ldots x_2x_1$. By definition, mi $(\lambda) = \lambda$. The mirror image mi (L) of a language L consists of the mirror images of the words in L. Using the fact that mi (mi (L)) $= L$, show that mi (L) is regular iff L is regular.

EXERCISE 1.3. Let L be the language over the alphabet $\{0, 1\}$ consisting of all words P such that 1 is the last letter of P and 000 is not a subword of P. (Hence, $\lambda \notin L$.) Find a regular expression denoting L.

EXERCISE 1.4. Let L_1 be a language obtained from a language L by adding or deleting finitely many words. Show that L_1 is regular iff L is regular.

EXERCISE 1.5. (For those familiar with universal algebras.) Clearly, $W(I)$ is the free semigroup with identity generated by I, where the semigroup operation is written multiplicatively and denoted by juxtaposition. How can $W(I)$ be regarded as a free algebra with one generator?

§ 2. Analysis and synthesis theorems

We shall now show how regular expressions characterize the behavior of finite deterministic automata. The latter are recognition devices which discriminate between input words over a fixed finite alphabet I by the terminal state of the device in the following fashion. The device is capable of a finite number of internal states, among which are a specified initial state s_0 and a designated set S_1 of final states. Given a word $y_1y_2 \ldots y_k$, the device first scans the letter y_1 in the state s_0 (cf. Fig. 1). Then it moves into another state s_1 (eventually, $s_1 = s_0$) and scans the letter y_2 in s_1, and so on, until it comes to the right end of

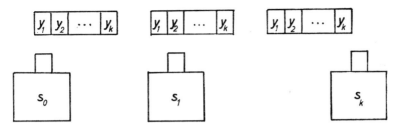

FIG. 1.

the word. At each step, the next state s_{i+1} $(0 \le i \le k-1)$ is uniquely determined by the state s_i and the scanned letter y_{i+1}. Thus, the input word $P = y_1y_2 \ldots y_k$ determines uniquely the terminal state s_k. If s_k belongs to the designated set S_1, then the word P is accepted by the automaton. Otherwise, it is rejected. Thus, one may ask any questions formulated using the letters of I, and always gets a "yes" or "no" answer. All words accepted by a given finite deterministic automaton constitute a language, called the behavior of the automaton. We shall prove that a language is the behavior of some finite deterministic automaton iff it is regular.

After these heuristic remarks, we shall now give the formal definitions.

DEFINITION. Let I be a finite alphabet. A *finite deterministic automaton* over the alphabet I is an ordered triple $\mathbf{A} = (S, s_0, f)$, where S is a finite non-empty set, referred to as the set of (*internal*) *states*, $s_0 \in S$ is called the *initial state* and f is a function mapping the Cartesian product $S \times I$ into the set S, referred to as the *transition function*.

Because the domain of the transition function f is always finite, the definition of the function can be given using a table or a graph. For instance, the following three tables each define the transition function f_i of a finite deterministic automaton $\mathbf{A}_i$ $(i = 1, 2, 3)$ over the alphabet $I_2 = \{x_1, x_2\}$:

f_1	s_0	s_1	s_2
x_1	s_1	s_1	s_0
x_2	s_2	s_1	s_1

f_2	s_0	s_1	s_2
x_1	s_1	s_0	s_2
x_2	s_0	s_1	s_2

f_3	s_0	s_1	s_2	s_3
x_1	s_1	s_2	s_2	s_3
x_2	s_1	s_0	s_2	s_1

Thus, $\mathbf{A_1}$ and $\mathbf{A_2}$ possess three states and $\mathbf{A_3}$ possesses four states. The transition functions f_i, $i = 1, 2, 3$, can be defined also by the graphs in Fig. 2.

We shall now extend the domain of the transition function f from $S \times I$ to $S \times W(I)$. This is done by defining

$$f(s, \lambda) = s, \quad \text{for all} \quad s \in S; \tag{2.1}$$

$$f(s, Px) = f(f(s, P), x), \quad \text{for all} \quad s \in S, \ P \in W(I), \ x \in I. \tag{2.1}'$$

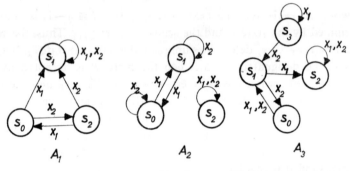

FIG. 2.

It is immediate that the function obtained is unique and that it is an extension of the original transition function, i.e. coincides with the latter for values from $S \times I$. For $s \in S$ and $P \in W(I)$, $f(s, P)$ is said to be the state to which the considered automaton will go if it is in the state s and receives the input word P. Thus, in the previous examples,

$$f_1(s_0, x_2x_1x_1) = f_1(f_1(s_0, x_2x_1), x_1)$$
$$= f_1(f_1(f_1(s_0, x_2), x_1), x_1) = f_1(f_1(s_2, x_1), x_1) = f_1(s_0, x_1) = s_1;$$
$$f_2(s_0, x_2x_1x_1) = s_0;$$
$$f_3(s_0, x_2x_1x_1) = s_2.$$

In most cases, the fastest way to evaluate $f(s, P)$ is to consider a graph like the ones in Fig. 2.

If we are dealing with a fixed automaton, or the transition function f is otherwise uniquely understood, then instead of $f(s, P)$ we write simply sP.

DEFINITION. Let $\mathbf{A} = (S, s_0, f)$ be a finite deterministic automaton over the alphabet I, $S_1 \subset S$ and

$$L(\mathbf{A}, S_1) = \{P \mid s_0 P \in S_1\}. \tag{2.2}$$

Then it is said that the set S_1 *represents* the language $L(\mathbf{A}, S_1)$ in the automaton $\mathbf{A}$, or that the language $L(\mathbf{A}, S_1)$ is the *behavior* of the set S_1 in the automaton $\mathbf{A}$. A language L_1 is *representable* in a finite deterministic automaton (shortly, L_1 is *f.a.r.*) iff, for some $\mathbf{A}$ and S_1, $L_1 = L(\mathbf{A}, S_1)$.

Clearly, $L(\mathbf{A}, S) = W(I)$. It is also clear that the empty set of states represents the empty language L_ϕ. As regards the preceding examples, we obtain, for instance, the following results:

$$L(\mathbf{A}_1, \{s_0\}) = |(x_2 x_1)^*|; \quad L(\mathbf{A}_1, \{s_2\}) = |(x_2 x_1)^* x_2|;$$
$$L(\mathbf{A}_1, \{s_1\}) = |(x_2 x_1)^* (x_1 + x_2 x_2)(x_1 + x_2)^*|;$$
$$L(\mathbf{A}_2, \{s_2\}) = L(\mathbf{A}_3, \{s_3\}) = L_\phi;$$
$$L(\mathbf{A}_2, \{s_0\}) = |(x_1 x_2^* x_1 + x_2)^*|;$$
$$L(\mathbf{A}_2, \{s_1\}) = |(x_1 x_2^* x_1 + x_2)^* x_1 x_2^*|;$$
$$L(\mathbf{A}_3, \{s_0\}) = |((x_1 + x_2) x_2)^*|;$$
$$L(\mathbf{A}_3, \{s_1\}) = |((x_1 + x_2) x_2)^* (x_1 + x_2)|;$$
$$L(\mathbf{A}_3, \{s_2\}) = |((x_1 + x_2) x_2)^* (x_1 + x_2) x_1 (x_1 + x_2)^*|.$$

The verification of these results is left to the reader. Because obviously

$$L(\mathbf{A}, S_1 \cup S_2) = L(\mathbf{A}, S_1) + L(\mathbf{A}, S_2), \tag{2.3}$$

we may, using these results, write a regular expression for any language represented in some of the automata $\mathbf{A}_1$, $\mathbf{A}_2$ and $\mathbf{A}_3$. In general, we shall consider the following

Analysis problem. Given a finite deterministic automaton $\mathbf{A} = (S, s_0, f)$ and $S_1 \subset S$, to determine the language $L(\mathbf{A}, S_1)$ represented by S_1 in $\mathbf{A}$.

In Theorem 2.2 it will be shown that we are always able to determine the language $L(\mathbf{A}, S_1)$ in an effective manner, namely, that there is an algorithm which produces a regular expression denoting $L(\mathbf{A}, S_1)$. Hence, every language which is f.a.r. is regular. We shall also consider the following converse problem.

Synthesis problem. Given a language L, to construct a finite deterministic automaton $\mathbf{A} = (S, s_0, f)$ such that L is represented by a subset S_1 of S in $\mathbf{A}$.

Because non-regular languages are not f.a.r., it suffices to consider the case where a regular expression is given. It will be shown in Theorem 2.3 that, for any finite set of regular expressions, one can construct a finite deterministic automaton such that every language denoted by some regular expression in the given set is represented by some set of states in this automaton. Before we prove the basic Theorems 2.2 and 2.3, we give a simple example of a language which is not f.a.r.

THEOREM 2.1. *The language*

$$\{x^p | p \text{ prime}\} \tag{2.4}$$

over the alphabet $\{x\}$ is not f.a.r.

Proof. Assume the contrary: The language (2.4) is represented by a set $S_1 \subset S$ in a finite deterministic automaton $\mathbf{A} = (S, s_0, f)$ over an alphabet I. Consider the states $s_0 x^i$, $i = 1, 2, \ldots$. They cannot all be distinct, because the number of states is finite. This implies the existence of two natural numbers k and l such that

$$s_0 x^k = s_0 x^l, \quad k > l. \tag{2.5}$$

We now choose a prime number $q \geqq l$ such that the number $q+(k-l)$ is not prime. (Note that we use the symbol "$+$" both to denote union of languages and in its ordinary arithmetical sense. No confusion will arise because the meaning is clear from the context.) Such a choice of q is always possible. By (2.5) and the fact that, for all words P, Q and R over the alphabet I, the equation $s_0 P = s_0 Q$ implies the equation $s_0(PR) = s_0(QR)$, we obtain the result

$$s_0 x^{q+(k-l)} = s_0 x^q. \tag{2.6}$$

On the other hand, by our assumption,

$$s_0 x^{q+(k-l)} \notin S_1, \quad s_0 x^q \in S_1. \tag{2.7}$$

Because conditions (2.6) and (2.7) are contradictory, we conclude that Theorem 2.1 holds true. □

THEOREM 2.2. *If a language is f.a.r. then it is regular. There is an algorithm of finding a regular expression denoting the language represented by a set of states in a finite deterministic automaton.*

Proof. Obviously, it suffices to prove the latter part of the theorem. Furthermore, by (2.3), it suffices to consider the case where the set of representing states consists of only one state.

Let $A = (\{s_1, \ldots, s_n\}, s_1, f)$ be a finite deterministic automaton over an alphabet I. If a word $P = y_1y_2 \ldots y_m$ over I, where $m \geqq 2$ and the letters y_ν need not be distinct, satisfies the condition $s_iP = s_j$, for some i and j such that $1 \leqq i, j \leqq n$, then we say that A goes from the state s_i to the state s_j through the *intermediate* states

$$s_iy_1, \quad s_iy_1y_2, \quad \ldots, s_iy_1y_2 \ldots y_{m-1},$$

after receiving the input P. Let L_{ij}^k ($0 \leqq k \leqq n$; $1 \leqq i, j \leqq n$) be the language consisting of all words P which have the following property: after receiving the input P, A goes from s_i to s_j in such a way that no state s_u, where $u > k$, is an intermediate state. Thus, by definition, L_{ij}^0 consists of all words P which have the following property: after receiving the input P, A goes from s_i to s_j through no intermediate states. Hence, for all i and j, either L_{ij}^0 is the empty language L_ϕ or is a finite language consisting of some words of length 1 or 0. ($\lambda \in L_{ij}^0$ iff $i = j$.) A regular expression α_{ij}^0 denoting L_{ij}^0 is immediately found.

We shall now make the following inductive hypothesis: for some k, where $1 \leqq k \leqq n$, and for each of the languages

$$L_{ij}^0, \quad L_{ij}^1, \ldots, L_{ij}^{k-1} \qquad (i, j = 1, \ldots, n),$$

we have found a regular expression α_{ij}^ν such that $L_{ij}^\nu = |\alpha_{ij}^\nu|$, for $\nu = 0$, $\ldots, k-1$. To complete the proof, it suffices to establish the formula

$$L_{ij}^k = L_{ij}^{k-1} + L_{ik}^{k-1}(L_{kk}^{k-1})^*L_{kj}^{k-1} \qquad (i, j = 1, \ldots, n). \tag{2.8}$$

Namely, it follows from (2.8) that

$$L_{ij}^k = |\alpha_{ij}^{k-1} + \alpha_{ik}^{k-1}(\alpha_{kk}^{k-1})^*\alpha_{kj}^{k-1}| \qquad (i, j = 1, \ldots, n),$$

which completes the inductive step. Because (cf. (2.2))

$$L(A, \{s_j\}) = L_{1j}^n \qquad (j = 1, \ldots, n),$$

we have thus found, for each $j = 1, \ldots, n$, a regular expression denoting the language represented in A by the set $\{s_j\}$.

To establish (2.8) we note first that every word belonging to the right side has the property characterizing L_{ij}^k and, hence, the right side is contained in the left side. Conversely, assume that $P \in L_{ij}^k$. Hence, after receiving the input P, A goes from s_i to s_j in such a way that no state s_u, where $u > k$, is an intermediate state. If s_k is not an intermediate state, then $P \in L_{ij}^{k-1}$. If s_k is an intermediate state, then P is of the

form
$$P = P_1P_2 \ldots P_{v-1}P_v \qquad (v \geqq 2),$$

where
$$P_1 \in L_{ik}^{k-1}, \quad P_2 \in L_{kk}^{k-1}, \ldots, \quad P_{v-1} \in L_{kk}^{k-1}, \quad P_v \in L_{kj}^{k-1}.$$

Hence,
$$P \in L_{ik}^{k-1}(L_{kk}^{k-1})^*L_{kj}^{k-1}.$$

This implies that the left side of (2.8) is contained in the right side. Therefore, (2.8) follows. $\square$

THEOREM 2.3. *If a language is regular then it is f.a.r. There is an algorithm yielding, for each finite set $\mathscr{M}$ of regular expressions over an alphabet I, a finite deterministic automaton $A(\mathscr{M})$ over I where each language denoted by some regular expression belonging to $\mathscr{M}$ is represented. Furthermore, if the regular expressions belonging to $\mathscr{M}$ contain altogether k non-empty letters of I, where each letter is counted as many times as it occurs, then the number of states of $A(\mathscr{M})$ is at most 2^k+1.*

Proof. Again, the first sentence in the statement of the theorem is implied by the second sentence. Simultaneously with the general proof, we give an example which will be separated from the general proof by double parentheses.

Let $\mathscr{M}$ be the given finite set of regular expressions over an alphabet I.
$$((\mathscr{M} = \{x(x^*+y)^*, \ yxy^*xy^*\}, \quad I = \{x,y\}.))$$

Assume that these regular expressions contain k non-empty letters. Different occurrences of the same letter are counted separately. Each occurrence is assigned a distinct number $1, \ldots, k$. If an occurrence of $z \in I$ is assigned the number i, then this occurrence of z is replaced by the letter z_i, and z_i is referred to as a *descendant* of z. The resulting set of regular expressions is denoted by $\mathscr{M}'$ and the corresponding alphabet by I'. (($k = 8$, $\mathscr{M}' = \{x_1(x_2^*+y_3)^*, \ y_4x_5y_6^*x_7y_8^*\}$, $I' = \{x_1, x_2, y_3, y_4, x_5, y_6, x_7, y_8\}$. The letters x_1, x_2, x_5, x_7 are descendants of the letter x, and the letters y_3, y_4, y_6, y_8 are descendants of the letter y.))

It is immediately seen from the regular expressions belonging to the set $\mathscr{M}'$:

(i) which two letters of I' immediately follow one another in some word in some language denoted by some regular expression in $\mathcal{M}'$ $((x_1x_2, x_1y_3, x_2x_2, x_2y_3, y_3x_2, y_3y_3, y_4x_5, x_5y_6, x_5x_7, y_6y_6, y_6x_7, x_7y_8, y_8y_8))$;

(ii) which letters of I' begin some word (i.e. are initial subwords) in some language denoted by some regular expression in $\mathcal{M}'$ $((x_1, y_4))$;

(iii) which letters of I' end some word (i.e. are final subwords) in some language denoted by some regular expression in $\mathcal{M}'$ $((x_1, x_2, y_3, x_7, y_8))$.
(Cf. Exercise 2.7.)

A finite deterministic automaton $A(\mathcal{M}) = (S, s_0, f)$ over the alphabet I will now be introduced. The set S of states consists of s_0 and, in addition, of certain subsets of I' which, as well as the transition function f, are specified in the following recursive definition.

For $z \in I$, define $f(s_0, z)$ to be the subset of I' consisting of those descendants of z which satisfy condition (ii).

$$((f(s_0, x) = \{x_1\} = s_1, \quad f(s_0, y) = \{y_4\} = s_2.))$$

Assume that s_i is a subset of I', possibly empty, which has been defined to be a state of $A(\mathcal{M})$ and that z belongs to I. Then define $f(s_i, z)$ to be the subset of I' consisting of those descendants of z which immediately follow some letter belonging to s_i in some word in some language denoted by some regular expression in $\mathcal{M}'$. The procedure is carried on until, for all subsets s_i and s_j of I' and all $x, y \in I$, the equation $f(s_i, x) = s_j$ implies that also the function value $f(s_j, y)$ has been defined. It follows that the number of states of $A(\mathcal{M})$ is at most $2^k + 1$.

$$
\begin{aligned}
&((f(s_1, x) = \{x_2\} = s_3, & &f(s_1, y) = \{y_3\} = s_4, \\
&f(s_2, x) = \{x_5\} = s_5, & &f(s_2, y) = \phi = s_6, \\
&f(s_3, x) = s_3, & &f(s_3, y) = s_4, \\
&f(s_4, x) = s_3, & &f(s_4, y) = s_4, \\
&f(s_5, x) = \{x_7\} = s_7, & &f(s_5, y) = \{y_6\} = s_8, \\
&f(s_6, x) = s_6, & &f(s_6, y) = s_6, \\
&f(s_7, x) = s_6, & &f(s_7, y) = \{y_8\} = s_9, \\
&f(s_8, x) = s_7, & &f(s_8, y) = s_8, \\
&f(s_9, x) = s_6, & &f(s_9, y) = s_9. \text{ Clearly, } 10 \leq 2^8 + 1.))
\end{aligned}
$$

Let $L_1, \ldots, L_u$ be the languages denoted by the regular expressions in the set $\mathcal{M}$.

$$((L_1 = |x(x^*+y)^*|, \quad L_2 = |yxy^*xy^*|.))$$

Let $L_1', \ldots, L_u'$ be the languages denoted by the regular expressions in the set $\mathcal{M}'$.

$$((L_1' = |x_1(x_2^*+y_3)^*|, \quad L_2' = |y_4x_5y_6^*x_7y_8^*|.))$$

The domain of the transition function f is now extended from $S \times I$ to $S \times W(I)$. (Cf. equations (2.1) and (2.1)'.) Then, for any $P \in W(I)$, where $P \neq \lambda$, and any $i = 1, \ldots, u$, $P \in L_i$ iff $f(s_0, P)$ is a subset of I' containing at least one letter which ends some word in L_i'. Furthermore, $f(s_0, P) = s_0$ iff $P = \lambda$. Thus, the language L_i is represented in $A(\mathcal{M})$ by a set $S_i \subset S$ such that S_i contains s_0 iff $\lambda \in L_i$ and S_i contains the element $s_j \neq s_0$ iff s_j contains at least one letter which ends some word in the language L_i'. Because it can be immediately verified whether or not $\lambda \in L_i$ (cf. Exercise 2.8), we have completed the proof of Theorem 2.3. $\square$

((For L_1, the corresponding final letters are x_1, x_2, y_3, and for L_2, they are x_7, y_8. Hence, $S_1 = \{s_1, s_3, s_4\}$ and $S_2 = \{s_7, s_9\}$. The graph of $A(\mathcal{M})$ is given in Fig. 3, where the states representing L_1 are triangles and those representing L_2 are squares. It is easy to see that the same result is obtained with fewer than ten states. The general problem of minimization will be discussed in Section 6.))

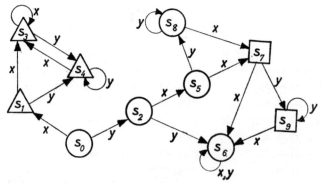

Fig. 3.

Let L_1 and L_2 be two regular languages over an alphabet I which are denoted by regular expressions α_1 and α_2 and are represented by sets S_1 and S_2 in an automaton $\mathbf{A} = (S, s_0, f)$ over I. Assuming that $\mathbf{A}$ is constructed by the method of Theorem 2.3 (which implies that $\mathbf{A}$ is *connected*, cf. Exercise 2.5) we conclude that $L_1 = L_2$ iff $S_1 = S_2$. Furthermore, the language $L_1 \cap L_2$ is represented by the set $S_1 \cap S_2$, and the language $\sim L_1$ by the set $S - S_1$ in the automaton $\mathbf{A}$. Hence, by Theorems 2.2 and 2.3, we obtain the following results.

THEOREM 2.4. *A language is f.a.r. iff it is regular.*

THEOREM 2.5. *There is an algorithm of deciding whether or not an equation between two regular expressions is valid.*

THEOREM 2.6. *The intersection of two regular languages is regular. The complement of a regular language is regular. Hence, the regular languages over a given finite alphabet form a Boolean algebra of sets. Furthermore, there is an algorithm of constructing a regular expression which denotes the intersection of the languages denoted by two given regular expressions, and also an algorithm of constructing a regular expression which denotes the complement of the language denoted by a given regular expression.*

It is immediately verified from Fig. 3 that if L_1 and L_2 are the languages considered in the proof of Theorem 2.3, then

$$L_1 \cap L_2 = L_\phi, \quad \sim L_1 = |\phi^* + y(x+y)^*|,$$
$$\sim L_2 = |\phi^* + x(x+y)^* + y + yxy^* + yy(x+y)^* + yxy^*xy^*x(x+y)^*|.$$

The algorithms referred to in Theorems 2.5 and 2.6 are based on the analysis and synthesis procedures of Theorems 2.2 and 2.3. They are not convenient in practice. In the following section, more practical analysis and synthesis methods are given.

EXERCISE 2.1. Show that the conditions (2.1) and

$$f(s, xP) = f(f(s, x), P), \quad \text{for all} \quad s \in S, \ x \in I, \ P \in W(I)$$

define the same extension of f as (2.1) and (2.1)'.

EXERCISE 2.2. Show that, for all $s \in S$ and $P, Q \in W(I)$,

$$s(PQ) = (sP)Q.$$

EXERCISE 2.3. Calculate the number of finite deterministic automata with n states over an alphabet with r letters.

EXERCISE 2.4. Let $A = (S, s_0, f)$ be a finite deterministic automaton with n states. A state $s \in S$ is *accessible* iff there is a word P such that $s = s_0 P$. (In the examples of Fig. 2, the state s_2 of A_2 and the state s_3 of A_3 are not accessible.) Show that

  (i) if s is accessible, then $s = s_0 P$, for some P with $\lg (P) < n$;
  (ii) if s is not accessible, then $L(A, S_1) = L(A, S_1 \cup \{s\})$, for any S_1.

EXERCISE 2.5. Let $A = (S, s_0, f)$ be a finite deterministic automaton over an alphabet I. The *connected subautomaton* of A is the finite deterministic automaton $C(A) = (S^a, s_0, f^a)$, where S^a consists of all accessible states of A and f^a is the restriction of f from $S \times I \to S$ to $S^a \times I \to S^a$. A is *connected* iff $A = C(A)$. Show that, for all words P, the state $s_0 P$ of A is the same as the state $s_0 P$ of $C(A)$. Prove also that $C(C(A)) = C(A)$.

EXERCISE 2.6. Given a finite deterministic automaton and a specified set of representing states, one must first order the states to be able to follow the analysis procedure of Theorem 2.2. Show by examples that different orderings of the states may lead to different regular expressions (although they denote the same language). Can you give some heuristic characterization of those orderings which lead to the "simplest" regular expressions?

EXERCISE 2.7. Following the recursive definition of regular expressions, present a detailed formal verification of points (i) − (iii) in the proof of Theorem 2.3. Cf. McNaughton and Yamada (1960).

EXERCISE 2.8. Following the recursive definition of regular expressions, give a necessary and sufficient condition for $\lambda \in |\alpha|$.

EXERCISE 2.9. The *initial restriction* ir (L) of a language L consists of all words P such that every initial subword of P belongs to L. The *initial extension* ie (L) of a language L consists of all initial subwords of the words in L. Show that the initial restriction and the initial extension of a regular language are regular. Study interconnections between ir, ie and the Boolean operators. Define similarly the notions of a final restriction and a final extension and show that the corresponding operators preserve the regularity of languages.

EXERCISE 2.10. Consider an infinite sequence

$$y_1, \ y_2, \ y_3, \ \ldots \tag{i}$$

of letters belonging to a given alphabet. The sequence (i) is termed f.a.r. iff the language

$$\{y_1, \ y_1y_2, \ y_1y_2y_3, \ \ldots\}$$

is f.a.r. Show that an infinite sequence is f.a.r. iff it is ultimately periodic. Define a sequence (i) over the alphabet $\{x_1, x_2\}$ as follows: $y_i = x_1$ if i is a square of a natural number; $y_i = x_2$ otherwise. Is this sequence f.a.r.?

EXERCISE 2.11. (For those familiar with universal algebras.) A finite deterministic automaton $A = (S, s_0, f)$ over the alphabet I_r can be viewed as a universal algebra $(S, \varphi_1, \ldots, \varphi_r, s_0)$, where $\varphi_i(s) = f(s, x_i)$, for $i = 1, \ldots, r$. Using this approach, define the basic notions presented in this section. Cf. Thatcher and Wright (1966) for a generalization where the functions φ_i are not necessarily monadic.

PROBLEM 2.1. Cf. Büchi (1960) and Kobrinskij and Trakhtenbrot (1962) for a definition of regular languages by formulas of predicate calculus. Study methods of translating these formulas into the language of regular expressions, and vice versa. (In Kobrinskij and Trakhtenbrot (1962, pp. 278–80) a method of translating regular expressions into predicate calculus is indicated. It contains several minor errors.) Cf. also Elgot and Mezei (1963).

§ 3. Characteristic equations

The analysis and synthesis methods presented in this section are based on results concerning equations between regular expressions and systems of such equations. These results will be proved in Chapter III. The reader who wants all proofs at the same time the results are given may either at this point read Chapter III (especially Sections III.2 and III.7) or omit the present section on a first reading.

The fact that two regular expressions α and β are identical, i.e. contain the same symbols in the same order is denoted by $\alpha \equiv \beta$.

THEOREM 3.1. *Assume that* $A = (\{s_0, \ldots, s_n\}, s_0, f)$ *is a finite deterministic automaton over an alphabet* I *and that the language represented* *by the set $\{s_{ij}\}$ in* $\mathbf{A}$ *is denoted by the regular expression* α_i, $i = 0, \ldots, n$. *Then the following equations are valid:*

$$\alpha_0 = \sum_{j=0}^{n} \alpha_j \gamma_{0j} + \phi^*,$$

$$\alpha_i = \sum_{j=0}^{n} \alpha_j \gamma_{ij} \qquad (i = 1, \ldots, n), \tag{3.1}$$

where, for $0 \leq i, j \leq n$, $\gamma_{ij} \equiv \sum_{x \in I_{ij}} x$ *and* I_{ij} *consists of those letters* $x \in I$ *which satisfy the condition* $f(s_j, x) = s_i$. *If there are no such letters* x, *then* $\gamma_{ij} \equiv \phi$.

Proof. Clearly, $\lambda \in |\alpha_i|$ iff $i = 0$. Thus, it suffices to prove that, for each $i = 0, \ldots, n$, a non-empty word P belongs to the language denoted by the left side of (3.1) iff P belongs to the language denoted by the right side of (3.1). Let i be an arbitrary number, $0 \leq i \leq n$, and assume that $P = P_1 x$, for some word P_1 and some $x \in I$. Denote $s_0 P_1 = s_j$. Then all of the following conditions are equivalent: (i) $P \in |\alpha_i|$; (ii) $s_0 P = s_i$; (iii) $x \in I_{ij}$; (iv) $P \in |\alpha_j \gamma_{ij}|$. Hence, for each $i = 0, \ldots, n$, the language denoted by the left side of (3.1) contains the same non-empty words as the language denoted by the right side of (3.1). $\square$

For instance, if $|\alpha_0|$, $|\alpha_1|$ and $|\alpha_2|$ are the languages represented by $\{s_0\}$, $\{s_1\}$ and $\{s_2\}$ in the second automaton ($\mathbf{A}_2$) given in Fig. 2, then the corresponding equations are as follows:

$$\alpha_0 = \alpha_0 x_2 + \alpha_1 x_1 + \alpha_2 \phi + \phi^*,$$

$$\alpha_1 = \alpha_0 x_1 + \alpha_1 x_2 + \alpha_2 \phi, \tag{3.2}$$

$$\alpha_2 = \alpha_0 \phi + \alpha_1 \phi + \alpha_2 (x_1 + x_2).$$

We obtain now the following *analysis procedure*. Given an automaton $\mathbf{A} = (\{s_0, \ldots, s_n\}, s_0, f)$ and a set S_1 of representing states,

    (i) write the equations (3.1);

    (ii) solve them for the α's;

    (iii) having thus obtained, for each $i = 0, \ldots, n$, a regular expression denoting the language represented by $\{s_i\}$, form the sum of the regular expressions corresponding to the states in S_1.

The task (ii) in this procedure is carried out by applying the following *rule:* if the equation $\alpha = \alpha\beta + \gamma$ is valid and $\lambda \notin |\beta|$, then the equation

$\alpha = \gamma\beta^*$ is valid. Given a system of equations (3.1), this rule is applied to one of the equations and the result is substituted to the remaining ones. Thus, the number of equations and unknowns is reduced by one. This elimination is carried on until a solution is obtained. The solution of the system (3.1) is unique (up to equality of regular expressions). These results will be proved in Theorem III.2.5.

As regards the system (3.2), the last equation may be written in the form

$$\alpha_2 = \alpha_2(x_1 + x_2) + \phi.$$

Hence, an application of our rule gives the result

$$\alpha_2 = \phi(x_1 + x_2)^* = \phi.$$

By applying the rule to the second equation, we obtain

$$\alpha_1 = (\alpha_0 x_1)x_2^*.$$

This result is substituted to the first equation:

$$\alpha_0 = \alpha_0 x_2 + \alpha_0 x_1 x_2^* x_1 + \phi^* = \alpha_0(x_2 + x_1 x_2^* x_1) + \phi^*.$$

Hence,

$$\alpha_0 = \phi^*(x_2 + x_1 x_2^* x_1)^* = (x_2 + x_1 x_2^* x_1)^*$$

and

$$\alpha_1 = \alpha_0 x_1 x_2^* = (x_2 + x_1 x_2^* x_1)^* x_1 x_2^*.$$

As further illustrations of our analysis method, we consider the two automata A_1 and A_2 over the alphabet $\{0, 1\}$, defined by Fig. 4. The representing states are indicated by squares.

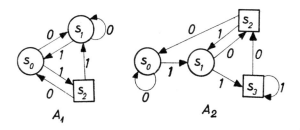

FIG. 4.

For A_1, we obtain the system of equations:

$$\alpha_0 = \alpha_1 1 + \alpha_2 0 + \phi^*,$$
$$\alpha_1 = \alpha_0 0 + \alpha_1 0 + \alpha_2 1,$$
$$\alpha_2 = \alpha_0 1.$$

(Terms of the form $\alpha_i \phi$ have been omitted.) We have to find the language represented by the set $\{s_2\}$, i.e. we have to determine α_2. By substituting according to the third equation to the second equation and then solving with respect to α_1, we obtain

$$\alpha_1 = \alpha_0 0 + \alpha_1 0 + \alpha_0 11 = \alpha_1 0 + \alpha_0(0+11),$$
$$\alpha_1 = \alpha_0(0+11)0^*.$$

According to the first equation,

$$\alpha_0 = \alpha_0(0+11)0^*1 + \alpha_0 10 + \phi^* = \alpha_0(10+(0+11)0^*1) + \phi^*.$$

Hence,

$$\alpha_0 = \phi^*(10+(0+11)0^*1)^* = (10+(0+11)0^*1)^*$$

which gives the final result

$$\alpha_2 = (10+(0+11)0^*1)^*1.$$

In order to determine the language represented by the set $\{s_2, s_3\}$ in A_2, we write first the equations characteristic to A_2:

$$\alpha_0 = \alpha_0 0 + \alpha_2 0 + \phi^*,$$
$$\alpha_1 = \alpha_0 1 + \alpha_2 1,$$
$$\alpha_2 = \alpha_1 0 + \alpha_3 0,$$
$$\alpha_3 = \alpha_1 1 + \alpha_3 1.$$

Because obviously $(\alpha_0 + \alpha_1 + \alpha_2 + \alpha_3) = (0+1)^*$, we obtain

$$\alpha_1 + \alpha_3 = \alpha_0 1 + \alpha_2 1 + \alpha_1 1 + \alpha_3 1 = (0+1)^*1. \qquad (3.3)$$

On the other hand,

$$\alpha_2 + \alpha_3 = \alpha_1 0 + \alpha_3 0 + \alpha_1 1 + \alpha_3 1 = (\alpha_1 + \alpha_3)(0+1).$$

Hence, by (3.3),

$$\alpha_2 + \alpha_3 = (0+1)^*1(0+1)$$

which solves the analysis problem of A_2. We note, finally, that different regular expressions, depending on the order of the eliminations, may be obtained as a solution, but the language denoted by them is unique.

We shall now proceed to the corresponding synthesis method.

DEFINITION. A finite set of regular expressions $\{\alpha_0, \ldots, \alpha_n\}$ over the alphabet $I_r = \{x_1, \ldots, x_r\}$ such that

$$\alpha_i = \sum_{j=1}^{r} x_j\alpha_{\varphi(i, j)} + \delta(\alpha_i) \qquad (i = 0, \ldots, n), \tag{3.4}$$

where, for each i, $\delta(\alpha_i) \equiv \phi$ or $\delta(\alpha_i) \equiv \phi^*$ and, for each i and j, $0 \leqq \varphi(i, j) \leqq n$, is said to be *closed*.

For instance, consider the regular expressions

$$\alpha_0 \equiv 1(11+0)^*1+\phi^*, \quad \alpha_1 \equiv (11+0)^*1, \quad \alpha_2 \equiv \phi$$

over the alphabet $\{0, 1\}$. Then the set $\{\alpha_0, \alpha_1, \alpha_2\}$ is closed because

$$\begin{aligned}
\alpha_0 &= 1\alpha_1 + 0\alpha_2 + \phi^*, \\
\alpha_1 &= 1\alpha_0 + 0\alpha_1 + \phi, \\
\alpha_2 &= 1\alpha_2 + 0\alpha_2 + \phi.
\end{aligned} \tag{3.5}$$

In the derivation of the equations (3.5), the following expansion

$$\alpha^* = \alpha\alpha^* + \phi^*, \tag{3.6}$$

which is valid for all regular expressions α, and the obvious associative, commutative and distributive laws are used. Note also that

$$\phi\alpha = \alpha\phi = \phi, \quad \phi^*\alpha = \alpha\phi^* = \alpha, \quad \alpha+\phi = \alpha.$$

As another illustration, we consider the regular expressions

$$\beta_0 \equiv 0^*1(0^*10^*1)^*, \quad \beta_1 \equiv (0^*10^*1)^*, \quad \beta_2 \equiv 0^*10^*1(0^*10^*1)^*.$$

Using (3.6), we obtain the equations

$$\begin{aligned}
\beta_0 &= 0\beta_0 + 1\beta_1 + \phi, \\
\beta_1 &= \beta_2 + \phi^* = 0\beta_2 + 1\beta_0 + \phi^*, \\
\beta_2 &= 0\beta_2 + 1\beta_0 + \phi.
\end{aligned} \tag{3.7}$$

Hence, the set $\{\beta_0, \beta_1, \beta_2\}$ is closed.

For a closed set $\{\alpha_0, \ldots, \alpha_n\}$ of regular expressions satisfying (3.4), we construct a finite deterministic automaton

$$\mathbf{A}(\alpha_0, \ldots, \alpha_n) = (\{s_0, \ldots, s_n\}, s_0, f) \tag{3.8}$$

by defining $f(s_i, x_j) = s_{\varphi(i, j)}$, where $\varphi(i, j)$ is the function defined by (3.4). For $i = 0, \ldots, n$, a state s_i of the automaton (3.8) is termed *designated* iff in (3.4) $\delta(\alpha_i) \equiv \phi^*$.

For the two closed sets $\{\alpha_0, \alpha_1, \alpha_2\}$ and $\{\beta_0, \beta_1, \beta_2\}$, the corresponding automata $\mathbf{A}_\alpha$ and $\mathbf{A}_\beta$ are obtained using (3.5) and (3.7). In Fig. 5, the designated states are indicated by squares. It is immediately verified that in these automata the languages $|\alpha_0|$ and $|\beta_0|$ are represented by the designated states. This is true also in general.

THEOREM 3.2. *If* $\{\alpha_0, \ldots, \alpha_n\}$ *is a closed set of regular expressions over the alphabet* I_r, *then the language* $|\alpha_0|$ *is represented in the corresponding automaton* $\mathbf{A}(\alpha_0, \ldots, \alpha_n)$ *by the set consisting of all designated states.*

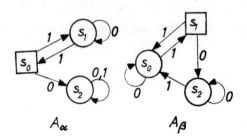

FIG. 5.

Proof. We have to show that, for any word P, $P \in |\alpha_0|$ iff $s_0 P$ is a designated state. This is a special case of the following more general assertion: (i) For $i = 0, \ldots, n$, $P \in |\alpha_i|$ iff $s_i P$ is a designated state. The assertion (i) will be established by induction on the length of P.

By the definition of a designated state and the equation $s_i \lambda = s_i$, (i) holds true if $\lg (P) = 0$. (Cf. also Exercise 3.1.) We shall make the following inductive hypothesis: (i) is satisfied for all P such that $\lg (P) = k$. Let $Q = x_j Q_1$, where $x_j \in I_r$ and Q_1 is of length k. By (3.4), $Q \in |\alpha_i|$ iff $Q_1 \in |\alpha_{\varphi(i,j)}|$. By our inductive hypothesis and the definition of f, $Q_1 \in |\alpha_{\varphi(i,j)}|$ iff $f(f(s_i, x_j), Q_1)$ is a designated state. But the latter condition is equivalent to the condition that $s_i(x_j Q_1) = s_i Q$ is a designated state. Hence, $Q \in |\alpha_i|$ iff $s_i Q$ is a designated state. Therefore, (i) is satisfied for all P such that $\lg (P) = k+1$. This completes the induction. $\square$

Theorem 3.2 yields the following *synthesis procedure*. Given a regular expression α_0 over I_r:

(i) determine a closed set $\{\alpha_0, \ldots, \alpha_n\}$ of regular expressions containing α_0;

(ii) form the corresponding automaton $\mathbf{A}(\alpha_0, \ldots, \alpha_n)$.

Task (i) in this procedure is carried out using (3.6) and the associative, commutative, distributive and idempotence laws. A finite closed set of regular expressions containing α_0 is always obtained. (Cf. Lemma III.7.7 and Exercise III.7.1.)

This synthesis procedure may be modified to yield, for any given finite set of regular expressions, a finite deterministic automaton where all of the corresponding languages are represented. We shall illustrate this (cf. also Exercise 3.4) by using the regular expressions

$$\alpha_0 \equiv x(x+y)^*, \quad \beta_0 \equiv yxy^*xy^*$$

considered in the proof of Theorem 2.3. (α_0 has been simplified because obviously $(x^*+y)^* = (x+y)^*$ is valid.)

We obtain first (the term ϕ is left out from the equations)

$$\alpha_0 = x(x+y)(x+y)^*+x\phi^* = x(\alpha_0+\phi^*+y(x+y)^*)+y\phi = x\alpha_1+y\alpha_2,$$

$$\alpha_1 = \alpha_0+\phi^*+y(x+y)^* = x\alpha_1+y\alpha_2+\phi^*+y(x+y)^*$$
$$= x\alpha_1+y(\alpha_2+(x+y)^*)+\phi^* = x\alpha_1+y\alpha_3+\phi^*,$$

$$\alpha_2 = x\alpha_2+y\alpha_2,$$

$$\alpha_3 = \alpha_2+(x+y)^* = (x+y)(x+y)^*+\phi^* = x\alpha_3+y\alpha_3+\phi^*$$

and have, thus, included α_0 in a closed set. The regular expression β_0 is handled similarly:

$$\beta_0 = x\phi+y(xy^*xy^*) = x\beta_1+y\beta_2,$$

$$\beta_1 = x\beta_1+y\beta_1,$$

$$\beta_2 = x(y^*xy^*)+y\phi = x\beta_3+y\beta_1,$$

$$\beta_3 = yy^*xy^*+xy^* = x\beta_4+y\beta_3,$$

$$\beta_4 = x\beta_1+y\beta_4+\phi^*.$$

We shall now consider pairs (α, β) of regular expressions. The addition and "scalar" multiplication is carried out termwise: $(\alpha, \beta)+(\gamma, \delta)$ defines the pair $(\alpha+\gamma, \beta+\delta)$ and $\gamma(\alpha, \beta)$ defines the pair $(\gamma\alpha, \gamma\beta)$. Furthermore, an equation $(\alpha, \beta) = (\gamma, \delta)$ is valid iff both of the equations $\alpha = \gamma$ and $\beta = \delta$ are valid.

Using the equations derived above, we obtain the following equations for pairs of regular expressions:

$$(s_0): \quad (\alpha_0, \beta_0) = x(\alpha_1, \beta_1) + y(\alpha_2, \beta_2),$$

$$(s_1): \quad (\alpha_1, \beta_1) = x(\alpha_1, \beta_1) + y(\alpha_3, \beta_1) + (\phi^*, \phi),$$

$$(s_2): \quad (\alpha_2, \beta_2) = x(\alpha_2, \beta_3) + y(\alpha_2, \beta_1),$$

$$(s_3): \quad (\alpha_3, \beta_1) = x(\alpha_3, \beta_1) + y(\alpha_3, \beta_1) + (\phi^*, \phi),$$

$$(s_4): \quad (\alpha_2, \beta_3) = x(\alpha_2, \beta_4) + y(\alpha_2, \beta_3),$$

$$(s_5): \quad (\alpha_2, \beta_1) = x(\alpha_2, \beta_1) + y(\alpha_2, \beta_1),$$

$$(s_6): \quad (\alpha_2, \beta_4) = x(\alpha_2, \beta_1) + y(\alpha_2, \beta_4) + (\phi, \phi^*).$$

We have, thus, included the pair (α_0, β_0) in a set of pairs which is closed. (Closure is defined similarly as above, cf. also Exercise 3.4.) Similarly as above, the corresponding automaton is now constructed. The state corresponding to each pair has been given together with the equations. The presence of ϕ^* indicates that the corresponding state is a representing one. Thus, $|\alpha_0|$ is represented by the set $\{s_1, s_3\}$ and $|\beta_0|$ by the set $\{s_6\}$.

The graph of the automaton is given in Fig. 6, where states representing $|\alpha_0|$ are triangles and those representing $|\beta_0|$ are squares. Note that the number of states is smaller than in the automaton given in Fig. 3. It is possible to obtain a still smaller automaton by identifying the states s_1 and s_3.

The synthesis procedure described above has also the advantage of being applicable when the notion of a regular expression is extended to include Boolean operators other than union. This is done by making

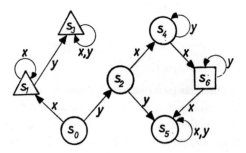

FIG. 6.

the convention that also $(\alpha \cap \beta)$ and $\sim(\alpha)$ are regular expressions over I whenever α and β are regular expressions over I. The former denotes the intersection of the languages denoted by α and β, and the latter the complement of $|\alpha|$ (with respect to $W(I)$). By Theorem 2.6, Theorem 2.4 remains valid also if the notion of a regular expression is modified in this way. Our synthesis procedure remains unaltered. However, task (i) is in this case more complicated. The equations

$$\begin{aligned}
\sim(x_1\alpha_1 + \ldots + x_r\alpha_r) &= x_1(\sim\alpha_1) + \ldots + x_r(\sim\alpha_r) + \phi^*, \\
\sim(x_1\alpha_1 + \ldots + x_r\alpha_r + \phi^*) &= x_1(\sim\alpha_1) + \ldots + x_r(\sim\alpha_r),
\end{aligned} \qquad (3.9)$$

which are valid for all regular expressions α_i over I_r, can be used to eliminate the complements.

As an illustration, we shall construct an automaton where the language denoted by the regular expression (in this wider sense)

$$\alpha_0 \equiv 0(\sim(1(00+01)^*0))11$$

is represented. Denoting $\beta_1 \equiv 1(00+01)^*0$, we obtain first

$$\beta_1 = 1((00+01)^*0) + 0\phi = 1\beta_2 + 0\beta_3,$$
$$\beta_2 = (00+01)(00+01)^*0 + 0 = 0((0+1)(00+01)^*0 + \phi^*) = 0\beta_4 + 1\beta_3,$$
$$\beta_3 = 0\beta_3 + 1\beta_3,$$
$$\beta_4 = 0\beta_2 + 1\beta_2 + \phi^*.$$

Hence, by (3.9),

$$\begin{aligned}
\sim\beta_1 &= 1(\sim\beta_2) + 0(\sim\beta_3) + \phi^*, \\
\sim\beta_2 &= 0(\sim\beta_4) + 1(\sim\beta_3) + \phi^*, \\
\sim\beta_3 &= 0(\sim\beta_3) + 1(\sim\beta_3) + \phi^*, \\
\sim\beta_4 &= 0(\sim\beta_2) + 1(\sim\beta_2).
\end{aligned}$$

Using these equations, we shall now include α_0 in a closed set of regular expressions.

$$\begin{aligned}
\alpha_0 &= 0(\sim\beta_1)11 + 1\beta_3 = 0\alpha_1 + 1\beta_3, \\
\beta_3 &= 0\beta_3 + 1\beta_3, \\
\alpha_1 &= (\sim\beta_1)11 = 0(\sim\beta_3)11 + 1((\sim\beta_2)11 + 1) = 0\alpha_2 + 1\alpha_3, \\
\alpha_2 &= (\sim\beta_3)11 = 0(\sim\beta_3)11 + 1((\sim\beta_3)11 + 1) = 0\alpha_2 + 1\alpha_4, \\
\alpha_3 &= (\sim\beta_2)11 + 1 = 0(\sim\beta_4)11 + 1((\sim\beta_3)11 + 1 + \phi^*) = 0\alpha_5 + 1\alpha_6,
\end{aligned}$$

$$\alpha_4 = (\sim\beta_3)11+1 = 0(\sim\beta_3)11+1((\sim\beta_3)11+1+\phi^*) = 0\alpha_2+1\alpha_6,$$
$$\alpha_5 = (\sim\beta_4)11 = 0(\sim\beta_2)11+1(\sim\beta_2)11 = 0\alpha_7+1\alpha_7,$$
$$\alpha_6 = (\sim\beta_3)11+1+\phi^* = 0(\sim\beta_3)11+1((\sim\beta_3)11+1+\phi^*)+\phi^*$$
$$= 0\alpha_2+1\alpha_6+\phi^*,$$
$$\alpha_7 = (\sim\beta_2)11 = 0(\sim\beta_4)11+1((\sim\beta_3)11+1) = 0\alpha_5+1\alpha_4.$$

Hence, $|\alpha_0|$ is represented by the set $\{s_6\}$ in the automaton given in Fig. 7. (The state corresponding to β_3 is s_8.)

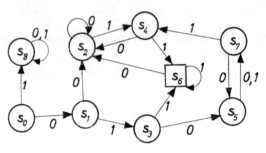

FIG. 7.

EXERCISE 3.1. Show that in (3.4) $\delta(\alpha_i) \equiv \phi^*$ iff $|\alpha_i|$ contains the empty word λ. What is the interconnection between the sets $|\alpha_i|$ and $|\alpha_{\varphi(i,j)}|$?

EXERCISE 3.2. Explain why in connection with analysis the coefficients are on the right (cf. (3.1)), whereas in connection with synthesis they are on the left (cf. (3.4)).

EXERCISE 3.3. Let $\{\alpha_0, \ldots, \alpha_n\}$ be a closed set of regular expressions. What language is represented in the automaton $(\{s_0, \ldots, s_n\}, s_i, f)$, $i = 0, \ldots, n$, by the set of designated states if f and the latter are defined as for (3.8)?

EXERCISE 3.4. For $m \geq 2$, consider ordered m-tuples $(\alpha_1, \ldots, \alpha_m)$ of regular expressions over I_r. Addition and scalar multiplication are carried out termwise. Using equations similar to (3.4), define the notion of closure for sets of such m-tuples. For closed sets, formulate and prove a theorem corresponding to Theorem 3.2. Assuming that any regular expression can be included in a closed set, prove that any ordered m-tuple of regular expressions can be included in a closed set of m-tuples. Conclude that these results give an algorithm yielding, for any finite set of regular expressions, a finite deterministic automaton where all of the languages denoted by these regular expressions are represented.

EXERCISE 3.5 (Frey, 1964). Given an automaton where a language L is represented, construct an automaton where (i) ir (L) is represented, (ii) ie (L) is represented. (Cf. Exercise 2.9. Cf. Frey (1964) also for a direct method to catenate two automata.)

§ 4. Equivalence relations induced by languages

We shall now derive another necessary and sufficient condition for a language to be f.a.r.

DEFINITION. An equivalence relation $\mathcal{E}$ over the set $W(I)$, where I is a finite alphabet, is of *finite index* iff the number of equivalence classes under $\mathcal{E}$ is finite. $\mathcal{E}$ is termed *right invariant* iff, whenever $P\mathcal{E}Q$ holds, then also $(PR)\mathcal{E}(QR)$ holds for all words $R \in W(I)$. $\mathcal{E}$ is termed *left invariant* iff, whenever $P\mathcal{E}Q$ holds, then also $(RP)\mathcal{E}(RQ)$ holds for all words $R \in W(I)$. $\mathcal{E}$ is a *congruence* iff it is both right and left invariant.

For instance, define the relation $\mathcal{E}$ as follows: for any $P, Q \in W(I)$, $P\mathcal{E}Q$ iff $\lg(P) = \lg(Q)$. Then $\mathcal{E}$ is right and left invariant and, hence, it is a congruence. This relation $\mathcal{E}$ is not of finite index.

DEFINITION. Let L be a language over a finite alphabet I. Two relations $\mathcal{E}_L$ and $\mathcal{C}_L$ over $W(I)$, referred to as the *equivalence* and *congruence* relation *induced* by L, are defined as follows. $P\mathcal{E}_L Q$ iff, for each $R \in W(I)$, PR being in L is equivalent to QR being in L. $P\mathcal{C}_L Q$ iff, for all $R_1, R_2 \in W(I)$, $R_1 P R_2$ being in L is equivalent to $R_1 Q R_2$ being in L.

It is immediately verified that $\mathcal{E}_L$ is a right invariant equivalence relation and $\mathcal{C}_L$ is a congruence. A new characterization of f.a.r. languages will now be given.

THEOREM 4.1. *For a language L over a finite alphabet I, the following three conditions are equivalent:*

(i) *L is f.a.r.;*

    (ii) *L is the union of some equivalence classes of a right invariant equivalence relation (over $W(I)$) of finite index;*

    (iii) *the equivalence relation induced by L is of finite index.*

Proof. We assume first that condition (i) is satisfied. Let L be represented by the set S_1 in the finite deterministic automaton $\mathbf{A} = (S, s_0, f)$ over I. We define a binary relation $\mathcal{E}$ over $W(I)$ as follows: $P\mathcal{E}Q$ iff $s_0P = s_0Q$. Clearly, $P\mathcal{E}P$. If $P\mathcal{E}Q$, then $Q\mathcal{E}P$. If $P\mathcal{E}Q$ and $Q\mathcal{E}R$, then $P\mathcal{E}R$. Hence, $\mathcal{E}$ is an equivalence relation. Assume that $P\mathcal{E}Q$ and $R \in W(I)$. Then

$$s_0(PR) = (s_0P)R = (s_0Q)R = s_0(QR).$$

Therefore, $(PR)\mathcal{E}(QR)$, which proves that $\mathcal{E}$ is right invariant. Because the number of equivalence classes of $\mathcal{E}$ does not exceed the number of states of $\mathbf{A}$, we conclude that $\mathcal{E}$ is of finite index. Finally, if $P \in L$ and $P\mathcal{E}Q$ then $s_0P = s_0Q$ and hence $Q \in L$. This implies that condition (ii) is satisfied.

    Assume next that (ii) is satisfied. Let $\mathcal{F}$ be the right invariant equivalence relation in question. Assume that $P \mathcal{F} Q$ and $PR \in L$. Because $\mathcal{F}$ is right invariant, we obtain $(PR) \mathcal{F} (QR)$. Because L is the union of some equivalence classes of $\mathcal{F}$, we obtain also the result $QR \in L$. By the symmetry of $\mathcal{F}$, we conclude that if $P \mathcal{F} Q$ and $PR \notin L$, then $QR \notin L$. Hence, if $P \mathcal{F} Q$ then, for all R, PR being in L is equivalent to QR being in L, i.e. $P\mathcal{E}_L Q$. This proves that the number of equivalence classes of $\mathcal{E}_L$ is at most that of $\mathcal{F}$ and, therefore, finite. Thus, (iii) is satisfied.

    Finally, we assume that (iii) is satisfied. Let the number of equivalence classes of $\mathcal{E}_L$ be $n+1$. We choose representatives $P_0, \ldots, P_n$ from each class and denote by $[P]$ the equivalence class determined by the word P. The choice of representatives can be made in such a way that $P_0 = \lambda$. Consider the finite deterministic automaton

$$\mathbf{A}_L = (S_L, [P_0], f_L),$$

where $S_L = \{[P_0], \ldots, [P_n]\}$ and the transition function f_L is defined by the equation

$$f_L([P_i], x) = [P_ix] \qquad (i = 0, \ldots, n; x \in I). \qquad (4.1)$$

It is clear that (4.1) defines a mapping of the set $S_L \times I$ into the set S_L because, by the right invariance of $\mathcal{E}_L$, the equation $[P_i] = [P_i']$

implies the equation $[P_i x] = [P_i' x]$. Denote by S_L' the subset of S_L consisting of the equivalence classes $[P_i]$ such that $P_i \in L$. The set S_L' is well defined because, by the definition of $\mathcal{E}_L$, if $[P_i] = [P_i']$ then P_i being in L is equivalent to P_i' being in L. It follows that, for any word P, $f_L([P_0], P) = [\lambda P] = [P]$ belongs to S_L' iff $P \in L$. Hence, L is represented in $\mathbf{A}_L$ by the set S_L'. This implies that (i) is satisfied. □

In some cases, Theorem 4.1 is more useful than the technique of regular expressions to decide whether or not a given language is f.a.r. For instance, let L be the language over the alphabet $\{x, y\}$ defined by the equation

$$L = \{x^n y^n \mid n = 0, 1, \ldots\}.$$

Assume that the relation $\mathcal{E}_L$ induced by L is of finite index. Hence, the words x^n, $n = 0, 1, \ldots$, cannot all belong to different equivalence classes. Therefore, for some m and n where $m < n$, $x^m \mathcal{E}_L x^n$. By the right invariance of $\mathcal{E}_L$, $x^m y^m \mathcal{E}_L x^n y^m$. But this is a contradiction because $x^m y^m \in L$ and $x^n y^m \notin L$. Hence, $\mathcal{E}_L$ is not of finite index and L is not f.a.r.

THEOREM 4.2. *For a language L over a finite alphabet I, the following three conditions are equivalent:*

(i) *L is f.a.r.;*
(ii) *L is the union of some equivalence classes of a congruence (over $W(I)$) of finite index;*
(iii) *the congruence $\mathcal{Q}_L$ induced by L is of finite index.*

The proof of Theorem 4.2, being almost the same as that of Theorem 4.1, is left to the reader. When it is shown that condition (i) implies condition (ii), then the binary relation $\mathcal{E}$ over $W(I)$ is defined as follows: $P\mathcal{E}Q$ iff $sP = sQ$, for all states s of the corresponding automaton.

DEFINITION. The *weight* of a regular language L is the least natural number $w(L)$ such that L is represented in a finite deterministic automaton with $w(L)$ states. The weight of an (unordered) m-tuple of regular languages $(L_1, \ldots, L_m)$ is the least natural number $w(L_1, \ldots, L_m)$ such that each of the languages $L_1, \ldots, L_m$ is represented in a finite deterministic automaton with $w(L_1, \ldots, L_m)$ states.

Theorem 2.3 gives an upper bound for the weight of an m-tuple of regular languages (and, hence, for the weight of a regular language). However, in most instances the weight is much smaller than this upper bound. For example, it is easy to verify that the weight of the pair of regular languages

$$(|x^2|, \quad |x(x^3)^*|)$$

over the alphabet $\{x\}$ equals 6. An automaton, where both of these languages are represented, is given in Fig. 8, where the states representing the former language are triangles and those representing the latter language are squares.

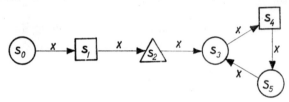

FIG. 8.

THEOREM 4.3. *The weight of a regular language L equals the number of equivalence classes of the right invariant equivalence relation $\mathcal{E}_L$ induced by L.*

Proof. Let n be the number of equivalence classes of $\mathcal{E}_L$. By the last part of the proof of Theorem 4.1, L is represented in an automaton with n states. Hence, $w(L) \leqq n$. Assume that L is represented in an automaton with $n_1 < n$ states and with the initial state s_0. This implies the existence of two words P_1 and P_2 such that $s_0 P_1 = s_0 P_2$ but not $P_1 \mathcal{E}_L P_2$. Therefore, there is a word Q such that $s_0(P_1 Q) = s_0(P_2 Q)$ and exactly one of the words $P_1 Q$ and $P_2 Q$ belongs to L. This is a contradiction. Hence, $w(L) = n$. $\square$

EXERCISE 4.1. Use the results established in this section to prove that the mirror image mi (L) of a language L is f.a.r. iff L is f.a.r. (Cf. Exercise 1.2 and Theorem 2.4 which give the same result.)

EXERCISE 4.2. Give examples of m-tuples of regular languages whose weight equals the upper bound of Theorem 2.3.

EXERCISE 4.3 (Rabin and Scott, 1959). Prove that the language represented by a set S_1 in a finite deterministic automaton A is not empty iff it contains a word of length less than the number of states of A. Conclude that there is an algorithm of deciding whether or not the language represented by a given set in a given automaton is empty.

EXERCISE 4.4 (Rabin and Scott, 1959). Using the results of this section, prove that f.a.r. languages form a Boolean algebra of sets.

EXERCISE 4.5 (Rabin and Scott, 1959). Assume that P is a word belonging to a language L represented in an n-state automaton and that $\lg(P) \geqq n$. Show that there are words $P_1, Q, P_2, Q \neq \lambda$, such that $P = P_1 Q P_2$ and all words $P_1 Q^i P_2$, $i = 0, 1, 2, \ldots$, belong to L. Using this result, prove that a language represented in an n-state automaton is infinite iff it contains a word P such that $n \leqq \lg(P) < 2n$. Conclude that there is an algorithm of deciding whether or not the language represented by a given set in a given (finite deterministic) automaton is infinite.

EXERCISE 4.6. Prove that a finite language represented in an n-state automaton over I_r, $r \geqq 2$, contains at most $(r^{n-1} - 1)/(r - 1)$ words.

EXERCISE 4.7. Prove Theorem 4.1 with "right invariant" replaced by "left invariant" and with the corresponding change in the definition of the induced equivalence relation.

EXERCISE 4.8. Define equivalence and congruence relations corresponding to $\mathcal{E}_L$ and $\mathcal{C}_L$, induced by (unordered) m-tuples of languages. State and prove theorems analogous to Theorems 4.1–4.3.

§ 5. Sequential machines

So far we have considered devices with no outputs; the only response given is the final state of the device. We shall now introduce devices whose response is a word of the same length as the input word.

DEFINITION. A *finite sequential Mealy machine*, or shortly, a *Mealy machine* is an ordered quintuple $\mathbf{ME} = (I, O, S, f, \varphi)$, where I and O are finite alphabets, called the *input* and the *output* alphabet, S is a finite non-empty set, called the set of *states*, and f and φ are functions mapping the set $S \times I$ into S and O, respectively, called the *transition* and *output* function. An ordered pair $(\mathbf{ME}, s)$, where $\mathbf{ME}$ is a Mealy machine and s is a state of $\mathbf{ME}$, called the *initial state*, is termed an *initial* Mealy machine. A *finite sequential Moore machine,* or shortly, a *Moore machine* is an ordered quintuple $\mathbf{MO} = (I, O, S, f, \varphi)$, where I, O, S and f are as above but φ (which is also now called the output function) is a function mapping the set S into the set O. An ordered pair $(\mathbf{MO}, s)$, where $\mathbf{MO}$ is a Moore machine and s is a state of $\mathbf{MO}$, called the *initial state,* is termed an *initial* Moore machine. The term *(initial) sequential machine* is used to refer to both (initial) finite sequential Mealy machines and (initial) finite sequential Moore machines.

Because of the finiteness of the sets I, O, S, a sequential machine can always be defined using a table or a graph. For instance, the following table defines a Mealy machine $\mathbf{ME}$ with $I = \{x_1, x_2\}$, $O = \{y_1, y_2, y_3\}$ and $S = \{s_1, s_2, s_3, s_4\}$.

f/φ	s_1	s_2	s_3	s_4
x_1	s_2/y_2	s_3/y_2	s_4/y_1	s_4/y_2
x_2	s_1/y_2	s_1/y_2	s_1/y_2	s_1/y_3

The following table defines a Moore machine $\mathbf{MO}$ with I and O as above and $S = \{s_1, s_2, s_3, s_4, s_5, s_6\}$.

φ	y_2	y_2	y_2	y_1	y_2	y_3
f	s_1	s_2	s_3	s_4	s_5	s_6
x_1	s_2	s_3	s_4	s_5	s_5	s_2
x_2	s_1	s_1	s_1	s_6	s_6	s_1

These two sequential machines are given also in Fig. 9.

For sequential machines, the domain of the transition function f is extended from $S \times I$ to $S \times W(I)$ in the same way as for automata. (Cf. equations (2.1) and (2.1)$'$.) As in connection with automata, if f is understood then the notation $f(s, P) = sP$ may be used. It is said that the sequential machine goes to the state sP if it is in the state s and receives the input P. Obviously, sequential machines are deterministic in the sense that s and P uniquely determine the state sP. They are deterministic also in the sense that the initial state and the input uniquely determine the response. The latter notion will now be formally defined.

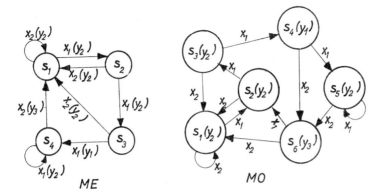

FIG. 9.

DEFINITION. For a Mealy machine $\mathbf{ME} = (I, O, S, f, \varphi)$, the *response function induced by a state $s \in S$*, in symbols resp_s, is a mapping of the set $W(I)$ into the set $W(O)$, defined as follows:

$$\text{resp}_s (\lambda) = \lambda, \tag{5.1}$$
$$\text{resp}_s (xP) = \varphi(s, x)\,\text{resp}_{sx}(P), \quad x \in I, \quad P \in W(I).$$

Hence, if $P = x_1 x_2 \ldots x_k \in W(I)$ (where the letters x_i are not necessarily distinct) and we denote

$$sx_1 = s^1, \; sx_1x_2 = s^2, \ldots, sx_1x_2 \ldots x_k = s^k,$$

then

$$\text{resp}_s (P) = \varphi(s, x_1)\varphi(s^1, x_2) \ldots \varphi(s^{k-1}, x_k).$$

The situation may be illustrated by the following table:

Time instant	0	1	2	...	k
Input	—	x_1	x_2	...	x_k
State	s	s^1	s^2	...	s^k
Response	—	$\varphi(s, x_1)$	$\varphi(s^1, x_2)$	...	$\varphi(s^{k-1}, x_k)$

For instance, we obtain the following result for the sequential machine **ME** of Fig. 9:

$\text{resp}_{s_1}\ (x_2x_1x_1x_2x_1x_1x_1x_1x_1x_2) = y_2y_2y_2y_2y_2y_2y_2y_1y_2y_2y_3.$

It is a consequence of (5.1) that the function resp_s is *length preserving*, i.e. we have always

$$\text{lg}\ (\text{resp}_s\ (P)) = \text{lg}\ (P).$$

DEFINITION. For a Moore machine $\mathbf{MO} = (I, O, S, f, \varphi)$, the *response function* resp_s *induced by a state* $s \in S$ is a function mapping the set $W(I)$ into the set $W(O)$, defined as follows:

$$\text{resp}_s\ (\lambda) \quad = \lambda, \tag{5.2}$$
$$\text{resp}_s\ (xP) = \varphi(sx)\ \text{resp}_{sx}(P), \quad x \in I, \quad P \in W(I).$$

Again, by (5.2), resp_s is length preserving. For instance, for the Moore machine **MO** of Fig. 9,

$$\text{resp}_{s_3}\ (x_1x_1x_1x_1x_2) = y_1y_2y_2y_2y_3.$$

DEFINITION. Let s and s' be states either in the same sequential machine or in two sequential machines with the same input alphabet I. The states s and s' are termed *equivalent* iff $\text{resp}_s = \text{resp}_{s'}$, i.e. for all $P \in W(I)$, $\text{resp}_s\ (P) = \text{resp}_{s'}\ (P)$. Two sequential machines $\mathbf{M}_1$ and $\mathbf{M}_2$ are termed *equivalent* iff, for each state in $\mathbf{M}_1$, there is an equivalent state in $\mathbf{M}_2$ and, for each state in $\mathbf{M}_2$, there is an equivalent state in $\mathbf{M}_1$. Finally, two initial sequential machines are termed equivalent iff their initial states are equivalent.

It is obvious that sequential machines $\mathbf{M}_1$ and $\mathbf{M}_2$ with the sets of states S_1 and S_2 are equivalent iff the family of response functions generated by S_1 equals the family of response functions generated by S_2:

$$\{\text{resp}_s\,|\,s \in S_1\} = \{\text{resp}_s\,|\,s \in S_2\}.$$

Two sequential machines $\mathbf{M}_1$ and $\mathbf{M}_2$ are equivalent iff, for each initial sequential machine $(\mathbf{M}_1, s_1)$, there is an equivalent initial sequential machine $(\mathbf{M}_2, s_2)$, and vice versa.

As regards the sequential machines **ME** and **MO** of Fig. 9, it is easy to verify that the state s_1 of **ME** and the state s_1 of **MO** are equivalent. From this it follows (cf. Exercise 5.4) that **ME** and **MO** are equivalent. We shall now prove the general result. For a finite set X, the notation card (X) is used to mean the number of elements in X.

THEOREM 5.1. *For any Moore machine, there is an equivalent Mealy machine with the same number of states. Conversely, for any Mealy machine* $\mathbf{ME} = (I, O, S, f, \varphi)$, *there is an equivalent Moore machine with* card $(S) \cdot$ card (O) *states. Hence, for any initial Moore machine, there is an equivalent initial Mealy machine, and vice versa.*

Proof. Given a Moore machine $\mathbf{MO} = (I, O, S, f, \varphi)$, we consider the ordered quintuple $\mathbf{ME} = (I, O, S, f, \varphi_1)$, where

$$\varphi_1(s, x) = \varphi(f(s, x)), \quad s \in S, \ x \in I. \tag{5.3}$$

Clearly, φ_1 maps the set $S \times I$ into the set O and, hence, $\mathbf{ME}$ is a Mealy machine. It follows from (5.3) that, for any s, the state s of $\mathbf{MO}$ is equivalent to the state s of $\mathbf{ME}$. Therefore, the first sentence of the theorem is true. It is also obvious that the last sentence follows from the first two sentences. Hence, it suffices to prove the second sentence.

Let $\mathbf{ME} = (I, O, S, f, \varphi)$ be a given Mealy machine. Consider the ordered quintuple $\mathbf{MO} = (I, O, S \times O, f_1, \varphi_1)$, where the functions f_1 and φ_1 are defined as follows:

$$f_1((s, y), x) = (f(s, x), \varphi(s, x)), \quad x \in I, \ y \in O, \ s \in S,$$
$$\varphi_1((s, y)) = y, \quad y \in O, \ s \in S.$$

Clearly, f_1 maps the set $(S \times O) \times I$ into the set $S \times O$, and φ_1 maps the set $S \times O$ into the set O. This implies that $\mathbf{MO}$ is a Moore machine with card $(S) \cdot$ card (O) states. To prove the equivalence of $\mathbf{ME}$ and $\mathbf{MO}$, we consider an arbitrary state $s_0 \in S$ and an arbitrary word $P = x_1 x_2 \ldots x_k \in W(I)$. Denote

$$f(s_{i-1}, x_i) = s_i; \quad \varphi(s_{i-1}, x_i) = y_i \quad (i = 1, \ldots, k).$$

We choose an arbitrary $y_0 \in O$ and claim that the state s_0 of $\mathbf{ME}$ and (s_0, y_0) of $\mathbf{MO}$ are equivalent. In fact,

$$f_1((s_{i-1}, y_{i-1}), x_i) = (f(s_{i-1}, x_i), \varphi(s_{i-1}, x_i)) = (s_i, y_i)$$

and

$$\varphi_1((s_i, y_i)) = y_i,$$

for $i = 1, \ldots, k$. Hence,

$$\mathrm{resp}_{s_0} (x_1 x_2 \ldots x_k) = \mathrm{resp}_{(s_0, y_0)} (x_1 x_2 \ldots x_k) = y_1 y_2 \ldots y_k.$$

Because the word $x_1 x_2 \ldots x_k$ was arbitrary, we conclude that $\text{resp}_{s_0} = \text{resp}_{(s_0, y_0)}$ and, therefore, s_0 and (s_0, y_0) are equivalent. This implies that also **ME** and **MO** are equivalent. $\square$

As an illustration, consider the Mealy machine

$$\mathbf{ME} = (\{x_1, x_2\}, \quad \{y_1, y_2\}, \quad \{s_1, s_2\}, \ f, \ \varphi),$$

where the functions f and φ are defined by the following table:

f/φ	s_1	s_2
x_1	s_2/y_1	s_2/y_2
x_2	s_1/y_2	s_1/y_1

Denote $\sigma_1 = (s_1, y_1)$, $\sigma_2 = (s_1, y_2)$, $\sigma_3 = (s_2, y_1)$, $\sigma_4 = (s_2, y_2)$. The sequential machine

$$\mathbf{MO} = (\{x_1, x_2\}, \quad \{y_1, y_2\}, \quad \{\sigma_1, \sigma_2, \sigma_3, \sigma_4\}, \ f_1, \ \varphi_1),$$

where f_1 and φ_1 are defined by the table

φ_1	y_1	y_2	y_1	y_2
f_1	σ_1	σ_2	σ_3	σ_4
x_1	σ_3	σ_3	σ_4	σ_4
x_2	σ_2	σ_2	σ_1	σ_1

is a Moore machine with four states which is equivalent to **ME**. The graphs of both machines are given in Fig. 10.

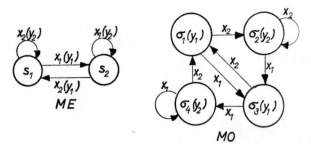

FIG. 10.

We shall now study languages represented in initial sequential machines. In connection with finite deterministic automata, words were distinguished according to the final state of the automaton. They will now be distinguished according to the last letter of the response.

DEFINITION. Let $(\mathbf{M}, s_0)$ be an initial sequential machine with input and output alphabets I and O and let O_1 be a subset of O. Then O_1 *represents* in $(\mathbf{M}, s_0)$ the language over $W(I)$

$$L(\mathbf{M}, s_0, O_1) = \{P \mid \mathrm{resp}_{s_0}(P) = Qy,\ Q \in W(O),\ y \in O_1\}. \quad (5.4)$$

A language L is *representable* in a sequential machine, or shortly, L is *f.m.r.* iff, for some $\mathbf{M}$, s_0 and O_1, $L = L(\mathbf{M}, s_0, O_1)$.

It is an immediate consequence of (5.4) that a f.m.r. language can never contain the empty word. It turns out that this is the only difference between f.m.r. and f.a.r. languages. The following theorem is an immediate consequence of the definition and Theorem 5.1.

THEOREM 5.2. *The same languages are represented in two equivalent initial sequential machines. If the languages* $L_1, \ldots, L_m$ *are represented in an initial Moore machine they are represented also in an initial Mealy machine, and vice versa.*

For instance, as regards the equivalent sequential machines **ME** and **MO** of Fig. 10, we obtain the following results:

$$L(\mathbf{ME}, s_1, \phi) = L(\mathbf{MO}, \sigma_1, \phi) = L_\phi,$$

$$L(\mathbf{ME}, s_1, \{y_1, y_2\}) = L(\mathbf{MO},\ \sigma_1,\ \{y_1, y_2\}) = |(x_1 + x_2)(x_1 + x_2)^*|,$$

$$L(\mathbf{ME}, s_1, \{y_1\}) = L(\mathbf{MO}, \sigma_1, \{y_1\}) = |(x_1 + x_2)^*(x_1 x_2 + x_2 x_1)|,$$

$$L(\mathbf{ME}, s_1, \{y_2\}) = L(\mathbf{MO}, \sigma_1, \{y_2\}) = |(x_1 + x_2)^*(x_1 x_1 + x_2 x_2)|.$$

It is obvious that any finite deterministic automaton $\mathbf{A} = (S, s_0, f)$ over an alphabet I can be converted into an initial Mealy or Moore machine by introducing an output alphabet O and an output function φ. For any O and any function φ (which maps either $S \times I$ or S into O), the initial sequential machine $(\mathbf{M}, s_0)$, where $\mathbf{M} = (I, O, S, f, \varphi)$, is referred to as an *extension* of $\mathbf{A}$. Similarly, any initial sequential machine $(\mathbf{M}, s_0)$, where $\mathbf{M} = (I, O, S, f, \varphi)$, can be converted into the finite deterministic automaton $\mathbf{A} = (S, s_0, f)$ over I, referred to as the *restriction* of $(\mathbf{M}, s_0)$, by omitting O and φ. Note that restriction is unique, whereas extension is not unique.

THEOREM 5.3. *The set of f.m.r. languages coincides with the set of such f.a.r. languages which do not contain the empty word. If a language L is represented in a finite deterministic automaton* $\mathbf{A} = (S, s_0, f)$ *over an alphabet I, then* $L - \{\lambda\}$ *or L is represented in an initial Moore machine which is an extension of* $\mathbf{A}$, *depending upon whether or not* s_0 *is one of the representing states. If a language L is represented in an initial Moore machine* $(\mathbf{M}, s_0)$, *where* $\mathbf{M} = (I, O, S, f, \varphi)$, *by a set* $O_1 \subset O$, *then* $L + \{\lambda\}$ *or L is represented in the restriction of* $(\mathbf{M}, s_0)$, *depending upon whether or not* $\varphi(s_0) \in O_1$, *by the set consisting of all states s such that* $\varphi(s) \in O_1$.

Proof. The first sentence of the theorem follows from the other two sentences, by Theorem 5.2. To prove the second sentence, consider an extension $(\mathbf{M}, s_0)$ of $\mathbf{A}$, where $\mathbf{M} = (I, \{y_1, y_2\}, S, f, \varphi)$ and φ is defined as follows: $\varphi(s) = y_1$, if s is a state representing L; $\varphi(s) = y_2$, otherwise. Then $(\mathbf{M}, s_0)$ is an initial Moore machine, where $L - \{\lambda\}$ or L is represented by $\{y_1\}$, depending on whether or not s_0 is a representing state in the original automaton $\mathbf{A}$. Finally, the last sentence of Theorem 5.3 is an immediate consequence of the definitions. □

It is easy to see that Theorem 5.3 holds true also for m-tuples of languages. In particular, if the languages $L_1, \ldots, L_m$ are represented in a finite deterministic automaton $\mathbf{A} = (S, s_0, f)$, then the languages $L_1 - \{\lambda\}, \ldots, L_m - \{\lambda\}$ are represented in an extension of $\mathbf{A}$. One way to obtain such an extension is to map each state of $\mathbf{A}$ into a different output. However, one may accomplish this with fewer than card (S) output letters. (Cf. Exercise 5.9.)

EXERCISE 5.1. Can you formulate an equivalent definition of resp_s by replacing the left sides of the latter equations (5.1) and (5.2) by $\text{resp}_s (Px)$? (Cf. Exercise 2.1.)

EXERCISE 5.2. Prove that, for all P and Q,

$$\text{resp}_s (PQ) = \text{resp}_s (P) \, \text{resp}_{sP} (Q).$$

EXERCISE 5.3. Prove that if the states s and s' are equivalent then, for any word P, the states sP and $s'P$ are equivalent.

EXERCISE 5.4. An initial sequential machine $(\mathbf{M}, s_0)$ is termed *connected* (cf. Exercise 2.5) iff, for any state s of $\mathbf{M}$, there is a word P such that $s = s_0 P$. Show that if two connected initial sequential machines

(M_1, s_1) and (M_2, s_2) are equivalent then also the sequential machines M_1 and M_2 are equivalent.

EXERCISE 5.5 (Blokh, 1960). Given a Mealy machine $ME = (I, O, S, f, \varphi)$, consider the sequential machine

$$MO = (I, O, S \cup S \times I, f_1, \varphi_1),$$

where

$$f_1(s, x) = (s, x), \quad f_1((s, x,), x^1) = (f(s, x), x^1)$$

and

$$\varphi_1(s) = y_1, \quad \varphi_1((s,x)) = \varphi(s, x),$$

where $s \in S$, $x, x^1 \in I$ and y_1 is an arbitrary fixed element of O. Prove that MO is a Moore machine equivalent to ME. Combine this result and Theorem 5.1 to obtain an upper bound for the number of states in a Moore machine which is equivalent to a given Mealy machine.

EXERCISE 5.6. Modify the definition of languages represented in initial sequential machines to concern all sequential machines. State and prove theorems analogous to Theorems 5.2 and 5.3.

EXERCISE 5.7. Modify the definition of f.m.r. languages in such a way that they may contain also the empty word and that the set of f.m.r. languages equals the set of f.a.r. languages. Study the validity of Theorems 5.2 and 5.3 in this case.

EXERCISE 5.8. Develop techniques analogous to those presented in Section 3 for the solving of the analysis problem of sequential machines. (Cf. equations (3.1).)

EXERCISE 5.9. m distinct non-empty languages $L_1, \ldots, L_m$ are represented in an n-state automaton A. The same languages L_i, or $L_i - \{\lambda\}$, are represented in an extension MO of A, MO being a Moore machine. What is the least number of output letters MO can have?

EXERCISE 5.10. Instead of the given definition, define a sequential machine as an ordered quadruple (I, O, S, f), where I, O and S are finite non-empty sets and f maps the set $S \times I$ into the set $S \times O$. How do you now characterize the difference between Mealy and Moore machines?

§ 6. Experiments and minimization

According to the definition in the previous section, the states s and s' are equivalent iff $\mathrm{resp}_s = \mathrm{resp}_{s'}$. We shall now prove that to decide whether or not the equation mentioned is valid, it suffices to test it for words whose length does not exceed a certain bound. We shall also consider algorithms of eliminating superfluous states from a given sequential machine.

Let s and s' be states either in the same sequential machine or in two machines with the same input alphabet I, and let P be a word over I. We say that P *distinguishes* s and s' iff

$$\mathrm{resp}_s\,(P) \neq \mathrm{resp}_{s'}\,(P).$$

Clearly, two states are equivalent iff they are indistinguishable by all words.

THEOREM 6.1. *Let* $\mathbf{M} = (I, O, S, f, \varphi)$ *be a sequential machine with at least two states. For a natural number k, let $\mathcal{E}_k$ be the equivalence relation over S defined by the condition: $s\mathcal{E}_k s'$ holds iff s and s' are indistinguishable by all words of length not exceeding k. Then there is a number $u \leqq card(S) - 1$ such that $\mathcal{E}_u = \mathcal{E}_{u+1}$ and, furthermore, for any states s and s', s and s' are equivalent iff $s\mathcal{E}_u s'$.*

Proof. (By the equation $\mathcal{E}_u = \mathcal{E}_{u+1}$ we mean that $\mathcal{E}_u$ and $\mathcal{E}_{u+1}$ are the same relation, i.e. that the partitions corresponding to $\mathcal{E}_u$ and $\mathcal{E}_{u+1}$ coincide.) We note first that obviously each $\mathcal{E}_k$ is an equivalence relation. By the definition of $\mathcal{E}_k$, the partition corresponding to $\mathcal{E}_{k+1}$ refines that corresponding to $\mathcal{E}_k$, i.e. for each k, every equivalence class under $\mathcal{E}_{k+1}$ is contained in some equivalence class under $\mathcal{E}_k$. This is denoted by

$$\mathcal{E}_{k+1} \subset \mathcal{E}_k \qquad (k = 1, 2, \ldots). \tag{6.1}$$

If m_k is the number of equivalence classes under $\mathcal{E}_k$, then (6.1) implies the inequalities

$$m_{k+1} \geqq m_k \qquad (k = 1, 2, \ldots). \tag{6.2}$$

We now claim that if, for some k,

$$\mathcal{E}_{k+1} = \mathcal{E}_k, \tag{6.3}$$

then

$$\mathcal{E}_{k+j} = \mathcal{E}_k \qquad (j = 1, 2, \ldots). \qquad (6.4)$$

Assume the contrary: for some j, there is a word of length less than or equal to $k+j$ which distinguishes two states s and s' indistinguishable by all words of length not exceeding k. Let

$$P = x_1 \ldots x_k x_{k+1} \ldots x_{k+v}$$

be the shortest word which distinguishes s and s'. By (6.3), $2 \leqq v \leqq j$. Consider the states

$$s_1 = sx_1 \ldots x_{v-1}, \quad s_1' = s'x_1 \ldots x_{v-1}.$$

If s_1 and s_1' are not equivalent under $\mathcal{E}_k$, then there is a word Q of length at most k which distinguishes them. But this implies that the word $x_1 \ldots x_{v-1}Q$, which is of length less than $k+v$, distinguishes s and s'. Because this contradicts the choice of P, we conclude that $s_1\mathcal{E}_k s_1'$. On the other hand, because P distinguishes s and s', the word $P_1 = x_v \ldots x_{k+v}$ distinguishes s_1 and s_1'. But lg $(P_1) = k+1$, which contradicts (6.3). Hence, (6.3) implies (6.4). In particular, if (6.3) holds for some k, then two states s and s' are equivalent iff $s\mathcal{E}_k s'$.

If $m_1 = 1$, then obviously $\mathcal{E}_2 = \mathcal{E}_1$. Thus, we may choose $u=1$. Assume that

$$m_1 \geqq 2. \qquad (6.5)$$

Because, for all k, $m_k \leqq$ card (S), it follows from (6.2) and (6.5) that there is a number $u \leqq$ card $(S)-1$ such that $m_u = m_{u+1}$. Consequently, by (6.1), $\mathcal{E}_{u+1} = \mathcal{E}_u$. □

THEOREM 6.2. *Two states s and s' of a sequential machine* $\mathbf{M} = (I, O, S, f, \varphi)$ *are equivalent iff*

$$\text{resp}_s (P) = \text{resp}_{s'} (P), \qquad (6.6)$$

for all words P of length less than or equal to card $(S)-1$. This upper bound is the best possible in the general case.

Proof. The theorem is true if card $(S)=1$. Therefore, we assume that card $(S) \geqq 2$. The equation (6.6) holds for all words P of length less than or equal to card $(S)-1$ iff it holds for all words P of length card $(S)-1$. Clearly, if s and s' are equivalent, then (6.6) holds for all words P of length card $(S)-1$. Conversely, if (6.6) holds for all words P of length card $(S)-1$, then it follows from Theorem 6.1 that s and s' are equivalent. To prove that the upper bound is the best possible, we consider the Mealy machine

$$(\{x_1, x_2\}, \{0, 1\}, \{s_1, \ldots, s_n\}, f, \varphi),$$

defined by Fig. 11. The states s_n and s_{n-1} are indistinguishable by any word of length less than $n-1$. $\square$

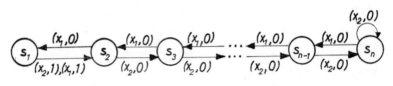

FIG. 11.

THEOREM 6.3. *A state s_1 of a sequential machine* $\mathbf{M}_1 = (I, O_1, S_1, f_1, \varphi_1)$ *and a state s_2 of a sequential machine* $\mathbf{M}_2 = (I, O_2, S_2, f_2, \varphi_2)$ *are equivalent iff they are indistinguishable by all words of length not exceeding* card $(S_1)+$ card $(S_2)-1$. *This upper bound is the best possible in the general case.*

Proof. Without loss of generality, we may assume that the sets S_1 and S_2 are disjoint. By Theorem 5.1 (first sentence), we may also assume that both machines are Mealy machines. Consider the "sum" of the machines $\mathbf{M}_1$ and $\mathbf{M}_2$:

$$\mathbf{M} = (I, O_1 \cup O_2, \quad S_1 \cup S_2, f, \varphi),$$

where, for $s \in S_i$ $(i = 1, 2), f(s, x) = f_i(s, x)$ and $\varphi(s, x) = \varphi_i(s, x)$. Then a state s_1 of $\mathbf{M}_1$ and a state s_2 of $\mathbf{M}_2$ are equivalent iff they are equivalent, regarded as states of $\mathbf{M}$. Hence, by Theorem 6.2, the first part of the theorem follows.

To prove the second part, we consider the Mealy machines

$$\mathbf{M}_1 = (\{x_1, x_2\}, \{0, 1\}, \{s_1, \ldots, s_n\}, f_1, \varphi_1)$$

and

$$\mathbf{M}_2 = (\{x_1, x_2\}, \{0, 1\}, \{s_1' \ldots, s_n'\}, f_2, \varphi_2),$$

defined by Fig. 12, where $n \geqq 3$. The states s_1 and s_1' are distinguished by the word $x_2^n x_1^{n-1}$ but are indistinguishable by any shorter word. This proves the assertion in the case where both $\mathbf{M}_1$ and $\mathbf{M}_2$ possess an equal number $\geqq 3$ states. The task of presenting similar examples for the other cases is left to the reader. $\square$

We shall now determine the "minimal" machine, i.e. the machine with the smallest number of states which is equivalent to a given machine. In the following discussion there is a slight difference between Mealy and Moore machines. In both cases the minimal machine will be unique.

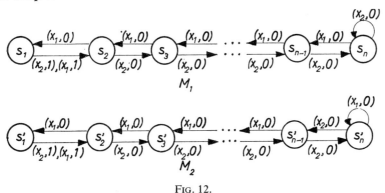

FIG. 12.

DEFINITION. A Mealy machine $\mathbf{M}_1 = (I, O, S_1, f_1, \varphi_1)$ is *isomorphic* to a Mealy machine $\mathbf{M}_2 = (I, O, S_2, f_2, \varphi_2)$ iff there exists a one-to-one mapping ϱ of S_1 *onto* S_2 such that, for all $x \in I$ and $s \in S_1$,

$$\varrho(f_1(s, x)) = f_2(\varrho(s), x); \quad \varphi_1(s, x) = \varphi_2(\varrho(s), x).$$

A Moore machine $\mathbf{M}_1 = (I, O, S_1, f_1, \varphi_1)$ is *isomorphic* to a Moore machine $\mathbf{M}_2 = (I, O, S_2, f_2, \varphi_2)$ iff there exists a one-to-one mapping ϱ of S_1 *onto* S_2 such that, for all $x \in I$ and $s \in S_1$,

$$\varrho(f_1(s, x)) = f_2(\varrho(s), x); \quad \varphi_1(s) = \varphi_2(\varrho(s)).$$

Such mappings ϱ are referred to as *isomorphisms*.

Clearly, the relation "$\mathbf{M}_1$ is isomorphic to $\mathbf{M}_2$" is an equivalence relation. Two sequential machines are isomorphic iff they have the same graph, except for a relabeling of the states.

DEFINITION. A Mealy machine is *reduced* iff it possesses no two equivalent states. Two states, either in the same Moore machine or in two different Moore machines, are termed *Moore-equivalent* iff they are equivalent and, furthermore, both are mapped into the same output. Two Moore machines $\mathbf{M}_1$ and $\mathbf{M}_2$ are termed *Moore-equivalent* iff, for each state in $\mathbf{M}_1$, there is a Moore-equivalent state in $\mathbf{M}_2$, and vice versa. A Moore machine is *reduced* iff no two of its states are Moore-equivalent.

THEOREM 6.4. *Among all Mealy machines equivalent to a given Mealy machine there is a unique (up to isomorphism) one with the smallest number of states. More specifically, let* $\mathbf{M} = (I, O, S, f, \varphi)$ *be a given Mealy machine. Then there exists a Mealy machine* $\mathbf{M}_1 = (I, O, S_1, f_1, \varphi_1)$ *with the following properties:*

(i) $\mathbf{M}_1$ *is equivalent to* $\mathbf{M}$;
(ii) *there is no Mealy machine* $\mathbf{M}_2$ *which is equivalent to* $\mathbf{M}$ *and has fewer states than* $\mathbf{M}_1$;
(iii) *if a Mealy machine* $\mathbf{M}_2$ *is equivalent to* $\mathbf{M}$ *and has equally many states as* $\mathbf{M}_1$, *then* $\mathbf{M}_2$ *and* $\mathbf{M}_1$ *are isomorphic;*
(iv) $\mathbf{M}_1$ *is reduced;*
(v) *there is an algorithm which yields, for any* $\mathbf{M}$, *the corresponding machine* $\mathbf{M}_1$.

Proof. Given a Mealy machine $\mathbf{M} = (I, O, S, f, \varphi)$, we first define the equivalence relations $\mathcal{E}_k$ as in Theorem 6.1 and determine a number u such that $\mathcal{E}_u = \mathcal{E}_{u+1}$. By Theorem 6.1, two states s and s' are equivalent, in symbols $s\mathcal{E}s'$, iff $s\mathcal{E}_u s'$. The equivalence class under $\mathcal{E}$ determined by a state s is denoted by $[s]$. The set of all equivalence classes under $\mathcal{E}$ is denoted by S_1.

To complete the definition of the machine $\mathbf{M}_1$, we define functions f_1 and φ_1 as follows:

$$f_1([s], x) = [f(s, x)]; \quad \varphi_1([s], x) = \varphi(s, x), \qquad (6.7)$$

for all $s \in S$ and $x \in I$. Clearly, if $s_1 \mathcal{E} s_2$ and $x \in I$, then $f(s_1, x)\mathcal{E}f(s_2, x)$. (Cf. Exercise 5.3.) Therefore, we may conclude that the definitions (6.7) are independent of the representatives chosen from each equivalence class and, hence, $\mathbf{M}_1 = (I, O, S_1, f_1, \varphi_1)$ is a Mealy machine.

Obviously, $\mathbf{M}_1$ satisfies condition (v). It satisfies also condition (i) because, for any $s \in S$, the state s of $\mathbf{M}$ and $[s]$ of $\mathbf{M}_1$ are equivalent.

Assume that $\mathbf{M}_2$ is a Mealy machine with a set of states S_2 such that $\mathbf{M}$ and $\mathbf{M}_2$ are equivalent. To each state $s_2 \in S_2$, there corresponds an equivalent state $s \in S$. On the other hand, to each $s \in S$, there corresponds a unique $[s] \in S_1$ which is equivalent to s. To each state $s_2 \in S_2$, we associate the element $[s] \in S_1$, thus defined. The element $[s] \in S_1$ does not depend on the choice of $s \in S$ and, hence, this association ϱ is a mapping of the set S_2 into the set S_1. It is immediately verified that ϱ is a mapping onto S_1. Hence, card $(S_2) \geqq$ card (S_1), and $\mathbf{M}_1$ satisfies condition (ii). Furthermore, if card $(S_2) =$ card (S_1) then ϱ is a one-to-one mapping and, by (6.7), also an isomorphism. Consequently, $\mathbf{M}_1$ satisfies condition (iii).

If $\mathbf{M}_1$ contains two equivalent states, then the sequential machine $\mathbf{M}_3$ obtained from $\mathbf{M}_1$, using the same construction as in the transition from $\mathbf{M}$ to $\mathbf{M}_1$, has fewer states than $\mathbf{M}_1$ and is equivalent to $\mathbf{M}_1$ and to $\mathbf{M}$. But this contradicts the fact that $\mathbf{M}_1$ satisfies (ii). Hence, $\mathbf{M}_1$ contains no two equivalent states and, thus, satisfies (iv). $\square$

The proof of the following theorem, being almost the same as that of Theorem 6.4, is omitted. The only difference is that one has to add a condition corresponding to Moore-equivalence to the definition of the equivalence relations $\mathcal{E}_k$.

THEOREM 6.5. *Among all Moore machines Moore-equivalent to a given Moore machine there is a unique (up to isomorphism) one with the smallest number of states. More specifically, let* $\mathbf{M} = (I, O, S, f, \varphi)$ *be a given Moore machine. Then there exists a Moore machine* $\mathbf{M}_1 = (I, O, S_1, f_1, \varphi_1)$ *with the following properties:*

(i) $\mathbf{M}_1$ *is Moore-equivalent to* $\mathbf{M}$;

(ii) *there is no Moore machine* $\mathbf{M}_2$ *which is Moore-equivalent to* $\mathbf{M}$ *and has fewer states than* $\mathbf{M}_1$;

(iii) *if a Moore machine* $\mathbf{M}_2$ *is Moore-equivalent to* $\mathbf{M}$ *and has equally many states as* $\mathbf{M}_1$, *then* $\mathbf{M}_2$ *and* $\mathbf{M}_1$ *are isomorphic;*

(iv) $\mathbf{M}_1$ *is reduced;*

(v) *there is an algorithm of constructing* $\mathbf{M}_1$, *given* $\mathbf{M}$.

As an illustration of Theorem 6.5, we consider the Moore machine defined by Fig. 3. (The output alphabet consists of three letters 0, 1, 2. The circles are mapped into 0, triangles into 1 and squares into 2.) First the equivalence classes under the relations $\mathcal{E}_k$ are computed:

$$\mathcal{E}_1: \quad \{s_1, s_3, s_4\}, \quad \{s_0\}, \quad \{s_2, s_6\}, \quad \{s_5, s_8\}, \quad \{s_7, s_9\};$$
$$\mathcal{E}_2: \quad \{s_1, s_3, s_4\}, \quad \{s_0\}, \quad \{s_2\}, \quad \{s_6\}, \quad \{s_5, s_8\}, \quad \{s_7, s_9\}.$$

$\mathcal{E}_3 = \mathcal{E}_2$, hence we may choose $u = 2$ (cf. Theorem 6.1). The minimal machine is given in Fig. 13.

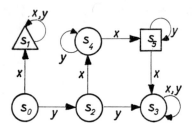

FIG. 13.

EXERCISE 6.1. Assume that the machines considered in Theorems 6.2 and 6.3 are Moore machines. Can you obtain in this case a better upper bound for the length of the experiments needed?

EXERCISE 6.2. Prove Theorem 6.5. Why is it necessary to add the requirement $\varphi(s) = \varphi(s')$ to the definition of a reduced Moore machine? Compare the proofs of Theorems 4.1 (especially the last part), 6.4 and 6.5.

EXERCISE 6.3. Find a method, as simple as possible, to determine the equivalence classes under $\mathcal{E}_{k+1}$ (cf. Theorem 6.1), provided the equivalence classes under $\mathcal{E}_k$ are known. Describe the analogous method for Moore machines. (Cf. the remark preceding Theorem 6.5.)

EXERCISE 6.4. Prove that isomorphic Mealy machines are equivalent and isomorphic Moore machines are Moore-equivalent. Show by counter examples that the converses of these statements do not hold true.

EXERCISE 6.5. Prove that two reduced Mealy machines are equivalent iff they are isomorphic.

EXERCISE 6.6. Let $M_1 = (I, O, S_1, f_1, \varphi_1)$ and $M_2 = (I, O, S_2, f_2, \varphi_2)$ be Mealy machines and ϱ a mapping of S_1 onto S_2 such that

$$\varrho(f_1(s, x)) = f_2(\varrho(s), x); \quad \varphi_1(s, x) = \varphi_2(\varrho(s), x), \quad x \in I, \quad s \in S_1.$$

Then M_2 is said to be a *homomorphic image* of M_1 and ϱ is said to be a *homomorphism*. Show that M_1 and M_2 are equivalent. Conclude that two homomorphic images of the same Mealy machine are equivalent. Show that the Mealy machine M_1 of Theorem 6.4 is a homomorphic image of any machine equivalent to M. Define homomorphisms and state and prove the corresponding results for Moore machines.

EXERCISE 6.7. Let M_1 and M_2 be sequential machines with the same input alphabet. Assume that, for each state s_1 of M_1 and each word P, there is a state s_2 of M_2 such that

$$\mathrm{resp}_{s_1}(P) = \mathrm{resp}_{s_2}(P),$$

and vice versa. Does it follow that M_1 and M_2 are equivalent? If not, give a counter example.

EXERCISE 6.8. Assume that M is a reduced Mealy machine. Does there exist a word P which distinguishes any two states of M? If not, give a counter example.

EXERCISE 6.9. Apply results established in this section to finite deterministic automata. In particular, show that there is an algorithm of determining the weight of a regular language and, more generally, the weight of an m-tuple of regular languages. (Consider an algorithm corresponding to Theorems 6.4 and 6.5 and not the trivial one: synthesize first by Theorem 2.3 and then check through all automata with fewer states.)

EXERCISE 6.10. (Preferably after reading Chapter III.) Modify the synthesis procedure presented in Section 3 in such a way that the resulting automaton is always minimal. Cf. also Brzozowski (1964).

§ 7. Sequential functions and relations

To each state s of a sequential machine $\mathbf{M} = (I, O, S, f, \varphi)$ there corresponds a function (resp$_s$) mapping the set $W(I)$ into the set $W(O)$. Conversely, one may ask under what conditions a mapping of $W(I)$ into (WO) is a response function of some sequential machine. We shall first solve the corresponding simpler problem for finite deterministic automata.

DEFINITION. A finite deterministic automaton $\mathbf{A} = (S, s_0, f)$ over an alphabet I is said to *realize* the function $\mathbf{A}_f : W(I) \to S$, where $\mathbf{A}_f(P) = s_0 P$, for all $P \in W(I)$. A function ψ mapping $W(I)$ into S, where I is a finite alphabet and S a finite non-empty set, is said to be *realizable* in a finite deterministic automaton iff, for some $\mathbf{A}$ over I, $\psi = \mathbf{A}_f$.

THEOREM 7.1. *Let I be a finite alphabet and S a finite non-empty set. A mapping ψ of $W(I)$ into S is realizable in a finite deterministic automaton iff, for all $P_1, P_2 \in W(I)$ and $x \in I$, the equation $\psi(P_1) = \psi(P_2)$ implies the equation $\psi(P_1 x) = \psi(P_2 x)$.*

Proof. Because, for any automaton $\mathbf{A}$ over I, the equation $s_0 P_1 = s_0 P_2$ implies the equation $s_0 P_1 x = s_0 P_2 x$, we conclude that the given condition is necessary for the realizability of ψ.

Assume, conversely, that $\psi : W(I) \to S$ satisfies the given condition. Let S_1 be the subset of S such that ψ is a mapping onto S_1. Denote $\psi(\lambda) = s_0$. Clearly, $s_0 \in S_1$. Consider the finite deterministic automaton $\mathbf{A} = (S_1, s_0, f)$, where f is defined as follows. For an element $s \in S_1$, choose a word $P_s \in W(I)$ such that $\psi(P_s) = s$. For $x \in I$, define

$$f(s, x) = \psi(P_s x).$$

This definition is independent of the choice of P_s, because if $s = \psi(P_s) = \psi(P'_s)$, then also $\psi(P_s x) = \psi(P'_s x)$. It is clear that $\psi = \mathbf{A}_f$. $\square$

DEFINITION. Let ψ be a mapping of $W(I)$ into $W(O)$, where I and O are alphabets. ψ is termed *length preserving* iff $\lg(\psi(P)) = \lg(P)$, for all $P \in W(I)$. ψ is termed *initial subwords preserving* iff, for all $P, Q \in W(I)$, $\psi(PQ)$ is of the form $\psi(P)R$, where $R \in W(O)$. For an initial subwords preserving function ψ and $P \in W(I)$, the mapping ψ_P of $W(I)$ into $W(O)$, defined by the equation $\psi_P(Q) = R$ is termed a *derivative* of ψ (where Q and R are as in the previous sentence). Finally, ψ is termed a *sequential function* iff, for some Mealy machine $\mathbf{M} = (I, O, S, f, \varphi)$ and some $s \in S$, $\psi = \text{resp}_s$. In this case ψ is said to be *realized* by $\mathbf{M}$.

Note that $\psi(\lambda) = \lambda$, for a length preserving ψ, and that all derivatives are initial subwords preserving. Furthermore, all derivatives of a length preserving function are length preserving.

THEOREM 7.2. *A mapping of $W(I)$ into $W(O)$, where I and O are finite alphabets, is a sequential function iff it is* (i) *length preserving,* (ii) *initial subwords preserving and* (iii) *possesses only a finite number of distinct derivatives. Furthermore, the number of derivatives (if finite) equals the number of states in a Mealy machine with fewest states which realizes the mapping.*

Proof. Let ψ be a mapping of $W(I)$ into $W(O)$ which satisfies (i)–(iii). Let

$$D(\psi) = \{\psi_{P_1}, \ldots, \psi_{P_n}\}$$

be the set of distinct derivatives of ψ. Because ψ itself is a derivative of ψ, we may assume that $P_1 = \lambda$. Consider the ordered quintuple $\mathbf{M} = (I, O, D(\psi), f, \varphi)$, where

$$f(\psi_{P_i}, x) = \psi_{P_i x}, \quad \varphi(\psi_{P_i}, x) = \psi_{P_i}(x),$$

for $\psi_{P_i} \in D(\psi)$, $x \in I$. By our assumption, all derivatives $\psi_{P_i x}$ belong to $D(\psi)$. Because ψ is length preserving, we conclude that $\psi_{P_i}(x)$ is a letter of O. Hence, $\mathbf{M}$ is a Mealy machine. We now claim that $\text{resp}_{s_0} = \psi$, where $s_0 = \psi_{P_1} = \psi_\lambda$. To prove this we show by induction on the length of Q that

$$\text{resp}_{s_0}(Q) = \psi(Q). \tag{7.1}$$

By the definition of the function resp_{s_0} and because ψ is length preserving, (7.1) holds if $\lg(Q) = 0$. Assume that (7.1) holds for words of length k and let $Q_1 = Q_2 x$, $x \in I$, be of length $k+1$. Then

$$\text{resp}_{s_0}(Q_1) = \text{resp}_{s_0}(Q_2)\,\varphi(s_0 Q_2, x) = \psi(Q_2)\,\psi_{Q_2}(x) = \psi(Q_2 x) = \psi(Q_1),$$

because, for any word Q_2, $s_0 Q_2 = \psi_{Q_2}$, by the definition of f. Hence, (7.1) holds for all words Q, and we conclude that the conditions (i)–(iii) are sufficient for ψ to be a sequential function.

Conversely, assume that ψ is a sequential function, realized by a Mealy machine $\mathbf{M} = (I, O, S, f, \varphi)$. In particular, let

$$\psi = \text{resp}_{s_1}, \quad s_1 \in S. \tag{7.2}$$

Clearly, for all $P, Q \in W(I)$,

$$\text{lg}\,(\text{resp}_{s_1}(P)) = \text{lg}\,(P); \quad \text{resp}_{s_1}(PQ) = \text{resp}_{s_1}(P)R,$$

for some $R \in W(O)$. Therefore, ψ is length and initial subwords preserving. For $P \in W(I)$, associate with the derivative ψ_P the state $s_1 P$ and denote the association by ϱ:

$$\varrho(\psi_P) = s_1 P.$$

Assume that the derivatives ψ_{P_1} and ψ_{P_2} are distinct, and let Q be a word such that $\psi_{P_1}(Q) \neq \psi_{P_2}(Q)$. Clearly, by (7.2),

$$\text{resp}_{s_1 P_1}(Q) = \psi_{P_1}(Q) \neq \psi_{P_2}(Q) = \text{resp}_{s_1 P_2}(Q),$$

which proves that $s_1 P_1 \neq s_1 P_2$. Hence, ϱ is a one-to-one mapping of the set $D(\psi)$, consisting of the derivatives of ψ, into the set S. Because S is finite this implies that $D(\psi)$ is finite and, furthermore,

$$\text{card}\,(D(\psi)) \leq \text{card}\,(S).$$

We conclude that the conditions (i)–(iii) are also necessary for ψ to be a sequential function and that the second sentence of the theorem holds true. $\square$

As an illustration, we consider the length and initial subwords preserving function ψ mapping $W(\{x\})$ into $W(\{0, 1\})$ such that the last letter of $\psi(x^n)$ is 1 iff $n = 3k$, for some natural number k. (Cf. also Exercise 7.2.) Thus,

$$\psi(\lambda) = \lambda, \quad \psi(x) = 0, \quad \psi(x^2) = 00, \quad \psi(x^3) = 001, \quad \psi(x^4) = 0010,$$
$$\psi(x^5) = 00100, \quad \psi(x^6) = 001001, \quad \psi(x^7) = 0010010, \ldots.$$

It is immediately verified that ψ possesses only three distinct derivatives, namely, ψ, ψ_x, ψ_{x^2}. Hence, ψ is a sequential function. It is realized by the Mealy machine defined by Fig. 14, where $\psi = \text{resp}_{s_0}$.

Given finite alphabets I and O, we shall consider binary relations $\mathcal{F}(P, Q)$ over $W(I) \times W(O)$, i.e. P ranges over $W(I)$ and Q over $W(O)$.

Such a relation $\mathcal{F}(P, Q)$ can be identified with the set of ordered pairs

$$\{(P, Q) | \mathcal{F}(P, Q)\}.$$

Hence, set theoretical operations may be performed on these relations. One may also identify a function f mapping $W(I)$ into $W(O)$ with the relation $\mathcal{F}(P, Q)$ such that $\mathcal{F}(P, Q)$ holds iff $Q = f(P)$.

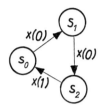

FIG. 14.

DEFINITION. The *sequential relation* $\mathcal{SR}_M$ *realized* by a Mealy machine $\mathbf{M} = (I, O, S, f, \varphi)$ is defined by the condition: $\mathcal{SR}_M(P, Q)$ iff $P \in W(I)$ and $Q = \text{resp}_s(P)$, for some $s \in S$. A binary relation $\mathcal{F}$ over $W(I) \times W(O)$ is termed *sequential* iff, for some $\mathbf{M}$, $\mathcal{F} = \mathcal{SR}_M$.

THEOREM 7.3. *A relation $\mathcal{F}$ over $W(I) \times W(O)$ is sequential iff there exists a finite number n of sequential functions $\psi_1, \ldots, \psi_n$ mapping $W(I)$ into $W(O)$ such that*

(i) $\mathcal{F} = \bigcup_{i=1}^{n} \psi_i$;

(ii) *for each $x \in I$ and each i, $1 \leq i \leq n$, there exists a j such that, for all $P \in W(I)$, $\psi_i(xP) = \psi_i(x) \psi_j(P)$.*

Proof. If $\mathcal{F}$ is a sequential relation realized by a Mealy machine with the states $s_1, \ldots, s_n$ then the functions $\psi_i = \text{resp}_{s_i}$, $i = 1, \ldots, n$, satisfy conditions (i) and (ii). (In particular, j in condition (ii) is determined by the equation $s_i x = s_j$.)

Conversely, assume that there are sequential functions $\psi_1, \ldots, \psi_n$ such that (i) and (ii) are satisfied. Consider the ordered quintuple $\mathbf{M} = (I, O, S, f, \varphi)$, where $S = \{\psi_1, \ldots, \psi_n\}$ and, for $x \in I$ and $1 \leq i \leq n$, $\varphi(\psi_i, x) = \psi_i(x)$ and $f(\psi_i, x) = \psi_j$ where

$$j = \min \{k \,|\, \psi_i(xP) = \psi_i(x) \psi_k(P), \quad \text{for all} \quad P \in W(I)\}.$$

Condition (ii) guarantees that f is well defined and, hence, **M** is a Mealy machine. Furthermore,

$$\mathcal{SR}_{\mathbf{M}} = \{(P, Q) \mid P \in W(I), \quad Q = \mathrm{resp}_s(P), \ s \in S\}$$

$$= \bigcup_{i=1}^{n} \bigcup_{P \in W(I)} (P, \psi_i(P)) = \bigcup_{i=1}^{n} \psi_i = \mathcal{F}.$$

Therefore, $\mathcal{F}$ is sequential. $\square$

EXERCISE 7.1. Instead of a Mealy machine, use a Moore machine in the definitions of sequential functions and relations. Are Theorems 7.2 and 7.3 still valid?

EXERCISE 7.2. Assume that a mapping ψ of $W(I)$ into $W(O)$ is length and initial subwords preserving. Define a mapping φ_1 of $W(I)$ into O by the condition that $\psi_1(P)$ equals the last letter of $\psi(P)$, for all $P \in W(I)$. Show that there is a one-to-one correspondence between functions ψ and ψ_1 and, furthermore, that the values of ψ can be effectively determined from the values of ψ_1. Cf. also Karp (1967).

EXERCISE 7.3. Assume that ψ is a length and initial subwords preserving mapping of $W(I)$ into $W(O)$ and, furthermore, that ψ^{-1} preserves regularity of languages (i.e. whenever $L \subset W(O)$ is regular then also $\{P \mid \psi(P) \in L\}$ is regular). Prove that ψ is a sequential function. Does the same conclusion hold true if the last assumption is replaced by the assumption that ψ preserves regularity of languages? (In Ginsburg and Rose (1966) this result is credited to J. Rhodes and E. Shamir.)

EXERCISE 7.4 (Gray and Harrison, 1966). Assume that $\mathcal{F}$ is a sequential relation over $W(I) \times W(O)$ which is a function, i.e. for each $P \in W(I)$, there is exactly one $Q \in W(O)$ such that $\mathcal{F}(P, Q)$. Prove that $\mathcal{F}$ is a sequential function. Show by a counter example that a sequential function need not be a sequential relation.

EXERCISE 7.5 (Elgot, 1961; Gray and Harrison, 1966). A binary relation $\mathcal{F}$ over $W(I) \times W(O)$ is said to be *length preserving* iff, for all P and Q, $\mathcal{F}(P, Q)$ implies that $\lg(P) = \lg(Q)$. A length preserving relation is *closed* under *initial (final) subwords* iff, for all P_1, P_2, Q_1, Q_2, the conditions $\mathcal{F}(P_1 P_2, Q_1 Q_2)$ and $\lg(P_1) = \lg(Q_1)$ ($\lg(P_2) = \lg(Q_2)$) imply the condition $\mathcal{F}(P_1, Q_1)$ ($\mathcal{F}(P_2, Q_2)$). Prove that sequential relations are closed under initial and final subwords.

EXERCISE 7.6 (Gray and Harrison, 1966). Study closure properties of sequential relations under Boolean operations.

EXERCISE 7.7 (Gill, 1966; Gray and Harrison, 1966). Study the following synthesis problem of sequential machines: to construct **M**, given some pairs (P, Q) such that $\mathcal{SR}_\mathbf{M}(P, Q)$, or given some values of a sequential function realized by **M**.

EXERCISE 7.8 (Spivak, 1965, 3). Let f be a length and initial subwords preserving mapping of $W(I)$ into $W(O)$ (where I and O are finite alphabets). For $P = x_1 \ldots x_k \in W(I)$ and $f(P) = y_1 \ldots y_k \in W(O)$, define

$$P_f = (x_1, y_1) \ldots (x_k, y_k)$$

and regard P_f as a word over the alphabet $I \times O$. Prove that f is a sequential function iff the language consisting of all words P_f, where $P \in W(I)$, is regular over the alphabet $I \times O$.

§ 8. Definite languages and non-initial automata

Two families of regular languages, definite and finite languages, will be studied in the next two sections. Definite languages are completely characterized by final subwords of a given length k. The behavior of definite automata depends exclusively on the latest k input letters, for some k. Thus, the behavior is independent of inputs which have occurred at sufficiently remote past moments. All languages and automata considered in this section are over a finite alphabet I.

DEFINITION. Let k be a non-negative integer and L a language such that, for any $P \in W(I)$ satisfying $\lg(P) \geqq k$, P belongs to L iff the final subword of P consisting of k letters belongs to L. Such languages L are termed *weakly k-definite*. For $k > 0$, a language L is *k-definite* iff L is weakly k-definite but not weakly $(k-1)$-definite. A language L is *0-definite* iff it is weakly 0-definite.

Clearly, for $k \geqq 1$, a weakly k-definite language L is k-definite iff there are words $P \in L$ and $Q \notin L$ such that $\lg(P) \geqq k-1$ and $\lg(Q) \geqq k-1$, and P and Q have the same final subword of $k-1$ letters. This implies our first theorem.

THEOREM 8.1. *A weakly k-definite language is weakly k_1-definite, for all $k_1 \geqq k$. A weakly k-definite language is k'-definite, for some k' where $0 \leqq k' \leqq k$. A language is k-definite for at most one k.*

Theorem 8.1 guarantees the unambiguity of the following.

DEFINITION. If L is k-definite, k is called the *degree* of L, in symbols, deg $(L) = k$. A language L is called *definite* iff there is an integer k such that L is k-definite.

For instance, every finite language is definite. The degree of the empty language L_ϕ equals 0. For a non-empty finite language L,

$$\deg (L) = 1 + \max \{\lg (P)|P \in L\}.$$

The language represented by A_2 in Fig. 4 (where representing states are squares) is definite with degree 2, whereas the language represented by $\{s_1\}$ in the automaton of Fig. 13 is not definite.

THEOREM 8.2. *All definite languages are regular. More specifically, for any definite language L, there are finite languages L_1 and L_2 such that*

$$L = L_1 + W(I)L_2. \tag{8.1}$$

Furthermore, the length of the longest word in the language $L_1 + L_2$ does not exceed the degree of L. Conversely, all languages of the form (8.1), where L_1 and L_2 are finite, are definite.

Proof. The last sentence is obvious. To prove the other sentences, we note first that the only 0-definite languages over I are L_ϕ and $W(I)$ which both are of the form (8.1), where $L_1 + L_2$ does not contain words of length greater than 0.

Assume that L is k-definite, for $k \geqq 1$. If L is finite, we may choose $L_2 = L_\phi$ and $L_1 = L$, and also the assertion concerning the degree of L holds true. If L is infinite, denote by $L^{(k)}$ the subset of L consisting of all words of length k. Because L is k-definite, we obtain

$$L = L_1 + W(I)L^{(k)},$$

where every word in L_1 is of length less than k and, hence, L_1 is finite. Clearly, the assertion concerning the degree of L holds true also in this case. □

We shall now introduce the notion of definiteness also for the transition function of a finite deterministic automaton. To say that a transition function f is weakly k-definite means that, for all words P of length at least k, the state $f(s, P) = sP$ does not depend on s and depends only on the last k letters of P, i.e. with respect to sufficiently long words, the behavior of the automaton remains unchanged if the initial state is changed and also if the input letters, other than the k last ones, are changed.

DEFINITION. Let f be the transition function of a finite deterministic automaton with the set of states S, and let $k \geqq 0$. The function f is *weakly k-definite* iff, for all $P \in W(I)$, the inequality $\lg(P) \geqq k$ implies that $f(s, P) = f(s', P)$, for all states $s, s' \in S$. For $k > 0$, the function f is *k-definite* iff it is weakly k-definite but not weakly $(k-1)$-definite. The function f is *0-definite* iff it is weakly 0-definite. The function f is *definite* iff, for some $k \geqq 0$, f is k-definite. Then k is called the *degree* of f.

In the next two theorems it will be shown how the two notions of definiteness, one concerning languages and the other concerning transition functions, are interrelated.

THEOREM 8.3. *Any language represented in a finite deterministic automaton with a definite transition function is definite, whereby the degree of the language does not exceed the degree of the function.*

Proof. Assume that the transition function f of a finite deterministic automaton $\mathbf{A} = (S, s_0, f)$ is k-definite. Let L be a language represented in $\mathbf{A}$ by the set $S_1 \subset S$. Consider two words $P_1 = Q_1 Q$ and $P_2 = Q_2 Q$, where Q is a word of length k. Denote $s_0 Q_1 = s_1$ and $s_0 Q_2 = s_2$. Because f is k-definite, $s_1 Q = s_2 Q$. Hence, $s_0 P_1 = s_0 P_2$. Therefore, for any $P \in W(I)$ satisfying $\lg(P) \geqq k$, P belongs to L iff the final subword of P consisting of k letters belongs to L. This implies that L is weakly k-definite and hence, by Theorem 8.1, L is k'-definite, for some $k' \leqq k$. □

THEOREM 8.4. *Assume that a k-definite language L is represented in a finite deterministic automaton* $\mathbf{A} = (S, s_0, f)$ *such that* card (S) *equals the weight of L. Then f is k-definite.*

Proof. Let $s, s' \in S$. There are words P and P' such that $s_0 P = s$ and $s_0 P' = s'$ because, otherwise, s or s' could be removed from S without changing any language represented in $\mathbf{A}$ and, thus, we would have $w(L) < $ card (S). Choose an arbitrary word $Q \in W(I)$ such that $\lg(Q) \geqq k$. Denote $sQ = s_1$, $s'Q = s_2$. Assume that L is represented by $S_1 \subset S$. Since L is k-definite, $PQQ' \in L$ iff $P'QQ' \in L$, for all words $Q' \in W(I)$.

Hence, $s_0 P Q Q' \in S_1$ iff $s_0 P' Q Q' \in S_1$. Thus, for all $Q' \in W(I)$, $s_1 Q' \in S_1$ iff $s_2 Q' \in S_1$. Because $w(L) = \text{card } (S)$, this implies that $s_1 = s_2$ (since, otherwise, we could reduce the number of states by identifying s_1 and s_2). We have shown that, for arbitrary $s, s' \in S$ and $Q \in W(I)$, where $\lg (Q) \geqq k$, $s Q = s' Q$. This implies that f is weakly k-definite.

If $k = 0$, then f is k-definite. Assume that $k \geqq 1$. Because L is not weakly $(k-1)$-definite, there are words $P_1, P_1', P_2 \in W(I)$, where $\lg (P_2) = k - 1$, such that $P_1 P_2 \in L$ and $P_1' P_2 \notin L$. Thus, $s_0 P_1 P_2 \in S_1$ and $s_0 P_1' P_2 \notin S_1$. This implies that $f(s_0 P_1, P_2) \neq f(s_0 P_1', P_2)$, and hence, f is not weakly $(k-1)$-definite. Therefore, f is k-definite. $\square$

THEOREM 8.5. *If a k-definite language L is represented in a finite deterministic automaton $\mathbf{A} = (S, s_0, f)$, then card $(S) \geqq k+1$.*

Proof. Because always card $(S) \geqq 1$, the theorem holds true for $k = 0$. Assume that $k \geqq 1$ and let L be represented in $\mathbf{A}$ by the set S_1. For $i \geqq 0$, let $\mathscr{E}_i$ be the equivalence relation over S defined by the condition: $s \mathscr{E}_i s'$ holds iff, for all words P of length $\geqq i$, $s P \in S_1$ exactly in case $s' P \in S_1$. (Thus, s and s' are indistinguishable by words of sufficient length, as far as transitions to S_1 are concerned. Cf. the definition of the equivalence relations $\mathscr{E}$ in the proof of Theorem 6.1.) Denote by m_i the number of equivalence classes under $\mathscr{E}_i$. Then obviously

$$m_{i+1} \leqq m_i \qquad (8.2)$$

and

$$1 \leqq m_i \leqq \text{card } (S), \qquad (8.3)$$

for all $i \geqq 0$. (Inequality (8.2) follows because the partition corresponding to $\mathscr{E}_i$ refines that corresponding to $\mathscr{E}_{i+1}$.) Because L is not weakly $(k-1)$-definite, there exist words P_1 and P_2 (one of which is possibly empty), and letters $x_1, \ldots, x_{k-1}$ belonging to I such that

$$P_1 x_1 \ldots x_{k-1} \in L, \quad P_2 x_1 \ldots x_{k-1} \notin L. \qquad (8.4)$$

Let u be fixed, $0 \leqq u \leqq k - 1$. Consider the states

$$a_u = s_0 P_1 x_1 \ldots x_u, \quad b_u = s_0 P_2 x_1 \ldots x_u. \qquad (8.5)$$

(If $u = 0$, then $a_u = s_0 P_1$ and $b_u = s_0 P_2$.) By (8.4),

$$a_u x_{u+1} \ldots x_{k-1} \in S_1, \quad b_u x_{u+1} \ldots x_{k-1} \notin S_1.$$

Because $\lg(x_{u+1} \ldots x_{k-1}) = k - u - 1$, we conclude that a_u and b_u are not equivalent under $\mathcal{E}_{k-u-1}$.

Choose an arbitrary word $Q \in W(I)$, $\lg(Q) \geq k - u$. Because L is k-definite, $P_1 x_1 \ldots x_u Q \in L$ iff $P_2 x_1 \ldots x_u Q \in L$. Hence, by (8.5), $a_u Q \in S_1$ iff $b_u Q \in S_1$. This implies that a_u and b_u are equivalent under $\mathcal{E}_{k-u}$. Because u was arbitrary, $0 \leq u \leq k - 1$, we obtain

$$m_{i+1} < m_i,$$

for $0 \leq i \leq k - 1$. Hence, by (8.3),

$$1 \leq m_k < m_{k-1} < \ldots < m_1 < m_0 \leq \text{card}(S).$$

Therefore, card $(S) \geq k + 1$. □

Using Theorem 8.5, we shall now present an algorithm of deciding whether or not a language L represented by a set S_1 in a given finite deterministic automaton $\mathbf{A} = (S, s_0, f)$ is definite. The algorithm also gives the degree of definite languages. Without loss of generality, we may assume that, for all $s \in S$, there is a word P such that $s_0 P = s$. For $i \geq 0$, let $\mathcal{E}_i$ be the equivalence relation over S defined by the condition: $s\mathcal{E}_i s'$ holds iff, for all words P of length i, $sP \in S_1$ exactly in case $s'P \in S_1$.

Note that $s\mathcal{E}_0 s'$ iff either $s, s' \in S_1$ or $s, s' \in S - S_1$, and also that $s\mathcal{E}_{i+1}s'$ iff, for all $x \in I$, $(sx)\mathcal{E}_i(s'x)$. This gives a practical method of computing the relations $\mathcal{E}_i$.

L is weakly k-definite iff $s\mathcal{E}_k s'$ holds for all states $s, s' \in S$. The degree of L is the smallest k such that $s\mathcal{E}_k s'$ holds for all states $s, s' \in S$. By Theorem 8.5, L is not definite if

$$s\mathcal{E}_{\text{card }(S)-1} s'$$

does not hold for all states $s, s' \in S$.

We shall now establish an interconnection between definite languages and such automata where the initial state is not specified.

DEFINITION. A *finite deterministic non-initial automaton* over a finite alphabet I is an ordered pair $\mathbf{A} = (S, f)$, where S is a finite non-empty set and f maps the set $S \times I$ into the set S.

As before, the domain of the function f can be extended from $S \times I$ to $S \times W(I)$ (cf. equations (2.1) and (2.1)′). We shall now extend the notion of representation to concern also non-initial automata. Consider first the straightforward generalization of the definition presented in Section 2. A language L is represented by a set $S_1 \subset S$ in a non-initial automaton $\mathbf{A} = (S, f)$ iff (i) whenever $P \in L$, then $sP \in S_1$, for all $s \in S$, and (ii) whenever $P \notin L$, then $sP \notin S_1$, for all $s \in S$. It is easy to see (cf. Exercise 8.9) that, by this definition, the only languages represented in non-initial automata are $W(I)$ and L_ϕ. To avoid this situation, we weaken conditions (i) and (ii) to concern only words of sufficient length. This leads to the following

DEFINITION. Assume that $\mathbf{A} = (S, f)$ is a finite deterministic non-initial automaton, $S_1 \subset S$ and $k \geq 0$. A language L is k-represented in $\mathbf{A}$ by S_1 iff (i) whenever $P \in L$ and $\lg(P) \geq k$ then, for all $s \in S$, $sP \in S_1$ and (ii) whenever $P \notin L$ and $\lg(P) \geq k$ then, for all $s \in S$, $sP \notin S_1$.

Note that if $k = 0$ we obtain our original notion. The following definition is useful for the solution of the analysis and synthesis problems.

DEFINITION. Two languages L_1 and L_2 which differ only by finitely many words, i.e.

$$\text{card} \left((L_1 - L_2) + (L_2 - L_1) \right)$$

is a finite number, are termed *almost equal*.

It is obvious that almost equality of languages is an equivalence relation.

It may happen that no language is k-represented by a given set of states in a given non-initial automaton. Necessary and sufficient conditions for k-representability are presented in our next theorem.

THEOREM 8.6. *A set S_1 k-represents some language in a finite deterministic non-initial automaton $\mathbf{A} = (S, f)$ iff (i) the languages $L_i = L(\mathbf{A}, s_i, S_1)$, $s_i \in S$, represented in the finite deterministic automata obtained from $\mathbf{A}$ by choosing an initial state s_i, are weakly k-definite and almost equal. If (i) is satisfied, then any weakly k-definite language which is almost equal to the languages L_i is represented by S_1, and only such languages are represented by S_1.*

Proof. Assume first that a language L is k-represented in $\mathbf{A}$ by S_1. Choose an $s_i \in S$, and consider the language $L_i = L(\mathbf{A}, s_i, S_1)$. Assume that

$$P_1Q \in L_i, \tag{8.6}$$

where $\lg(Q) = k$, and let $P_2 \in W(I)$ be arbitrary. By (8.6),

$$s_iP_1Q \in S_1 \tag{8.7}$$

and hence $P_1Q \in L$. Writing (8.7) in the form $(s_iP_1)Q \in S_1$, we obtain the result $Q \in L$ (because L is k-represented by S_1 and $\lg(Q) = k$). Hence, $(s_iP_2)Q = s_i(P_2Q) \in S_1$, which implies that $P_2Q \in L_i$. Therefore, L_i is weakly k-definite.

We have also seen that every word of L_i with a length at least k is contained in L. Conversely, if $P \in L$ and $\lg(P) \geq k$ then $s_iP \in S_1$ and, therefore, $P \in L_i$. Hence, for all i, L and L_i are almost equal. This implies that the languages L_i are almost equal.

Conversely, assume that the languages L_i are weakly k-definite and almost equal. This implies that, for each i, $L_i = L_i' + W(I)L'$, where every word in L_i' is of length less than k and every word in L' is of length k. Let L be any weakly k-definite language which is almost equal to the languages L_i. Hence, $L = L'' + W(I)L'$, where every word in L'' is of length less than k. It now follows by the definition of the languages L_i that L is k-represented by S_1 in A. Clearly, only weakly k-definite languages which are almost equal to the languages L_i are k-represented by S_1. □

Theorem 8.6 suggests the following *analysis procedure* for non-initial automata. Given a finite deterministic non-initial automaton $\mathbf{A} = (S, f)$ and a set $S_1 \subset S$, we have to decide whether or not, for some k, S_1 k-represents a language in A and if it does, to determine the language. We apply first the algorithm presented after Theorem 8.5 to decide whether or not the languages

$$L_i = L(\mathbf{A}, s_i, S_1)$$

are definite and to determine their degrees. If they are not all definite, then no language is k-represented by S_1 (for any k). If they are all definite and u is the greatest degree (whence they are all weakly u-definite), we check whether or not they contain the same words of length u. If this is not the case, then no language is k-represented by S_1 (for any k). Otherwise, any weakly u-definite language which is almost equal to the languages L_i is u-represented by S_1. This analysis procedure is not practical and can be essentially simplified (cf. Exercise 8.12).

Finally, the *synthesis problem* of non-initial automata will be solved. Given a language L, we have to construct a non-initial automaton where L is k-represented by some set. We assume that $k \geqq 1$, the case $k = 0$ being trivial. We may also assume that L is of the form

$$L = W(I)L^{(k)}, \tag{8.8}$$

where $L^{(k)}$ contains only words of length k. (Namely, by Theorem 8.6, L has to be weakly k-definite and we may choose (8.8) from the class of all almost equal weakly k-definite languages.) Denote by $I^{(k)}$ the set of all words of length k. Consider the non-initial automaton $\mathbf{A} = (I^{(k)}, f)$, where

$$f(x_1 x_2 \ldots x_k, x) = x_2 \ldots x_k x,$$

for all x_i, $x \in I$. Clearly, L is k-represented in $\mathbf{A}$ by the subset of $I^{(k)}$ consisting of words belonging to $L^{(k)}$.

For instance, the language $|(0+1)^*(001+100)|$, or any almost equal weakly 3-definite language, is represented in the non-initial automaton given in Fig. 15, where representing states are squares.

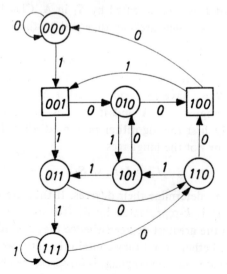

FIG. 15.

EXERCISE 8.1. A language is termed *quasifinite* iff it is either finite or the complement of a finite language. Show that a language over the alphabet $\{x\}$ is definite iff it is quasifinite.

EXERCISE 8.2. Show that the following definition of weakly k-definite languages is equivalent to the one given in the text: L is weakly k-definite iff, for all $P, Q \in W(I)$ satisfying $\lg(P) \geq k$, $\lg(Q) \geq k$ and having the same final subwords consisting of k letters, the conditions $P \in L$ and $Q \in L$ are equivalent.

EXERCISE 8.3. Show that the definite languages form a Boolean algebra of sets. Estimate the degree of the sum and the intersection of two languages and the degree of the complement of a language.

EXERCISE 8.4. Assume that L is a language represented in a finite deterministic automaton A with a k-definite transition function. Under what conditions (for A) is L k-definite?

EXERCISE 8.5. An alternative algorithm for the one presented after Theorem 8.5 is to use Theorem 2.2 to obtain a regular expression α, and then decide from the form of α whether or not $|\alpha|$ is definite. Accomplish the last step in this procedure. (This exercise is easier with the additional knowledge of regular expressions given in Chapter III.)

EXERCISE 8.6. Prove that the transition function of a finite deterministic automaton (S, s_0, f) is definite iff it is weakly $(\text{card}(S) - 1)$-definite. Conclude that there is an algorithm of deciding whether or not the transition function of a given finite deterministic automaton is definite.

EXERCISE 8.7 (Paz and Peleg, 1965, 2). A language L over I is termed *ultimate definite* iff, for some language L_1, $L = W(I)L_1$. Prove that there exist non-regular ultimate definite languages. Prove also that there is an algorithm of deciding whether or not an ultimate definite language is represented in a given finite deterministic automaton.

EXERCISE 8.8 (Paz and Peleg, 1965, 2). A language L over I is termed *reverse ultimate definite* iff, for some L_1, $L = L_1W(I)$, and *symmetric definite* iff, for some L_1 and L_2, $L = L_1W(I)L_2$. Prove that there exist algorithms to decide whether or not a reverse ultimate definite or a symmetric definite language is represented in a given finite deterministic automaton. Cf. also Ginzburg (1966).

EXERCISE 8.9. Show that the only languages 0-represented in non-initial automata are $W(I)$ and L_ϕ.

EXERCISE 8.10. (Preferably after reading Chapter III.) Construct an algorithm of deciding, given two regular expressions α and β, whether or not the languages $|\alpha|$ and $|\beta|$ are almost equal.

EXERCISE 8.11. Let L be a weakly k-definite language over the alphabet I_r. Determine the number of weakly k-definite languages almost equal to L.

EXERCISE 8.12 (Brzozowski, 1963; Steinby, 1967). For a language L and word P, denote $\partial_P(L) = \{Q \mid PQ \in L\}$. (These so-called *left derivatives* will be studied later on.) Prove that if L is k-definite then, for any P, $\partial_P(L)$ is a definite language with a degree $\leq k$ which is almost equal to L. Using this result, improve the analysis procedure presented after Theorem 8.6, assuming that at least one of the initial automata obtained from the non-initial one is connected (cf. Exercise 2.5).

§ 9. Finite languages

In this section we shall study a subfamily of the family of definite languages, namely, the family of finite languages. A method will be developed which yields the most economical representation of any finite language.

DEFINITION. For a regular language L, let $w_1(L)$ be the least integer k such that L is represented by a set S_1 in a finite deterministic automaton, where card $(S_1) = k$. The number $w_1(L)$ is referred to as the *representation number* of L.

Given a finite language L, we shall determine the weight $w(L)$ and representation number $w_1(L)$ of L. A trivial algorithm is to construct an automaton where L is represented and then to check through all automata with fewer states, or to apply the minimization procedures of Section 6. (Cf. Exercises 6.9 and 9.1.) In the algorithm developed below, the regular expression denoting the given language L is transformed into a "representation form" from which the numbers $w(L)$ and $w_1(L)$ can directly be seen.

We shall exclude two special cases. The empty language L_ϕ is represented by the empty set of states in the one-state automaton. The language consisting of the empty word λ is represented by the initial state of a two-state automaton. In these special cases the representation numbers are 0 and 1, whereas the weights are 1 and 2, respectively. In the remaining part of this section, we assume that all languages considered contain at least one non-empty word.

Every finite language is denoted by a regular expression α, where either the star (*) does not occur, or $\alpha \equiv \alpha_1 + \phi^*$, and the star does not occur in α_1. Such regular expressions α are brought into a "normal form" by applying the distributive law

$$\beta\gamma + \beta\delta = \beta(\gamma + \delta)$$

whenever possible. For instance, the regular expression

$$0^2 + 01 + 02 + 012 + 02^2 + 10^2 + 12^3 + 2010 + 201^2 + 2012$$
$$+ 12^4 + 2201^2 + 2012^2 \quad (9.1)$$

over the alphabet $\{0, 1, 2\}$ possesses the normal form

$$0(0 + 1(\phi^* + 2) + 2(\phi^* + 2)) + 1(0^2 + 2^3(\phi^* + 2))$$
$$+ 201(0 + 1(\phi^* + 2) + 2(\phi^* + 2)). \quad (9.2)$$

It is easy to prove, by induction on the number of words in the finite language considered, that normal forms are unique up to the order of terms in various sums.

Let α_1 be a regular expression appearing as a consecutive part in a normal form α. Assume, furthermore, that there exists a non-empty α_2 such that $\alpha_2\alpha_1$ is a term in a sum occurring in α. Then α_1 is termed a *final branch* of α. For instance, each of the following

$$01(0 + 1(\phi^* + 2) + 2(\phi^* + 2)); \quad (\phi^* + 2); \quad 2^2(\phi^* + 2)$$

is a final branch of (9.2), whereas

$$1(\phi^* + 2); \quad 2^3(\phi^* + 2); \quad 0 + 1(\phi^* + 2); \quad 2$$

are not final branches of (9.2). If a normal form α contains two occurrences of a final branch α_1, then we erase the other one, provided it is not part of a final branch α_1' which could also be erased (i.e. α does not contain two occurrences of such an α_1'). The procedure is carried on until each final branch of the *original normal form* α occurs only once. (Note that if we have erased the final branch α_1 from a term $\alpha_2\alpha_1$, then no part of α_2 can be erased during the next steps of the procedure.) The resulting regular expression is termed a *representation form* of α or of the language $L = |\alpha|$.

Representation forms are not unique. For instance, each of the following is a representation form of (9.2):

$$0+1(0^2+2^3(\phi^*+2))+201(0+1+2),$$
$$0+1(0^2+2^3)+201(0+1(\phi^*+2)+2),$$
$$0+1(0^2+2^3)+201(0+1+2(\phi^*+2)), \qquad (9.3)$$
$$0(0+1+2)+1(0^2+2^3(\phi^*+2))+201,$$
$$0(0+1(\phi^*+2)+2)+1(0^2+2^3)+201,$$
$$0(0+1+2(\phi^*+2))+1(0^2+2^3)+201.$$

(Uniqueness can be obtained by erasing the final branches in some alphabetical order.)

A certain non-negative integer is determined by the original language alone and is independent of the representation form chosen. We define the notion of the *characteristic number* for regular expressions of the type considered recursively as follows:

(i) The characteristic number of every letter and of ϕ^* equals 0.

(ii) If x is a letter and $\alpha\,(\not\equiv\phi^*)$ a regular expression with the characteristic number k, then the characteristic number of $x(\alpha)$ equals $k+1$.

(iii) The characteristic number of a sum equals the sum of the characteristic numbers of its terms.

The *characteristic number of a finite language* is defined to be the characteristic number of its representation form. It is easy to see that the characteristic number is independent of the representation form chosen. For instance, the characteristic number of the language denoted by (9.1) can be computed from any of the representation forms (9.3). It equals 8.

THEOREM 9.1. *If $c(L)$ is the characteristic number of a finite language L, then $w(L) = c(L)+3$. If $c_1(L)$ is the number of occurrences of ϕ^* in a representation form of L, then $w_1(L) = c_1(L)+1$.*

Proof. We note first that the number $c_1(L)$ is uniquely determined by the language L.

The theorem holds true if L consists of one (non-empty) word

$$P = x_1 \ldots x_k, \quad k \geq 1, \tag{9.4}$$

only. Then $w(L) = k+2$ and $w_1(L) = 1$. On the other hand, $c(L) = k-1$ and $c_1(L) = 0$.

Assume that the theorem holds true for a language L and let $L_1 = PL$, where P is as in (9.4). Clearly, $w_1(L_1) = w_1(L)$ and $w(L_1) = w(L)+k$. It is also obvious that $c_1(L_1) = c_1(L)$ and $c(L_1) = c(L)+k$. Hence, the theorem holds true for the language L_1.

Assume, finally, that the theorem holds true for the languages L_1 and L_2, both containing at least one non-empty word. Assume, furthermore, that L_1 and L_2 are denoted by the normal forms α_1 and α_2 which possess no common final branches and that $\alpha_1 + \alpha_2$ is a normal form. Then

$$w_1(L_1+L_2) = w_1(L_1)+w_1(L_2)-1. \tag{9.5}$$

The equation (9.5) follows because the same state may be chosen to represent all words $P \in L_1+L_2$ such that no word possessing P as a proper initial subword belongs to L_1+L_2. Similarly,

$$w(L_1+L_2) = w(L_1)+w(L_2)-3. \tag{9.6}$$

The equation (9.6) follows because, as seen above, we may choose one common representing state and, furthermore, common initial and terminal states. No other reductions are possible. On the other hand, by the definition of the numbers $c(L)$ and $c_1(L)$,

$$c(L_1+L_2) = c(L_1)+c(L_2) \tag{9.7}$$

and

$$c_1(L_1+L_2) = c_1(L_1)+c_1(L_2). \tag{9.8}$$

By (9.5)–(9.8), the theorem holds true for L_1+L_2.

It can be directly verified that if the theorem holds true for L_1, then it holds true for $L_1+\phi^*$. Hence, we may conclude that the theorem holds true for all languages defined by a representation form. On the other hand, it is obvious that weight and representation number remain invariant if final branches are erased in order to transform a normal form into a representation form. □

According to Theorem 9.1, the language denoted by (9.1) with the representation forms (9.3) can be represented by a set of 2 states in an automaton with 11 states (but neither one of these numbers can be reduced). The automaton is given in Fig. 16, where representing states are squares.

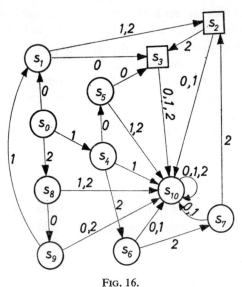

FIG. 16.

EXERCISE 9.1. Establish an interconnection between the number $w_1(L)$ and the equivalence relation $\mathscr{E}_L$ induced by L. Prove that if L is represented by a set S_1 in an automaton $\mathbf{A} = (S, s_0, f)$, where card $(S) = w(L)$, then card $(S_1) = w_1(L)$.

EXERCISE 9.2. Let L_k^r be the language over $I_r = \{x_1, \ldots, x_r\}$ consisting of all words with the same number $\leq k$ of occurrences of $x_1, \ldots, x_r$. Prove that

$$w(L_k^r) = (k+1)^r + 1; \quad w_1(L_k^r) = k+1.$$

EXERCISE 9.3. Extend the theory developed in this section to concern all quasifinite languages. (Cf. Exercise 8.1.)

EXERCISE 9.4. Assume that $w_1(L) = k$, where L is a finite language. Prove that, for any word P, $w_1(L+P) \leqq 2k$. Show that this upper bound is the smallest possible in the general case.

EXERCISE 9.5. A language L is termed *reducible* iff $w_1(L)$ is less than the number of words in L. Otherwise, L is *irreducible*. Prove that a finite language is irreducible iff it consists of the words

$$P_1, P_1P_2, \ldots, P_1P_2 \ldots P_k,$$

for some $k \geqq 1$ and words $P_1, P_2, \ldots, P_k$, where $P_2, \ldots, P_k$ are not empty.

§ 10. Two-way automata

We shall now generalize the notion of a finite deterministic automaton and consider devices which are not confined to a strict one-way motion while scanning the input word. Such a *two-way automaton* can move back and forth. At each moment, the scanned letter x and the state of the automaton uniquely determine the next state as well as the move, after which the automaton may continue to scan x or may scan the letter to the right or to the left of x. (For finite deterministic automata, there is only one possible move, after which the automaton scans the letter to the right of x.) The represented language is defined in the same way as in connection of finite deterministic automata. In Section IV.6 we shall study a further generalization which is also capable of replacing letters by other letters.

After these preliminary remarks we shall now give the formal definitions.

DEFINITION. A *finite deterministic two-way automaton*, or shortly, a *two-way automaton* over a finite alphabet I is an ordered triple **TWA** = (S, s_0, f), where S is a finite non-empty set (called the set of *internal states*), $s_0 \in S$ (the *initial state*) and f is a mapping of the set $S \times I$ into the set $S \times \{1, 0, -1\}$ (the *move function*).

An *instantaneous description* is a word of the form PsQ, where $P, Q \in W(I)$ and $s \in S$. The instantaneous description U_1 *directly yields* the instantaneous description U_2, in symbols $U_1 \vdash_{\text{TWA}} U_2$ or shortly $U_1 \vdash U_2$, iff one of the following conditions (i)–(iii) is satisfied, where $s, s' \in S$, $x, y \in I$ and $P, Q \in W(I)$.

(i) $U_1 = PsxQ,$ $U_2 = Pxs'Q$ and $f(s, x) = (s', 1)$.

(ii) $U_1 = PysxQ,$ $U_2 = Ps'yxQ$ and $f(s, x) = (s', -1)$.

(iii) $U_1 = PsxQ,$ $U_2 = Ps'xQ$ and $f(s, x) = (s', 0)$.

The instantaneous description U *yields* the instantaneous description U', in symbols $U \vdash^*_{\mathbf{TWA}} U'$ or shortly $U \vdash^* U'$, iff there is a finite sequence

$$U_0, U_1, \ldots, U_k \qquad (k \geqq 0)$$

of instantaneous descriptions such that $U_0 = U$, $U_k = U'$ and, for each $i = 0, \ldots, k-1$, U_i directly yields U_{i+1}.

For $S_1 \subset S$, the language $L(\mathbf{TWA}, S_1)$ *represented* in $\mathbf{TWA}$ by S_1 consists of all words P such that the instantaneous description s_0P yields an instantaneous description Ps_1, where $s_1 \in S_1$, i.e.

$$L(\mathbf{TWA}, S_1) = \{P | s_0P \vdash^* Ps_1, s_1 \in S_1\}.$$

A language L is *representable* in a two-way automaton iff, for some $\mathbf{TWA}$ and S_1, $L = L(\mathbf{TWA}, S_1)$.

Thus, an instantaneous description $PsxQ$ indicates the fact that the automaton is scanning the letter x of the input word PxQ in the state s. The numbers 1, -1 and 0 give the three possible moves. Note that by choosing $k = 0$ and $U_0 = U_k = U$, it is seen that $U \vdash^* U$. Hence, $\lambda \in L(\mathbf{TWA}, S_1)$ iff $s_0 \in S_1$. Note also that instead of saying "S is a finite non-empty set" we could say "S is a finite alphabet". In our definitions we prefer the former expression for the state set because we do not consider strings of elements of S.

It is obvious that a finite deterministic automaton can be regarded as a two-way automaton, where the values $f(s, x)$ are always of the form $(s', 1)$. Thus, a two-way automaton is more general than a finite deterministic automaton. Every f.a.r. language is also representable in a two-way automaton. However, as shown in our next theorem, also the converse holds true and, hence, these two types of automata represent the same family of languages.

THEOREM 10.1. *Every language representable in a two-way automaton is f.a.r.*

Proof. Let $L = L(\mathbf{TWA}, S_1)$, where $\mathbf{TWA} = (S, s_0, f)$ is a two-way automaton over I and $S_1 \subset S$. Consider the set $S' = S \cup \{s'\}$, where

$s' \notin S$. To each non-empty word P over I we associate a mapping φ_P of the set S' into itself, defined as follows. Assume that $P = P_1 x$, where $x \in I$. Then

$$\varphi_P(s') = \begin{cases} \bar{s} & \text{if } s_0 P \vdash^* P\bar{s}, \\ s' & \text{if, for no } s_\nu \in S, \ s_0 P \vdash^* P s_\nu; \end{cases}$$

$$\varphi_P(s) = \begin{cases} \bar{s} & \text{if } P_1 s x \vdash^* P\bar{s}, \\ s' & \text{if, for no } s_\nu^\doteq \in S, \ P_1 s x \vdash^* P s_\nu, \end{cases}$$

where $s \in S$. The mapping φ_P is well defined because the state $\bar{s}$, if it exists, is unique. It is also easy to verify that if $\varphi_{P_1} = \varphi_{P_2}$, then $P_1 \mathcal{E}_L P_2$, where $\mathcal{E}_L$ is the equivalence relation induced by the language L. (In fact, if $\varphi_{P_1} = \varphi_{P_2}$ and $Q \in W(I)$, then the instantaneous descriptions $s_0 P_1 Q$ and $s_0 P_2 Q$ either yield, respectively, the instantaneous descriptions $P_1 \bar{s} Q$ and $P_2 \bar{s} Q$, for some $\bar{s}$, or do not yield any instantaneous description of the form $P_1 s_\nu Q$ or $P_2 s_\nu Q$. If $P_1 = P_1' x_1$ and $P_2 = P_2' x_2$, then the same conclusion holds true, for any $s \in S$, with respect to the instantaneous descriptions $P_1' s x_1 Q$ and $P_2' s x_2 Q$. From these facts and the definition of the language L it follows that $P_1 Q \in L$ iff $P_2 Q \in L$.)

Thus, the number of equivalence classes of $\mathcal{E}_L$ does not exceed the number $n+1$, where n is the number of distinct mappings φ_P. (The number $n+1$ is chosen rather than n because the empty word may constitute another equivalence class.) But each φ_P is a mapping of the finite set S' into itself and, hence, n is finite. By Theorem 4.1, L is f.a.r. $\square$

Given **TWA** $= (S, s_0, f)$ and S_1, there is an algorithm of deciding whether or not a word P belongs to the language $L(\textbf{TWA}, S_1)$. One has to check through a sequence of at most

$$\lg (P) \text{ card } (S) + 1$$

instantaneous descriptions, beginning with $s_0 P$, where each instantaneous description immediately yields the next one. Furthermore, it follows from Theorems 4.1 and 4.3 that every equivalence class of $\mathcal{E}_L$ contains a word of length at most n (where n is the number of distinct mappings φ_P). Comparing the proofs of Theorems 4.1 and 10.1, the following theorem is seen to be a consequence of Theorem 2.5.

THEOREM 10.2. *There is an algorithm of deciding whether or not two languages* $L(\mathbf{TWA}, S_1)$ *and* $L(\mathbf{TWA'}, S_1')$ *represented in two two-way automata are equal.*

EXERCISE 10.1. Introduce the notion of an instantaneous description also for finite deterministic automata and modify the definition of the represented language accordingly. Note that in this approach one does not need the extension of f defined by (2.1) and (2.1)'. Can you introduce this notion also for sequential machines?

EXERCISE 10.2. Define the language represented in a two-way automaton without introducing the notion of an instantaneous description, i.e., by extending the domain of f.

EXERCISE 10.3 (Shepherdson, 1959). For a two-way automaton $\mathbf{TWA} = (S, s_0, f)$ and $S_1 \subset S$, consider the language

$$L_R(\mathbf{TWA}, S_1) = \{P \mid s_0 P \vdash {}^*Ps, s \in S - S_1\}$$

"rejected" by the set S_1. Prove that $L_R(\mathbf{TWA}, S_1)$ is regular.

EXERCISE 10.4 (Shepherdson, 1959). For a two-way automaton $\mathbf{TWA} = (S, s_0, f)$, define formally the language consisting of all words (i) for which $\mathbf{TWA}$ "goes off" the left end of the word and (ii) which give rise to a non-stop behavior of $\mathbf{TWA}$. Prove that both of these languages are regular.

EXERCISE 10.5 (Shepherdson, 1959). Introduce the notion of a two-way Mealy machine and study whether or not Theorem 10.1 is valid for two-way Mealy machines.

EXERCISE 10.6 (Shepherdson, 1959). Modify the notion of a two-way automaton in such a way that the input word is given between two "boundary markers" B, where $B \notin I$, and the represented language is defined by

$$L(\mathbf{TWA}, S_1) = \{P \mid s_0 BPB \vdash {}^*BPBs_1, s_1 \in S_1\}.$$

Prove that (for this modification) every representable language is regular. (Note that the unmodified two-way automaton has no way of knowing when it has reached the other end of the input word.)

EXERCISE 10.7. Construct an example of a two-way automaton representing a language L and possessing fewer than $w(L)$ states.

EXERCISE 10.8. Give a detailed proof of Theorem 10.2.

CHAPTER II

FINITE NON-DETERMINISTIC AND PROBABILISTIC AUTOMATA

THE automata and sequential machines studied in Chapter I are strictly deterministic in their actions: at each moment, the next state (and the output letter) is uniquely determined by the present state and the scanned letter. Thus, the output (both the final state and the output word) is uniquely determined by the input and the initial state.

The condition of determinism will be relaxed in this chapter. We shall consider automata which possess several choices for their actions. The moves are chosen at random, possibly with prefixed probabilities. The automata studied in Chapter I are special cases of these more general devices. It turns out that probabilistic automata are capable of representing also non-regular languages.

§ 1. Non-deterministic automata

Finite non-deterministic automata introduced in this section are direct generalizations of finite deterministic automata. When scanning the letter x in the internal state s, a non-deterministic automaton is at liberty to choose one of possible next states. These possible next states are determined by x and s. It may also happen that, for some x and s, there are no possible next states. A non-deterministic automaton **NA** may also possess several initial states. Given a designated set S_1 of final states, the language represented by S_1 in **NA** consists of all words which cause at least one sequence of state transitions from an initial state to a final state. The same word may cause a sequence of state transitions from an initial state to a final state as well as another sequence of state transitions from an initial state to a non-final state. However, all failures of the latter kind are disregarded and the word is accepted if there is at least one sequence of state transitions of the former kind.

These notions will be made explicit in the following

DEFINITION. A *finite non-deterministic automaton* over a finite alphabet I is an ordered triple $\mathbf{NA} = (S, S_0, f)$, where S is a finite non-empty set (the set of *internal states*), $S_0 \subset S$ (the set of *initial states*) and f is a mapping of the set $S \times I$ into the set of all subsets of S (the *transition function*).

Let S_1 be a subset of S. The language *represented* by S_1 in $\mathbf{NA}$, in symbols $L(\mathbf{NA}, S_1)$, consists of all words $P = x_0 x_1 \ldots x_{n-1}$ (where $n \geqq 1$ and $x_i \in I$) for which there is a sequence $s_0, s_1, \ldots, s_n$ of elements of S such that (i) $s_0 \in S_0$, (ii) $s_n \in S_1$ and (iii) $s_i \in f(s_{i-1}, x_{i-1})$, for $i = 1, \ldots, n$. Furthermore, by definition, $\lambda \in L(\mathbf{NA}, S_1)$ iff $S_0 \cap S_1 \neq \phi$. A language L is *representable* in a finite non-deterministic automaton iff, for some $\mathbf{NA}$ and S_1, $L = L(\mathbf{NA}, S_1)$.

It is obvious that finite deterministic automata can be considered as special cases, where S_0 and each $f(s, x)$ consists of one state. Hence, every language which is f.a.r. is also representable in a finite non-deterministic automaton. The next theorem shows that also the converse holds true.

THEOREM 1.1. *Every language representable in a finite non-deterministic automaton is f.a.r.*

Proof. Assume that $L = L(\mathbf{NA}, S_1)$, where $\mathbf{NA} = (S, S_0, f)$ is a finite non-deterministic automaton over I and $S_1 \subset S$. Denote by 2^S the set of all subsets of S. Let $\mathbf{A}' = (2^S, S_0, f')$ be the finite deterministic automaton over I, where for $x \in I$ and $\sigma = \{s_1, \ldots, s_h\} \in 2^S$,

$$f'(\sigma, x) = \bigcup_{i=1}^{h} f(s_i, x). \tag{1.1}$$

Furthermore, by definition, $f'(\phi, x) = \phi$. Let S_1' be the subset of 2^S consisting of all subsets of S which contain at least one element of S_1, and let $L' = L(\mathbf{A}', S_1')$. We claim that

$$L' = L. \tag{1.2}$$

In fact, $\lambda \in L$ iff $S_0 \cap S_1 \neq \phi$ iff $S_0 \in S_1'$ iff $\lambda \in L'$. Let P be any non-empty word over I. We conclude, by (1.1), that if P causes a sequence of state transitions of **NA** from a state in S_0 to a state in S_1, then also $f'(S_0, P) \in S_1'$, and conversely. This implies that $P \in L$ iff $P \in L'$. □

EXERCISE 1.1. Define the notion of the language represented by a set of states in a finite non-deterministic automaton by extending the domain of the transition function f. (Cf. equations (I.2.1) and (I.2.1)'.)

EXERCISE 1.2. What are the differences between a non-initial automaton introduced in Section I.8 and a finite non-deterministic automaton possessing several initial states?

EXERCISE 1.3. Introduce the notion of a finite non-deterministic two-way automaton and prove that every representable language is regular.

EXERCISE 1.4 (Starke, 1966, 1). Introduce the notion of a non-deterministic sequential machine (both of Mealy and Moore type). Study the represented languages, as well as problems of equivalence.

EXERCISE 1.5. Compare the proofs of Theorems 1.1 and I.2.3. Can you obtain Theorem 1.1 as a corollary of Theorem I.2.3?

PROBLEM 1.1. For the representation of a given language, a non-deterministic automaton is in general more economical as regards the number of states than a deterministic automaton. Introduce the notion of a "non-deterministic weight" of a language and develop a method to compute it (or find at least some relation between weight and non-deterministic weight). If possible, extend the comparison to deterministic and non-deterministic two-way automata. Cf. Karp (1967).

§ 2. Probabilistic automata and cut-point representation

We shall now introduce the notion of a finite probabilistic automaton (**PA**) which is a further generalization of a finite deterministic and non-deterministic automaton. If the states of **PA** are $s_1, \ldots, s_n$, then after scanning a letter x in a state s, **PA** goes to the state s_i with a probability $p_i(s, x)$, where for all s and x,

$$\sum_{i=1}^{n} p_i(s, x) = 1, \quad p_i(s, x) \geq 0.$$

Instead of a fixed initial state, **PA** has an *initial distribution* of states, i.e. each state is an initial state with a prefixed probability. The represented language $L(\mathbf{PA}, S_1, \eta)$ depends on the set S_1 of final states and also on a real number η, so-called *cut-point*, where $0 \leqq \eta < 1$. The language $L(\mathbf{PA}, S_1, \eta)$ consists of all words which cause a sequence of state transitions, after which the probability of **PA** being in one of the states of S_1 is greater than η.

We shall first introduce some terminology concerning vectors and matrices.

By an *(n-dimensional) stochastic matrix* we mean an $(n \times n)$ square matrix

$$M = ||p_{ij}||_{1 \leqq i, j \leqq n},$$

where for every i and j, p_{ij} is a non-negative real number and

$$\sum_{j=1}^{n} p_{ij} = 1 \qquad (i = 1, \ldots, n).$$

By an *n-dimensional stochastic row (column) vector* we mean an n-dimensional row (column) vector with non-negative components, the sum of which equals 1. A stochastic row vector is a *coordinate vector* iff one of its components equals 1. The n-dimensional *identity matrix* is denoted by E_n. Clearly, E_n is a stochastic matrix.

DEFINITION. A *finite probabilistic automaton* over a finite alphabet I is an ordered triple $\mathbf{PA} = (S, s_0, M)$, where $S = \{s_1, \ldots, s_n\}$ is a finite set with $n \geqq 1$ elements (the set of *internal states*), s_0 is an n-dimensional stochastic row vector (the *initial distribution*) and M is a mapping of I into the set of n-dimensional stochastic matrices. For $x \in I$, the (i, j)th entry in the matrix $M(x)$ is denoted by $p_j(s_i, x)$ and referred to as the *transition probability* of **PA** to enter into the state s_j, after being in the state s_i and receiving the input x.

As an example, consider the finite probabilistic automaton $\mathbf{PA}_1 = (\{s_1, s_2\}, (1, 0), M)$ over the alphabet $\{x, y\}$, where

$$M(x) = \left\| \begin{matrix} 0 & 1 \\ 1 & 0 \end{matrix} \right\|, \qquad M(y) = \left\| \begin{matrix} 1/2 & 1/2 \\ 1/2 & 1/2 \end{matrix} \right\|.$$

The initial distribution indicates that s_1 is the initial state. From the matrices M we see that, for instance, if $\mathbf{PA}_1$ is in the state s_1 and receives the input y, then the probability of entering into s_2 equals the probability of staying in s_1.

A finite probabilistic automaton can always be defined also by a graph. For the graph corresponding to $\mathbf{PA}_1$, cf. Fig. 17, where transition probabilities $\neq 1$ are given in parentheses and arrows with probability 0 are omitted. The components of the initial distribution are given together with the states.

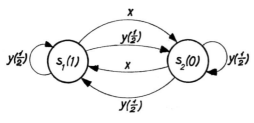

FIG. 17.

For a finite probabilistic automaton

$$\mathbf{PA} = (\{s_1, \ldots, s_n\}, s_0, M)$$

over I, we extend the domain of the function M from I to $W(I)$ by defining

$$M(\lambda) = E_n,$$
$$M(x_1 x_2 \ldots x_k) = M(x_1) M(x_2) \ldots M(x_k),$$

where $k \geqq 2$, $x_i \in I$ and juxtaposition on the right side denotes matrix multiplication. For $P \in W(I)$, the (i, j)th entry in the matrix $M(P)$ is denoted by $p_j(s_i, P)$ and referred to as the transition probability of $\mathbf{PA}$ to enter into the state s_j, after being in the state s_i and receiving the input P. (Cf. Exercise 2.1.)

DEFINITION. Let $\mathbf{PA} = (\{s_1, \ldots, s_n\}, s_0, M)$ be a finite probabilistic automaton over I and $P \in W(I)$. The stochastic row vector $s_0 M(P)$ is termed the *distribution of states* caused by the word P, and is denoted by $\mathbf{PA}(P)$.

Thus, the distribution of states caused by the empty word equals the initial distribution.

DEFINITION. Let $\bar{S}_1$ be an n-dimensional column vector, each component of which equals either 0 or 1, and $\mathbf{PA}$ as in the previous definition. Let η be a real number such that $0 \leqq \eta < 1$. The language *represented* in **PA** by $\bar{S}_1$ with the *cut-point* η is defined by

$$L(\mathbf{PA}, \bar{S}_1, \eta) = \{P \mid s_0 M(P) \bar{S}_1 > \eta\}. \qquad (2.1)$$

A language L is η-*stochastic* iff, for some **PA** and $\bar{S}_1$, $L = L(\mathbf{PA}, \bar{S}_1, \eta)$. A language L is *stochastic* iff, for some η (such that $0 \leqq \eta < 1$), L is η-stochastic.

Clearly, there is a one-to-one correspondence between the subsets S_1 of the set $\{s_1, \ldots, s_n\}$ and the column vectors $\bar{S}_1$: to each subset S_1 there corresponds the column vector $\bar{S}_1$ whose ith component equals 1 iff s_i belongs to S_1. The language represented by the column vector $\bar{S}_1$ in **PA** with cut-point η consists of all words P such that the sum of the components corresponding to the states of S_1 in the distribution **PA**(P) is greater than η. (Cf. Exercise 2.2.)

For the automaton defined by Fig. 17, we obtain

$$\mathbf{PA}_1(x^n) = (1, 0) M(x^n) = (1, 0) \text{ if } n \text{ is even;}$$
$$\mathbf{PA}_1(x^n) = (0, 1) \text{ if } n \text{ is odd;}$$
$$\mathbf{PA}_1(P) = (1/2, 1/2) \text{ if } P \text{ contains at least one } y.$$

Thus, for $\bar{S}_1 = \binom{0}{1}$,

$$L(\mathbf{PA}_1, \bar{S}_1, \eta) = \begin{cases} W(\{x, y\}) - |(x^2)^*| & \text{if} \quad 0 \leqq \eta < 1/2, \\ |x(x^2)^*| & \text{if} \quad 1/2 \leqq \eta < 1. \end{cases}$$

(Cf. also Exercise 2.3.)

Finite deterministic automata can be considered as a special case of finite probabilistic automata, where the initial distribution and the matrices $M(x)$ consist only of 0's and 1's. If we rewrite a finite deterministic automaton $\mathbf{A} = (S, s_0, f)$ over I in this fashion as a finite probabilistic automaton $\mathbf{PA} = (S, s_0, M)$ it is obvious that, for any S_1 and $P \in W(I)$, $f(s_0, P) \in S_1$ iff $s_0 M(P) \bar{S}_1 = 1$. (Here S_1 means a subset of S and $\bar{S}_1$ the corresponding column vector.) Hence,

$$L(\mathbf{A}, S_1) = L(\mathbf{PA}, \bar{S}_1, \eta),$$

for any η such that $0 \leqq \eta < 1$. This implies the following result.

THEOREM 2.1. *Every regular language is stochastic. Furthermore, every regular language is η-stochastic, for any η such that $0 \leqq \eta < 1$.*

The converse of Theorem 2.1 does not hold true: we shall prove in Section 4 that there are non-regular stochastic languages. However, the subsequent weaker result holds true.

THEOREM 2.2. *Every 0-stochastic language is regular.*

Proof. Let $L = L(\mathbf{PA}, \bar{S}_1, 0)$, where $\mathbf{PA} = (S, s_0, M)$ is a finite probabilistic automaton over an alphabet I, $S = \{s_1, \ldots, s_n\}$ and $\bar{S}_1$ is an n-dimensional column vector whose components are 0's and 1's. We construct a finite non-deterministic automaton $\mathbf{NA} = (S, S_0, f)$ over I as follows. The set S_0 consists of the elements s_i of S such that the ith component in the initial distribution s_0 is greater than 0. For $s_i \in S$ and $x \in I$, $f(s_i, x)$ consists of those elements s_j of S for which $p_j(s_i, x)$ (i.e., the (i, j)th entry in the matrix $M(x)$) is greater than 0.

Let S_1 be the subset of S corresponding to the column vector $\bar{S}_1$. Then it is obvious that

$$L(\mathbf{NA}, S_1) = L(\mathbf{PA}, \bar{S}_1, 0).$$

Theorem 2.2 now follows, by Theorems 1.1 and I.2.4. □

EXERCISE 2.1. Assume that, for each $x \in I$, $p_j(s_i, x)$ is the probability of $\mathbf{PA}$ to enter into s_j, after being in s_i and receiving the input x. Compute the (i, j)th entry in the matrix $M(x_1 x_2)$ and show that it equals (according to the basic laws of probability) the probability of $\mathbf{PA}$ to enter into s_j, after being in s_i and receiving the input $x_1 x_2$. Extend this result for the entries of the matrix $M(x_1 \ldots x_k)$. (Use induction on k.) Prove also that the product of stochastic matrices is a stochastic matrix.

EXERCISE 2.2. What does the inequality $s_0 M(P) \bar{S}_1 > \eta$ mean in terms of transition probabilities?

EXERCISE 2.3. Prove that, for all η and $\bar{S}_1$, the language $L(\mathbf{PA}_1, \bar{S}_1, \eta)$, where $\mathbf{PA}_1$ is the automaton defined by Fig. 17, is regular.

EXERCISE 2.4. Which languages are represented in a finite probabilistic automaton with one state?

EXERCISE 2.5. Characterize the languages represented in a two-state probabilistic automaton over the alphabet $\{x\}$. (*Hint:* each of the languages is denoted by a regular expression of one of the following forms:

$$\phi, \; \phi^*, \; x^*, \; \phi^*+x+ \; \ldots \; +x^k, \; x^kx^*, \; (x^2)^*, \; x(x^2)^*, \; \phi^*+x^2+ \; \ldots \; +x^{2k},$$

$$x+x^3+ \; \ldots \; +x^{2k-1}, \; \phi^*+x^2+ \; \ldots \; +x^{2k-2}+x^{2k-1}x^*,$$

$$x+x^3+ \; \ldots \; +x^{2k-1}+x^{2k}\,x^*,$$

where $k = 1, 2, \ldots.)$

EXERCISE 2.6. Prove that any language represented in any two-state probabilistic automaton over $\{x\}$ is represented either in the automaton $\mathbf{PA}_1 = (\{s_1, \; s_2\}, \; (1, \; 0), \; M_1)$ or in the automaton $\mathbf{PA}_2 = (\{s_1, \; s_2\}, (1, \; 0), \; M_2)$, where

$$M_1(x) = \left\| \begin{matrix} 1/2 & 1/2 \\ 0 & 1 \end{matrix} \right\|, \qquad M_2(x) = \left\| \begin{matrix} 0 & 1 \\ 1/2 & 1/2 \end{matrix} \right\|.$$

§ 3. Theorems concerning stochastic languages

We shall first establish a result which is a useful lemma in constructions involving finite probabilistic automata.

THEOREM 3.1. *Every stochastic language is η-stochastic, for any η such that $0 < \eta < 1$.*

Proof. Let L be a stochastic language. By definition, there is a real number η' $(0 \leqq \eta' < 1)$ such that L is η'-stochastic. If $\eta' = 0$ then L is η-stochastic, for any η such that $0 < \eta < 1$, by Theorems 2.1 and 2.2. Assume that $L = L(\mathbf{PA}, \bar{S}_1, \eta')$, where $\mathbf{PA} = (\{s_1, \ldots, s_n\}, s_0, M)$ is a finite probabilistic automaton over an alphabet I and $\eta' > 0$.

For every real number u satisfying $0 < u < 1$, we consider the finite probabilistic automaton

$$\mathbf{PA}_u = (\{s_1, \; \ldots, \; s_n, \; s_{n+1}\}, \; s_0^u, \; M_1)$$

over I, where s_0^u and M_1 are defined as follows. The vector s_0^u is an $(n+1)$-dimensional stochastic row vector whose $(n+1)$th component equals u and whose ith component equals the ith component of s_0 multiplied by $1-u$, for $i = 1, \ldots, n$, i.e.

$$s_0^u = ((1-u)\,s_0, \; u).$$

For each $x \in I$,

$$M_1(x) = \left\| \begin{array}{ccc} & & 0 \\ M(x) & & \vdots \\ & & 0 \\ 0 \ldots 0 & & 1 \end{array} \right\|.$$

Consequently, for every $P \in W(I)$,

$$M_1(P) = \left\| \begin{array}{ccc} & & 0 \\ M(P) & & \vdots \\ & & 0 \\ 0 \ldots 0 & & 1 \end{array} \right\|. \qquad (3.1)$$

To prove that L is η-stochastic, for any η such that $0 < \eta < 1$, we consider first a fixed value of η satisfying $0 < \eta < \eta'$. Let $\bar{S}_1'$ be the $(n+1)$-dimensional column vector whose first n components equal, respectively, the components of $\bar{S}_1$ and whose $(n+1)$th component equals 0. By (3.1) and the definition of s_0^u,

$$\mathbf{PA}_u(P)\, \bar{S}_1' = (1-u)\, \mathbf{PA}(P)\, \bar{S}_1,$$

for all words P. Hence, for $u = 1 - \eta/\eta'$,

$$L = L(\mathbf{PA}_u, \bar{S}_1', \eta). \qquad (3.2)$$

Consider a fixed value of η satisfying $\eta' < \eta < 1$. In this case we let $\bar{S}_1'$ be the $(n+1)$-dimensional column vector whose first n components equal, respectively, the components of $\bar{S}_1$ and whose $(n+1)$th component equals 1. Consequently,

$$\mathbf{PA}_u(P)\, \bar{S}_1' = (1-u)\, \mathbf{PA}(P)\, \bar{S}_1 + u,$$

for all words P. Hence, for $u = (\eta - \eta')/(1 - \eta')$, (3.2) is satisfied. □

Theorem 3.1 cannot be extended to cover the point $\eta = 0$. This is due to the existence of non-regular stochastic languages (which will be established in the next section) and to Theorem 2.2.

We shall now derive a characterization of stochastic languages. For this purpose, we introduce the notion of a derivative of a language.

DEFINITION. Let L be a language over a finite alphabet I and $P \in W(I)$. The *(left) derivative* of L with respect to P is defined by

$$\partial_P(L) = \{Q \mid PQ \in L\}.$$

Thus, the derivative of L with respect to P is obtained by choosing all words of L which possess P as an initial subword and then erasing the initial subword P from these words. Clearly, for any L, $\partial_\lambda(L) = L$ and, for all $P, Q \in W(I)$,

$$\partial_{PQ}(L) = \partial_Q(\partial_P(L)).$$

THEOREM 3.2. *All derivatives of a stochastic language are stochastic languages. Conversely, if there is an integer k such that all derivatives of a language L with respect to words of length k are stochastic languages, then L is a stochastic language.*

Proof. Assume that $L_1 = L(\mathbf{PA}, \bar{S}_1, \eta)$, where $\mathbf{PA} = (S, s_0, M)$ is a finite probabilistic automaton over an alphabet I and $P \in W(I)$. Then

$$\partial_P(L_1) = L(\mathbf{PA}_1, \bar{S}_1, \eta), \tag{3.3}$$

where $\mathbf{PA}_1 = (S, s_0 M(P), M)$. The equation (3.3) follows because, for any word Q over I,

$$\mathbf{PA}_1(Q) = s_0 M(P) M(Q) = s_0 M(PQ) = \mathbf{PA}(PQ),$$

and hence, $Q \in L(\mathbf{PA}_1, \bar{S}_1, \eta)$ iff $PQ \in L(\mathbf{PA}, \bar{S}_1, \eta) = L_1$.

The converse part of the theorem is obvious for $k = 0$. Assume that L is a language over a finite alphabet I such that all derivatives $\partial_x(L)$, where $x \in I$, are stochastic languages. By Theorems 3.1, 2.1 and 2.2, this implies that all derivatives $\partial_x(L)$, where $x \in I$, are η-stochastic languages, for some η such that $0 < \eta < 1$. (In fact, we may choose $\eta = \frac{1}{2}$.) Therefore, for each $x \in I$, there is a finite probabilistic automaton $\mathbf{PA}_x = (S_x, (s_0)_x, M_x)$ over I and a column vector $(\bar{S}_1)_x$ such that

$$\partial_x(L) = L(\mathbf{PA}_x, (\bar{S}_1)_x, \eta). \tag{3.4}$$

Without loss of generality, we may assume that the sets S_x are mutually disjoint. Let

$$S' = \bigcup_{x \in I} S_x \cup \{s'\},$$

where s' does not belong to any of the sets S_x. For $I = \{x_1, \ldots, x_r\}$, we index the elements of S' (using natural numbers) in such a way that s' is given the index 1, and after that come the elements of S_{x_1} and so on and, finally, the elements of S_{x_r}. Consider the finite probabilistic automaton

$$\mathbf{PA}' = (S', s_0', M')$$

over I, where s_0' is the card (S')-dimensional coordinate vector whose first component (i.e. the component corresponding to s') equals 1 and, for each $x \in I$, the (i, j)th entry $p_j'(s_i, x)$ in the card (S')-dimensional stochastic matrix $M'(x)$ is defined as follows. If $i = 1$ and j corresponds to some state s_μ in the set S_x, then $p_j'(s_i, x)$ equals the component corresponding to s_μ in $(s_0)_x$. If i and j correspond to the states s_μ and s_ν in the same set S_y, then $p_j'(s_i, x)$ equals the (μ, ν)th entry in the matrix $M_y(x)$. Finally, $p'(\cdot, x)$ equals 0 in all other cases. Thus, for instance,

$$M'(x_1) = \begin{Vmatrix} 0 & (s_0)_{x_1} & 0 & \ldots & 0 \\ 0 & M_{x_1}(x_1) & 0 & \ldots & 0 \\ 0 & 0 & M_{x_2}(x_1) & \ldots & 0 \\ & & & & \vdots \\ \vdots & \vdots & & & 0 \\ 0 & 0 & \ldots & 0 & M_{x_r}(x_1) \end{Vmatrix}.$$

Let $\bar{S}_1'$ be the card (S')-dimensional column vector whose first component equals 1 or 0, depending on whether $\lambda \in L$ or $\lambda \notin L$, and is followed by the vectors $(\bar{S}_1)_{x_1}, \ldots, (\bar{S}_1)_{x_r}$. Then it is easily verified that

$$(s_0)_x M_x(P) (\bar{S}_1)_x = s_0' M'(xP) \bar{S}_1', \tag{3.5}$$

for any $x \in I$ and $P \in W(I)$. (In fact, $\mathbf{PA}'$ is able to simulate all automata $\mathbf{PA}_x$ and our construction of $\mathbf{PA}'$ causes a "delay" of one time instant compared to the automata $\mathbf{PA}_x$. Furthermore, the first letter x of an input word for $\mathbf{PA}'$ determines the automaton $\mathbf{PA}_x$ which $\mathbf{PA}'$ is going to simulate.) Because the conditions $xP \in L$ and $P \in \partial_x(L)$ are equivalent, we infer from (3.4) and (3.5) that

$$L = L(\mathbf{PA}', \bar{S}_1', \eta).$$

(Note that $s_0' \bar{S}_1'$ equals 1 or 0, depending on whether $\lambda \in L$ or $\lambda \notin L$. Hence, $\lambda \in L(\mathbf{PA}', \bar{S}_1', \eta)$ iff $\lambda \in L$.) Thus, L is stochastic.

We shall now make the following inductive hypothesis: the converse part of the theorem holds true for a fixed value of $k \geqq 1$. Assume that all derivatives of a language L over I with respect to words of length $k+1$ are stochastic languages. Let P be an arbitrary word over I of length k. Hence, for any $x \in I$, the language $\partial_{Px}(L)$ is stochastic. Because $\partial_{Px}(L) = \partial_x(\partial_P(L))$ we conclude, by the proof for the case

$k = 1$, that $\partial_P(L)$ stochastic. Since P was arbitrary this implies, by our inductive hypothesis, that L is stochastic. Hence, the converse part of the theorem holds true for the value $k+1$. $\square$

As an immediate corollary of Theorem 3.2, we obtain the following

THEOREM 3.3. *A language L is stochastic iff, for some integer k, all derivatives of L with respect to words of length k are stochastic. If, for some k, all derivatives of a language L with respect to words of length k are stochastic, then all derivatives of L (including L itself) are stochastic.*

DEFINITION. A *Rabin automaton* is a finite probabilistic automaton, where the initial distribution is a coordinate vector.

THEOREM 3.4. *Any stochastic language is representable in a Rabin automaton. More specifically, for any η-stochastic language L, there is a Rabin automaton* **PA**$'$ *and a column vector $\bar{S}_1'$ such that*

$$L = L(\mathbf{PA'}, \bar{S}_1', \eta). \tag{3.6}$$

Proof. Assume that $L = L(\mathbf{PA}, \bar{S}_1, \eta)$, where $\mathbf{PA} = (S, s_0, M)$ is a finite probabilistic automaton over an alphabet I and $\bar{S}_1$ is a card (S)-dimensional column vector (consisting of 0's and 1's). Denote $S' = S \cup \{s'\}$, where $s' \notin S$, and index the elements of S' in such a way that s' is given the index 1. Consider the Rabin automaton

$$\mathbf{PA'} = (S', s_0', M')$$

over I, where $s_0' = (1, 0, \ldots, 0)$ and, for each $x \in I$, the (i, j)th entry $p'(s_i, x)$ in the card (S')-dimensional stochastic matrix $M'(x)$ is defined as follows. For $i > 1$ and $j > 1$ $p'(s_i, x)$ equals the corresponding entry (i.e. the entry corresponding to the states with the indices i and j) in the matrix $M(x)$. For each i, $p_1'(s_i, x) = 0$. For $j > 1$, $p_j'(s_1, x)$ equals the component corresponding to the state with the index j in the vector $s_0 M(x)$. Thus,

$$M'(x) = \left\| \begin{matrix} 0 & s_0 M(x) \\ 0 & M(x) \end{matrix} \right\|.$$

Furthermore, let $\bar{S}_1'$ be the card (S')-dimensional column vector whose first component equals 1 or 0, depending on whether $\lambda \in L$ or $\lambda \notin L$, and is followed by the vector $\bar{S}_1$.

For any word of the form xP, where $x \in I$, we obtain

$$s_0' M'(xP) \bar{S}_1' = (1, 0, \ldots, 0) \, M'(x) \, M'(P) \bar{S}_1'$$
$$= (0, s_0 M(x)) \, M'(P) \, \bar{S}_1' = s_0 M(x) \, M(P) \, \bar{S}_1 = s_0 M(xP) \, \bar{S}_1.$$

(Here $(0, s_0 M(x))$ denotes the card (S')-dimensional row vector whose first component equals 0 and is followed by the components of $s_0 M(x)$.) Because $s_0' \bar{S}_1'$ equals 1 or 0, depending on whether $\lambda \in L$ or $\lambda \notin L$, we conclude that (3.6) is satisfied. $\square$

We shall now introduce a special type of cut-points and prove that the resulting languages are regular.

DEFINITION. Let $\mathbf{PA} = (S, s_0, M)$ be a finite probabilistic automaton over an alphabet I, S_1 a subset of S and $\bar{S}_1$ the corresponding column vector. A real number η, where $0 \leqq \eta < 1$, is termed *isolated* with respect to the pair $(\mathbf{PA}, \bar{S}_1)$ iff there is a positive number δ such that, for all $P \in W(I)$,

$$|s_0 M(P) \bar{S}_1 - \eta| \geqq \delta. \tag{3.7}$$

We shall show that a language represented with an isolated cut-point is regular.

THEOREM 3.5. *Assume that* $L = L(\mathbf{PA}, \bar{S}_1, \eta)$, *where the cut-point η is isolated with respect to* $(\mathbf{PA}, \bar{S}_1)$. *Then L is regular.*

Proof. We shall prove that the equivalence relation $\mathcal{E}_L$ induced by the language L is of finite index. Theorem 3.5 then follows, by Theorem I.4.1.

Let $\mathbf{PA} = (\{s_1, \ldots, s_n\}, s_0, M)$ and let the alphabet be I. By the assumption, there is a positive number δ such that (3.7) is satisfied, for all words P over I. Let U_i be the set of real numbers ξ defined by the equation

$$U_i = \{\xi \mid i2\delta/n \leqq \xi < (i+1) \, 2\delta/n\}, \quad i = 0, 1, 2, \ldots.$$

The sets U_i are mutually disjoint and there is a natural number k such that every real number in the closed interval $[0, 1]$ belongs to exactly one of the sets $U_0, U_1, \ldots, U_k$. Let $P \in W(I)$ and consider the distribution of states

$$\mathbf{PA}(P) = (p_1(P), \ldots, p_n(P)).$$

Assume that, for $1 \leqq i \leqq n$, $p_i(P)$ belongs to the set U_{j_i}, where $0 \leqq j_i \leqq k$. We denote

$$U(P) = (j_1, \ldots, j_n). \tag{3.8}$$

The equation (3.8) defines a mapping U of the set $W(I)$ into the set of n-dimensional vectors whose components are non-negative integers less than or equal to k. Clearly, the number of such vectors is finite.

To complete the proof, it suffices to show that if, for some words P_1 and P_2 over I,

$$U(P_1) = U(P_2) \tag{3.9}$$

then $P_1 \mathcal{E}_L P_2$. (This proves, namely, that the number of equivalence classes under $\mathcal{E}_L$ does not exceed the number of vectors belonging to the range of U.) Assume the contrary: there is a word $Q \in W(I)$ such that $P_1 Q \in L$ and $P_2 Q \notin L$. (This is no loss of generality, for if $P_1 Q \notin L$ and $P_2 Q \in L$, then we interchange the roles of P_1 and P_2.) Hence, by (3.7),

$$s_0 M(P_1 Q) \bar{S}_1 \geqq \eta + \delta, \quad s_0 M(P_2 Q) \bar{S}_1 \leqq \eta - \delta.$$

Consequently,

$$s_0 M(P_1 Q) \bar{S}_1 - s_0 M(P_2 Q) \bar{S}_1 \geqq 2\delta$$

and, hence,

$$(s_0 M(P_1) - s_0 M(P_2)) M(Q) \bar{S}_1 \geqq 2\delta. \tag{3.10}$$

On the other hand, by (3.9), every component of the n-dimensional vector $s_0 M(P_1) - s_0 M(P_2)$ is of absolute value less than $2\delta/n$. Because $M(Q)$ is a stochastic matrix, each component of the column vector $M(Q)\bar{S}_1$ is in the interval $[0, 1]$. This implies that

$$|(s_0 M(P_1) - s_0 M(P_2)) M(Q) \bar{S}_1| < n(2\delta/n) = 2\delta,$$

which contradicts (3.10). Therefore, (3.9) implies that P_1 and P_2 are equivalent under $\mathcal{E}_L$. $\square$

It is not known whether or not the family of stochastic languages is closed under Boolean operations. The simple argument by which Theorem I.2.6 was established is not applicable for probabilistic automata. For instance, if $L = L(\mathbf{PA}, \bar{S}_1, \eta)$ and $\bar{S}_2$ corresponds to the complement of S_1, i.e. a component of $\bar{S}_2$ equals 1 iff the same component of $\bar{S}_1$ equals 0, then the language

$$L_1 = L(\mathbf{PA}, \bar{S}_2, 1-\eta)$$

does not necessarily equal the complement of L. However, L_1 coincides
with $\sim L$ as regards words P for which $\mathbf{PA}(P)\bar{S}_1 \neq \eta$, i.e.

$$((\sim L) - L_1) + (L_1 - (\sim L)) \subset \{P \mid \mathbf{PA}(P)\bar{S}_1 = \eta\} = \{P \mid \mathbf{PA}(P)\bar{S}_2 = 1 - \eta\}.$$

The following partial result concerning closure under Boolean operations will now be established.

THEOREM 3.6. *The sum $L_1 + L_2$ and the intersection $L_1 \cap L_2$ of a stochastic language L_1 and a regular language L_2 are both stochastic languages.*

Proof. Without loss of generality, we may assume that L_1 and L_2 are both languages over the same alphabet I. Let $L_1 = L(\mathbf{PA}', \bar{S}_1', \eta)$, where

$$\mathbf{PA}' = (\{s_1, \ldots, s_n\}, \quad (p_1, \ldots, p_n), M').$$

Let $L_2 = L(\mathbf{PA}'', \bar{S}_1'', 0)$, where

$$\mathbf{PA}'' = (\{s_{n+1}, \ldots, s_{n+m}\}, \quad (1, 0, \ldots, 0), M'')$$

and every row in each stochastic matrix $M''(x)$ is a coordinate vector. (Thus, $\mathbf{PA}''$ is the finite deterministic automaton, where L_2 is represented, rewritten as a probabilistic automaton.) Consider the finite probabilistic automaton

$$\mathbf{PA} = (\{s_1, \ldots, s_n, s_{n+1}, \ldots, s_{n+m}\}, \quad (p_1/2, \ldots, p_n/2, 1/2, 0, \ldots, 0), M)$$

over I, where for each $x \in I$,

$$M(x) = \left\| \begin{matrix} M'(x) & 0 \\ 0 & M''(x) \end{matrix} \right\|.$$

Consequently, for every word P over I,

$$M(P) = \left\| \begin{matrix} M'(P) & 0 \\ 0 & M''(P) \end{matrix} \right\|. \tag{3.11}$$

Define

$$\bar{S}_1 = \begin{pmatrix} \bar{S}_1' \\ \bar{S}_2'' \end{pmatrix}.$$

Then by (3.11), for any word P over I,

$$\mathbf{PA}(P)\bar{S}_1 = \tfrac{1}{2}(\mathbf{PA}'(P)\bar{S}_1' + \mathbf{PA}''(P)\bar{S}_1''). \tag{3.12}$$

Because $\mathbf{PA}''(P)\bar{S}_1''$ equals 1 or 0, depending on whether $P \in L_2$ or $P \notin L_2$,

(3.12) implies the equations

$$L_1 + L_2 = L(\mathbf{PA}, \bar{S}_1, \eta/2)$$

and

$$L_1 \cap L_2 = L(\mathbf{PA}, \bar{S}_1, (\eta+1)/2). \qquad \square$$

As an immediate corollary of Theorems 3.6 and I.2.6, we obtain the following

THEOREM 3.7. *If L_1 is a stochastic language and L_2 a regular language, then the language L_1–L_2 is stochastic. Let L' be a language obtained from a language L by adding or removing finitely many words. Then L' is stochastic iff L is stochastic.*

For a finite probabilistic automaton $\mathbf{PA} = (S, s_0, M)$, a subset S_1 of S and a real number η such that $0 \leqq \eta < 1$, we denote

$$L_{(=)}(\mathbf{PA}, \bar{S}_1, \eta) = \{P \,|\, \mathbf{PA}(P)\bar{S}_1 = \eta\},$$

where $\bar{S}_1$ is the column vector corresponding to S_1. Then the following result concerning closure under complementation can be established.

THEOREM 3.8. *Assume that $L = L(\mathbf{PA}, \bar{S}_1, \eta)$ is a stochastic language such that the language $L_{(=)}(\mathbf{PA}, \bar{S}_1, \eta)$ is regular. Then the complement of L is a stochastic language.*

Proof. Denote by S_2 the column vector corresponding to the complement of S_1. Then

$$\sim L = \{P \,|\, \mathbf{PA}(P)\bar{S}_1 \leqq \eta\}$$
$$= \{P \,|\, \mathbf{PA}(P)\bar{S}_2 > 1-\eta\} + L_{(=)}(\mathbf{PA}, \bar{S}_1, \eta),$$

whence the theorem follows, by Theorem 3.6. $\square$

We shall see in the next section that the hypothesis of Theorem 3.8 is not satisfied for all stochastic languages.

EXERCISE 3.1. Prove that any finite set of stochastic languages can be represented in the same finite probabilistic automaton with the same cut-point. Prove also that the representing sets of states can be chosen to be mutually disjoint.

EXERCISE 3.2. Let L' be a language obtained from a language L by adding or removing the empty word. Prove, without using Theorem 3.7, that L' is stochastic iff L is stochastic.

EXERCISE 3.3. Consider an example of the construction of the automaton **PA**, as in the proof Theorem 3.2, for given automata $\mathbf{PA}_x$. Verify that (3.5) is satisfied.

EXERCISE 3.4. Prove that if, for some **PA** and $\bar{S}_1$, the function $\mathbf{PA}(P)S_1$ assumes only finitely many values when P ranges over $W(I)$, then the language $L(\mathbf{PA}, \bar{S}_1, \eta)$ is regular, for any η. (Cf. also Exercise 4.9.)

EXERCISE 3.5. Consider the automaton $\mathbf{PA}_1$ introduced in Exercise 2.6. Let $\bar{S}_1 = \binom{1}{0}$. Prove that infinitely many languages are represented in $\mathbf{PA}_1$ by $\bar{S}_1$. More specifically, prove that, for all integers $k \geqq 2$, there is a regular language L_k of weight k and a cut-point η_k such that

$$L_k = L(\mathbf{PA}_1, \bar{S}_1, \eta_k).$$

EXERCISE 3.6. Prove that all derivatives of a regular language are regular. Describe an algorithm which yields, given a regular expression α and a word P, a regular expression denoting the language $\partial_P(|\alpha|)$.

PROBLEM 3.1. Introduce the notion of a *right derivative* of a language. Is Theorem 3.2 valid for right derivatives?

PROBLEM 3.2. Introduce the notion of the weight (and of the "Rabin weight") for a stochastic language, i.e. consider the number of states in the smallest probabilistic automaton (Rabin automaton), where the language can be represented. Develop a method to determine the weight and the Rabin weight. For which languages is the latter greater than the former? (Cf. also Exercise 3.5.)

PROBLEM 3.3. Determine an upper bound, as sharp as possible, for the weight of a regular language represented with an isolated cut-point. (The proof of Theorem 3.5 gives the bound $(n/2\delta+1)^n$. A better bound is obtained in Rabin (1963) and Paz (1966).)

PROBLEM 3.4. Is there an algorithm to decide whether or not two given stochastic languages are equal? (You have to specify the meaning of the word "given": all real numbers involved have to be generated by some effective procedure. Cf. also Theorem 5.9.)

PROBLEM 3.5. Is the family of stochastic languages closed under Boolean operations? Study also other operations, for instance, catenation and catenation closure.

§ 4. Non-regular stochastic languages

It was established in Theorem 2.1 that every regular language is stochastic. We shall now prove that the converse of this result does not hold true. Moreover, we obtain a non-denumerable family of non-regular stochastic languages.

For an integer $m \geqq 2$ and a real number η such that $0 \leqq \eta < 1$, we define a language over the alphabet $\{0, 1, \ldots, m-1\}$ by the equation

$$L(m, \eta) = \{x_1 \ldots x_i | .x_1 \ldots x_i > \eta, i \geqq 1\}.$$

Thus, $L(m, \eta)$ consists of all those non-empty words $x_1 \ldots x_i$ for which the number $.x_1 \ldots x_i$, considered as an m-adic expansion, is greater than η. The language $L(m, \eta)$ is referred to as the *m-adic language* with cut-point η.

For a word P (over any alphabet), the *mirror image* of P, in symbols mi(P), is obtained by writing P backwards. If $P = \lambda$ or P consists of only one letter then, by definition, mi(P) = P. The mirror image mi(L) of a language L consists of the mirror images of the words belonging to L. It is easy to prove (cf. Exercise I.1.2) that a language L is regular iff mi(L) is regular.

THEOREM 4.1. *For any m and η, the mirror image* mi($L(m, \eta)$) *of the m-adic language is represented in a two-state probabilistic automaton with cut-point η.*

Proof. Given m and η, consider the finite probabilistic automaton $\mathbf{PA}_m = (\{s_1, s_2\}, (1, 0), M)$ over the alphabet $I = \{0, 1, \ldots, m-1\}$, where for each $x \in I$,

$$M(x) = \left\| \begin{matrix} (m-x)/m & x/m \\ (m-x-1)/m & (x+1)/m \end{matrix} \right\|.$$

Let $\bar{S}_1 = \binom{0}{1}$. We claim that

$$\text{mi}(L(m, \eta)) = L(\mathbf{PA}_m, \bar{S}_1, \eta). \tag{4.1}$$

Note first that, by definition, $\lambda \notin \text{mi}(L(m, \eta))$. Because $(1, 0)\bar{S}_1 = 0$, we conclude that $\lambda \notin L(\mathbf{PA}_m, \bar{S}_1, \eta)$. Thus, to establish (4.1) it suffices to prove that, for every non-empty word P over I,

$$\mathbf{PA}_m(P)\bar{S}_1 = .\mathrm{mi}(P), \tag{4.2}$$

where the right side denotes m-adic expansion. We shall prove (4.2) by induction on the length of P. Assume that $\lg(P) = 1$, i.e. $P = x \in I$ and $\mathrm{mi}(P) = P$. Then both sides of (4.2) equal x/m.

We make the following inductive hypothesis: (4.2) is valid for all words P of length k ($\geqq 1$). Consider an arbitrary word

$$Q = x_1 \ldots x_k x_{k+1}$$

of length $k+1$. By the inductive hypothesis, the (1,2)th entry in the matrix $M(x_1 \ldots x_k)$ equals $.x_k \ldots x_1$. Because the product of stochastic matrices is a stochastic matrix, the (1,1)th entry in the matrix $M(x_1 \ldots x_k)$ equals $1 - .x_k \ldots x_1$. Hence,

$$\mathbf{PA}_m(Q)\bar{S}_1 = (1,0)M(x_1 \ldots x_k) \begin{Vmatrix} (m-x_{k+1})/m & x_{k+1}/m \\ (m-x_{k+1}-1)/m & (x_{k+1}+1)/m \end{Vmatrix} \binom{0}{1}$$

$$= (1 - .x_k \ldots x_1)(x_{k+1}/m) + .x_k \ldots x_1((x_{k+1}+1)/m)$$

$$= x_{k+1}/m + .x_k \ldots x_1(1/m) = .x_{k+1}x_k \ldots x_1 = .\mathrm{mi}(Q).$$

Thus, (4.2) is valid for all words of length $k+1$. This completes the induction. □

THEOREM 4.2. *The m-adic language $L(m, \eta)$ is regular iff the cut-point η is rational.*

Proof. We prove that $L(m, \eta)$ is f.a.r. iff η is rational. Assume first that η is rational. Then there are natural numbers u and v such that the m-adic expansion of η is of the form

$$\eta = .a_1 \ldots a_u a_{u+1} \ldots a_{u+v} a_{u+1} \ldots a_{u+v} \ldots .$$

We choose such an expansion of η which does not end with an infinite sequence of $(m-1)$'s. The language $L(m, \eta)$ is represented by the set $\{s''\}$ in the finite deterministic automaton

$$(\{s_0, s_1, \ldots, s_{u+v-1}, s', s''\}, s_0, f)$$

over the alphabet $\{0, 1, \ldots, m-1\}$, where the transition function f is defined as follows:

$$f(s_i, a_{i+1}) = s_{i+1} \qquad (i = 0, \ldots, u+v-2),$$

$$f(s_{u+v-1}, a_{u+v}) = s_u;$$

$$f(s_i, x) = \begin{cases} s' & \text{if } x < a_{i+1} \\ s'' & \text{if } x > a_{i+1} \end{cases} \qquad (i = 0, \ldots, u+v-1);$$

$$f(s', x) = s', \text{ for all } x,$$

$$f(s'', x) = s'' \text{ for all } x.$$

(Cf. Fig. 18.)

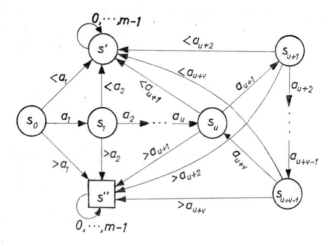

Fig. 18.

Assume that $\eta = .b_1 \ldots b_i \ldots$ is irrational. We claim that $L(m, \eta)$ is not f.a.r. Assume the contrary: $L(m, \eta)$ is represented by the set S_1 in a finite deterministic automaton, where s_0' is the initial state and f' the transition function. There are natural numbers k and l, $k < l$, such that

$$f'(s_0', b_1 \ldots b_k) = f'(s_0', b_1 \ldots b_k b_{k+1} \ldots b_l) \qquad (4.3)$$

(because the number of states is finite). Let h be the smallest natural number such that $b_{k+h} \neq b_{l+h}$. Since the expansion of η is not almost periodic, such a number h exists. Thus, by (4.3),

$$f'(s_0', b_1 \ldots b_k b_{k+1} \ldots b_{k+h-1} x) = f'(s_0', b_1 \ldots b_l b_{l+1} \ldots b_{l+h-1} x),$$

$$(4.4)$$

for all letters x.

If $b_{k+h} < b_{l+h}$, then we choose in (4.4) $x = b_{l+h}$. This implies that the left side of (4.4) is a state belonging to S_1 whereas the right side of (4.4) does not belong to S_1, which is a contradiction. If $b_{k+h} > b_{l+h}$, then we choose $x = b_{k+h}$. This implies that the right side of (4.4) belongs to S_1 whereas the left side does not belong to S_1, which is also a contradiction. Thus, $L(m, \eta)$ is not f.a.r. $\square$

It follows by the definition of m-adic languages that if $\eta_1 < \eta_2$ then $L(m, \eta_1) \supset L(m, \eta_2)$ and, hence, also

$$\mathrm{mi}(L(m, \eta_1)) \supset \mathrm{mi}(L(m, \eta_2)),$$

where the inclusion is proper. (Cf. Exercise 4.1.) It is an immediate consequence of Theorem 4.2 that mi $(L(m, \eta))$ is regular iff η is rational. Hence, by Theorems 4.1 and 3.1, we obtain the following

THEOREM 4.3. *For every real number η such that $0 < \eta < 1$ and every alphabet I consisting of at least two letters, there is a non-regular η-stochastic language over I. The family of stochastic languages over I is non-denumerable.*

Theorem 4.3 can be established also using Theorems 4.2, 3.1 and Exercise 4.3. It is easy to prove (using Theorems 3.8, 4.1 and Exercise 4.3) that all of the languages $L(m, \eta)$, $\mathrm{mi}(L(m, \eta))$, as well as their complements, are stochastic.

We shall finally show by an example that the language

$$L_{(=)}(\mathbf{PA}, \bar{S}_1, \eta)$$

considered in Section 3 is sometimes non-regular. Thus, the hypothesis of Theorem 3.8 is not always satisfied.

Consider the Rabin automaton **PA** over the alphabet $\{x, y\}$ defined by Fig. 19, where s_1 is the initial state and the transition probabilities $\neq 1$ are given within parentheses. Let $S_1 = \{s_5\}$ and let $\bar{S}_1$ be the corresponding column vector. A straightforward calculation shows that

$$L_{(=)}(\mathbf{PA}, \bar{S}_1, \tfrac{1}{2}) = \{x^{m+1} y x^m \mid m \geq 0\}. \qquad (4.5)$$

Clearly, the language (4.5) is not f.a.r. and, hence, it is not regular.

It is also seen that

$$L(\mathbf{PA}, \bar{S}_1, \tfrac{1}{2}) = \{x^m y x^n \,|\, 0 < m \leq n\}. \tag{4.6}$$

Hence, the language (4.6) is stochastic.

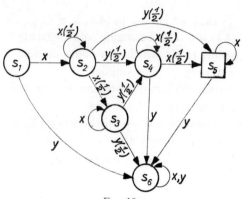

FIG. 19.

(*Remark*. The latter result is significant from the point of view of the theory of formal languages which will be studied in Chapter IV. Namely, (4.6) is an example of a stochastic language which is context-free and non-regular. This shows that some self-embedding languages can be represented in finite probabilistic automata.)

EXERCISE 4.1. For $\eta_1 < \eta_2$, give an example of a word belonging to the language $L(m, \eta_1)$ which does not belong to the language $L(m, \eta_2)$.

EXERCISE 4.2. Give an example of a finite probabilistic automaton, where a non-regular language is represented with cut-point $\tfrac{1}{3}$.

The Exercises 4.3–4.7 are from Salomaa, 1967.

EXERCISE 4.3. Prove that the language $L(m, \eta)$ is represented in the three-state probabilistic automaton

$$\mathbf{PA}'_m = (\{s_1, s_2, s_3\}, (1, 0, 0), M')$$

over the alphabet $\{0, 1, \ldots, m-1\}$, where for each letter x of the alphabet,

$$M'(x) = \left\| \begin{array}{ccc} 1/m & (m-x-1)/m & x/m \\ 0 & 1 & 0 \\ 0 & 0 & 1 \end{array} \right\|.$$

What is the representing column vector? Conclude that the language $L(m, \eta)$ is η-stochastic.

EXERCISE 4.4. Prove that $L(m, \eta)$ cannot be represented in a two-state probabilistic automaton.

EXERCISE 4.5. Prove that any set of n-dimensional stochastic matrices $(n \geq 2)$

$$M(x) = \|a_{\mu\nu}^x\|_{1 \leq \mu, \nu \leq n} \qquad (x = 0, \ldots, m-1)$$

where, for some $k \, (1 < k \leq n)$,

$$\sum_{\nu=k}^{n} a_{\mu\nu}^x = x/m \qquad (\mu = 1, \ldots, k-1; \; x = 0, \ldots, m-1)$$

and

$$\sum_{\nu=k}^{n} a_{\mu\nu}^x = (x+1)/m \qquad (\mu = k, \ldots, n; \; x = 0, \ldots, m-1)$$

determines an n-state probabilistic automaton, where $\mathrm{mi}(L(m, \eta))$ is represented with cut-point η.

EXERCISE 4.6. Consider the alphabet $I = \{0, \ldots, m-1\}$. Let $\varphi(P)$ be a real-valued function defined for words P over the alphabet I such that $\varphi(\lambda) = 0$ and, for all words P and letters x,

$$\varphi(xP) = a(x)\,\varphi(P) + b(x),$$

where $a(x)$ and $b(x)$ are non-negative and $a(x) + b(x) \leq 1$. Prove that the language

$$L(m, \eta, \varphi) = \{P \,|\, \varphi(P) > \eta\}$$

is represented in a three-state probabilistic automaton.

EXERCISE 4.7. Let φ be a mapping of I into $W(\mathrm{I})$, where the alphabet I is as in Exercise 4.6. By defining $\varphi(\lambda) = \lambda$ and

$$\varphi(x_1 \ldots x_i) = \varphi(x_1) \ldots \varphi(x_i)$$

we obtain a mapping of $W(I)$ into $W(I)$. Prove that if φ is a *constant length code*, i.e. the function values $\varphi(x)$, where $x \in I$, are words of equal length, then the language $\{P \,|\, .\varphi(P) > \eta\}$ is non-regular iff η is an irrational number of the form

$$\eta = .\varphi(x_1) \ldots \varphi(x_i) \ldots .$$

Study the general case, where φ is an arbitrary mapping of I into $W(I)$.

EXERCISE 4.8 (Starke, 1966, 3). Prove that, for every η such that $0 < \eta < 1$, there are **PA** and $\bar{S}_1$ such that

$$L_{(=)}(\mathbf{PA}, \bar{S}_1, \eta)$$

is non-regular.

EXERCISE 4.9 (Starke, 1966, 3). A real number η $(0 \leqq \eta < 1)$ is *weakly isolated* with respect to the pair $(\mathbf{PA}, \bar{S}_1)$ iff (3.7) holds for all words P such that $s_0 M(P)\bar{S}_1 \neq \eta$. Prove that if η is weakly isolated with respect to the pair $(\mathbf{PA}, \bar{S}_1)$, then the language $L_{(=)}(\mathbf{PA}, \bar{S}_1, \eta)$ is regular.

Some knowledge of the eigenvalues of stochastic matrices is needed in Exercises 4.10–4.13.

EXERCISE 4.10. The most simple probabilistic automaton, where a non-regular language is represented, is a three-state automaton over a one-letter alphabet. Prove that the language $L(\mathbf{PA}, \bar{S}_1, 4/11)$, where $\mathbf{PA} = (\{s_1, s_2, s_3\}, (0, 0, 1), M)$ is over the alphabet $\{x\}$ and

$$M(x) = \begin{Vmatrix} 2/3 & 0 & 1/3 \\ 5/9 & 1/3 & 1/9 \\ 1/4 & 1/4 & 1/2 \end{Vmatrix}, \qquad \bar{S}_1 = \begin{pmatrix} 0 \\ 0 \\ 1 \end{pmatrix},$$

is non-regular. (This example is from Paz (1966).) Note that a non-regular language may result although, as in this example, all numbers in the initial distribution and in the matrices as well as the cut-point, are rational.

EXERCISE 4.11 (Turakainen, 1966). Prove the following general result concerning three-state probabilistic automata

$$\mathbf{PA} = (\{s_1, s_2, s_3\}, \quad (p_1, p_2, p_3), \quad M)$$

over the alphabet $\{x\}$. Let y_1, y_2, y_3 be the components of the row eigenvector corresponding to the eigenvalue 1 of the matrix $M(x)$. Denote

$$\xi_i = y_i/(y_1 + y_2 + y_3),$$
$$\xi_{ij} = (y_i + y_j)/(y_1 + y_2 + y_3) \qquad (i, j = 1, 2, 3; i \neq j).$$

Then a non-regular language is representable in **PA** iff

$$(p_1, p_2, p_3) \neq (\xi_1, \xi_2, \xi_3)$$

and $M(x)$ has an eigenvalue μ such that arg μ is irrational in degrees. Moreover, if these two conditions are satisfied then, for each set S_1 of representing states consisting of one or two states, there is exactly one cut-point η such that the language $L(\mathbf{PA}, \bar{S}_1, \eta)$ is non-regular. This cut-point is ξ_i if $S_1 = \{s_i\}$, and ξ_{ij} if $S_1 = \{s_i, s_j\}$ $(i \neq j)$.

Conclude that if all eigenvalues of $M(x)$ are real, then only regular languages are represented. In fact, this result is valid for all probabilistic automata over $\{x\}$. Cf. also Turakainen (1967) for results concerning regularity of languages represented in an arbitrary finite probabilistic automaton over a one-letter alphabet.

EXERCISE 4.12 (Turakainen, 1967). Show by an example that the catenation of a regular language ($\neq L_\phi$, $W(I)$) and of a stochastic non-regular language may be a regular language.

EXERCISE 4.13 (Salomaa, 1965; Turakainen, 1966). Let **PA** be a probabilistic automaton over a one-letter alphabet and S_1 a subset of the set of states. Give an upper bound for the number of real numbers η such that the language $L(\mathbf{PA}, \bar{S}_1, \eta)$ is non-regular.

PROBLEM 4.1. Is the mirror image of a stochastic language stochastic? (This holds true for the language $L(m, \eta)$.)

PROBLEM 4.2. Study criteria for deciding whether or not a given language is stochastic. (Bukharaev (1965, 1967) has developed a general criterion resembling Theorem I.4.1. It is based on an equivalence relation, induced by the given language, in the space of infinite-dimensional vectors, the sum of whose components converges absolutely to 1. A language is stochastic iff the space spanned by the equivalence classes is of finite dimension. In Bukharaev (1965) an example is given of a language representable in a Turing machine, which is not stochastic.)

§ 5. Probabilistic sequential machines

We shall now introduce probabilistic devices which convert input words into output words. Special types of these devices resemble Mealy and Moore machines considered in Section I.5. We shall prove theorems concerning the equivalence and non-equivalence of various types of probabilistic sequential machines. The main result is that a language representable in any finite probabilistic sequential machine is representable in a finite probabilistic automaton.

We denote by $\mathcal{M}(i, j)$ the set of all $i \times j$ matrices consisting of non-negative real numbers whose sum equals 1. Thus, $\mathcal{M}(1, j)$ denotes the set of all j-dimensional stochastic row vectors.

DEFINITION. A *finite probabilistic sequential machine* is an ordered quintuple $\mathbf{PM} = (I, O, S, \delta, F)$, where I and O are finite alphabets (*input* and *output alphabet*), S is a finite non-empty set (the set of *internal states*), δ is an element of $\mathcal{M}(1, \text{card}(S))$ (the *initial distribution*) and F is a mapping of the set $S \times I$ into the set $\mathcal{M}(\text{card}(S), \text{card}(O))$.

Assume that $S = \{s_1, \ldots, s_n\}, I = \{x_1, \ldots, x_r\}$ and $O = \{y_1, \ldots, y_m\}$. The (i, j)th entry in the matrix $F(s_u, x_v)$, where $1 \leq i, u \leq n$ and $1 \leq v \leq r$ and $1 \leq j \leq m$ is denoted by

$$p_{\mathbf{PM}}(s_i, y_j / s_u, x_v) \tag{5.1}$$

and referred to as the probability of $\mathbf{PM}$ to enter into the state s_i and produce the output y_j, after being in the state s_u and receiving the input x_v.

Assume that $k \geq 1$ and $s^1, \ldots, s^k \in S$, $y^1, \ldots, y^k \in O$ and $x^1, \ldots, x^k \in I$. Denote

$$p_{\mathbf{PM}}(s^1 \ldots s^k, y^1 \ldots y^k / x^1 \ldots x^k) = \sum_{s^0 \in S} \delta(s^0) \prod_{i=1}^{k} p_{\mathbf{PM}}(s^i, y^i / s^{i-1}, x^i),$$

where $\delta(s^0)$ equals, for $s^0 = s_j$, the jth component of the vector δ. Furthermore, denote

$$p_{\mathbf{PM}}(y^1 \ldots y^k / x^1 \ldots x^k) = \sum p_{\mathbf{PM}}(s^1 \ldots s^k, y^1 \ldots y^k / x^1 \ldots x^k), \tag{5.2}$$

where the sum is taken over all k-tuples $(s^1, \ldots, s^k)$ with each $s^i \in S$. The number (5.2) is referred to as the probability of $\mathbf{PM}$ to give the response $y^1 \ldots y^k$ to the input $x^1 \ldots x^k$. By definition,

$$p_{\mathbf{PM}}(\lambda / \lambda) = 1.$$

If each of the matrices $F(s_u, x_v)$ satisfies the condition

$$F(s_u, x_v) = f(s_u, x_v) \, \varphi \, (s_u, x_v), \tag{5.3}$$

where f is an n-dimensional stochastic column vector and φ is an

m-dimensional stochastic row vector, then **PM** is termed a *(finite) probabilistic Mealy machine*. The components of the vectors f and φ are referred to, respectively, as *transition probabilities* and *output probabilities*.

Assume that, for each $s_u \in S$ and $x_v \in I$, there is an n-dimensional stochastic vector $f(s_u, x_v)$ and, for each $s_i \in S$, there is an m-dimensional stochastic vector $\varphi(s_i)$ such that (5.1) satisfies the condition

$$p_{PM}(s_i, y_j/s_u, x_v) = f(s_i/s_u, x_v)\, \varphi\,(y_j/s_i), \tag{5.4}$$

where $f(s_i/s_u, x_v)$ equals the ith component of the vector $f(s_u, x_v)$ and $\varphi(y_j/s_i)$ equals the jth component of the vector $\varphi(s_i)$. Then **PM** is termed a *(finite) probabilistic Moore machine*. If all of the vectors φ in (5.4) are coordinate vectors, then **PM** is said to possess a *deterministic output function*. In this case **PM** is called, shortly, a *d.o. machine*.

A probabilistic Mealy (Moore) machine **PM** is said to possess a *deterministic transition function* iff all of the vectors $f(s_u, x_v)$ appearing in (5.3) (in (5.4)) are coordinate vectors. Then **PM** is called, shortly, a *d.t. Mealy (Moore) machine*. The term *d.t. machine* is used to refer to both d.t. Mealy machines and d.t. Moore machines.

Two finite probabilistic sequential machines **PM** and **PM'** with the same input and output alphabets are termed *equivalent* iff

$$p_{PM}(Q/P) = p_{PM'}(Q/P), \tag{5.5}$$

for any $P \in W(I)$ and $Q \in W(O)$ such that $\lg(P) = \lg(Q)$.

It will be shown in Theorem 5.9 that it suffices to test finitely many pairs (P, Q) to see whether (5.5) is satisfied for all pairs (P, Q). It is easy to see that probabilistic Mealy and Moore machines are generalizations of the notions considered in Section I.5. (Cf. Exercise 5.1.) Any d.o. machine may be considered as a finite probabilistic automaton, where to each state there corresponds a unique output letter.

DEFINITION. For a finite probabilistic sequential machine **PM** $= (I, O, S, \delta, F)$ and for $x^1, \ldots, x^k \in I$ ($k \geq 2$) and $y \in O$, define

$$p_{PM}(y/x^1 \ldots x^k) = \sum p_{PM}(y^1 \ldots y^{k-1} y/x^1 \ldots x^k), \tag{5.6}$$

where the sum is taken over all $(k-1)$-tuples $(y^1, \ldots, y^{k-1})$ with each $y^i \in O$. (For $k = 1$, $p_{PM}(y/x^1)$ is defined by (5.2).) Let η be a real number such that $0 \leqq \eta < 1$. Then the output y *represents* in **PM** the language

$$L(\mathbf{PM}, y, \eta) = \{P \mid p_{\mathbf{PM}}(y/P) > \eta\}$$

with *cut-point* η. A language L is *representable* in a finite probabilistic sequential machine, or shortly, L is *p.m.r.* iff $L = L(\mathbf{PM}, y, \eta)$, for some **PM**, y and η.

Thus, the language represented in **PM** by y consists of such words P which have the following property: the probability of **PM** to give a response, ending with the letter y, to the input P is greater than η. If a language is p.m.r. then it does not contain the empty word because, by (5.2) and (5.6), $p_{\mathbf{PM}}(y/P)$ is defined for non-empty words P only. Our first theorem is a direct consequence of the definitions.

THEOREM 5.1. *Let* **PM** *and* **PM**′ *be equivalent finite probabilistic sequential machines. Then, for any y and η,*

$$L(\mathbf{PM}, y, \eta) = L(\mathbf{PM}', y, \eta).$$

THEOREM 5.2. *If a stochastic language L does not contain the empty word, then it is p.m.r. Furthermore, there is a d.o. machine, where L is represented.*

Proof. The theorem follows because any finite probabilistic automaton together with a set of representing states can be considered as a d.o. machine, where the output alphabet consists of two letters. □

We shall now study the problem whether it suffices to have probabilistic transition functions or probabilistic output functions, i.e. whether, given a finite probabilistic sequential machine, one can construct an equivalent d.o. machine or an equivalent d.t. machine. As regards d.o. machines, this is always possible. As regards d.t. machines, such a construction is not, in general, possible.

THEOREM 5.3. *Only regular languages are represented in a d.t. Moore machine.*

Proof. Assume that $L = L(\mathbf{PM}, y, \eta)$, for some d.t. Moore machine **PM** $= (I, O, S, \delta, F), y \in O$ and $0 \leqq \eta < 1$. By the definition of a d.t. Moore machine,

$$p_{\mathbf{PM}}(s^1 \ldots s^k, y^1 \ldots y^k / x^1 \ldots x^k) = \sum_{s^0 \in S} \delta(s^0) \prod_{i=1}^{k} f(s^i/s^{i-1}, x^i)\, \varphi(y^i/s^i),$$

where each of the numbers $f(s^i/s^{i-1}, x^i)$ equals either 0 or 1 (and the notations are the same as before). In particular, for each word $x^1 \ldots x^k$ over I and each state $s^0 \in S$, there is exactly one sequence of states $s^1, \ldots, s^k$ such that

$$f(s^i/s^{i-1}, x^i) = 1 \quad (i = 1, \ldots, k). \tag{5.7}$$

Denote $s^k = s^0 x^1 \ldots x^k$. Then, for any (non-empty) P over I,

$$p_{\text{PM}}(y/P) = \sum_{s^0 \in S} \delta(s^0)\, \varphi\,(y/s^0 P). \tag{5.8}$$

Let $S = \{s_1, \ldots, s_n\}$, and consider the language $L(i,j)$ represented by the set $\{s_j\}$ in the finite deterministic automaton $\mathbf{A}_i = (S, s_i, f)$ over I, where $1 \leqq i, j \leqq n$. (Here the *function* $f:S \times I \to S$ is defined by $f(s_u, x_v) = s_v$, if the vth component of the *vector* $f(s_u, x_v)$ equals 1.) By Theorems I.2.4 and I.2.6 each intersection of the form

$$L(1, i_1) \cap \ldots \cap L(n, i_n) \quad (1 \leqq i_j \leqq n) \tag{5.9}$$

is regular. Every word P over I belongs to exactly one of the intersections (5.9) and, by (5.8), $p_{\text{PM}}(y/P)$ assumes the same value for all words P belonging to the same intersection. Thus, the language $L = L(\text{PM}, y, \eta)$ is the union of some of the intersections (5.9) and, therefore, it is regular. $\square$

THEOREM 5.4. *For every d.t. Mealy machine, there is an equivalent d.t. Moore machine.*

Proof. Assume that $\mathbf{PM} = (I, O, S, \delta, F)$ is a d.t. Mealy machine such that

$$F(s_u, x_v) = f(s_u, x_v)\, \varphi\,(s_u, x_v),$$

where the vectors f are n-dimensional coordinate vectors and the vectors φ are m-dimensional stochastic vectors. (We use our previous notation and, accordingly, card$(S) = n$, card$(I) = r$, card$(O) = m$.) Consider the set $S_1 = S \cup S \times I$. For each $\sigma \in S_1$, we define an m-dimensional stochastic vector $\varphi_1(\sigma)$ as follows:

$$\varphi_1\big((s_u, x_v)\big) = \varphi(s_u, x_v),$$
$$\varphi_1(s_u) = \varphi_0,$$

where φ_0 is an arbitrary fixed m-dimensional stochastic vector. For each pair $(\sigma,\ x)$, where $\sigma \in S_1$ and $x \in I$, we define an $(nr+n)$-dimensional coordinate vector $f_1(\sigma, x)$ as follows. We assume that the elements of S_1 are indexed and, thus, each component of an $(nr+n)$-dimensional vector corresponds to some state in S_1. In the vector $f_1(s, x)$ the component corresponding to the state (s, x) equals 1. In the vector $f_1((s, x^1), x^2)$ the component corresponding to the state $(a(f(s, x^1)), x^2)$ equals 1, where $a(f(s, x^1))$ denotes the state s_u such that in the vector $f(s, x^1)$ the uth component equals 1. Finally, let δ_1 be the $(nr+n)$-dimensional stochastic vector such that the components corresponding to the states s equal the same components of the vector δ, whereas the components corresponding to the states (s, x) equal 0.

Consider the d.t. Moore machine $\mathbf{PM}_1 = (I, O, S_1, \delta_1, F_1)$, where F_1 is determined by the vectors f_1 and φ_1. We claim that $\mathbf{PM}$ and $\mathbf{PM}_1$ are equivalent. In fact, for each state $s^0 \in S$ and each word $x^1 \ldots x^k$ over I, there is exactly one sequence of states $s^1, \ldots, s^k$ such that (5.7) is satisfied, where $f(s^i/s^{i-1}, x^i)$ denotes the component of the vector $f(s^{i-1}, x^i)$ corresponding to the state s^i. Hence, we obtain

$$p_{\mathbf{PM}}(y^1 \ldots y^k/x^1 \ldots x^k) = \sum_{s^0 \in S} \delta(s^0) \prod_{i=1}^{k} \varphi(y^i/s^{i-1}, x^i), \qquad (5.10)$$

where $\varphi(y^i/s^{i-1},\ x^i)$ denotes the component of the vector $\varphi(s^{i-1}, x^i)$ corresponding to y^i. (Note that the states s^{i-1} appearing in the product depend on s^0.) Similarly, for each $\sigma^0 \in S_1$ and each word $x^1 \ldots x^k$ over I, there is exactly one sequence of states $\sigma^1, \ldots, \sigma^k \in S_1$ such that

$$f_1(\sigma^i/\sigma^{i-1}, x^i) = 1 \qquad (i = 1, \ldots, k),$$

where the left side denotes the component of $f_1 (\sigma^{i-1}, x^i)$ corresponding to the state σ^i. Furthermore, if $\sigma^0 = s^0 \in S$, then $\sigma^i = (s^{i-1}, x^i)$, for $i = 1, \ldots, k$, where $s^1, \ldots, s^k$ are defined as above. Therefore, by the definition of the initial distribution δ_1, we obtain the result

$$p_{\mathbf{PM}_1} (y^1 \ldots y^k/x^1 \ldots x^k) = \sum_{\sigma^0 \in S} \delta_1(\sigma^0) \prod_{i=1}^{k} \varphi_1(y^i/\sigma^i),$$

where $\delta_1(\sigma^0)$ denotes the component of δ_1 corresponding to σ_0 and

$\varphi_1(y^i/\sigma^i)$ denotes the component of $\varphi_1(\sigma^i)$ corresponding to y^i. Hence, by (5.10) and the definition of the vectors φ_1, we obtain the result

$$p_{\mathbf{PM}_1}(y^1 \ldots y^k/x^1 \ldots x^k) = p_{\mathbf{PM}}(y^1 \ldots y^k/x^1 \ldots x^k). \quad \square$$

The next theorem is an immediate consequence of Theorems 5.1, 5.3 and 5.4.

THEOREM 5.5. *Only regular languages are represented in a d.t. machine.*

On the other hand, it follows by Theorem 4.3 that there are d.o. machines, where non-regular languages can be represented. (In fact, the automaton $\mathbf{PA}_m$ and the vector $\bar{S}_1$ considered in the proof of Theorem 4.1 can immediately be extended to a d.o. machine whose output alphabet consists of two letters.) Thus, we obtain the following

THEOREM 5.6. *There is a d.o. machine* **PM** *such that no d.t. machine is equivalent to* **PM**.

We shall now prove that it suffices to have a probabilistic transition function in a finite probabilistic sequential machine.

THEOREM 5.7. *For any finite probabilistic sequential machine, there is an equivalent d.o. machine. Hence, all p.m.r. languages are stochastic.*

Proof. We note first that the latter part of the theorem is a consequence of the former part because any language representable in a d.o. machine is stochastic. (The detailed verification of this fact is left as an exercise.)

To prove the former part, we assume that $\mathbf{PM} = (I, O, S, \delta, F)$ is a finite probabilistic sequential machine. (We use our earlier notations: $\operatorname{card}(S) = n$, $\operatorname{card}(O) = m$.) Consider the set $S_1 = S \times O$. For each $\sigma \in S_1$, we define an m-dimensional coordinate vector $\varphi(\sigma)$ such that, in each $\varphi((s, y))$, the component corresponding to the output y equals 1. For each pair (σ, x), where $\sigma = (s, y) \in S_1$ and $x \in I$, we define an nm-dimensional stochastic vector $f(\sigma, x)$ such that

$$f((s', y')/\sigma, x) = F(s', y'/s, x),$$

where we use the same notation as before. (Thus, the vector $f((s, y), x)$ is independent of y.) Finally, we define an nm-dimensional stochastic vector δ_1 arbitrarily in such a way that

$$\sum_{y \in O} \delta_1((s,y)) = \delta(s),$$

where $\delta_1((s, y))$ denotes the component corresponding to the element $(s, y) \in S_1$ and $\delta(s)$ denotes the component corresponding to the element $s \in S$.

Consider the d.o. machine $\mathbf{PM}_1 = (I, O, S_1, \delta_1, F_1)$, where F_1 is determined by the vectors f and φ. By the definition of F_1 and δ_1, we obtain the result

$$p_{\mathbf{PM}_1}\big((s^1, y^1) \ldots (s^k, y^k), y^1 \ldots y^k / x^1 \ldots x^k\big)$$

$$= \sum_{(s^0, y^0) \in S_1} \delta_1\big((s^0, y^0)\big) \prod_{i=1}^{k} F_1\big((s^i, y^i), y^i / (s^{i-1}, y^{i-1}), x^i\big)$$

$$= \sum_{s^0 \in S} \delta(s^0) \prod_{i=1}^{k} F(s^i, y^i / s^{i-1}, x^i) = p_{\mathbf{PM}}(s^1 \ldots s^k, y^1 \ldots y^k / x^1 \ldots x^k). \quad (5.11)$$

On the other hand

$$p_{\mathbf{PM}_1}\big((s^1, y^{i_1}) \ldots (s^k, y^{i_k}), y^1 \ldots y^k / x^1 \ldots x^k\big) = 0$$

if, for some j, $y^{i_j} \neq y^j$. Thus, by (5.11), the equation

$$p_{\mathbf{PM}_1}(y^1 \ldots y^k / x^1 \ldots x^k) = p_{\mathbf{PM}}(y^1 \ldots y^k / x^1 \ldots x^k)$$

follows. $\square$

By Theorems 5.2 and 5.7, a language is p.m.r. iff it is stochastic and does not contain the empty word. Thus, p.m.r. languages bear the same relation to stochastic languages as f.m.r. languages do to regular (f.a.r.) languages. As an immediate corollary of Theorem 5.7, we obtain the following

THEOREM 5.8. *For any probabilistic Mealy machine, there is an equivalent probabilistic Moore machine.*

We shall now prove that there is an algorithm of deciding whether or not two finite probabilistic sequential machines are equivalent. Theorem 5.9 is analogous to Theorem I.6.3.

THEOREM 5.9. *Let* **PM** *and* **PM'** *be two finite probabilistic sequential machines with n and n' states and with the same input and output alphabets. Then* **PM** *and* **PM'** *are equivalent iff* (5.5) *is satisfied for all words P and Q of length* $n+n'-1$.

Proof. Assume that $\textbf{PM} = (I, O, S, (p_1, \ldots, p_n), F)$ and $\textbf{PM'} = (I, O, S', (q_1, \ldots, q_{n'}), F')$. For $x_v \in I$ and $y_j \in O$, let $M(y_j/x_v)$ ($M'(y_j/x_v)$) be the n-dimensional (n'-dimensional) square matrix whose (u, i)th entry equals (5.1) (equals (5.1) with **PM** replaced by **PM'**). Furthermore, define

$$\overline{M}(y_j/x_v) = \left\| \begin{matrix} M(y_j/x_v) & 0 \\ 0 & M'(y_j/x_v) \end{matrix} \right\|.$$

Let $V_{n+n'}$ be the linear space of all $(n+n')$-dimensional column vectors with real components and let $c \in V_{n+n'}$ be the vector whose every component equals 1. We define a mapping $\bar{p}$ of the set of pairs (Q, P), where $Q \in W(O)$, $P \in W(I)$, $\lg(Q) = \lg(P)$, into $V_{n+n'}$ recursively as follows:

$$\bar{p}(\lambda/\lambda) = c,$$
$$\bar{p}(y_j Q/x_v P) = \overline{M}(y_j/x_v)\bar{p}(Q/P) \quad \text{if} \quad \lg(Q) = \lg(P). \quad (5.12)$$

Let ω be a mapping of $V_{n+n'}$ into the set of real numbers defined by

$$\omega(\gamma) = (p_1, \ldots, p_n, -q_1, \ldots, -q_{n'})\gamma, \quad \gamma \in V_{n+n'}.$$

Then it is easily verified that, for all $Q \in W(O)$, $P \in W(I)$ such that $\lg(Q) = \lg(P)$,

$$p_{\textbf{PM}}(Q/P) - p_{\textbf{PM'}}(Q/P) = \omega(\bar{p}(Q/P)). \quad (5.13)$$

For $k = 0, 1, 2, \ldots$, denote by U_k the linear subspace of $V_{n+n'}$ spanned by the vectors $\bar{p}(Q/P)$, where $Q \in W(O)$, $P \in W(I)$ and $\lg(Q) = \lg(P) = k$. Because, for any $x \in I$,

$$\bar{p}(Q/P) = \sum_{y \in O} \bar{p}(Qy/Px)$$

we obtain, for all k,

$$U_k \subset U_{k+1}. \quad (5.14)$$

On the other hand, we claim that if, for some k,

$$U_k = U_{k+1}, \quad (5.15)$$

then also

$$U_{k+1} = U_{k+2} \qquad (5.16)$$

and hence $U_k = U_{k+l}$, for all l.

Assume that (5.15) is satisfied, for some k. Every vector in U_{k+2} is spanned by the vectors

$$\bar{p}(y_j Q / x_v P)(y_j \in O, \ x_v \in I, \ Q \in W(O), \ P \in W(I), \ \mathrm{lg}(P) = \mathrm{lg}(Q) = k+1).$$
$$(5.17)$$

By (5.12) and (5.15), each of the vectors (5.17) is a linear combination of vectors of the form

$$\bar{M}(y/x)\,\bar{p}(Q'/P') \ (y \in O, x \in I, Q' \in W(O), P' \in W(I), \mathrm{lg}(Q')$$
$$= \mathrm{lg}(P') = k).$$

Therefore, by (5.12), each of the vectors (5.17) is a linear combination of vectors in U_{k+1}. This proves the equation (5.16).

Because U_0 is 1-dimensional and every U_k is a subspace of an $(n+n')$-dimensional space we conclude, by (5.14), that (5.15) is satisfied, for some $k \leq n+n'-1$. Hence, (5.15) is always satisfied for $k = n+n'-1$. This implies that the function ω vanishes for all vectors $\bar{p}(Q/P)$ iff it vanishes on the subspace $U_{n+n'-1}$. By (5.13), we conclude that **PM** and **PM'** are equivalent iff (5.5) is satisfied for all words P and Q of length $n+n'-1$. $\square$

EXERCISE 5.1. Prove that if in (5.3) (in (5.4)) also the vectors φ, as well as the initial distribution δ, are coordinate vectors, then the d.t. Mealy (Moore) machine can be rewritten as an initial Mealy (Moore) machine (in the sense of Section I.5). Explain why there is no deterministic device corresponding to the general finite probabilistic sequential machine.

EXERCISE 5.2. Give examples of finite probabilistic sequential machines which are neither probabilistic Mealy machines nor probabilistic Moore machines.

EXERCISE 5.3. Prove that a finite probabilistic sequential machine is a probabilistic Mealy machine iff every matrix $F(s, x)$ is of rank 1.

EXERCISE 5.4. Verify in detail (by referring to the definitions and performing the matrix calculations involved) the statement made in the proof of Theorem 5.2.

EXERCISE 5.5. Prove that any language representable in a d.o. machine is stochastic.

EXERCISE 5.6. Compare the proofs of Theorems 5.4 and 5.7 to the proofs showing the equivalence of finite sequential Mealy and Moore machines. (The proof of Theorem 5.7 resembles that of Theorem I.5.1, whereas the proof of Theorem 5.4 resembles that sketched in Exercise I.5.5.)

EXERCISE 5.7. Define the notion of a language represented in **PM** by a subset of O (rather than by a single element of O). Does this properly increase the family of p.m.r. languages?

EXERCISE 5.8. Explain $\bar{p}$ (in the proof of Theorem 5.9) in terms of probabilities and verify (5.13).

EXERCISE 5.9. Define finite probabilistic sequential machines without including the initial distribution in the definition. (Cf. the definition of sequential machines in Section I.5.) Define then the notion of equivalence for two initial distributions in the same machine, and prove that $(n-1)$-equivalence is a sufficient condition for equivalence, where n is the number of states. (Cf. Theorems I.6.1 and I.6.2.) Apply this result to the equivalence of states, i.e. to the case where initial distributions are coordinate vectors. Cf. Carlyle (1963) and Paz (1966) for results concerning *reduced* probabilistic machines, i.e. machines with no two equivalent states.

EXERCISE 5.10 (Page, 1966). Let $\mathbf{PA} = (S, s_0, M)$ and $\mathbf{PA}' = (S, s_0', M)$ be two finite probabilistic automata over I (which, thus, differ only with respect to initial distributions), $S_1 \subset S$ and $\bar{S}_1$ the corresponding column vector. Prove that the equation

$$s_0 M(P) \bar{S}_1 = s_0' M(P) \bar{S}_1$$

holds for all $P \in W(I)$ iff it holds for all $P \in W(I)$ with length less than or equal to $\operatorname{card}(S) - 2$. (It is assumed that $\operatorname{card}(S) \geq 3$.)

EXERCISE 5.11. Prove that the numbers $n-1$ and $n+n'-1$ given in Exercise 5.9 and Theorem 5.9 cannot be reduced in the general case. (Hint: consider the degenerate case of a d.o.d.t. machine.)

PROBLEM 5.1. Does the family of stochastic languages remain unaltered if in (2.1) the symbol ">" is replaced by "$\geqq$"? Study the same problem in the case where the components of $\bar{S}_1$ as well as η are allowed to be arbitrary real numbers. (This approach is due to Page (1966).)

PROBLEM 5.2. Study cases where the number of states becomes smaller in the transition from a probabilistic automaton or sequential machine of a certain type into a device of another type. (This is a more general problem than Problem 3.2.)

§ 6. Realizability of functions

We shall now consider problems analogous to the ones discussed in Section I.7. Considerations are restricted to finite probabilistic automata (rather than sequential machines).

DEFINITION. Let $\mathbf{PA} = (\{s_1, \ldots, s_n\}, s_0, M)$ be a finite probabilistic automaton over I. The mapping

$$Z_{\mathbf{PA}}(P) = s_0 M(P)$$

of $W(I)$ into the set $\mathcal{M}(1, n)$ of n-dimensional stochastic row vectors is termed the *function realized* by **PA**. A function Z mapping $W(I)$ into $\mathcal{M}(1, n)$ is said to be *realizable* by a finite probabilistic automaton iff, for some **PA**, $Z = Z_{\mathbf{PA}}$.

Thus, the value $Z_{\mathbf{PA}}(P)$ equals the distribution of states caused by the word P. Clearly, for $I = \{x_1, \ldots, x_r\}$, a function $Z:W(I) \to \mathcal{M}(1, n)$ is realized by a finite probabilistic automaton iff there are n-dimensional stochastic matrices $M(x_1), \ldots, M(x_r)$ such that

$$Z(Px_i) = Z(P)M(x_i), \tag{6.1}$$

for all $P \in W(I)$ and all i, $1 \leq i \leq r$. The following theorem is a direct consequence of the definitions.

THEOREM 6.1. *A necessary and sufficient condition for a language L over I to be stochastic is the existence of* (i) *a natural number n,* (ii) *a mapping Z of $W(I)$ into $\mathcal{M}(1, n)$ realizable by a finite probabilistic automaton,* (iii) *an n-dimensional column vector U consisting of 0's and 1's and* (iv) *a real number η satisfying $0 \leq \eta < 1$ such that, for any word P over I, $P \in L$ iff $Z(P)U > \eta$.*

Hence, criteria for deciding whether or not a language is stochastic and whether or not a function is realizable are interrelated. The next theorem gives a necessary and sufficient condition for a function to be realizable.

THEOREM 6.2. *Let n be a natural number and I a finite alphabet. A function $Z: W(I) \to \mathcal{M}(1, n)$ is realized by a finite probabilistic automaton iff the following two conditions are satisfied:*

(i) *For all $P \in W(I)$ and all $x \in I$, if $Z(P) = \sum_{i=1}^{k} \gamma_i Z(P_i)$ then also $Z(Px) = \sum_{i=1}^{k} \gamma_i Z(P_i x)$.*

(ii) *If $Z(P_1), \ldots, Z(P_v)$, where $1 \leq v \leq n$, are linearly independent and $x \in I$, then there are n-dimensional row vectors $Z_{v+1}, \ldots, Z_n$ and $U_{v+1}, \ldots, U_n$ such that*

$$
\begin{Vmatrix} Z(P_1) \\ \vdots \\ Z(P_v) \\ Z_{v+1} \\ \vdots \\ Z_n \end{Vmatrix}^{-1} \begin{Vmatrix} Z(P_1 x) \\ \vdots \\ Z(P_v x) \\ U_{v+1} \\ \vdots \\ U_n \end{Vmatrix} \tag{6.2}
$$

is a stochastic matrix.

Proof. We shall first prove the "only if" part. Assume that, for each $x_i \in I$, there is an $n \times n$ stochastic matrix $M(x_i)$ such that (6.1) is satisfied. Condition (i) follows, by the distributive law for matrix multiplication. Given linearly independent vectors $Z(P_1), \ldots, Z(P_v)$, we choose n-dimensional row vectors Z_i, $v+1 \leq i \leq n$, such that all of the vectors Z are linearly independent. For $x \in I$, denote $U_i = Z_i M(x)$, $v+1 \leq i \leq n$. Then, by (6.1),

$$
\begin{Vmatrix} Z(P_1) \\ \vdots \\ Z(P_v) \\ Z_{v+1} \\ \vdots \\ Z_n \end{Vmatrix} \cdot M(x) = \begin{Vmatrix} Z(P_1 x) \\ \vdots \\ Z(P_v x) \\ U_{v+1} \\ \vdots \\ U_n \end{Vmatrix}
$$

and hence, by the assumption concerning $M(x)$, the matrix (6.2) is an $n \times n$ stochastic matrix. Thus, also condition (ii) is satisfied.

For the "if" part, assume that (i) and (ii) are satisfied. We choose words $P_1, \ldots, P_v \in W(I)$, $1 \leqq v \leqq n$, such that $Z(P_1), \ldots, Z(P_v)$ are linearly independent and, for no words $Q_1, \ldots, Q_{v+1} \in W(I)$, $Z(Q_1), \ldots, Z(Q_{v+1})$ are linearly independent. This implies that, for any $P \in W(I)$, there are real numbers γ_j, $1 \leqq j \leqq v$, such that

$$Z(P) = \sum_{j=1}^{v} \gamma_j Z(P_j). \tag{6.3}$$

By (ii) there is, for $x \in I$, a stochastic matrix $M(x)$ (not necessarily unique) such that

$$Z(P_j)M(x) = Z(P_j x) \qquad (j = 1, \ldots, v). \tag{6.4}$$

Let $P \in W(I)$ and $x \in I$ be arbitrary. Because the condition (i) is satisfied we obtain, by (6.3),

$$Z(Px) = \sum_{j=1}^{v} \gamma_j Z(P_j x)$$

and thus, by (6.4), the equation (6.1) with $x_i = x$ follows. $\square$

For an analogous result concerning finite deterministic automata, condition (i) is both necessary and sufficient (provided deterministic automata are rewritten as degenerate probabilistic ones). This was shown in Theorem I.7.1. It is also easy to see that condition (ii) is satisfied iff it is satisfied for the maximal number v of linearly independent vectors $Z(P_1), \ldots, Z(P_v)$. If $v = n$, then the stochastic matrices $M(x)$ defining the automaton are unique.

One may also consider mappings Z of $W(I)$ into the set of real numbers in the closed interval $[0, 1]$ and study under what conditions there exist a finite probabilistic automaton **PA** and a column vector $\bar{S}_1$ such that, for all words P over I,

$$Z(P) = \mathbf{PA}(P) \, \bar{S}_1. \tag{6.5}$$

Then Z is said to be *realized* by **PA**. (Cf. Exercises 6.6 and 6.7.) One may also ask under what conditions such a mapping Z can be approximated by a finite deterministic automaton in the sense of the following

DEFINITION. Let I be a finite alphabet and Z a mapping of the set $W(I)$ into the set of real numbers in the closed interval $[0, 1]$. For

$\varepsilon > 0$, a finite deterministic automaton $\mathbf{A} = (S, s_0, f)$ over I, *ε-approximates* Z iff there is a function $\psi : S \to [0, 1]$ such that, for all $P \in W(I)$,

$$|Z(P) - \psi(f(s_0, P))| \leq \varepsilon.$$

The mapping Z is *ε-approximable* iff there is a finite deterministic automaton which ε-approximates Z. The mapping Z is *quasidefinite* iff, for any $\varepsilon > 0$, there is a natural number $k(\varepsilon)$ such that for all $P, Q \in W(I)$ with $\lg(Q) = k(\varepsilon)$,

$$|Z(PQ) - Z(Q)| \leq \varepsilon.$$

We shall now prove that quasidefiniteness is a sufficient condition for ε-approximability.

THEOREM 6.3. *If Z is quasidefinite then it is ε-approximable, for any $\varepsilon > 0$.*

Proof. Given a quasidefinite $Z : W(I) \to [0, 1]$ and $\varepsilon > 0$, we define a finite deterministic automaton $\mathbf{A} = (S, s_0, f)$ over I as follows.

Because Z is quasidefinite, there is a natural number $k(\varepsilon)$ such that

$$|Z(PQ) - Z(Q)| \leq \varepsilon, \qquad (6.6)$$

whenever $P, Q \in W(I)$ and $\lg(Q) = k(\varepsilon)$. Let $P_1 = \lambda, P_2, \ldots, P_m$ be all the words over I with length less than $k(\varepsilon)$ and $P_{m+1}, \ldots, P_{m+n}$ all the words over I with length equal to $k(\varepsilon)$. We define

$$S = \{U_1, \ldots, U_m, U_{m+1}, \ldots, U_{m+n}\}, \quad s_0 = U_1,$$

where each U_i is a set of real numbers defined as follows:

$$U_i = \{Z(P_i)\} \qquad (i = 1, \ldots, m),$$
$$U_i = \{\xi \mid Z(PP_i) = \xi, \quad P \in W(I)\} \qquad (i = m+1, \ldots, m+n). \quad (6.7)$$

Furthermore, for $x \in I$ and $1 \leq i \leq m+n$, define

$$F(U_i, x) = \{\xi \mid Z(Px) = \xi, Z(P) \in U_i\}.$$

It follows that, for each $P \in W(I)$, there is an i such that $Z(P) \in U_i$. Moreover, for any $x \in I$ and $1 \leq i \leq m+n$, there is a j such that

$$F(U_i, x) \subset U_j. \qquad (6.8)$$

For $i \leq m$, (6.8) is obvious because in this case $F(U_i, x)$ contains only one element. For $i > m$, (6.8) follows by (6.7) because the words determining the elements of $F(U_i, x)$ possess the same final subword of length $k(\varepsilon)$. Let $x \in I$ and $1 \leq i \leq m+n$. We define

$$f(U_i, x) = U_j, \tag{6.9}$$

where j is the smallest number such that (6.8) is satisfied.

Having completed the definition of the automaton **A**, we show that **A** ε-approximates Z. Define

$$\psi(U_i) = \tfrac{1}{2}\left(\sup\{\xi|\xi \in U_i\}+\inf\{\xi|\xi \in U_i\}\right) \qquad (i = 1, \ldots, m+n).$$

We prove now that, for $P \in W(I)$,

$$Z(P) \in f(s_0, P) \tag{6.10}$$

using induction on the length of P. If $P = \lambda$, (6.10) is obvious because $s_0 = U_1$ and $Z(\lambda) \in U_1$. Assuming (6.10) to be true for words of length v, it is seen to be true for words of length $v+1$, by the definition (6.9).

Let $Q_1 \in W(I)$ be arbitrary. Then

$$|Z(Q_1)-\psi(f(s_0, Q_1))| \leq \varepsilon. \tag{6.11}$$

In fact, if $\lg(Q_1) < k(\varepsilon)$ then the left side of (6.11) equals 0. If $\lg(Q_1) \geq k(\varepsilon)$ then (6.11) follows, by (6.6) and (6.10). $\qquad\square$

EXERCISE 6.1. Show that $k(\varepsilon)$ can be replaced by $k(2\varepsilon)$ in the proof of Theorem 6.3.

EXERCISE 6.2 (Paz, 1967). For a function $Z : W(I) \to [0, 1]$ and $\varepsilon > 0$, an ε-cover induced by Z is a collection

$$\{U_1, \ldots, U_k\},$$

where each U_i is a set of real numbers in the interval $[0, 1]$ such that (i) every value of the function Z belongs to at least one of the sets U_i, (ii) the absolute value of the difference of any two numbers in U_i ($1 \leq i \leq k$) does not exceed ε and (iii) for any $x \in I$ and U_i, there is a U_j such that (6.8) is satisfied. Prove that the two conditions (i) for all $\varepsilon > 0$, Z is ε-approximable and (ii) for all $\varepsilon > 0$, there is an ε-cover induced by Z, are equivalent.

EXERCISE 6.3 (Paz, 1967). For a function $Z : W(I) \to [0, 1]$ and a real number η ($0 \leq \eta < 1$), define the language

$$L(Z, \eta) = \{P|Z(P) > \eta\}.$$

For $\varepsilon > 0$, a finite deterministic automaton **A** $= (S, s_0, f)$ ε-approximates the language $L_1 = L(Z, \eta)$ iff there is a set $S_1 \subset S$ such that the language $L_2 = L(\mathbf{A}, S_1)$ satisfies the condition

$$(L_1-L_2)+(L_2-L_1) \subset \{P \,|\, |Z(P)-\eta| \leq \varepsilon\}.$$

Prove that the conditions (i) for all $\varepsilon > 0$, Z is ε-approximable and (ii) for all $\varepsilon > 0$ and $\eta \,(0 \leq \eta < 1)$, $L(Z, \eta)$ is ε-approximable, are equivalent. Show that there exists a finite probabilistic automaton **PA**, a column vector $\bar{S}_1$ and real numbers η_1, η_2 such that, for the function

$$Z(P) = \mathbf{PA}(P)\,\bar{S}_1,$$

$L(Z, \eta_1)$ is ε-approximable for all $\varepsilon > 0$ but $L(Z, \eta_2)$ is not ε-approximable for any sufficiently small ε. (In Paz (1967) such an example, credited to H. Kesten and R. E. Stearns, is given.)

EXERCISE 6.4 (Paz, 1966). For $\varepsilon \geq 0$, a language L_2 *ε-approximates* an η-stochastic language $L_1 = L(\mathbf{PA}, \bar{S}_1, \eta)$ iff

$$(L_1-L_2)+(L_2-L_1) \subset \{P \,|\, |\mathbf{PA}(P)\,\bar{S}_1-\eta| \leq \varepsilon\}.$$

The family of stochastic languages is *closed* under ε-approximation of complement iff, for every stochastic language L, there is a stochastic language L' such that $\sim L$ ε-approximates L'. Prove that the family of stochastic languages is closed under 0-approximation of complement.

EXERCISE 6.5 (Turakainen, 1967). Show that in the statement of Theorem 6.2 condition (ii) may be replaced by the following condition (ii)': Assume that v, $1 \leq v \leq n$, is the maximal number of linearly independent vectors $Z(P)$ and that $Z(P_1)$, ..., $Z(P_v)$ are linearly independent. Then there are n-dimensional row vectors Z_{v+1}, ..., Z_n and U_{v+1}, ..., U_n such that (6.2) is an $n \times n$ matrix consisting of non-negative elements and, furthermore, the sum of the components of Z_i equals the sum of the components of U_i, for $i = v+1, ..., n$. (Cf. also the work of Bukharaev (1965, 1967) for another criterion.)

EXERCISE 6.6 (Starke, 1966, 3). Consider a function $Z : W(I) \rightarrow [0, 1]$ which assumes only finitely many values. Prove that Z is realized by a finite probabilistic automaton iff, for any η such that $0 \leq \eta \leq 1$, the language

$$\{P \,|\, Z(P) = \eta\}$$

is regular.

EXERCISE 6.7 (Starke, 1966, 3). Prove that, for any finite alphabet I and any η_1 such that $0 < \eta_1 \leqq 1$, there exists a mapping $Z : W(I) \to [0, 1]$ such that (i) for all η such that $0 \leqq \eta < 1$, the language

$$\{P \,|\, Z(P) > \eta\}$$

is regular, and (ii) the languages

$$\{P \,|\, Z(P) = \eta_1\}, \quad \{P \,|\, Z(P) < \eta_1\}$$

are non-regular.

EXERCISE 6.8 (Starke, 1965). Let I and O be finite alphabets. A function $Z : W(I) \times W(O) \to [0, 1]$ which satisfies, for all $P \in W(I)$,

$$\sum_{Q \in W(O)} Z(P, Q) = 1$$

is termed a *stochastic operator*. A stochastic operator is *sequential* iff, for all $P \in W(I)$, $Q \in W(O)$, $x \in I$, we have $Z(P, Q) = 0$ if $\lg(P) \neq \lg(Q)$ and

$$\sum_{y \in O} Z(Px, Qy) = Z(P, Q).$$

A stochastic operator Z is *generated* by the state s_1 of a finite probabilistic sequential machine

$$\mathbf{PM} = (I', O', \{s_1, \ldots, s_n\}, (1, 0, \ldots, 0), F), \quad I \subset I', O \subset O',$$

iff, for all $P \in W(I)$ and $Q \in W(O)$ such that $\lg(P) = \lg(Q)$,

$$Z(P, Q) = p_{\mathbf{PM}}(P/Q).$$

Prove that a stochastic operator is generated by some state of some finite probabilistic sequential machine iff it is sequential.

EXERCISE 6.9 (Starke, 1965). Let $Z : W(I) \times W(O) \to [0, 1]$ be a sequential stochastic operator and $P_1 \in W(I)$, $Q_1 \in W(O)$ such that $Z(P_1, Q_1) > 0$. The mapping Z_{P_1, Q_1} of $W(I) \times W(O)$ into $[0, 1]$ defined by the equation

$$Z_{P_1, Q_1}(P, Q) = \frac{Z(P_1 P, Q_1 Q)}{Z(P_1, Q_1)}$$

is termed a *derivative* of Z. Prove that every derivative of Z is a sequential stochastic operator. Study the interconnection between the number of distinct derivatives of Z and the number of states in the smallest probabilistic sequential machine, where Z is generated by some state. Cf. also Starke (1966, 2) for various related results.

PROBLEM 6.1. Let I be a finite alphabet and Z a mapping of $W(I)$ into the set of real numbers in the interval $[0, 1]$. Under what conditions are there **PA** and $\bar{S}_1$ such that (6.5) is satisfied? In particular, study the case where I consists of one letter. Study also the case, where Z maps $W(I)$ into the set of all real numbers and the components of $\bar{S}_1$ are allowed to be arbitrary real numbers.

PROBLEM 6.2. Consider various (Boolean and other) operations defined for languages. Study whether or not the family of stochastic languages is closed under ε-approximation of a given operation. (Cf. Exercise 6.4 and Paz (1966).)

CHAPTER III

ALGEBRA OF REGULAR EXPRESSIONS

IT WAS seen in Chapter I that the star operator (*) is fundamental in the theory of finite deterministic automata. In this chapter, a more detailed discussion of the algebraic properties of this operator and its compositions with other regular operators is presented.

§ 1. Star height

Consider regular expressions over a finite alphabet

$$I_r = \{x_1, \ldots, x_r\}.$$

Our main objective in this chapter is to present a formal characterization of the set of valid equations between regular expressions. For instance, the following equations are members of this set:

$$\alpha + (\beta + \gamma) = (\alpha + \beta) + \gamma, \tag{1.1}$$

$$\alpha(\beta\gamma) = (\alpha\beta)\gamma, \tag{1.2}$$

$$\alpha + \beta = \beta + \alpha, \tag{1.3}$$

$$\alpha(\beta + \gamma) = \alpha\beta + \alpha\gamma, \tag{1.4}$$

$$(\alpha + \beta)\gamma = \alpha\gamma + \beta\gamma, \tag{1.5}$$

$$\alpha + \alpha = \alpha, \tag{1.6}$$

$$\phi^*\alpha = \alpha, \tag{1.7}$$

$$\alpha\phi^* = \alpha, \tag{1.7}'$$

$$\phi\alpha = \phi, \tag{1.8}$$

$$\alpha\phi = \phi, \tag{1.8}'$$

$$\alpha + \phi = \alpha, \tag{1.9}$$

$$\alpha^* = \phi^* + \alpha^*\alpha, \tag{1.10}$$

114

$$\alpha^* = (\phi^* + \alpha)^*, \tag{1.11}$$

$$(\alpha^*)^* = \alpha^*, \tag{1.12}$$

$$\alpha^*\alpha^* = \alpha^*, \tag{1.13}$$

$$(\alpha + \beta)^* = (\alpha^*\beta^*)^*, \tag{1.14}$$

$$(\alpha + \beta)^* = (\alpha^*\beta)^*\alpha^*, \tag{1.15}$$

$$(\alpha + \beta)^* = \beta^*(\alpha\beta^*)^*, \tag{1.16}$$

$$(\alpha + \beta)^* = \alpha^* + \alpha^*\beta(\alpha + \beta)^*, \tag{1.17}$$

$$(\alpha + \beta)^* = (\alpha^*\beta)^* + (\beta^*\alpha)^*_{\ ,} \tag{1.18}$$

$$(\alpha\beta)^*\alpha = \alpha(\beta\alpha)^*, \tag{1.19}$$

$$(\alpha^*\beta)^* = \phi^* + (\alpha + \beta)^*\beta, \tag{1.20}$$

$$(\alpha\beta^*\gamma)^* = \phi^* + \alpha(\beta + \gamma\alpha)^*\gamma, \tag{1.21}$$

$$\alpha^m(\alpha^n)^* = (\alpha^n)^*\alpha^m, \tag{1.22}$$

$$\alpha^* = (\phi^* + \alpha + \ldots + \alpha^{n-1})(\alpha^n)^*. \tag{1.23}$$

In (1.22) and (1.23), m and n are arbitrary natural numbers. In fact, (1.1)–(1.23) are infinite schemas of valid equations, i.e. a valid equation results whenever some regular expressions are substituted for the variables α, β and γ. The validity of most of the schemas (1.1)–(1.23) is obvious. The easiest method to establish the validity of (1.15)–(1.21) is to show that an arbitrary word in the language denoted by one side belongs to the language denoted by the other side. The schemas (1.1)–(1.23) are valid for any alphabet I_r, whereas, for instance, the schema $(\alpha + \beta)^* = \alpha^*\beta^*$ is valid for the case $r = 1$ only.

The main topic of this chapter, the characterization of the set of valid equations between regular expressions, will be discussed in Sections 3–8. We shall first consider other problems concerning regular expressions, namely, star height and solution of equations.

DEFINITION. The *star height* of a regular expression over the alphabet I is a non-negative integer defined recursively as follows:

(i) The letters of I and ϕ have star height 0.

(ii) If α and β have star heights i and j, then $(\alpha + \beta)$ and $(\alpha\beta)$ have star height max (i, j).

(iii) If α has star height i, then α^* has star height $i+1$.

The *star height of a regular language L*, in symbols sh(L), is the least integer i such that, for some regular expression α, $L = |\alpha|$ and the star height of α equals i.

In this section, we shall discuss the problem whether or not the star height of every regular expression can be reduced below some bound, i.e. whether or not the star height of a regular language L over I_r is always less than some constant which possibly depends on r. For $r \geqq 2$, the answer is negative. However, it will be shown in Section 3 that the star height of every regular language over I_1 equals 0 or 1.

Define recursively an infinite sequence of regular expressions α_1, α_2, ... over the two-letter alphabet $\{0, 1\}$ as follows:

$$\alpha_1 = (01)^*,$$
$$\alpha_i = \left(0^{2^{i-1}}\alpha_{i-1}1^{2^{i-1}}\alpha_{i-1}\right)^*, \qquad i = 2, 3, \ldots.$$

Thus, for instance,

$$\alpha_3 = (0000(00(01)^*11(01)^*)^*1111(00(01)^*11(01)^*)^*)^*.$$

Let L_i be the language denoted by α_i, for $i = 1, 2, \ldots$.

THEOREM 1.1. *For any $i \geqq 1$, the star height of the language L_i equals i. Hence, there are regular languages with any preassigned star height over any alphabet containing at least two letters.*

Proof. Since any finite language which does not contain the empty word has star height 0 and the construction of the sequence of languages L_i is possible whenever the alphabet contains at least two letters, we conclude that the second part of the theorem is a consequence of the first part.

Thus, we have to show that

$$\text{sh } (L_i) = i \qquad (i = 1, 2, \ldots). \tag{1.24}$$

It follows immediately from the definition of the regular expressions α_i that

$$\text{sh } (L_i) \leqq i \qquad (i = 1, 2, \ldots). \tag{1.25}$$

Consider words $P(i, j)$ $(i, j \geqq 1)$ over the alphabet $\{0, 1\}$, defined as follows:

$P(1, j) = 01$, for all j;

$P(i, j) = 0^{2^{i-1}}(P(i-1, j))^j 1^{2^{i-1}}(P(i-1, j))^j$, for $i \geqq 2$ and all j.

Thus, for instance,

$$P(3, 2) = 0000(000101110101)^2 1111(000101110101)^2.$$

For any word P over the alphabet $\{0, 1\}$, denote by $N_j(P)$, $j = 0,1$, the number of occurrences of the letter j in the word P. Thus,

$$N_0(P(3, 2)) = N_1(P(3, 2)) = 28.$$

For $i = 1, 2, \ldots$, denote by $\mathcal{F}_i$ the family of regular languages L over $\{0, 1\}$ satisfying the following three conditions:

(a) There is an integer a such that, for every word $P \in L$,

$$N_0(P) = N_1(P) + a.$$

(b_i) There are infinitely many values of j such that $(P(i, j))^j$ is a subword of at least one word in L.

(c) There is no language L' satisfying conditions (a) and (b_i) such that $\text{sh}(L') < \text{sh}(L)$.

For any i, the language L_i satisfies conditions (a) (with $a = 0$) and (b_i). Thus, for $i = 1, 2, \ldots$, the family $\mathcal{F}_i$ is not empty. Denote by h_i the common star height of the languages in $\mathcal{F}_i$. Then, by (1.25),

$$h_i \leq \text{sh}(L_i) \leq i \quad (i = 1, 2, \ldots). \tag{1.26}$$

Because any language satisfying (b_1) is infinite, we conclude that

$$h_1 = 1. \tag{1.27}$$

Consider an arbitrary but fixed $i \geq 2$ and an arbitrary $K \in \mathcal{F}_i$. Because $\text{sh}(K) = h_i$, there are regular expressions $\beta_1, \ldots, \beta_m$ such that

$$K = |\beta_1 + \ldots + \beta_m|$$

and each regular expression β_μ, $\mu = 1, \ldots, m$, is of the form

$$\beta_\mu = \gamma_0^* \gamma_1 \gamma_2^* \cdots \gamma_{2n-1} \gamma_{2n}^*, \tag{1.28}$$

where the star height of each of the regular expressions γ_ν, $\nu = 0, \ldots, 2n$, is at most $h_i - 1$. (Note that γ_0 or γ_{2n} may be the regular expression ϕ.) Because K satisfies condition (a), each of the languages $|\beta_\nu|$ satisfies (a). Because K satisfies condition (b_i), at least one of the languages $|\beta_\nu|$, say the language denoted by (1.28), satisfies (b_i). Furthermore, each of the languages $|\gamma_\nu|$, $\nu = 0, \ldots, 2n$, satisfies (a). This follows because $|\beta_\mu|$ satisfies (a) and, for any $\nu = 0, \ldots, 2n$, there are words Q_1

and Q_2 (possibly empty) such that $Q_1 Q Q_2 \in |\beta_\mu|$, for all $Q \in |\gamma_\nu|$. The same argument shows that each of the languages $|\gamma_{2u}|$, $0 \leqq u \leqq n$, satisfies condition (a) with $a = 0$, because the empty word is contained in each of the languages $|\gamma_{2u}^*|$. We shall now establish three lemmas.

LEMMA 1.1. *None of the languages* γ_ν, $\nu = 0, \ldots, 2n$, *satisfies condition* (b_i).

Proof of Lemma 1.1. Assume the contrary: for some ν, $|\gamma_\nu|$ satisfies (b_i). Because $|\gamma_\nu|$ satisfies (a) and $\mathrm{sh}\,(|\gamma_\nu|) < \mathrm{sh}\,(K)$, we conclude that K does not satisfy condition (c). This is a contradiction and, hence, Lemma 1.1 follows.

LEMMA 1.2. *For some* u, $0 \leqq u \leqq n$, *the language* $|\gamma_{2u}^*|$ *satisfies condition* (b_i).

Proof of Lemma 1.2. Assume the contrary. Then, by Lemma 1.1, none of the languages

$$|\gamma_0^*|, \ |\gamma_1|, \ \ldots, \ |\gamma_{2n-1}|, \ |\gamma_{2n}^*| \tag{1.29}$$

satisfies (b_i). Because the number of the languages (1.29) is finite, this implies the existence of an integer j_0 such that, whenever $j > j_0$, the word $\big(P(i, j)\big)^j$ is not a subword of any word belonging to one of the languages (1.29).

Let the language $|\beta_\mu|$ be represented in a finite deterministic automaton with j_1 states, among which s_0 is the initial state. Assume that Q^j, where $j > j_1$, is a subword of a word in $|\beta_\mu|$, i.e. $Q_3 Q^j Q_4 \in |\beta_\mu|$, for some words Q_3 and Q_4. Because the states

$$s_0 Q_3 Q, \ s_0 Q_3 Q^2, \ \ldots, \ s_0 Q_3 Q^j$$

are not all distinct, there are natural numbers k and l such that

$$s_0 Q_3 Q^k = s_0 Q_3 Q^l \quad (1 \leqq k < l \leqq j).$$

This implies that $Q_3 Q^{j+\nu(l-k)} Q_4 \in |\beta_\mu|$, for $\nu = 0, 1, 2, \ldots$, and thus $Q^{j+\nu(l-k)}$ is a subword of a word in $|\beta_\mu|$, for all values of $\nu \geqq 0$.

Because the language $|\beta_\mu|$ satisfies the condition (b_i), there is an integer $j_2 > \max(j_0, j_1)$ such that $\big(P(i, j_2)\big)^{j_2}$ is a subword of some word in $|\beta_\mu|$. By what we have shown, this implies the existence of a natural number d such that $\big(P(i, j_2)\big)^{j_2+\nu d}$ is a subword of some word in $|\beta_\mu|$, for all integers $\nu \geqq 0$. On the other hand, because $\big(P(i, j_2)\big)^{j_2}$ is not a subword of any word belonging to one of the languages (1.29), it follows by (1.28) that $(P(i, j_2))^j$ is not a subword of any word in $|\beta_\mu|$, provided $j > (2n+1)j_2$. This is a contradiction which completes the proof of Lemma 1.2.

LEMMA 1.3. *For some u such that $0 \leqq u \leqq n$, the language $|\gamma_{2u}|$ satisfies condition (b_{i-1}).*

Proof of Lemma 1.3. By Lemma 1.2, there is a u, $0 \leqq u \leqq n$, such that the language $|\gamma_{2u}^*|$ satisfies (b_i). We shall prove that $|\gamma_{2u}|$ satisfies (b_{i-1}). Again, assume the contrary: there is a natural number j_0 such that, whenever $j > j_0$, the word $(P(i-1, j))^j$ is not a subword of any word in $|\gamma_{2u}|$. Because $|\gamma_{2u}^*|$ satisfies condition (b_i), there is a natural number $j_1 > j_0$ such that the word

$$(P(i, j_1))^{j_1} = \left(0^{2^{i-1}}(P(i-1, j_1))^{j_1} 1^{2^{i-1}}(P(i-1, j_1))^{j_1}\right)^{j_1}$$

is a subword of some word in $|\gamma_{2u}^*|$. This implies the existence of words $P_1, \ldots, P_v \in |\gamma_{2u}|$ such that

$$P(i, j_1) = 0^{2^{i-1}}\left(P(i-1, j_1)\right)^{j_1} 1^{2^{i-1}}\left(P(i-1, j_1)\right)^{j_1} \tag{1.30}$$

is a subword of the word $P_1 \ldots P_v$.

As seen above, the language $|\gamma_{2u}|$ satisfies condition (a) with $a = 0$, i.e. in any word belonging to $|\gamma_{2u}|$ the number of occurrences of the letter 0 equals the number of occurrences of the letter 1. In particular, this is true of the words $P_1, \ldots, P_v$. This implies that if the first occurrence of

$$\left(P(i-1, j_1)\right)^{j_1}$$

in (1.30) is not a subword of any of the words P_ν, then the second occurrence is a subword of some P_ν. In both cases a contradiction arises. Thus, Lemma 1.3 follows.

Hence, the language $|\gamma_{2u}|$ satisfies the conditions (a) and (b_{i-1}). This implies the inequality $h_{i-1} \leqq \mathrm{sh}\left(|\gamma_{2u}|\right)$. On the other hand, $\mathrm{sh}\left(|\gamma_{2u}|\right) \leqq h_i - 1$. Because $i \geqq 2$ was arbitrary, we conclude that the inequality

$$h_i \geqq h_{i-1} + 1 \tag{1.31}$$

holds for all values of $i \geqq 2$. The equation (1.24) is an immediate consequence of (1.26), (1.27) and (1.31). This completes the proof of Theorem 1.1. □

EXERCISE 1.1. Draw the graphs of automata representing some of the languages L_i (for instance $i = 2, 3, 4$). How does the number i describe the loop structure of these graphs? (For a general discussion on the interrelation between star height and loop complexity, cf. the work of Eggan (1963) and McNaughton (1965, 1966).)

PROBLEM 1.1. Extend the notion of star height to concern regular expressions involving intersections and complements. Can the proof of Theorem 1.1 be modified for this case? (This problem has been proposed by J. Brzozowski.)

PROBLEM 1.2 (McNaughton, 1966). Is there an algorithm to determine the star height of the language denoted by a given regular expression? To prove the existence of such an algorithm, it suffices to show that, for any regular expression α of star height h, there is a finite number k of regular expressions $\alpha_1, \ldots, \alpha_k$ of star height $h-1$ such that if $\mathrm{sh}\,(|\alpha|) < h$ then $\alpha = \alpha_i$, for some $i = 1, \ldots, k$. The number k may depend, for instance, on the number of letters and operators in α.

The same problem may be stated also for the extended notion of star height introduced in Problem 1.1. Cf. also McNaughton (1964) for another approach to proofs concerning star height.

§ 2. Solution of equations

In this section we study equations and systems of equations involving languages and regular operations (sum, catenation and catenation closure). The languages involved need not necessarily be regular. However, the form of the equations studied is suitable especially for regular languages (cf. Exercise 2.4). All languages are considered to be over some alphabet $I_r = \{x_1, \ldots, x_r\}$.

Let n be a natural number, and consider the system of equations

$$
\begin{aligned}
y_1 &= y_1 L_{11} + y_2 L_{21} + \ldots + y_n L_{n1} + R_1, \\
y_2 &= y_1 L_{12} + y_2 L_{22} + \ldots + y_n L_{n2} + R_2, \\
&\quad\ldots \\
y_n &= y_1 L_{1n} + y_2 L_{2n} + \ldots + y_n L_{nn} + R_n,
\end{aligned}
\tag{2.1}
$$

where L_{ij}, $1 \leqq i, j \leqq n$, and R_i, $1 \leqq i \leqq n$, are given languages over the alphabet $I_r = \{x_1, \ldots, x_r\}$. Any n-tuple $(y_1, \ldots, y_n)$ of languages over I_r satisfying the equations (2.1) is called a *solution* of this system.

We consider also n-dimensional row vectors Y and $n \times n$ matrices Z whose elements are languages. Then $(Y)_i$ denotes the ith component of Y, and $(Z)_{ij}$ the (i, j)th entry in Z. Addition and multiplication are defined in the usual fashion. In this matrix notation, the system (2.1) may be written in the form

$$Y = YM + R, \qquad (2.2)$$

where $(Y)_i = y_i$, $(R)_i = R_i$ and $(M)_{ij} = L_{ij}$, for $1 \leq i, j \leq n$. Furthermore, we introduce the star operator for $n \times n$ matrices (whose elements are languages) by defining

$$M^* = \sum_{i=0}^{\infty} M^i,$$

where M^0 is the identity matrix E for which $(E)_{ij} = \{\lambda\}$ if $i = j$, and $(E)_{ij} = L_\phi$ if $i \neq j$.

DEFINITION. An $n \times n$ matrix

$$M = \|L_{ij}\|_{1 \leq i, j \leq n}$$

possesses the *empty word property (e.w.p.)* iff there is sequence of numbers $i_1, \ldots, i_k$ $(k \geq 1)$ such that $\lambda \in L_{i_\nu i_{\nu+1}}$, for $1 \leq \nu \leq k-1$, and $\lambda \in L_{i_k i_1}$. Each number in every such sequence is termed *cyclic* with respect to M.

Note that any matrix, where a language containing the empty word appears on the main diagonal, possesses e.w.p.

THEOREM 2.1. *If the matrix M does not possess e.w.p., then the system* (2.2) *has a unique solution, namely,*

$$Y = RM^*. \qquad (2.3)$$

Proof. Because

$$(RM^*)M + R = R(M^*M + E) = RM^*,$$

we conclude that (2.3) is a solution of (2.2). Let Y_0 be an arbitrary solution of (2.2), i.e.

$$Y_0 = Y_0 M + R.$$

By substituting, we obtain

$$Y_0 = (Y_0 M + R)M + R = Y_0 M^2 + RM + R.$$

Similarly, by successive substitutions, we obtain the result

$$Y_0 = Y_0 M^{k+1} + RM^k + \ldots + RM + R, \qquad (2.4)$$

for any natural number k. Consequently,

$$RM^* \subset Y_0, \qquad (2.5)$$

i.e. $(RM^*)_i \subset (Y_0)_i$, for each $i = 1, \ldots, n$.

Obviously, the catenation of two languages contains the empty word λ iff λ is contained in both languages, and the sum of two languages contains λ iff λ is contained in at least one of the terms. Because M does not possess e.w.p. none of the languages $(M^k)_{ij}$, where $k \geq n$ and $1 \leq i, j \leq n$ contains the empty word.

Let now i $(1 \leq i \leq n)$ and $P \in (Y_0)_i$ be arbitrary, and let $\lg(P) = u$. We choose in (2.4) $k+1 = (u+1)n$. Then every word in every non-empty language $(M^{k+1})_{ji}$, $j = 1, \ldots, n$, is of length at least $u+1$. This implies that $P \notin (Y_0 M^{k+1})_i$. By (2.4),

$$P \in (RM^k + \ldots + RM + R)_i \subset (RM^*)_i.$$

Consequently, $Y_0 \subset RM^*$ and thus, by (2.5), $Y_0 = RM^*$. $\square$

The following theorem is an immediate corollary of Theorem 2.1.

THEOREM 2.2. *Assume that L is a language not containing the empty word. Then the equation $y = yL + R$ possesses a unique solution, namely, $y = RL^*$.*

We shall now study the case where the solution of (2.2) is not unique.

THEOREM 2.3. *An n-dimensional vector Y is a solution of (2.2) iff*

$$Y = (R+T)M^*, \qquad (2.6)$$

where T is a vector such that $(T)_i = L_\phi$ if i is not cyclic with respect to M.

Proof. Let Y_0 be an arbitrary solution of (2.2). As in the proof of Theorem 2.1 we conclude that (2.5) holds and, thus,

$$Y_0 = RM^* + T, \qquad (2.7)$$

for some vector T. By (2.7) and (2.2) we obtain

$$RM^* + T = RM^*M + TM + R = RM^* + TM.$$

This implies the relation $TM \subset RM^* + T$ and, hence,

$$TM^2 \subset RM^*M + TM \subset RM^*M + RM^* + T = RM^* + T.$$

Similarly, we deduce the relation

$$TM^k \subset RM^* + T, \tag{2.8}$$

for all natural numbers k. Since (2.8) obviously is satisfied also for $k = 0$, we conclude that

$$TM^* \subset RM^* + T = Y_0.$$

Thus,

$$Y_0 = Y_0 + TM^* = (R+T)M^*. \tag{2.9}$$

We have shown that every solution of (2.2) is of the form (2.9), for some vector T. On the other hand, a vector of the form (2.9) is a solution of (2.2) iff

$$(R+T)M^* = (R+T)M^*M + R,$$

i.e.

$$RM^* + TM^* = RM^* + TM^*M$$

which condition is satisfied iff

$$T \subset RM^* + TM^*M. \tag{2.10}$$

Hence, the set of solutions of (2.2) equals the set of vectors (2.9) such that the condition (2.10) is satisfied.

Consider now an arbitrary vector Y_0 of the form (2.6), i.e. T satisfies the condition mentioned in the statement of the theorem. Let i be a number which is not cyclic with respect to M. Then it is obvious that

$$(T)_i \subset (RM^* + TM^*M)_i \tag{2.11}$$

On the other hand, if i is cyclic with respect to M then, for some $k \geqq 1$, $\lambda \in (M^k)_{ii}$ and thus

$$(T)_i \subset (TM^k)_i.$$

Consequently, (2.11) holds true also if i is cyclic with respect to M. This implies that (2.10) is satisfied and, thus, Y_0 is a solution of (2.2).

Conversely, let Y_0 be an arbitrary solution of (2.2). This implies that Y_0 is of the form (2.9). We write the vector T in the form

$$T = T_1 + T_2, \tag{2.12}$$

where $(T_1)_i = (T)_i$ if i is cyclic and $(T_1)_i = L_\phi$ if i is not cyclic with respect to M and, furthermore, $(T_2)_i = (T)_i$ if i is not cyclic and $(T_2)_i = L_\phi$

if i is cyclic with respect to M. We have to show that

$$Y_0 = (R + T_1)M^*. \tag{2.13}$$

For this purpose, we write for Y_0 and R the decompositions corresponding to (2.12):

$$Y_0 = Y_1 + Y_2, \quad R = R_1 + R_2.$$

Because Y_0 satisfies (2.7), we conclude that

$$Y_1 \subset RM^* + T_1, \quad Y_2 \subset RM^* + T_2. \tag{2.14}$$

Furthermore, we define two matrices M_1 and M_2 as follows:

$$(M_1)_{ij} = \begin{cases} (M)_{ij} & \text{if } i \text{ is cyclic and } j \text{ is not,} \\ L_\phi, & \text{otherwise;} \end{cases}$$

$$(M_2)_{ij} = \begin{cases} (M)_{ij} & \text{if neither } i \text{ nor } j \text{ is cyclic,} \\ L_\phi, & \text{otherwise.} \end{cases}$$

Using the fact that $Y_1 + Y_2 = (Y_1 + Y_2)M + R$, we deduce the equation

$$Y_2 = Y_2 M_2 + Y_1 M_1 + R_2. \tag{2.15}$$

(The equation (2.15) is easily verified by considering first components $(Y_2)_i$ such that i is cyclic and then components $(Y_2)_i$ such that i is not cyclic.) Clearly, the matrix M_2 does not possess e.w.p. Therefore, by Theorem 2.1,

$$Y_2 = (Y_1 M_1 + R_2) M_2^*.$$

Consequently,

$$Y_0 = Y_1 + Y_2 = Y_1(E + M_1 M_2^*) + R_2 M_2^*.$$

Because obviously $M_1 \subset M$, $M_2 \subset M$ and $R_2 \subset R$, we obtain

$$Y_0 \subset Y_1 M^* + RM^* = (Y_1 + R) M^*.$$

Hence, by (2.14),

$$Y_0 \subset (RM^* + T_1 + R)M^* = (R + T_1)M^*.$$

Because obviously $(R + T_1) M^* \subset (R + T)M^* = Y_0$, we obtain the equation (2.13). □

Theorem 2.1 is a special case of Theorem 2.3 because if M does not possess e.w.p., then no number i is cyclic with respect to M. The following theorem is a corollary of Theorem 2.3 corresponding to Theorem 2.2.

THEOREM 2.4. *Assume that L is a language containing the empty word.*

Then the set of solutions of the equation $y = yL + R$ *equals the set of languages of the form* $y = (R + T)L^*$, *where T is an arbitrary language.*

THEOREM 2.5. *Assume that all the coefficients* L_{ij} *and* R_i *in the system* (2.1) *are regular languages and that the solution Y of the system is unique. Then all components of Y are regular languages. Furthermore, there is an algorithm of finding the solution Y.*

Proof. By Theorems 2.1 and 2.3, the matrix $M = \|L_{ij}\|$ does not possess e.w.p. The proof of Theorem 2.5 is by induction on the number n. The case $n = 1$ is clear, by Theorem 2.2. Assuming that $n \geqq 2$ and having established the theorem for the numbers $1, \ldots, n-1$, we consider the system (2.1). Because $\lambda \notin L_{nn}$ we obtain, by Theorem 2.2,

$$y_n = (y_1 L_{1n} + \ldots + y_{n-1} L_{(n-1)n} + R_n) L_{nn}^* . \qquad (2.16)$$

Now eliminate y_n from the first $n-1$ equations according to (2.16):

$$y_i = y_1(L_{1i} + L_{1n}L_{nn}^*L_{ni}) + \ldots + y_{n-1}(L_{(n-1)i} + L_{(n-1)n}L_{nn}^*L_{ni})$$
$$+ R_n L_{nn}^* L_{ni} + R_i , \qquad (2.17)$$

where $i = 1, \ldots, n-1$. The elements of the matrix of the system (2.17) are of the form

$$L_{ji}' = L_{ji} + L_{jn}L_{nn}^*L_{ni} .$$

Thus, if $\lambda \in L_{ji}'$ then $\lambda \in L_{ji}$ or both $\lambda \in L_{jn}$ and $\lambda \in L_{ni}$. Because the matrix of the system (2.1) does not possess e.w.p., we conclude that the matrix of the system (2.17) does not possess e.w.p. Hence, by Theorem 2.1, the solution of the system (2.17) is unique. By our inductive hypothesis, the solution is a vector whose components are regular languages. The equation (2.16) implies that also y_n is a regular language, which completes the induction. It is obvious that the induction also gives an algorithm, consisting of successive eliminations, to find the solution. □

The validity of the analysis procedure presented in Section I.3 is now obvious.

As an illustration, we consider the alphabet {0, 1} and the following system of three equations:

$$y_1 = y_1 0 + y_2 + y_3 + \lambda,$$
$$y_2 = y_1 11 + y_2 0 + y_3 0 + 1^*,$$
$$y_3 = y_1 1 + y_2. \qquad (2.18)$$

(The language consisting of the empty word is the coefficient of y_2 and y_3 in the first and that of y_2 in the last equation. The empty language is the coefficient of y_3 in the last equation.) Substituting according to (2.18) we obtain

$$y_1 = y_1(0+1)+y_2+\lambda,$$

$$y_2 = y_1(11+10)+y_20+1^*.$$

We then solve the second equation:

$$y_2 = \left(y_1(11+10)+1^*\right)0^*, \tag{2.19}$$

and substitute the result to the first equation:

$$y_1 = y_1(0+1+(11+10)0^*)+1^*0^*,$$

whence

$$y_1 = 1^*0^*(0+1+(11+10)0^*)^* = (0+1)^*. \tag{2.20}$$

(Note that although the regular language y_1 is unique, different regular expressions for y_1 may be obtained, for instance, by changing the order of eliminations.) The equations (2.18)–(2.20) give the solution of our system.

EXERCISE 2.1. Instead of (2.1), consider systems of equations, where the coefficients L_{ij} appear on the left. State and prove for these systems results corresponding to those established for (2.1).

EXERCISE 2.2. Find simple regular expressions denoting the languages defined by (2.18) and (2.19).

EXERCISE 2.3. Modify the notion of regular expressions by omitting the symbol ϕ and defining $|\alpha^*|$ to be the sum of the languages $|\alpha^i|$, $i \geqq 1$. Prove that in this case the equation $y = yL+R$ possesses the unique solution $y = RL^*+R$. State and prove the result concerning the solutions of (2.1).

EXERCISE 2.4. (Preferably after reading Chapter IV.) Give reasons why systems of the form (2.1) are suitable for the study of regular languages.

EXERCISE 2.5. (Brzozowski, 1967) A language L is a *star language* iff, for some language L_1, $L = L_1^*$. In this case L_1 is termed a *root* of L.

Show by an example that a regular language may have a non-regular root. Prove that, for every star language L, there exists a unique root L_M of L which is contained in every other root of L. Prove that L is regular iff L_M is regular.

§ 3. The sets $\mathcal{S}_r$ and $\mathcal{O}_r$. Languages over a one-letter alphabet

We shall now turn to the discussion of valid equations between regular expressions. We consider the alphabets $I_r = \{x_1, \ldots, x_r\}$ and

$$A_\omega = \{\alpha, \beta, \gamma, \alpha_1, \beta_1, \gamma_1, \ldots\}.$$

Thus, A_ω is an infinite alphabet such that A_ω and each I_r are disjoint. The recursive definition of regular expressions presented in Section I.1 applies also to A_ω.

We denote by $\mathcal{O}_r$, $r = 1, 2, \ldots$, the set of all valid equations between regular expressions over the alphabet I_r. Thus, an equation $X = Y$ belongs to the set $\mathcal{O}_r$ iff X and Y are regular expressions over I_r, denoting the same language. For instance, the equation

$$x_1(x_1x_1+x_2)^*x_1+\phi^* = (x_1x_2^*x_1)^*$$

belongs to the set $\mathcal{O}_2$. It is obvious that

$$\mathcal{O}_1 \subset \mathcal{O}_2 \subset \mathcal{O}_3 \subset \ldots, \tag{3.1}$$

where all inclusions are proper. The union of all sets $\mathcal{O}_r$ is denoted by $\mathcal{O}_\omega$.

By $\mathcal{S}_r$, $r = 1, 2, \ldots$, we denote the set of all schemas of valid equations between regular expressions over the alphabet I_r. More specifically, $\mathcal{S}_r$ consists of equations of the form $X = Y$, where X and Y are regular expressions over A_ω such that always a valid equation results whenever each letter of A_ω appearing in X or Y is substituted by some regular expression over I_r. The intersection of all sets $\mathcal{S}_r$ is denoted by $\mathcal{S}_\omega$. For instance, the equations (1.1)–(1.21) belong to all sets $\mathcal{S}_r$, $r = 1, 2, \ldots$, and, hence, they belong also to $\mathcal{S}_\omega$. The equations (1.22) and (1.23) define both infinite subsets of $\mathcal{S}_\omega$. As regards the sets $\mathcal{S}_r$, the chain of inclusions (3.1) is reversed:

$$\mathcal{S}_1 \supset \mathcal{S}_2 \supset \mathcal{S}_3 \supset \ldots \supset \mathcal{S}_\omega \tag{3.2}$$

We shall now prove that only the first of the inclusions (3.2) is proper.

THEOREM 3.1. $\mathcal{S}_2 = \mathcal{S}_3 = \ldots = \mathcal{S}_\omega$. *Furthermore*, $\mathcal{S}_2$ *is properly included in* $\mathcal{S}_1$.

Proof. The second part of the theorem follows by (3.2) because, for instance, the equation $\alpha\beta = \beta\alpha$ belongs to the set $\mathcal{S}_1$ but does not belong to the set $\mathcal{S}_2$. To prove the first part, it suffices to show that

$$\mathcal{S}_2 = \mathcal{S}_\omega. \tag{3.3}$$

Assume the contrary: there is an equation

$$X = Y \tag{3.4}$$

which belongs to $\mathcal{S}_2$ but not to $\mathcal{S}_\omega$. This implies that there is a natural number $r \geqq 3$ such that (3.4) does not belong to $\mathcal{S}_r$. Hence, there are some regular expressions over I_r such that the equation $X_r = Y_r$, resulting from (3.4) by substituting these regular expressions for letters of A_ω appearing in X or Y, is not valid. Without loss of generality, we may assume that there is a word P over I_r such that $P \in |X_r|$ and $P \notin |Y_r|$.

Consider now the following function f mapping the set $W(I_r)$ into the set $W(I_2)$:

$$f(x_1) = x_1 x_2^{r-1},$$
$$f(x_2) = x_2 x_1 x_2^{r-2},$$
$$\ldots$$
$$f(x_r) = x_2^{r-1} x_1,$$
$$f(\lambda) = \lambda,$$
$$f(P'Q') = f(P')f(Q'), \text{ for } P',Q' \in W(I_r).$$

If α is a regular expression over I_r, then α_f is defined to be the regular expression over I_2, obtained from α by replacing each letter x_i by $f(x_i)$, $i = 1, \ldots, r$. Because f is a one-to-one mapping it follows that, for any word $Q \in W(I_r)$ and any regular expression α over I_r, $Q \in |\alpha|$ iff $f(Q) \in |\alpha_f|$. This implies that $f(P) \in |(X_r)_f|$ and $f(P) \notin |(Y_r)_f|$. But $f(P) \in W(I_2)$, and $(X_r)_f$ and $(Y_r)_f$ are regular expressions over I_2, resulting from (3.4). Hence, (3.4) does not belong to $\mathcal{S}_2$. This is a contradiction. Therefore, the equation (3.3) holds true. $\square$

If X and Y are regular expressions then, as in Section I.3, we use the notation $X \equiv Y$ to mean that X and Y are identical, i.e. contain the same symbols in the same order.

DEFINITION. Let X and Y be regular expressions over the same alphabet. Then X is a *well-formed part* of Y iff one of the following conditions is satisfied:

(i) $Y \equiv X$ or $Y \equiv X^*$.

(ii) There is a regular expression Z such that $Y \equiv (X+Z)$, $Y \equiv (Z+X)$, $Y \equiv (XZ)$ or $Y \equiv (ZX)$.

(iii) There is a regular expression Z such that X is a well-formed part of Z and Z is a well-formed part of Y.

Assume that X_1' is the result of replacing a well-formed part X_2 of a regular expression X_1 by a regular expression X_3. Assume, furthermore, that the equations $X_1 = X_4$ and $X_2 = X_3$ belong to the set $\mathscr{S}_r$ ($\mathcal{O}_r$), $r = 1, 2, \ldots, \omega$. Then also the equation $X_1' = X_4$ belongs to $\mathscr{S}_r$ ($\mathcal{O}_r$). In this sense, the sets $\mathscr{S}_r$ and $\mathcal{O}_r$ are closed under *replacement*.

Assume that the equation $X_1 = X_2$ belongs to the set $\mathscr{S}_r$ and the equation $X_1' = X_2'$ is the result of substituting all letters of A_ω appearing in X_1 or X_2 by some regular expressions over A_ω (by some regular expressions over I_r). Then $X_1' = X_2'$ belongs to $\mathscr{S}_r$ (to $\mathcal{O}_r$). Both types of *substitutions* are used in the sequel.

DEFINITION. Any equation which is obtained from a set $\mathscr{S}$ of equations by a finite number of substitutions and replacements is said to be *generated* by $\mathscr{S}$. An equation $X = Y$ is *transformable* by $\mathscr{S}$ into an equation $X_1 = Y_1$ iff both of the equations $X = X_1$ and $Y = Y_1$ are generated by $\mathscr{S}$. A subset $\mathscr{S}$ of $\mathscr{S}_r$, $r = 1, 2, \ldots, \omega$, is termed a *basis* of $\mathscr{S}_r$ (of $\mathcal{O}_r$) iff every equation in $\mathscr{S}_r$ (in $\mathcal{O}_r$) is generated by $\mathscr{S}$. The set $\mathscr{S}_r$ ($\mathcal{O}_r$) is *finitely generated* iff it possesses a finite basis.

Our main concern in Sections 3–6 is the problem whether or not the sets $\mathscr{S}_r$ and $\mathcal{O}_r$ are finitely generated. We shall also study some special cases, where bases can actually be exhibited.

In this section we shall prove that the equations (3.5)–(3.17) which belong to the set $\mathscr{S}_1$ constitute a basis of $\mathcal{O}_1$. Because (3.14) is a set consisting of an infinite number of equations, this basis is not finite. The equations (3.5)–(3.14) are among the equations (1.1)–(1.23) and, thus, belong to all sets $\mathcal{S}_r$. The equations (3.15)–(3.17) belong to the set $\mathcal{S}_1-\mathcal{S}_2$.

$$\alpha+(\beta+\gamma) = (\alpha+\beta)+\gamma, \tag{3.5}$$

$$\alpha(\beta\gamma) = (\alpha\beta)\,\gamma, \tag{3.6}$$

$$\alpha+\beta = \beta+\alpha, \tag{3.7}$$

$$\alpha(\beta+\gamma) = \alpha\beta+\alpha\gamma, \tag{3.8}$$

$$\alpha+\alpha = \alpha, \tag{3.9}$$

$$\phi^*\alpha = \alpha, \tag{3.10}$$

$$\phi\alpha = \phi, \tag{3.11}$$

$$\alpha+\phi = \alpha, \tag{3.12}$$

$$\alpha^* = (\phi^*+\alpha)^*, \tag{3.13}$$

$$\alpha^* = (\alpha^n)^*\,(\phi^*+\alpha+ \ \ldots \ +\alpha^{n-1}), \qquad n = 1, 2, \ldots, \tag{3.14}$$

$$\alpha\beta = \beta\alpha, \tag{3.15}$$

$$(\alpha\beta^*)^* = \phi^*+\alpha\alpha^*\beta^*, \tag{3.16}$$

$$(\alpha+\beta)^* = \alpha^*\beta^*. \tag{3.17}$$

THEOREM 3.2. *The set $\mathcal{S}$ consisting of the equations* (3.5)–(3.17) *is a basis of* $\mathcal{O}_1$.

Proof. It suffices to prove that an arbitrary equation $X = Y$ in the set $\mathcal{O}_1$ is transformable by the set $\mathcal{S}$ into an equation where both sides are identical. If X and Y denote finite languages this is obvious, in view of (3.5)–(3.12) and (3.15). We, therefore, assume that X and Y denote infinite languages. The equation $X = Y$ is transformable by $\mathcal{S}$ into an equation $X_1 = Y_1$, where the star height of the regular expressions X_1 and Y_1 equals 1. This follows because, by (3.16), the star height can be reduced and, by (3.15) and (3.17), it is possible to reach a situation where (3.16) can be applied. (Note that using (3.13), (3.16) and (3.17) the equations $(\phi^*)^* = \phi^*$, $\alpha^*\alpha^* = \alpha^*$ and $(\alpha^*)^* = \alpha^*$ are easily obtained.)

Substituting ϕ^* for β in (3.16) we obtain the equation (1.10) and hence, for any $n \geqq 1$,

$$\alpha^* = \phi^*+\alpha+ \ \ldots \ +\alpha^{n-1}+\alpha^n\alpha^*. \tag{3.18}$$

In view of (3.17), we may assume without loss of generality that X_1 and Y_1 are both sums of a finite number of regular expressions, each of which is a catenation of words and regular expressions of the form $(x_1^i)^*$. Consider all numbers i such that $(x_1^i)^*$ appears in either X_1 or Y_1. Assume that c is their least common multiple. Then, by (3.14), any regular expression $(x_1^i)^*$ appearing in X_1 or Y_1 may be replaced by the regular expression

$$(x_1^c)^*(\phi^* + x_1^i + x_1^{2i} + \ldots + x_1^{(d-1)i}),$$

where $di = c$. This implies that the equation $X_1 = Y_1$ is transformable by $\mathcal{S}$ into an equation

$$X_2 \equiv (x^c)^* X_3 + X_4 = (x^c)^* Y_3 + Y_4 \equiv Y_2,$$

where each of the regular expressions X_3, X_4, Y_3, Y_4 denotes a finite language. Using (3.18) it is easy to see that the equation $X_2 = Y_2$ is transformable by $\mathcal{S}$ into the equation $X_2 + Y_2 = X_2 + Y_2$. $\square$

As a corollary, we obtain the following

THEOREM 3.3. *The star height of every language over a one-letter alphabet equals 0 or 1.*

EXERCISE 3.1. Prove that every regular expression α over a one-letter alphabet possesses a unique normal form α_1 of star height ≤ 1 such that the equation $\alpha = \alpha_1$ is valid. Cf. Salomaa (1964, 3) where also another basis for $\mathcal{O}_1$ is constructed.

§ 4. Languages containing the empty word

In this section, we shall study a special case where the set of schemas of valid equations is finitely generated.

DEFINITION. A regular expression X (over any alphabet) possesses the *empty word property* (e.w.p.) iff one of the following conditions is satisfied:

(i) There is a regular expression Y such that $X \equiv Y^*$.

(ii) X is a sum of regular expressions, one of which possesses e.w.p.

(iii) X is a catenation of regular expressions, both of which possess e.w.p.

Obviously, a regular expression X possesses e.w.p. iff the language $|X|$ contains the empty word, i.e. iff the 1×1 matrix determined by the language $|X|$ possesses e.w.p.

We denote by $\mathcal{E}_r, r = 1, 2, \ldots$, the set of all schemas of valid equations between such regular expressions over the alphabet I_r which possess e.w.p. More specifically, $\mathcal{E}_r$ consists of equations of the form $X = Y$, where X and Y are regular expressions over A_ω such that always a valid equation results whenever each letter of A_ω appearing in X or Y is substituted by some regular expression over I_r which possesses e.w.p. To avoid unnecessary complications (cf. Exercise 4.1), we make here the additional assumption that ϕ occurs in neither X nor Y. The intersection of all sets $\mathcal{E}_r, r = 1, 2, \ldots$, is denoted by $\mathcal{E}_\omega$. An equation which belongs to $\mathcal{S}_r, r = 1, 2, \ldots, \omega$, and does not contain ϕ, belongs also to $\mathcal{E}_r$. The proof of the following theorem, being almost identical to the proof of Theorem 3.1, is omitted.

THEOREM 4.1. $\mathcal{E}_2 = \mathcal{E}_3 = \ldots = \mathcal{E}_\omega$. *Furthermore, $\mathcal{E}_2$ is properly included in $\mathcal{E}_1$.*

DEFINITION. A word P' which is obtained from a word P by omitting some letters (possibly all or none) is termed an *abbreviation* of P.

Thus, λ and P are abbreviations of P. A word of length n possesses at most 2^n abbreviations.

We define recursively the following mapping a of the set of regular expressions into itself:

(i) $a(\phi) = \phi$; $a(\alpha) = \alpha + \phi^*$, where α is a letter.

(ii) $a(X+Y) = a(X)+a(Y)$; $a(XY) = a(X)a(Y)$.

(iii) $a(X^*) = (a(X))^*$.

Clearly, for any regular expression X, $|a(X)|$ consists of all abbreviations of the words in $|X|$. It is also obvious that an equation $X = Y$, where X and Y do not contain ϕ, belongs to the set $\mathcal{E}_\omega$ iff the equation $a(X) = a(Y)$ belongs to the set $\mathcal{S}_\omega$.

We shall prove that a set consisting of twelve equations, namely (3.5)–(3.9) and (4.1)–(4.7), is a basis of $\mathcal{E}_\omega$. (Hereby, only regular expressions not involving ϕ are allowed in substitutions.) Hence, by Theorem 4.1, it is a basis of any set $\mathcal{E}_r, r \geq 2$. The equations (4.1)–(4.4) belong also to $\mathcal{S}_\omega$, but the equations (4.5)–(4.7) belong to $\mathcal{E}_\omega - \mathcal{S}_\omega$.

$$(\alpha+\beta)\gamma = \alpha\gamma+\beta\gamma, \tag{4.1}$$

$$\alpha^*\alpha^* = \alpha^*, \tag{4.2}$$

$$(\alpha+\beta)^*+\alpha = (\alpha+\beta)^*, \tag{4.3}$$

$$(\alpha+\beta)^* = (\alpha^*+\beta)^*, \tag{4.4}$$

$$(\alpha+\beta)^* = (\alpha\beta)^*, \tag{4.5}$$

$$\alpha\beta+\beta = \alpha\beta, \tag{4.6}$$

$$\alpha\beta+\alpha = \alpha\beta. \tag{4.7}$$

THEOREM 4.2. *The equations* (3.5)–(3.9) *and* (4.1)–(4.7) *form a basis of* $\mathcal{E}_\omega$. *Hence,* $\mathcal{E}_\omega$ *is finitely generated.*

Proof. The fact that an equation $X = Y$ is generated by the set of equations consisting of (3.5)–(3.9) and (4.1)–(4.7) is denoted by $\vdash X = Y$. Thus, we have to show that if $X = Y$ belongs to $\mathcal{E}_\omega$ then $\vdash X = Y$. The proof is separated into several lemmas. Lemma 4.1 is an immediate consequence of (3.9).

LEMMA 4.1. *If* $\vdash X+X_1+X_2 = X$ *then* $\vdash X+X_1 = X$.

LEMMA 4.2. *If* $P' \neq \lambda$ *is an abbreviation of* P *then* $\vdash P+P' = P$.

Proof of Lemma 4.2. We may assume that

$$P \equiv P_1\beta_1 P_2\beta_2 \ldots P_k\beta_k P_{k+1}, \quad P' \equiv \beta_1\beta_2 \ldots \beta_k,$$

where P's are words and β's are letters. By (4.6) (or (3.9)), we obtain the relations

$$\vdash P_1\beta_1 = P_1\beta_1+\beta_1, \quad \vdash P_2\beta_2 = P_2\beta_2+\beta_2, \ldots,$$

$$\vdash P_{k-1}\beta_{k-1} = P_{k-1}\beta_{k-1}+\beta_{k-1}. \tag{4.8}$$

By (4.7) and (4.6),

$$\vdash P_k\beta_k P_{k+1} = P_k\beta_k P_{k+1}+P_k\beta_k = P_k\beta_k P_{k+1}+P_k\beta_k+\beta_k$$

and hence, by Lemma 4.1,

$$\vdash P_k\beta_k P_{k+1} = P_k\beta_k P_{k+1}+\beta_k. \tag{4.9}$$

By (4.8) and (4.9), there is a regular expression X such that $\vdash P = P+P'+X$ and thus, by Lemma 4.1, $\vdash P+P' = P$.

LEMMA 4.3. *For all natural numbers* n,

$$\vdash (\alpha_1+ \ldots +\alpha_n)^* = (\alpha_1 \ldots \alpha_n)^*. \tag{4.10}$$

Proof of Lemma 4.3. By (4.5), we may assume that $n \geq 3$. Using (4.6) (or (3.9)) and (4.5), we infer

$$\vdash (\alpha^k)^* = (\alpha^k+\alpha)^* = (\alpha^{k+1})^*,$$

for all natural numbers k. Thus,

$$\vdash (\alpha^k)^* = \alpha^*, \qquad k = 1, 2, \ldots. \tag{4.11}$$

Using (4.5)–(4.7), we obtain

$$\vdash (\alpha_1 + \ldots + \alpha_n)^* = (\alpha_1(\alpha_2 + \ldots + \alpha_n))^*$$
$$= (\alpha_1\alpha_2 + \ldots + \alpha_1\alpha_n + \alpha_1 + \ldots + \alpha_n)^*$$
$$= (\alpha_1\alpha_2 + (\alpha_1 + \ldots + \alpha_n + \alpha_1\alpha_3 + \ldots + \alpha_1\alpha_n))^*$$
$$= (\alpha_1\alpha_2\alpha_3 + \alpha_1\alpha_2(\alpha_1 + \alpha_2 + \alpha_4 + \ldots + \alpha_n + \alpha_1\alpha_3 + \ldots + \alpha_1\alpha_n))^*$$
$$= (\alpha_1\alpha_2\alpha_3 + (\alpha_1 + \ldots + \alpha_n + X_2))^* = \ldots = (\alpha_1\alpha_2 \ldots \alpha_n + X_{n-1})^*,$$

where X_i is a sum of finitely many words over $\{\alpha_1, \ldots, \alpha_n\}$, each of which is an abbreviation of the word $(\alpha_1 \ldots \alpha_n)^i$. Hence, by (4.4),

$$\vdash (\alpha_1 + \ldots + \alpha_n)^* = ((\alpha_1 \ldots \alpha_n)^* + X_{n-1})^*. \tag{4.12}$$

On the other hand, using (4.11), Lemma 4.2 and (4.4), we deduce

$$\vdash (\alpha_1 \ldots \alpha_n)^* = ((\alpha_1 \ldots \alpha_n)^{n-1})^* = ((\alpha_1 \ldots \alpha_n)^{n-1} + X_{n-1})^*$$
$$= (((\alpha_1 \ldots \alpha_n)^{n-1})^* + X_{n-1})^* = ((\alpha_1 \ldots \alpha_n)^* + X_{n-1})^*.$$

Thus, by (4.12), the relation (4.10) follows.

LEMMA 4.4. *Assume that $n \geqq 1$ and $X(\alpha_1, \ldots, \alpha_n)$ is a regular expression over the alphabet $\{\alpha_1, \ldots, \alpha_n\}$ such that all letters $\alpha_1, \ldots, \alpha_n$ occur in X but ϕ does not occur in X. Then*

$$\vdash (X(\alpha_1, \ldots, \alpha_n))^* = (\alpha_1 \ldots \alpha_n)^* = (\alpha_1 + \ldots + \alpha_n)^*.$$

Proof of Lemma 4.4. We may assume that $X \equiv X_1 + \ldots + X_m$, where each X_i is a regular expression of the form

$$X_i \equiv Y_1^{(i)} \ldots Y_{j(i)}^{(i)}$$

such that each Y_ν either is a letter or of the form $Y_\nu \equiv (Y_\nu')^*$. By Lemmas 4.3 and 4.2, we obtain

$$\vdash (X(\alpha_1, \ldots, \alpha_n))^* = (X_1 \ldots X_m)^*$$
$$= (X_1 \ldots X_m + Y_1^{(1)} + \ldots + Y_{j(1)}^{(1)} + \ldots + Y_1^{(m)} + \ldots + Y_{j(m)}^{(m)})^*$$
$$= (Y_1^{(1)} + \ldots + Y_{j(1)}^{(1)} + \ldots + Y_1^{(m)} + \ldots + Y_{j(m)}^{(m)})^*.$$

By (4.4), we may replace each $(Y_\nu')^*$ by Y_ν' and, thus, we reduce the star height of X. Repeating the same procedure, we derive $\vdash X^* = Y^*$, where Y is a finite sum of words over $\{\alpha_1, \ldots, \alpha_n\}$. Hence, by Lemma 4.2,

$$\vdash X^* = (Y + \alpha_1 + \ldots + \alpha_n)^* = (\alpha_1 + \ldots + \alpha_n)^* = (\alpha_1 \ldots \alpha_n)^*.$$

We use the term *elementary product* to mean a catenation of regular expressions over A_ω, each of which either is a letter or is of the form $(X_1 \ldots X_n)^*$ where the X's are distinct letters of A_ω. As an immediate consequence of Lemma 4.4 and the fact that the set consisting of (3.5)–(3.9) and (4.1)–(4.7) generates only equations in $\mathcal{E}_\omega$, we obtain the following

LEMMA 4.5. *Let $X = Y$ be an arbitrary equation in the set E_ω. Then there are regular expressions X_1 and Y_1, each of which is a sum of finitely many elementary products, such that $\vdash X = X_1$, $\vdash Y = Y_1$ and $X_1 = Y_1$ belongs to the set $\mathcal{E}_\omega$.*

LEMMA 4.6. *Assume that*

$$|a(X)| \subset \left| a\left(\sum_{i=1}^{k} Y_i\right) \right|,$$

where X and Y_i, $i = 1, \ldots, k$, are elementary products. Then there is a number i_1, $1 \leq i_1 \leq k$, such that $|a(X)| \subset |a(Y_{i_1})|$.

Proof of Lemma 4.6. Suppose the contrary: for each $i = 1, \ldots, k$, there is a word P_i such that

$$P_i \in |a(X)|, \quad P_i \notin |a(Y_i)|. \tag{4.13}$$

Because X is an elementary product, there is a word $P \in |a(X)|$ such that all words P_i, $i = 1, \ldots, k$, are abbreviations of P. By the assumption,

$$P \in \left| a\left(\sum_{i=1}^{k} Y_i\right) \right| = \left| \sum_{i=1}^{k} a(Y_i) \right|.$$

This implies that, for some i_1, $P \in |a(Y_{i_1})|$. Because P_{i_1} is an abbreviation of P, also $P_{i_1} \in |a(Y_{i_1})|$ which contradicts (4.13).

LEMMA 4.7. *Let X and Y be elementary products such that $|a(X)| \subset |a(Y)|$. Then $\vdash Y + X = Y$.*

Proof of Lemma 4.7. If X is a letter then the lemma holds, for any Y, by (4.3) and Lemma 4.2. Assume next that $X \equiv (\alpha_1 \ldots \alpha_n)^*$. This implies that Y contains a factor of the form

$$Y' \equiv (\alpha_1 \ldots \alpha_n \beta_1 \ldots \beta_m)^*.$$

For if all factors of Y of the form $(Y_1 \ldots Y_v)^*$ contain at most $n-1$ of the letters $\alpha_1, \ldots, \alpha_n$ and the number of all factors of Y equals k, then

$$(\alpha_1 \ldots \alpha_n)^k \in |a(X)|, \quad (\alpha_1 \ldots \alpha_n)^k \notin |a(Y)|,$$

which contradicts our assumption.

Thus, by Lemma 4.3, (4.3) and (4.4), we obtain

$$\vdash Y' = (\alpha_1 \ldots \alpha_n + \beta_1 + \ldots + \beta_m)^* = (X + \beta_1 + \ldots + \beta_m)^* = Y' + X$$

and hence, by Lemma 4.2, $\vdash Y + X = Y$.

We shall now make the following inductive hypothesis: the lemma has been established for $X = X_1$ and for $X = X_2$. We shall prove that this implies that the lemma holds true for the product $X_1 X_2$. Let

$$|a(X_1 X_2)| \subset |a(Y)|, \tag{4.14}$$

where $Y \equiv Y_1 \ldots Y_k$. This implies that both $|a(X_1)| \subset |a(Y)|$ and $|a(X_2)| \subset |a(Y)|$. Let $u \geqq 1$ be the number such that $|a(X_1)| \subset |a(Y_1 \ldots Y_u)|$ but $|a(X_1)| \not\subset |a(Y_1 \ldots Y_{u-1})|$. Similarly, let $v \leqq k$ be the number such that $|a(X_2)| \subset |a(Y_v \ldots Y_k)|$ but $|a(X_2)| \not\subset |a(Y_{v+1} \ldots Y_k)|$. By our inductive hypothesis,

$$\vdash Y_1 \ldots Y_u + X_1 = Y_1 \ldots Y_u, \quad \vdash Y_v \ldots Y_k + X_2 = Y_v \ldots Y_k. \tag{4.15}$$

Assume first that $u < v$. Then, by (4.15),

$$\vdash Y_1 \ldots Y_k = (Y_1 \ldots Y_u + X_1) Y_{u+1} \ldots Y_{v-1}(Y_v \ldots Y_k + X_2).$$

Thus, by Lemmas 4.1 and 4.2,

$$\vdash Y_1 \ldots Y_k + X_1 X_2 = Y_1 \ldots Y_k. \tag{4.16}$$

Assume next that $u = v$ and $Y_u \equiv (\alpha_1 \ldots \alpha_n)^*$. By (4.2), we obtain

$$\vdash Y_1 \ldots Y_k = Y_1 \ldots Y_u Y_u \ldots Y_k.$$

The same argument as in the first case can now be used to deduce (4.16) from (4.15).

Assume that $u = v$ and Y_u is a letter. Then $Y \equiv Y^{(1)} Y_u Y^{(2)}$, where

$$|a(X_1)| \not\subset |a(Y^{(1)})|, \quad |a(X_2)| \not\subset |a(Y^{(2)})|.$$

Consequently, there are words P_i, $i = 1, 2$, such that

$$P_i \in |a(X_i)|, \quad P_i \notin |a(Y^{(i)})| \qquad (i = 1, 2).$$

This implies that

$$P_1 P_2 \in |a(X_1 X_2)|, \quad P_1 P_2 \notin |a(Y^{(1)} Y_u Y^{(2)})|,$$

which contradicts (4.14). If $u > v$ then a similar contradiction arises. Thus, these cases can actually never occur. This completes the proof of Lemma 4.7.

We are now in the position to establish Theorem 4.2. Let $X = Y$ be an arbitrary equation in the set $\mathscr{E}_\omega$. By Lemma 4.5, the equation $X = Y$ is transformable by the set consisting of (3.5)–(3.9) and (4.1)–(4.7) into an equation $X_1 = Y_1$, where both sides are sums of finitely many elementary products. Let X_1' be an arbitrary elementary product appearing in X_1. Then, by Lemmas 4.6 and 4.7, there is an elementary product Y_1' appearing in Y_1 such that $\vdash Y_1' + X_1' = Y_1'$. Hence, $\vdash Y_1 + X_1 = Y_1$. Similarly, $\vdash X_1 + Y_1 = X_1$. This implies that $\vdash X_1 = Y_1$ and $\vdash X = Y$. $\square$

EXERCISE 4.1. Prove that a contradiction arises if the regular expressions X and Y in the equations $X = Y$ of $\mathscr{E}_r$ are allowed to contain ϕ and no restrictions are imposed upon substitutions. Is it possible to allow X and Y to contain ϕ^*?

EXERCISE 4.2. Prove that the equations $(\alpha^*)^* = \alpha^*$, $(\alpha\beta)^* \alpha = (\alpha\beta)^*$ and $\alpha(\alpha\beta)^* = (\alpha\beta)^*$ are generated by the set consisting of (3.5)–(3.9) and (4.1)–(4.7). (These equations occur in the original formulation of Janov (1962).)

EXERCISE 4.3 (Janov, 1962). Prove that a basis of $\mathscr{E}_1$ is obtained by adding the equations $\alpha\beta = \beta\alpha$ and $(\alpha\beta)^* = \alpha^*\beta^*$ to the basis of $\mathscr{E}_\omega$. (*Hint:* establish first a criterion to decide whether or not an equation belongs to $\mathscr{E}_1$.)

EXERCISE 4.4. For a language L, let $a(L)$ be the language consisting of all abbreviations of the words in L. Prove that the operator a preserves the regularity of languages, i.e. if L is regular then $a(L)$ is regular.

PROBLEM 4.1. Study the independence of the equations (3.5)–(3.9) and (4.1)–(4.7).

PROBLEM 4.2. Construct a simple basis for $\mathcal{E}_1$ consisting of independent equations. (Cf. Exercise 4.3.)

§ 5. Commutative languages

In this section we shall assume that catenation is commutative, i.e. the order of letters in a word does not matter but only the number of occurrences of each letter.

More specifically, let c be the operator defined for languages such that $c(L)$ is the language consisting of all such words which are obtained by permuting the letters in some word belonging to L. Thus, for

$$L = \{x^n y^n \,|\, n = 0, 1, \ldots\},$$

$c(L)$ consists of all words where the number of occurrences of x equals the number of occurrences of y.

DEFINITION. For regular expressions X and Y, the equation $X = Y$ is said to be *c-valid* iff the languages $c(|X|)$ and $c(|Y|)$ are equal.

Clearly, all valid equations are c-valid but not vice versa. Denote by $\mathcal{E}_r$, $r = 1, 2, \ldots$, the set of equations $X = Y$, where X and Y are regular expressions over A_ω such that whenever the letters of A_ω appearing in X or Y are substituted by some regular expressions over I_r, then the resulting equation is c-valid. We denote by $\mathcal{E}_\omega$ the intersection of all sets $\mathcal{E}_r$, $r = 1, 2, \ldots$. It is obvious that

$$\mathcal{E}_1 \supset \mathcal{E}_2 \supset \mathcal{E}_3 \supset \ldots \supset \mathcal{E}_\omega . \tag{5.1}$$

Furthermore,

$$\mathcal{S}_r \subset \mathcal{E}_r \qquad (r = 1, 2, \ldots) \tag{5.2}$$

and also

$$\mathcal{S}_\omega \subset \mathcal{E}_\omega . \tag{5.3}$$

Because an equation between two regular expressions over a one-letter alphabet is valid iff it is c-valid, we conclude that the inclusion (5.2) is not proper for $r = 1$. On the other hand, the equation $\alpha\beta = \beta\alpha$ belongs to all sets $\mathcal{E}$ but does not belong to $\mathcal{S}_r$, $r > 1$. This shows that both the inclusion (5.2), for $r > 1$, and the inclusion (5.3) are proper. We shall now exhibit a basis for the set $\mathcal{E}_\omega$.

THEOREM 5.1. *The set $\mathcal{O}$ consisting of the equations* (3.5)–(3.17) *and of the equation*

$$(\alpha+\beta)^* = (\alpha\beta)^* (\alpha^*+\beta^*) \qquad (5.4)$$

is a basis of $\mathcal{C}_\omega$.

Proof. Assume that the equation $X = Y$ belongs to the set $\mathcal{C}_\omega$. By the same argument as in the proof of Theorem 3.2, we may restrict ourselves to the case where both X and Y are of star height 1. It follows, by (3.15) and (3.17), that the equation $X = Y$ is transformable by $\mathcal{O}$ into an equation $X_1 = Y_1$, where both sides are sums of finitely many terms of the form

$$(P_1+ \ldots +P_n)^* P_{n+1}, \qquad (5.5)$$

where $n \geqq 0$ and each P_i, $i = 1, \ldots, n+1$, is a word over A_ω. By (3.13), we may assume also that none of the words P_i, $i = 1, \ldots, n$, is empty. It is understood that, for $n = 0$, (5.5) is reduced to the word P_1. Regular expressions of the form (5.5), where none of the words P_i, $i = 1, \ldots, n$, is empty, are referred to as *normal products*.

The given equation $X = Y$ contains a finite number u of letters of A_ω; assume that they are $\alpha_1, \ldots, \alpha_u$. To each word of the form

$$\alpha_1^{i_1} \ldots \alpha_u^{i_u} \qquad (i_j \geqq 0, \, j = 1, \ldots, u) \qquad (5.6)$$

we associate the u-dimensional vector $(i_1, \ldots, i_u)$. A set of words of the form (5.6) is said to be *linearly independent* iff the set of the associated vectors is linearly independent. By (3.15) we may assume that, for the equation $X_1 = Y_1$, the words appearing in normal products are of the form (5.6). A normal product (5.5) is termed *linearly independent* iff either $n = 0$ or the set of words $\{P_1, \ldots, P_n\}$ is linearly independent.

It is clear that if a set of words $\{P_1, \ldots, P_n\}$ is linearly independent, then the languages

$$c(P_1^{i_1} \ldots P_n^{i_n}) \quad \text{and} \quad c(P_1^{j_1} \ldots P_n^{j_n}),$$

where the exponents are non-negative, are equal iff, for each $v = 1, \ldots, n$, $i_v = j_v$.

We shall now establish two lemmas.

LEMMA 5.1. *For any natural number $n \geq 2$, $\mathcal{U}$ generates the equation*

$$(\alpha_1 + \ldots + \alpha_n)^* = (\alpha_1 \ldots \alpha_n)^* ((\alpha_1 + \ldots + \alpha_{n-1})^*$$
$$+ (\alpha_1 + \ldots + \alpha_{n-2} + \alpha_n)^* + \ldots + (\alpha_2 + \ldots + \alpha_n)^*). \quad (5.7)$$

Proof of Lemma 5.1. We apply induction on the number n. By (5.4), the assertion follows for $n = 2$. Assume that the equation (5.7) is generated by $\mathcal{U}$. Then, by (5.4) and (3.17), we conclude that the following equations are generated by $\mathcal{U}$:

$$(\alpha_1 + \ldots + \alpha_n + \alpha_{n+1})^* = (\alpha_1 + \ldots + \alpha_n)^* \alpha_{n+1}^*$$
$$= (\alpha_1 \ldots \alpha_n)^* ((\alpha_1 + \ldots + \alpha_{n-1})^* + \ldots + (\alpha_2 + \ldots + \alpha_n)^*) \alpha_{n+1}^*$$
$$= (\alpha_1 \ldots \alpha_n + \alpha_1 + \ldots \alpha_{n-1} + \alpha_{n+1})^* + \ldots$$
$$+ (\alpha_1 \ldots \alpha_n + \alpha_2 + \ldots + \alpha_n + \alpha_{n+1})^*$$
$$= (\alpha_1 \ldots \alpha_n + \alpha_{n+1})^* (\alpha_1 + \ldots + \alpha_{n-1})^* + \ldots$$
$$+ (\alpha_1 \ldots \alpha_n + \alpha_{n+1})^* (\alpha_2 + \ldots + \alpha_n)^*$$
$$= (\alpha_1 \ldots \alpha_n \alpha_{n+1})^* (((\alpha_1 \ldots \alpha_n)^* + \alpha_{n+1}^*) (\alpha_1 + \ldots + \alpha_{n-1})^* + \ldots$$
$$+ ((\alpha_1 \ldots \alpha_n)^* + \alpha_{n+1}^*) (\alpha_2 + \ldots + \alpha_n)^*)$$
$$= (\alpha_1 \ldots \alpha_{n+1})^* ((\alpha_1 + \ldots + \alpha_n)^* + \ldots + (\alpha_2 + \ldots + \alpha_{n+1})^*).$$

This completes the induction.

LEMMA 5.2. *For any normal product Z, there is a sum Z' of linearly independent normal products such that the equation $Z = Z'$ is generated by $\mathcal{U}$.*

Proof of Lemma 5.2. Assume that (5.5) is the given normal product. If it is linearly independent, then we may choose $Z' \equiv Z$. Assume that (5.5) is linearly dependent. This implies that, after a suitable renumbering of the words $P_1, \ldots, P_n$, there is a natural number v, $1 \leq v < n$, such that

$$P_1^{i_1} \ldots P_v^{i_v} = P_{v+1}^{i_{v+1}} \ldots P_n^{i_n}, \quad (5.8)$$

where the exponents are positive on the left side and non-negative on the right side. By (3.14), (3.15) and (3.17), we conclude that $\mathcal{U}$ generates the following equations:

$$(P_1 + \ldots + P_n)^* = P_1^* \ldots P_n^* = (P_1^{i_1})^* Z_1 \ldots (P_n^{i_n})^* Z_n$$
$$= Z_{n+1}(P_1^{i_1} + \ldots + P_v^{i_v})^* (P_{v+1}^{i_{v+1}} + \ldots + P_n^{i_n})^*, \quad (5.9)$$

where Z_j, $j = 1, \ldots, n+1$, is a sum of finitely many words. By (5.8) and Lemma 5.1,

$$\left(P_1^{i_1} + \ldots + P_v^{i_v}\right)^* = \left(P_{v+1}^{i_{v+1}} \ldots P_n^{i_n}\right)^* \left(\left(P_1^{i_1} + \ldots + P_{v-1}^{i_{v-1}}\right)^* \right.$$
$$\left. + \ldots + \left(P_2^{i_2} + \ldots + P_v^{i_v}\right)^*\right) \quad (5.10)$$

is generated by $\mathcal{O}$. It is easy to see that the equation

$$\left(P_{v+1}^{i_{v+1}} + \ldots + P_n^{i_n}\right)^* = \left(P_{v+1}^{i_{v+1}} \ldots P_n^{i_n}\right)^* \left(P_{v+1}^{i_{v+1}} + \ldots + P_n^{i_n}\right)^*$$

is generated by $\mathcal{O}$. (For $v = 1$, the right side of (5.10) is $(P_2^{i_2} \ldots P_n^{i_n})^*$.) Hence, because (5.9) and (5.10) are generated, we conclude that $\mathcal{O}$ generates an equation $Z = \bar{Z}$, where $\bar{Z}$ is a sum of finitely many normal products

$$(Q_1 + \ldots + Q_m)^* Q_{m+1} \quad (5.11)$$

such that $m < n$. If some of the normal products (5.11) is linearly dependent, we repeat the same procedure, thus reducing the number of words within the scope of the star. In this fashion, we obtain a regular expression Z' as required in the lemma.

We are now in the position to establish Theorem 5.1. By Lemma 5.2, the equation $X_1 = Y_1$ is transformable by $\mathcal{O}$ into an equation $X_2 = Y_2$, where both sides are sums of finitely many linearly independent normal products. On the other hand, such an equation $X_2 = Y_2$ belonging to $\mathcal{C}_\omega$ is generated by $\mathcal{O}$. This is seen by considering first the case where each of the words $P_1, \ldots, P_n$ in every normal product (5.5) appearing in X_2 or Y_2 consists of a single letter. The proof for this case is obvious by an inductive argument. By Lemma 5.1, the general case is then reduced to this special case. □

EXERCISE 5.1. Prove that the operator c introduced in this section does not preserve the regularity of languages.

EXERCISE 5.2. By a *trace* of a word P we mean any word (including the empty word) obtained by catenating some letters of P. Thus, λ, x, y, xy, yx, yy, yyx, xyy, yxy are the traces of the word yxy. Let $t(L)$ be the language consisting of all traces of the words in L. Prove that $t(L) = a(c(L))$. Does t preserve regularity? Give an upper bound for the number of traces of a word of length n.

EXERCISE 5.3. Why is the proof of Theorem 5.1 not valid if $\mathcal{C}_\omega$ is replaced by $\mathcal{C}_1$?

EXERCISE 5.4. Study the interconnection between equations of $\mathcal{C}_\omega$ and equations involving sums of m-tuples of non-negative integers. (For the latter, cf. Ginsburg and Spanier (1966).)

PROBLEM 5.1. Are the inclusions (5.1) proper?

PROBLEM 5.2. Study the independence of the equations in the given basis of $\mathcal{C}_\omega$, especially the independence of (5.4). (If (5.4) is independent then, in the one-letter case, every substitution instance of (5.4) is generated but not (5.4) itself.)

§ 6. Non-existence of a finite basis for the sets $\mathcal{S}_r$

We shall now prove that the sets $\mathcal{S}_r$ and $\mathcal{U}_r$, $r = 2, 3, \ldots, \omega$, are not finitely generated. Thus, it is not possible to obtain such a simple characterization for the sets $\mathcal{S}_r$ as was given for the sets $\mathcal{E}_r$ in Section 4.

We shall first establish an independence result concerning the basis $\mathcal{U}$ of $\mathcal{C}_\omega$. Let p be an arbitrary prime number. We denote by $\mathcal{U}_p$ the finite subset of $\mathcal{U}$, obtained from $\mathcal{U}$ by removing all equations (3.14), where $n \geq p$.

THEOREM 6.1. *The equation*

$$\alpha^* = (\alpha^p)^*(\phi^* + \alpha + \ldots + \alpha^{p-1}) \tag{6.1}$$

is not generated by the set $\mathcal{U}_p$.

Proof. A regular expression X over the alphabet $\{\alpha\}$ is said to possess *p-property* iff, whenever X_1^* is a well-formed part of X, then every word in the language denoted by X_1 is of length divisible by p. Thus, for instance, the regular expression

$$\phi^* + \alpha^2 + \alpha(\alpha^3(\alpha^3 + \alpha^6)^* + \alpha((\alpha^9)^* + \phi^*)^* \alpha^2)^*$$

possesses 3-property. There is a simple algorithm of deciding whether or not a regular expression X possesses p-property. (Cf. Exercise 6.1.)

The set $\mathcal{U}_p$ generates only equations such that either both sides possess p-property or neither side possesses p-property. This follows because, by checking through $\mathcal{U}_p$, it is immediately verified that all substitution instances of members of $\mathcal{U}_p$ are equations of this type. On the other hand, if $X_1 = X_2$ and $X_3 = X_4$ are equations of this type generated by $\mathcal{U}_p$ then so is also any equation obtained from them by replacement. Theorem 6.1 now follows because the right side of (6.1) possesses p-property, whereas the left side does not possess p-property. □

Obviously, Theorem 6.1 holds true also with the equation

$$x_1^* = (x_1^p)^*(\phi^* + x_1 + \ldots + x_1^{p-1})$$

instead of (6.1).

THEOREM 6.2. *The set $\mathcal{S}_\omega$ is not finitely generated. Hence, none of the sets $\mathcal{S}_r$, $r \geqq 2$, is finitely generated.*

Proof. The second part of the theorem is a consequence of the first part, by Theorem 3.1. To prove the first part, we assume the contrary: there is a finite subset $\mathcal{S}$ of $\mathcal{S}_\omega$ which generates every equation in $\mathcal{S}_\omega$. By (5.3),

$$\mathcal{S} \subset \mathcal{C}_\omega$$

and thus, by Theorem 5.1, every equation in $\mathcal{S}$ is generated by the set $\mathcal{C}$ consisting of the equations (3.5)–(3.17) and (5.4). Furthermore, because $\mathcal{S}$ is finite, only a finite subset $\mathcal{C}'$ of $\mathcal{C}$ is needed to generate all equations in $\mathcal{S}$. There is a prime number p such that $\mathcal{C}' \subset \mathcal{C}_p$. Hence, by Theorem 6.1, the equation (6.1) is not generated by $\mathcal{C}'$. On the other hand, the equation (6.1) belongs to the set $\mathcal{S}_\omega$. Therefore, it is generated by $\mathcal{S}$. Because $\mathcal{C}'$ generates every equation in $\mathcal{S}$, the equation (6.1) is generated by $\mathcal{C}'$. This is a contradiction. □

THEOREM 6.3. *The set $\mathcal{O}_2$ is not finitely generated. Hence, none of the sets $\mathcal{O}_r$, $r = 2, 3, \ldots, \omega$, is finitely generated.*

Proof. The second part of the theorem follows from the first part, by Theorem 3.1 and the inclusions (3.1). To prove the first part, we again assume the contrary: there is a finite subset $\mathcal{S}'$ of $\mathcal{S}_2$ which generates every equation in $\mathcal{O}_2$. By Theorem 3.1 and the inclusion (5.3), we conclude that $\mathcal{S}' \subset \mathcal{C}_\omega$. Thus, we may conclude as in the proof of Theorem 6.2 that there is a finite subset $\mathcal{C}''$ of $\mathcal{C}$ which generates every equation in $\mathcal{S}'$. By the remark following the proof of Theorem 6.1, we obtain a contradiction as in the proof of Theorem 6.2. □

Theorems 6.2 and 6.3 can be established also without using Theorem 5.1. (Cf. Exercise 6.7.) It is an open problem whether or not the sets $\mathcal{S}_1$ and $\mathcal{O}_1$ are finitely generated. (Cf. also Problem 5.1 and Exercise 6.2.)

EXERCISE 6.1. Describe an algorithm for deciding whether or not a regular expression possesses p-property.

EXERCISE 6.2. Prove that if $\mathcal{C}_1 = \mathcal{C}_\omega$ (cf. Problem 5.1), then $\mathcal{S}_1$ and $\mathcal{O}_1$ are not finitely generated.

EXERCISE 6.3. Denote by $\mathcal{S}_1^{(1)}$ the subset of $\mathcal{S}_1$ consisting of equations involving only one (non-empty) letter. Prove that there is neither a finite subset of $\mathcal{S}_1^{(1)}$ which generates $\mathcal{S}_1^{(1)}$ nor a finite subset of $\mathcal{S}_1^{(1)}$ which generates $\mathcal{O}_1$.

EXERCISE 6.4. Instead of the three regular operators sum, catenation and catenation closure, consider an arbitrary finite number of operators $\varphi_1, \ldots, \varphi_n$. Define φ-*regular expressions* over an alphabet I by:

(i) each letter of I, as well as ϕ, is a φ-regular expression;
(ii) if φ_i is a k_i-place operator and $\alpha_1, \ldots, \alpha_{k_i}$ are φ-regular expressions, then so is
$$\varphi_i(\alpha_1, \ldots, \alpha_{k_i}).$$

Let ϕ denote the empty language, $x \in I$ denote the language $\{x\}$ and define the language $|\varphi_i(\alpha_1, \ldots, \alpha_k)|$ denoted by φ_i in terms of the languages denoted by the α's. Assume hereby that each φ_i possesses the replacement property: a word belongs to the language

$$|\varphi_i(\alpha_1, \ldots, \alpha_k)|$$

iff it is obtained from a word of $|\varphi_i(x_1, \ldots, x_k)|$, where each x_j is a letter of I, by replacing each x_j by a word belonging to $|\alpha_j|$. (This means that each operator φ_i commutes with the substitution operator.) A language is φ-*regular* iff it is denoted by a φ-regular expression. An equation $\alpha = \beta$ between two φ-regular expressions is valid iff α and β denote the same language. Let $\mathcal{S}_r^\varphi$ be defined as $\mathcal{S}_r$, with regular expressions replaced by φ-regular expressions.

Prove that if the family of φ-regular languages equals the family of regular languages (over I), then the set $\mathcal{S}_\omega^\varphi$ is not finitely generated. (Cf. Janov, 1964.)

EXERCISE 6.5. Omit ϕ from the definition of φ-regular expressions in Exercise 6.4. Assume that the family of φ-regular languages equals the family of regular languages (over I) containing the empty word.

Is the set of valid equations between φ-regular expressions finitely generated?

EXERCISE 6.6 (Janov, 1966). Let P be a non-empty word over the alphabet I_r, $r \geqq 2$. Let $\mathcal{E}_r(P)$ consist of all equations of the form $X = Y$, where X and Y are regular expressions over A_ω such that always a valid equation results whenever each letter of A_ω appearing in X or Y is substituted by either some regular expression over I_r which possesses e.w.p. or by P.

Prove that $\mathcal{E}_r(P) = \mathcal{S}_r$ ($= \mathcal{S}_2$). Conclude that $\mathcal{E}_r(P)$ is not finitely generated.

EXERCISE 6.7 (Murskij, 1964). Give a direct proof of Theorem 6.2 (i.e. without any reference to the results of Section 5) by the following argument. With every regular expression X over A_ω we associate a graph G_X whose edges are labeled by letters of A_ω and λ as follows. The graph associated with a letter of A_ω possesses two nodes, referred to as the initial and the terminal node, and an edge from the initial node to the terminal node which is labeled by the letter in question. The graph associated with ϕ possesses two nodes, referred to as the initial and the terminal node, and no edges. Proceeding inductively, we assume that we have associated with the regular expressions X and Y over A_ω the graphs G_X and G_Y which both possess exactly one initial node and exactly one terminal node. The graph G_{X+Y} associated with the regular expression $X+Y$ consists of the nodes of G_X and G_Y and of two additional nodes, referred to as the initial and terminal node of G_{X+Y}. All edges between the nodes of G_X and of G_Y are left unchanged. Edges labeled by λ are added from the initial node of G_{X+Y} to the initial nodes of G_X and G_Y, as well as from the terminal nodes of G_X and G_Y to the terminal node of G_{X+Y}. The graph G_{XY} associated with the regular expression XY consists of the nodes of G_X and G_Y. All edges between the nodes of G_X and of G_Y are left unchanged, and an edge labeled by λ is added from the terminal node of G_X to the initial node of G_Y. The initial node of G_X (the terminal node of G_Y) is referred to as the initial (terminal) node of G_{XY}. Finally, the graph G_{X*} associated with the regular expression X^* consists of all nodes of G_X, the edges between them being left unchanged, and of two additional nodes, referred to as the initial and terminal node of G_{X*}. Edges labeled by λ are added from the initial node of G_{X*} and from the terminal node of G_X to the initial node of G_X, as well as from the initial node of G_X to the terminal node of G_{X*}.

Assume that $\mathcal{S}$ is a finite subset of $\mathcal{S}_\omega$. For every equation $X = Y$ in $\mathcal{S}$, we consider the graphs G_X and G_Y associated with X and Y. Let p be a prime number greater than the maximal number of nodes in these graphs. Then the equation (6.1) is not generated by $\mathcal{S}$.

For similar arguments, cf. also Yoeli and Ginzburg (1964) and Hedetniemi (1966).

PROBLEM 6.1. Is there any way to replace a finite number of equation schemas by one schema?

PROBLEM 6.2. Construct an infinite basis for $\mathcal{S}_2$.

PROBLEM 6.3. Construct a subset of $\mathcal{S}_2$ which generates all equations in $\mathcal{U}_\omega$.

PROBLEM 6.4. Let U be a set of regular expressions over I_r, $r \geqq 1$. Let $\mathcal{E}_r(U)$ consist of all equations of the form $X = Y$, where X and Y are regular expressions over A_ω such that always a valid equation results whenever each letter of A_ω appearing in X or Y is substituted by some regular expression in U.

Is there a set U such that (i) $\mathcal{E}_r(U)$ is finitely generated and (ii) U properly includes the set of regular expressions possessing e.w.p.? Determine a "maximal" set U_1 which satisfies these two conditions (i.e. for which there is no set which satisfies (i) and (ii) and properly includes U_1). Cf. Theorems 4.2, 6.2 and Exercise 6.6. Note that, in view of the results of Sections 4–6, only the set of regular expressions possessing e.w.p. has a satisfactory algebraic characterization.

§ 7. Two complete axiom systems

In view of the negative results presented in Section 6, there are two possible approaches to the problem of characterizing the set of valid equations between regular expressions. In the first place, one may try to construct infinite bases for the set $\mathcal{S}_\omega$. (Cf. Problem 6.2. Cf. also Theorem 3.2.) Another approach is to allow rules of inference stronger than substitution. This procedure will be followed in this section. We shall present two axiom systems $\mathcal{F}_1$ and $\mathcal{F}_2$. In the system $\mathcal{F}_1$, one is allowed to *introduce stars* to regular expressions satisfying certain conditions. The validity of this rule is based on the representation theory of regular languages. The feature characteristic for the system $\mathcal{F}_2$ is that regular expression *equations* of the form $y = yL + R$ are solvable within the system. Both of the systems $\mathcal{F}_1$ and $\mathcal{F}_2$ are shown to be consistent and complete.

For a regular expression X (over any alphabet), we define

$$C(X) = 2^{s(X)} + 2,$$

where $s(X)$ is the number of (non-empty) letters occurring in X. (Each letter is counted as many times as it occurs.)

We shall now introduce the *axiom system* $\mathcal{F}_1$. The *axioms* in the system are the equations (1.1)–(1.10), including the equations (1.7)' and (1.8)'. By a *substitution instance* of an axiom we mean the result of substituting all letters of A_ω in the axiom (i.e. those of α, β, γ appearing in the axiom) by some regular expressions over some alphabet I_r. Thus, for example,

$$(x_1^* + x_2 x_3) + \left(x_9 + (x_2^* + x_3 x_4^*)\right) = \left((x_1^* + x_2 x_3) + x_9\right) + (x_2^* + x_3 x_4^*)$$

is a substitution instance of the axiom (1.1).

There are two *rules of inference*, R1 and R2, in the axiom system $\mathcal{F}_1$.

R1 (Replacement). Assume that a regular expression Y_1 is a well-formed part of a regular expression X_1 and that X_2 is the result of replacing (some occurrence of) Y_1 by a regular expression Y_2. Then from the equations $X_1 = Z$ and $Y_1 = Y_2$ one may infer the equation $X_2 = Z$ and the equation $X_2 = X_1$.

R2 (Introduction of stars). The equation

$$X + Y_1 Z^* Y_2 = X$$

may be inferred from the $C(X) + 1$ equations

$$X + Y_1 Z^i Y_2 = X, \quad i = 0, 1, \ldots, C(X).$$

DEFINITION. A *proof* of an equation $X = Y$ in the axiom system $\mathcal{F}_1$ is a finite sequence of equations such that each of them either is a substitution instance of an axiom or may be inferred from some equations occurring earlier in the sequence by R1 or R2 and, furthermore,

$X = Y$ is the last equation in the sequence. An equation $X = Y$ is *derivable* within $\mathcal{F}_1$, in symbols, $\vdash_1 X = Y$ iff there is a proof of $X = Y$ in $\mathcal{F}_1$. The axiom system $\mathcal{F}_1$ is *consistent* iff all derivable equations belong to the set $\mathcal{V}_\omega$. The axiom system $\mathcal{F}_1$ is *complete* iff every equation in the set $\mathcal{V}_\omega$ is derivable.

For instance, the following sequence of equations is a proof of the equation (7.1) in the axiom system $\mathcal{F}_1$:

$$x_1^* + x_1^* = x_1^*,$$
$$x_1^* = \phi^* + x_1^* x_1,$$
$$x_1^* + (\phi^* + x_1^* x_1) = x_1^*. \tag{7.1}$$

Note that according to the preceding definition all derivable equations are of the form $X = Y$, where X and Y are regular expressions over some alphabet I_r. Substitution and replacement are not applicable to equations involving regular expressions over A_ω. (Cf. also Exercise 7.10.)

THEOREM 7.1. *The axiom system $\mathcal{F}_1$ is consistent.*

Proof. It suffices to show that the set $\mathcal{V}_\omega$ is closed under the rules R1 and R2, i.e., if one of these rules is applied to some equations in the set $\mathcal{V}_\omega$, then the resulting equation is in $\mathcal{V}_\omega$. As regards the rule R1, this is obvious. As regards the rule R2, we note that, for any regular expression X over some I_r, the equation $X + Y = X$ belongs to the set $\mathcal{V}_\omega$ iff $|Y| \subset |X|$. Hence, it suffices to establish the following

LEMMA 7.1. *Assume that X, Y_1, Y_2 and Z are regular expressions over some I_r such that, for each i satisfying $0 \leq i \leq C(X)$, we have*

$$|Y_1 Z^i Y_2| \subset |X|. \tag{7.2}$$

Then also $|Y_1 Z^* Y_2| \subset |X|$.

Proof of Lemma 7.1. If the language $|Z|$ is empty, then the lemma follows because, by definition, $\phi^0 = \phi^*$. In what follows, we assume that $|Z|$ is not empty.

It suffices to show that the inclusion (7.2) holds for all values of $i \geq 0$. By the assumption, (7.2) holds for $i \leq C(X)$. We make the following inductive hypothesis: (7.2) holds for $i \leq C(X) + k$, where

$k \geqq 0$. To complete the induction, it must be proved that

$$|Y_1 Z^{C(X)+k+1} Y_2| \subset |X|. \qquad (7.3)$$

Assume the contrary: there is a word P such that

$$P \in |Y_1 Z^{C(X)+k+1} Y_2|, \quad P \notin |X|. \qquad (7.4)$$

Hence, P is of the form

$$P = P^{(Y_1)} P_1^{(Z)} \ldots P_{C(X)+k+1}^{(Z)} P^{(Y_2)}, \quad P^{(Y_1)} \in |Y_1|, \quad P_v^{(Z)} \in |Z|, \quad P^{(Y_2)} \in |Y_2|.$$

According to Theorem I.2.3, the language $|X|$ can be represented in a finite deterministic automaton with $C(X)-1$ states. This implies that the states

$$s_0 P^{(Y_1)} P_1^{(Z)}, \quad \ldots, \quad s_0 P^{(Y_1)} P_1^{(Z)} \ldots P_{C(X)+k}^{(Z)},$$

where s_0 is the initial state, cannot all be distinct. Hence, for some u and v,

$$s_0 P^{(Y_1)} P_1^{(Z)} \ldots P_u^{(Z)} = s_0 P^{(Y_1)} P_1^{(Z)} \ldots P_u^{(Z)} \ldots P_{u+v}^{(Z)},$$

where $1 \leqq u < u+v \leqq C(X)+k$. Consequently,

$$s_0 P' = s_0 P, \qquad (7.5)$$

where

$$P' = P^{(Y_1)} P_1^{(Z)} \ldots P_u^{(Z)} P_{u+v+1}^{(Z)} \ldots P_{C(X)+k+1}^{(Z)} P^{(Y_2)} \in |Y_1 Z^i Y_2|, \qquad (7.6)$$

for some $i \leqq C(X)+k$. By (7.4) and (7.5) we obtain

$$P' \notin |X|. \qquad (7.7)$$

Because (7.6) and (7.7) contradict our inductive hypothesis, we may conclude that (7.3) holds. This completes the proof of the lemma and, thus, Theorem 7.1 follows. □

THEOREM 7.2. *The axiom system $\mathcal{F}_1$ is complete.*

Proof. In the following proof X, Y and Z, possibly with subscripts, are regular expressions over some alphabet I_r. The proof is based on several lemmas. The replacement rule R1 and the results mentioned in Lemma 7.2 will be used without being explicitly referred to.

LEMMA 7.2. $\vdash_1 X = X$. *If* $\vdash_1 X = Y$, *then* $\vdash_1 Y = X$. *If* $\vdash_1 X = Y$ *and* $\vdash_1 Y = Z$, *then* $\vdash_1 X = Z$. *If* $\vdash_1 X_1 = X_2$ *and* $\vdash_1 Y_1 = Y_2$, *then* $\vdash_1 X_1+Y_1 = X_2+Y_2$, $\vdash_1 X_1 Y_1 = X_2 Y_2$ *and* $\vdash_i X_1^* = X_2^*$.

The proof of Lemma 7.2 is straightforward, by R1 and the axiom (1.6). For instance, by axiom (1.6) we obtain $\vdash_1 X + X = X$. We choose in R1

$$X_1 \equiv Y_1 \equiv X + X, \quad Y_2 \equiv Z \equiv X.$$

Hence, $X_2 \equiv X$, $\vdash_1 X_1 = Z$ and $\vdash_1 Y_1 = Y_2$. By R1, we may conclude that $\vdash_1 X_2 = Z$, i.e. the first assertion of the lemma follows. The rest of the proof is left to the reader.

LEMMA 7.3. *Assume that $k \geqq 1$ and*

$$\vdash_1 X + Y_1 Z_1^{n_1} Y_2 \ldots Y_k Z_k^{n_k} Y_{k+1} = X, \tag{7.8}$$

whenever $0 \leqq n_i \leqq C(X)$, $i = 1, \ldots, k$. Then also

$$\vdash_1 X + Y_1 Z_1^* Y_2 \ldots Y_k Z_k^* Y_{k+1} = X. \tag{7.9}$$

Proof of Lemma 7.3. The proof is by induction on the number k. The lemma holds true for $k = 1$ because, in this case, it is another formulation of the rule R2. As an inductive hypothesis, assume that it holds for the value k, i.e. (7.8) implies (7.9). Assume, furthermore, that

$$\vdash_1 X + Y_1 Z_1^{n_1} Y_2 \ldots Y_k Z_k^{n_k} Y_{k+1} Z_{k+1}^{n_{k+1}} Y_{k+2} = X, \tag{7.10}$$

whenever $0 \leqq n_i \leqq C(X)$, for all i. By (7.10) and the inductive hypothesis, we obtain the result

$$\vdash_1 X + Y_1 Z_1^* Y_2 \ldots Y_k Z_k^* Y_{k+1} Z_{k+1}^{n_{k+1}} Y_{k+2} = X. \tag{7.11}$$

Because (7.11) is satisfied for all values of n_{k+1}, $0 \leqq n_{k+1} \leqq C(X)$, an application of R2 gives the relation

$$\vdash_1 X + Y_1 Z_1^* Y_2 \ldots Y_k Z_k^* Y_{k+1} Z_{k+1}^* Y_{k+2} = X.$$

This completes the induction.

LEMMA 7.4. *Assume that the star height of the regular expression Y equals 0 and that $|Y| \subset |X|$. Then $\vdash_1 X + Y = X$.*

Proof of Lemma 7.4. By axioms (1.1)–(1.9) (including (1.7)′ and (1.8)′), there is a regular expression Y_1 such that $\vdash_1 Y = Y_1$ and Y_1 is a sum of finitely many words. Hence, it suffices to prove the lemma for the case where Y is a word. By (1.1)–(1.10), we obtain the relation

$$\vdash_1 Z^* = \phi^* + Z + \ldots + Z^{k-1} + Z^* Z^k, \tag{7.12}$$

for all natural numbers k. By applying (7.12) to all well-formed parts of X of the form Z^* (cf. Exercise 7.9), we obtain the relation $\vdash_1 X = X_1 + Y$, for some regular expression X_1. Hence, by (1.6), the relation $\vdash_1 X + Y = X$ follows.

LEMMA 7.5. *If* $|Y| \subset |X|$, *then* $\vdash_1 X + Y = X$.

Proof of Lemma 7.5. The proof is by induction on the star height of the regular expression Y. By the previous lemma, Lemma 7.5 holds (for all X) if the star height of Y equals 0. We shall make the following inductive hypothesis: Lemma 7.5 holds (for all X) if the star height of Y is less than or equal to k.

Assume that $|Y| \subset |X|$ and the star height of Y equals $k+1$. By (1.1)–(1.9), there is a regular expression Y' such that $\vdash_1 Y = Y'$ and Y' is a sum of finitely many terms of the form

$$U \equiv Y_1 Z_1^* Y_2 \ldots Y_u Z_u^* Y_{u+1}, \qquad (7.13)$$

where $u \geqq 1$ and the star height of each Z_i is less than or equal to k, and the star height of each Y_i is less than or equal to k or $Y_i \equiv \phi^*$. To complete the induction, it suffices to show that, for an arbitrary U of the form (7.13) occurring as a term in Y', we have

$$\vdash_1 X + U = X. \qquad (7.14)$$

Let $n_1, \ldots, n_u$ be arbitrary integers such that $0 \leqq n_i \leqq C(X)$ and consider the regular expression

$$U(n_1, \ldots, n_u) \equiv Y_1 Z_1^{n_1} Y_2 \ldots Y_u Z_u^{n_u} Y_{u+1}.$$

Clearly,

$$|U(n_1, \ldots, n_u)| \subset |U| \subset |Y| \subset |X|.$$

Furthermore, the star height of $U(n_1, \ldots, n_u)$ is less than or equa to k, except for the case where $k = 0$ and some $Y_i \equiv \phi^*$. By our induc tive hypothesis and by (1.7) and (1.7)', we obtain the result

$$\vdash_1 X + U(n_1, \ldots, n_u) = X.$$

Hence, by Lemma 7.3, we obtain the relation (7.14). This completes the induction, and we conclude that Lemma 7.5 holds true.

To prove Theorem 7.2, we now assume that $X = Y$ is an arbitrary equation in the set $\mathcal{O}_\omega$. Then we have both $|X| \subset |Y|$ and $|Y| \subset |X|$ and hence, by Lemma 7.5, $\vdash_1 Y + X = Y$ and $\vdash_1 X + Y = X$. Therefore, by

(1.3), we obtain the relation $\vdash_1 X = Y$ which proves the completeness of the axiom system $\mathcal{F}_1$. □

The axiom system $\mathcal{F}_1$ possesses an undesirable feature, namely, the characteristic rule of inference, R2, is rather difficult to apply. We shall now present another consistent and complete axiom system $\mathcal{F}_2$ with R2 replaced by a rule of inference which is easier to apply than R2. The *axioms* in the system $\mathcal{F}_2$ are (1.1)–(1.11) (without including (1.7)′ and (1.8)′). The *rules of inference* are R1 and the following

R3 (Solution of equations). If Y does not possess e.w.p., then the equation $X = ZY^*$ may be inferred from the equation $X = XY+Z$.

The notions of proof, derivability, consistency and completeness are defined as before, with $\mathcal{F}_1$ replaced by $\mathcal{F}_2$. Derivability within $\mathcal{F}_2$ is denoted by the symbol $\vdash_2$. It is a consequence of Theorem 2.2 that an application of R3 always leads from an equation in $\mathcal{O}_\omega$ to an equation in $\mathcal{O}_\omega$. Hence, we obtain the following

THEOREM 7.3. *The axiom system $\mathcal{F}_2$ is consistent.*

We shall now show that the axiom system $\mathcal{F}_2$ is complete. To do this, we consider an arbitrary equation belonging to the set $\mathcal{O}_\omega$ and show that it is derivable within $\mathcal{F}_2$. Both sides of the given equation are regular expressions over some alphabet $I_r (r \geqq 1)$, because the given equation belongs to some set $\mathcal{O}_r$. From now on we assume that the given equation and thus also the number r are fixed.

Lemma 7.2 holds true also with the symbol $\vdash_1$ replaced by the symbol $\vdash_2$, the proof being exactly the same as in connection with $\mathcal{F}_1$. The replacement rule R1 and the results mentioned in Lemma 7.2 will be used without being explicitly referred to. In view of (1.1) and (1.2), we shall write catenations and sums of more than two regular expressions associatively and use the customary Σ-notation for sums. We shall also consider ordered pairs (X, Y) of regular expressions. Then by the sum $(X_1, Y_1)+(X_2, Y_2)$ is meant the ordered pair (X_1+X_2, Y_1+Y_2), and by the product $(X, Y)Z$ is meant the ordered pair (XZ, YZ). The notation $\vdash_2 (X_1, X_2) = (Y_1, Y_2)$ is used to mean that both $\vdash_2 X_1 = Y_1$ and $\vdash_2 X_2 = Y_2$.

The subsequent proof of the completeness of the axiom system $\mathcal{F}_2$ is based on two lemmas. Firstly, because of the rule R3, certain systems of equations possess a solution which is unique up to derivability within $\mathcal{F}_2$. This is shown in Lemma 7.6. Secondly, for any given valid equation, such a system of equations can be constructed. This is a consequence of Lemma 7.7.

First let us show that any substitution instance of (1.7)′ and (1.8)′ is derivable within $\mathcal{F}_2$. Let X be an arbitrary regular expression over I_r. By (1.8), $\vdash_2 \phi\phi = \phi$ and hence, by (1.9),

$$\vdash_2 X\phi\phi = X\phi, \quad \vdash_2 X\phi = (X\phi)\phi+\phi.$$

This implies, by R3, that

$$\vdash_2 X\phi = \phi\phi^*.$$

Therefore, by (1.8), we have

$$\vdash_2 X\phi = \phi. \tag{7.15}$$

Consequently,

$$\vdash_2 X = X+\phi = X+X\phi = X\phi+X.$$

Hence, by R3,

$$\vdash_2 X\phi^* = X. \tag{7.16}$$

LEMMA 7.6. *Assume that n is a natural number and*

$$\vdash_2 (X_i, Y_i) = \sum_{j=1}^{n} (X_j, Y_j) Z_{ij}+(R_i, R_i), \qquad i = 1, \ldots, n,$$

where none of the regular expressions Z_{ij} possesses e.w.p. Then

$$\vdash_2 X_i = Y_i, \quad for \quad i = 1, \ldots, n.$$

Lemma 7.6 is essentially due to Theorems 2.1 and 2.5. Clearly, the matrix M, where $(M)_{ij} = |Z_{ij}|$, does not possess e.w.p. By Theorem 2.1, the solution of the system $X = XM+R$, where $(R)_i = R_i$, is unique. According to the proof of Theorem 2.5, the solution is found using R3 and successive eliminations. By (1.1)–(1.9), all equations involved are derivable within $\mathcal{F}_2$. The verification of this fact is left to the reader.

DEFINITION. A regular expression X over the alphabet $I_r = \{x_1, \ldots, x_r\}$ is *equationally characterized* iff there is a finite number n of regular expressions $X_1, \ldots, X_n$ such that $X \equiv X_1$ and

$$\vdash_2 X_i = \sum_{j=1}^{r} X_{ij}x_j+\delta(X_i), \qquad i = 1, \ldots, n, \tag{7.17}$$

where $\delta(X_i) \equiv \phi$ or $\delta(X_i) \equiv \phi^*$ and, for each i and j, there is a k, $1 \leq k \leq n$, such that $X_{ij} \equiv X_k$.

Thus, a regular expression is equationally characterized iff it can be included in a finite set of regular expressions, each of which satisfies a derivable equation of the form (7.17). (Cf. the notion of a closed set of regular expressions introduced in Section I.3.) The next lemma is the most important tool in the completeness proof.

LEMMA 7.7. *Every regular expression over the alphabet I_r is equationally characterized.*

Proof. We follow the recursive definition of regular expressions. Using axioms (1.6)–(1.9), the following relations are obtained:

$$\vdash_2 \phi = \sum_{j=1}^{r} \phi x_j + \phi,$$

$$\vdash_2 x_i = \phi x_1 + \ldots + \phi^* x_i + \ldots + \phi x_r + \phi, \qquad i = 1, \ldots, r,$$

$$\vdash_2 \phi^* = \sum_{j=1}^{r} \phi x_j + \phi^*.$$

Thus, it may be concluded that the regular expressions ϕ and x_i, $i = 1, \ldots, r$, are equationally characterized. (For ϕ the corresponding set consists of ϕ alone, and for x_i it consists of x_i, ϕ and ϕ^*.)

Assume that the regular expressions X and Y are equationally characterized. This implies that there are regular expressions $X_1, \ldots, X_n$ with $X_1 \equiv X$ such that (7.17) holds. Furthermore, there are regular expressions $Y_1, \ldots, Y_m$ with $Y_1 \equiv Y$ such that

$$\vdash_2 Y_i = \sum_{j=1}^{r} Y_{ij} x_j + \delta(Y_i), \qquad i = 1, \ldots, m, \tag{7.18}$$

where $\delta(Y_i) \equiv \phi$ or $\delta(Y_i) \equiv \phi^*$ and, for each i and j, there is a k, $1 \leq k \leq m$, such that $Y_{ij} \equiv Y_k$. To complete the proof of Lemma 7.7, it suffices to show that the regular expressions $X+Y$, XY and X^* are equationally characterized.

We denote

$$\xi(u, v) \equiv X_u + Y_v \qquad (1 \leq u \leq n, \quad 1 \leq v \leq m).$$

Because we have

$$\vdash_2 \phi + \phi = \phi, \quad \vdash_2 \phi + \phi^* = \phi^* + \phi = \phi^*, \quad \vdash_2 \phi^* + \phi^* = \phi^*,$$

we obtain, using (7.17) and (7.18) (and the commutative and distributive laws),

$$\vdash_2 \xi(u, v) = \sum_{j=1}^{r} (X_{uj} + Y_{vj}) x_j + \delta(u, v),$$

where $\delta(u, v) \equiv \phi$ or $\delta(u, v) \equiv \phi^*$ and all of the regular expressions $X_{uj} + Y_{vj}$ are among the regular expressions ξ. Since $\xi(1, 1) \equiv X + Y$, this implies that $X + Y$ is equationally characterized.

Let us consider next regular expressions

$$\eta(u, v_1, \ldots, v_h) \equiv XY_u + X_{v_1} + \ldots + X_{v_h}, \tag{7.19}$$

where $1 \leq u \leq m$, $h \geq 0$ and $1 \leq v_1 < v_2 < \ldots < v_h \leq n$. (Obviously, the number of the regular expressions (7.19) equals $m \cdot 2^n$.) Assume first that $\delta(Y_u) \equiv \phi$. Then, by (1.3)–(1.6), (1.9) and (7.15), the following result may be obtained:

$$\vdash_2 \eta(u, v_1, \ldots, v_h) = \sum_{j=1}^{r} (XY_{uj} + X_{v_1 j} + \ldots + X_{v_h j}) x_j + \delta(\eta), \tag{7.20}$$

where

$$\delta(\eta) \equiv \phi \quad \text{or} \quad \delta(\eta) \equiv \phi^*. \tag{7.21}$$

If $\delta(Y_u) \equiv \phi^*$, then we obtain, by (1.3)–(1.6), (1.9) and (7.16), the result

$$\vdash_2 \eta(u, v_1, \ldots, v_h) = \sum_{j=1}^{r} (XY_{uj} + X_{1j} + X_{v_1 j} + \ldots + X_{v_h j}) x_j + \delta(\eta), \tag{7.22}$$

where (7.21) is satisfied. Using axioms (1.3) and (1.6), the coefficients of x_j on the right sides of (7.20) and (7.22) may be replaced by some regular expressions (7.19). Because $\eta(1) \equiv XY$, it is concluded that XY is equationally characterized.

We denote, finally,

$$\zeta(0) \equiv X^*, \quad \zeta(u_1, \ldots, u_h) \equiv X^*(X_{u_1} + \ldots + X_{u_h}), \tag{7.23}$$

where $h \geq 1$ and $1 \leq u_1 < u_2 < \ldots < u_h \leq n$. (Obviously, the number of the regular expressions (7.23) equals 2^n.) By (7.17),

$$\vdash_2 X = \sum_{j=1}^{r} X_{1j} x_j + \delta(X).$$

Hence, by (1.9) or (1.11),

$$\vdash_2 X^* = \left(\sum_{j=1}^{r} X_{1j} x_j \right)^*.$$

From this relation we obtain, by (1.10),

$$\vdash_2 \zeta(0) = \sum_{j=1}^{r} X^* X_{1j} x_j + \phi^*. \tag{7.24}$$

Assume that the regular expression $X_{u_1} + \ldots + X_{u_h}$ does not possess e.w.p. Then we obtain the relation

$$\vdash_2 \zeta(u_1, \ldots, u_h) = \sum_{j=1}^{r} X^* (X_{u_1 j} + \ldots + X_{u_h j}) x_j + \phi. \tag{7.25}$$

If the regular expression $X_{u_1} + \ldots + X_{u_h}$ possesses e.w.p., then the following relation is derived:

$$\vdash_2 \zeta(u_1, \ldots, u_h) = \sum_{j=1}^{r} X^* (X_{1j} + X_{u_1 j} + \ldots + X_{u_h j}) x_j + \phi^*. \tag{7.26}$$

Again, using axioms (1.3) and (1.6), the coefficients of x_j on the right sides of (7.24)–(7.26) may be replaced by some regular expressions (7.23). Hence, by (7.23)–(7.26), it is concluded that X^* is equationally characterized. This proves Lemma 7.7.

A suitable position has now been reached to establish the completeness of $\mathcal{F}_2$.

THEOREM 7.4. *The axiom system $\mathcal{F}_2$ is complete.*

Proof. Assume that $X_1 = Y_1$ is the given equation belonging to the set $\mathcal{O}_r$. By Lemma 7.7, both X_1 and Y_1 are equationally characterized. Let the corresponding regular expressions be $X_1, \ldots, X_n$ and $Y_1, \ldots, Y_m$ such that the conditions (7.17) and (7.18) are satisfied. Obviously in (7.17), (in (7.18)), $\delta(X_i) \equiv \phi^*$ ($\delta(Y_i) \equiv \phi^*$) iff X_i (Y_i) possesses e.w.p. Because $X_1 = Y_1$ belongs to the set $\mathcal{O}_r$, we conclude, by Theorem 7.3, that $\delta(X_1) \equiv \delta(Y_1)$. Similarly, we conclude that each of the equations $X_{1j} = Y_{1j}, j = 1, \ldots, r$, belongs to $\mathcal{O}_r$. Thus, we obtain the result

$$\vdash_2 (X_1, Y_1) = \sum_{j=1}^{r} (X_{1j}, Y_{1j}) x_j + (\delta(X_1), \delta(X_1)), \tag{7.27}$$

where the pairs (X_{1j}, Y_{1j}) are among the pairs (X_h, Y_k), $1 \leq h \leq n$,

$1 \leqq k \leqq m$, and the equations $X_{1j} = Y_{1j}$, $j = 1, \ldots, r$, belong to the set $\mathcal{O}_r$. Hence, we obtain relations of the form (7.27), where each of the pairs (X_{1j}, Y_{1j}), $j = 1, \ldots, r$, appears on the left side of the equation. If there are some pairs distinct from (X_1, Y_1) and (X_{1j}, Y_{1j}) as coefficients on the right sides of the equations in question, then again a relation of the form (7.27) is derived for these pairs. The procedure is carried on until no new pairs appear as coefficients, which will eventually happen because the number of all possible pairs is mn. Thus, we obtain a set of pairs

$$(X^{(1)}, Y^{(1)}), (X^{(2)}, Y^{(2)}), \ldots, (X^{(u)}, Y^{(u)}) \qquad (7.28)$$

such that $X^{(1)} \equiv X_1$, $Y^{(1)} \equiv Y_1$, $u \leqq mn$ and, for some Z_i,

$$\vdash_2 (X^{(i)}, Y^{(i)}) = \sum_{j=1}^{r} (X_j^{(i)}, Y_j^{(i)}) x_j + (Z_i, Z_i), \qquad i = 1, \ldots, u, \quad (7.29)$$

where all of the pairs $(X_j^{(i)}, Y_j^{(i)})$ are among the pairs (7.28). By (7.15), we may write (7.29) in the form

$$\vdash_2 (X^{(i)}, Y^{(i)}) = \sum_{j=1}^{u} (X^{(j)}, Y^{(j)}) Z_{ij} + (Z_i, Z_i), \qquad i = 1, \ldots, u,$$

where, for each i and j, either $Z_{ij} \equiv \phi$ or $Z_{ij} \equiv x_{j_1} + \ldots + x_{j_v}$, for some $v \geqq 1$ and $1 \leqq j_1 < \ldots < j_v \leqq r$. Thus none of the regular expressions Z_{ij} possesses e.w.p. This implies, by Lemma 7.6, that $\vdash_2 X^{(i)} = Y^{(i)}$, $i = 1, \ldots, u$. In particular, we have $\vdash_2 X_1 = Y_1$. Thus, Theorem 7.4 follows. □

The given completeness proofs are *constructive* in the sense that, for any equation $X = Y$ in the set $\mathcal{O}_\omega$, they give a method to construct its proofs in $\mathcal{F}_1$ and $\mathcal{F}_2$. One may even compute an upper bound, depending on the number of regular operators included in X and Y, for the length of the shortest proof of $X = Y$ (cf. Exercise 7.7). However, the general method is in most cases not economical, and various short cuts can be taken.

As an illustration, let us now establish the derivability within $\mathcal{F}_2$ of the equation $X_1 = Y_1$, where

$$X_1 \equiv (0 + 01 + 10)^*, \quad Y_1 \equiv (10 + 0^*01)^* 0^*.$$

(Thus, instead of x_1 and x_2, the letters of the alphabet I_2 are written 0 and 1.)

We use also the notations

$$X_2 \equiv X_1 + X_1 1 \equiv (0+01+10)^* + (0+01+10)^* 1$$

and

$$Y_2 \equiv Y_1 + (10+0^*01)^* 1 \equiv (10+0^*01)^* 0^* + (10+0^*01)^* 1.$$

By (1.10), the following result is obtained:

$$\vdash_2 X_1 = \phi^* + X_1(0+01+10) = \phi^* + X_2 0 + X_1 01.$$

Because we have

$$\vdash_2 X_1 = \phi^* + X_1 0 + X_1 01 + X_1 10 = \phi^* + X_1 0 + X_1 0 + X_1 01 + X_1 10$$
$$= X_1 0 + X_1,$$

we may write

$$\vdash_2 X_2 = X_1 + X_1 1 = \phi^* + X_2 0 + X_1 01 + X_1 1$$
$$= \phi^* + X_2 0 + (X_1 0 + X_1)1 = \phi^* + X_2 0 + X_1 1.$$

Using (7.16) and the relation $\vdash_2 0^* = \phi^* + 0^* 0$, we obtain

$$\vdash_2 Y_1 = (10+0^*01)^* + Y_1 0 = \phi^* + (10+0^*01)^* (10+0^*01) + Y_1 0$$
$$= \phi^* + Y_2 0 + Y_1 01$$

and

$$\vdash_2 Y_2 = Y_1 + (10+0^*01)^* 1 = \phi^* + Y_2 0 + Y_1 01 + (10+0^*01)^* 1$$
$$= \phi^* + Y_2 0 + (Y_1 0 + (10+0^*01)^*) 1 = \phi^* + Y_2 0 + Y_1 1.$$

Thus we have established the relations

$$\vdash_2 (X_1, Y_1) = (X_2, Y_2)0 + (X_1, Y_1) 01 + (\phi^*, \phi^*)$$

and

$$\vdash_2 (X_2, Y_2) = (X_2, Y_2)0 + (X_1, Y_1) 1 + (\phi^*, \phi^*).$$

Two successive applications of R3 give, finally, the result

$$\vdash_2 X_1 = Y_1 = 0^*(01+10^*0)^*.$$

The method used in this example is, in principle, the same as the one used in the completeness proof of $\mathcal{F}_2$. However, the proof has been simplified by allowing the word 01 to appear as a coefficient (cf. Exercise 7.8).

EXERCISE 7.1. Prove in detail the validity of the analysis and synthesis procedures described in Section I.3. (Note that Lemma 7.7 remains valid if the definition of equational characterization is modified in such a way that the coefficients X_{ij} are on the right.)

EXERCISE 7.2. Is it necessary to assume in the definition of η and ζ in the proof of Lemma 7.7 that $u_1 < u_2 < \ldots < u_h$ and $v_1 < v_2 < \ldots < v_h$?

EXERCISE 7.3. Prove the consistency and completeness of the axiom system $\mathcal{F}_2'$, obtained from $\mathcal{F}_2$ by reversing the order of factors in products appearing in (1.7), (1.8), (1.10) and R3.

EXERCISE 7.4. Omit the symbol ϕ from regular expressions (cf. Exercise 2.3). Prove that a complete axiomatization for this restricted case consists of the axioms (1.1)–(1.6) and

$$\alpha^* = \alpha^*\alpha + \alpha \tag{1.10}'$$

and of the rules R1 and R3′: From the equation $X = XY + Z$ one may infer the equation $X = ZY^* + Z$. Furthermore, prove the independence of each of the axioms and rules. (Cf. Salomaa (1966, 3).)

EXERCISE 7.5. Let X and Y be regular expressions over I_r and let $U(k)$ be the set of words over I_r with length less than or equal to k. Define $C(X, Y) = 2^{s(X, Y)} + 1$, where $s(X, Y)$ is the number of (nonempty) letters occurring in the regular expressions X and Y, each letter being counted as many times as it occurs.

Prove that the equation $X = Y$ belongs to the set V_r iff

$$|X| \cap U(C(X, Y)) = |Y| \cap U(C(X, Y)).$$

Using this fact, construct another consistent and complete axiom system for valid equations between regular expressions.

EXERCISE 7.6. Introduce the notion of a right derivative (cf. Problem II.3.1) and of a two-sided derivative for languages. State Lemma 7.7 in terms of right derivatives. Prove formulas to the effect that left (right) derivatives commute with Boolean operators. Study interconnections between various types of derivatives. (Cf. the work of Brzozowski (1964) and Huzino (1966, 1967).)

EXERCISE 7.7. Define the *length* of a proof to be the number of equations occurring in the proof. Determine an upper bound for the length of the shortest proof in $\mathcal{F}_1$ (in $\mathcal{F}_2$) of an equation $X = Y$.

EXERCISE 7.8. In the proof of Theorem 7.4, nothing is assumed of the remainder (Z_i, Z_i) in (7.29). Using this fact, introduce modifications for the notion of equational characterization such that the proof of Theorem 7.4 remains valid.

EXERCISE 7.9. How is the choice of k determined in the proof of Lemma 7.4?

EXERCISE 7.10. Show that if the following substitution rule is added, then also all equations in $\mathcal{S}_\omega (= \mathcal{S}_2)$ are derivable both in $\mathcal{F}_1$ and $\mathcal{F}_2$: the letters in an equation may be substituted by letters of A_ω. (This solves the problem proposed by Büchi in *Math. Reviews* (1966, 7411).) Can you conclude that also all equations in $\mathcal{S}_1$ are derivable?

PROBLEM 7.1. Study the independence of the axioms and rules both in $\mathcal{F}_1$ and in $\mathcal{F}_2$. Study also whether or not R3 can be weakened, for instance, to the following form: If Y does not possess e.w.p. and $X = XY+\phi^*$, then $X = Y^*$.

§ 8. Operators preserving regularity

The notion of a regular expression can be extended to include operators other than union, catenation and catenation closure. (This was done already in Section I.3.) Many of these additional operators can also be formally characterized. In this section we shall show how complement and intersection can be added to the axiom system $\mathcal{F}_2$. Regular expressions not involving complements and intersections are referred to as *restricted* regular expressions.

The following additions are made to the definition of the empty word property (e.w.p.), presented in Section 4:

(iv) $X \equiv (Y \cap Z)$, where both Y and Z possess e.w.p.

(v) $X \equiv \sim(Y)$, where Y does not possess e.w.p.

We denote by $\mathcal{V}'_r$, $r = 1, 2, \ldots$, the set of all valid equations between regular expressions over the alphabet I_r. Thus, an equation $X = Y$ belongs to the set $\mathcal{V}'_r$ iff X and Y are regular expressions (possibly involving complements and intersections) over I_r and denote the same language.

Axiom systems $\mathcal{F}(r)$, $r = 1, 2, \ldots$, are now introduced. The *axioms* in the system $\mathcal{F}(r)$ are (1.1)–(1.11) (without including (1.7)′ and (1.8)′) and the following:

$$\alpha \cap \beta = \sim ((\sim \alpha) + (\sim \beta)), \tag{8.1}$$

$$\sim (\alpha_1 x_1 + \ldots + \alpha_r x_r) = (\sim \alpha_1) x_1 + \ldots + (\sim \alpha_r) x_r + \phi^*, \tag{8.2}$$

$$\sim (\alpha_1 x_1 + \ldots + \alpha_r x_r + \phi^*) = (\sim \alpha_1) x_1 + \ldots + (\sim \alpha_r) x_r. \tag{8.3}$$

The *rules of inference* are R1 and R3.

Derivability is defined as in the previous section. (Substitution instances of (8.1)–(8.3) are obtained whenever $\alpha, \beta, \alpha_1, \ldots, \alpha_r$ are substituted by some regular expressions over I_r.) The fact that an equation $X = Y$ is derivable within $\mathcal{F}(r)$ is denoted by $\vdash_{(r)} X = Y$. The axiom system $\mathcal{F}(r)$ is termed *consistent* iff all derivable equations belong to the set $\mathcal{O}'_r$. It is termed *complete* iff all equations belonging to the set $\mathcal{O}'_r$ are derivable.

Note that the axioms, as well as the notions of consistency and completeness, depend on r and, thus, an infinite sequence of axiom systems is obtained. (Cf. Exercise 8.4.)

THEOREM 8.1. *Each of the axiom systems* $\mathcal{F}(r)$, $r = 1, 2, \ldots$, *is consistent and complete.*

Proof. Obviously, all substitution instances of (8.1)–(8.3) belong to the set $\mathcal{O}'_r$. (Cf. also Exercise 7.6.) Thus, by Theorem 7.3, the consistency of $\mathcal{F}(r)$, $r = 1, 2, \ldots$, follows.

To prove the completeness of an arbitrary but fixed $\mathcal{F}(r)$, we assume that $Y = Z$ is an equation belonging to the set $\mathcal{O}'_r$. By (8.1), we may assume that the regular expressions Y and Z do not involve intersections. To establish the relation

$$\vdash_{(r)} Y = Z, \tag{8.4}$$

we use the same argument as in the completeness proof of $\mathcal{F}_2$ except that it has to be shown that the property of being equationally characterized is preserved under the forming of complements. Let X_1 be a regular expression which is equationally characterized and let (7.17), where the symbol $\vdash_2$ is replaced by the symbol $\vdash_{(r)}$, be the corresponding equations. By (8.2) and (8.3), we obtain the relations

$$\vdash_{(r)} \sim X_i = \sum_{j=1}^{r} (\sim X_{ij})\, x_j + \delta(\sim X_i), \qquad i = 1, \ldots, n,$$

where $\delta(\sim X_i) \equiv \phi$ for $\delta(X_i) \equiv \phi^*$, and $\delta(\sim X_i) \equiv \phi^*$ for $\delta(X_i) \equiv \phi$. This implies that $\sim X_1$ is equationally characterized. Hence, we may conclude by the same argument as in the completeness proof of $\mathcal{F}_2$ that (8.4) holds. $\square$

All Boolean properties of complement and intersection follow by the given axioms and rules. (Cf. also Exercise 8.2.) We shall now show how any regular expression can be reduced to a restricted regular expression.

THEOREM 8.2. *For any regular expression X_1 over the alphabet I_r, there is a restricted regular expression Y_1 over I_r such that $\vdash_{(r)} X_1 = Y_1$.*

Proof. The given regular expression X_1 is equationally characterized. Let (7.17), where the symbol $\vdash_2$ is replaced by the symbol $\vdash_{(r)}$, be the corresponding equations. These equations can be written in the form

$$\vdash_{(r)} X_i = \sum_{j=1}^{n} X_j Z_{ij} + \delta(X_i), \qquad i = 1, \ldots, n,$$

where, for each i and j, either $Z_{ij} \equiv \phi$ or $Z_{ij} \equiv x_{j_1} + \ldots + x_{j_v}$, for some $v \geqq 1$ and $1 \leqq j_1 < \ldots < j_v \leqq r$. Theorem 8.2 now follows, by Theorems 2.1 and 2.5, because the equations involved are derivable within $\mathcal{F}(r)$. The detailed verification of this fact is left to the reader.

The algorithm presented for eliminating complements from regular expressions is, finally, illustrated by an example. Let

$$X \equiv \sim ((x_1 x_2 + x_2)^*).$$

Denoting

$$Y \equiv (x_1 x_2 + x_2)^*, \quad Z \equiv (x_1 x_2 + x_2)^* (x_1 + \phi^*),$$

we obtain

$$\vdash_{(2)} Y = \phi x_1 + Z x_2 + \phi^*, \quad \vdash_{(2)} Z = Y x_1 + Y = Y x_1 + Z x_2 + \phi^*.$$

Hence, by (8.3),

$$\vdash_{(2)} X = (\sim \phi)\, x_1 + (\sim Z)\, x_2, \quad \vdash_{(2)} \sim Z = X x_1 + (\sim Z)\, x_2.$$

An application of R3, replacement and another application of R3 give
the results

$$\vdash_{(2)} \sim Z = Xx_1x_2{}^*,$$

$$\vdash_{(2)} X = (\sim \phi) x_1 + Xx_1x_2^*x_2,$$

$$\vdash_{(2)} X = (\sim \phi) x_1(x_1x_2^*x_2)^* = (x_1+x_2)^* x_1(x_1x_2^*x_2)^*.$$

EXERCISE 8.1. Add intersection and complement to the axiom system $\mathcal{F}_1$ of Section 7.

EXERCISE 8.2. Prove the equation $\sim \sim x_1 = x_1$ in the axiom system $\mathcal{F}(r)$.

EXERCISE 8.3. How can ϕ be eliminated when intersection and complement are available?

EXERCISE 8.4. Add intersection and complement to the axiom system $\mathcal{F}_2$ without using axioms (like (8.2) and (8.3)) which depend on the number of letters in the alphabet. Establish then the result corresponding to the one presented in Exercise 7.10. (Cf. Tixier (1967).)

EXERCISE 8.5. Investigate how other regularity preserving operators can be added to $\mathcal{F}_2$. In particular, consider the operators a (abbreviation), t (trace), mi (mirror image), ∂ (left derivative), ir (initial restriction), ie (initial extension). For definitions, cf. Exercises 5.2, I.1.2 and I.2.9. Cf. also Hartmanis and Stearns (1963).

PROBLEM 8.1. Define a (possibly unique) "canonical form" for regular expressions such that all regular expressions can be reduced to this form. Cf. Exercise 3.1 and Paz and Peleg (1965, 1).

CHAPTER IV

FORMAL LANGUAGES AND
GENERALIZED AUTOMATA

So FAR we have considered only rather restricted classes of languages, namely, regular and stochastic languages. We have also studied in detail the devices capable of recognizing these languages. In this chapter we shall introduce a hierarchy of languages, consisting of four classes. The lowest class in this hierarchy is the class of regular languages, and each class properly includes all lower classes. The hierarchy is introduced by defining a sequence of four classes of *generation* devices, each of which is more restricted than the previous one. To each class L in this hierarchy of languages there corresponds a class $\mathcal{A}(L)$ of *recognition* devices, referred to as automata, such that a language belongs to L iff it is represented in some automaton belonging to $\mathcal{A}(L)$. Thus we obtain also a hierarchy of automata.

§ 1. Hierarchy of languages

In Section I.1, a language over an alphabet I was defined to be a subset of the set $W(I)$. As regards finite languages, one may specify any language simply by listing all words in the language. As regards infinite languages, one has to give some rules which yield all the words in the language to be specified. This was done for regular languages in Section I.1, where a regular language was defined by a regular expression denoting the language. We shall now introduce the notion of a *grammar* which enables us to specify infinite languages in a much larger class than the class of regular languages.

We shall first take an example. Consider the language

$$L = \{x^n y^n \,|\, n = 1, 2, \ldots\} \tag{1.1}$$

over the alphabet $\{x, y\}$. It may be stated that

(i) xy is a word in L;
(ii) if X is a word in L, then so is xXy;
(iii) no string of letters is a word in L, unless its being so follows from a finite number of applications of (i) and (ii).

Conditions (i) and (ii) are expressed symbolically as follows:

$$X \to xy, \quad X \to xXy. \tag{1.2}$$

Formulas of the form (1.2) are referred to as *productions*. The chain

$$X \Rightarrow xXy \Rightarrow xxXyy \Rightarrow xxxXyyy \Rightarrow xxxxyyyy \tag{1.3}$$

is referred to as a *derivation* of the word x^4y^4 from the initial symbol X. These notions will now be made explicit.

DEFINITION. A *grammar* is an ordered quadruple $G = (I_N, I_T, X_0, F)$, where I_N and I_T are finite disjoint alphabets, X_0 is an element of I_N, and F is a finite set of ordered pairs (P, Q) such that Q is a word over the alphabet $I = I_N \cup I_T$ and P is a non-empty word over I containing at least one letter of I_N.

The elements of I_N are referred to as *non-terminals* (or *non-terminal letters*) and those of I_T as *terminals* (or *terminal letters*). X_0 is called the *initial* symbol or letter. Elements (P, Q) of F are called *productions* (or *rewriting rules*) and are written $P \to Q$.

For example,

$$(\{X\}, \{x, y\}, X, \{X \to xy, X \to xXy\}) \tag{1.4}$$

is a grammar, whereas

$$(\{X\}, \{x, y\}, X, \{X \to xy, X \to xXy, xy \to yx\})$$

is not a grammar because the left side of the last production does not contain any non-terminal.

DEFINITION. Let $G = (I_N, I_T, X_0, F)$ be a grammar, $I = I_N \cup I_T$, and P and Q words over I. Then P *directly generates* Q *according to* G, in symbols, $P \underset{G}{\Rightarrow} Q$ (or shortly $P \Rightarrow Q$ when G is understood) iff there are words P', Q', R_1, R_2 over I such that $P = R_1P'R_2$, $Q = R_1Q'R_2$ and $P' \to Q'$ is in F. P *generates* Q *according to* G, in symbols, $P \underset{G}{\overset{*}{\Rightarrow}} Q$

(or shortly $P \overset{*}{\Rightarrow} Q$) iff there is a finite sequence of words over I

$$P_0, P_1, \ldots, P_k, \quad k \geqq 0, \tag{1.5}$$

such that $P = P_0$, $Q = P_k$ and, for all $i = 0, \ldots, k-1$, P_i directly generates P_{i+1} according to G. The sequence (1.5) is said to be a *derivation* of P_k from P_0 (according to G) and is denoted by

$$P_0 \Rightarrow P_1 \Rightarrow \ldots \Rightarrow P_k.$$

The number k is referred to as the *length* of the derivation.

For example, (1.3) is a derivation of $x^4 y^4$ from X according to the grammar (1.4). Note that, by choosing $k = 0$, we get the result that P generates P.

DEFINITION. If $G = (I_N, I_T, X_0, F)$ is a grammar, then the language over I_T

$$L(G) = \{P \,|\, P \in W(I_T),\ X_0 \overset{*}{\underset{G}{\Rightarrow}} P\}$$

is said to be *generated* by G. Two grammars are termed *equivalent* iff they generate the same language.

Thus, the language $L(G)$ generated by a grammar $G = (I_N, I_T, X_0, F)$ consists of those words over the terminal alphabet I_T which are generated by the initial symbol X_0 according to G. Some examples will now be presented.

EXAMPLE 1. (1.1) is the language generated by the grammar (1.4).

EXAMPLE 2. The grammar $(\{X\}, I_T, X, \{X \to P_1, \ldots, X \to P_n\})$, where $P_1, \ldots, P_n$ are words over I_T, generates the finite language

$$\{P_1, \ldots, P_n\}.$$

EXAMPLE 3. The grammar

$$G = (\{X_0, X_1\}, \{x\}, X_0, \{X_0 \to \lambda, X_0 \to x^3, X_0 \to x^5, X_0 \to x^2 X_1 x^3,$$
$$X_1 \to \lambda, X_1 \to {}^{\mathfrak{r}}_{\mathfrak{t}} x^2 X_1\}) \tag{1.6}$$

generates the regular language

$$L(G) = |\phi^* + x^3 + x^5 (x^2)^*|.$$

The production $X_0 \to x^5$ is superfluous in the sense that $L(G)$ remains unchanged if it is removed.

EXAMPLE 4. For $n \geq 1$, the grammar

$$G_n = (\{X\}, \{x_1, \ldots, x_n, y_1, \ldots, y_n\}, X, \{X \to \lambda, X \to Xx_1Xy_1X,$$
$$\ldots, X \to Xx_nXy_nX\})$$

generates the so-called *Dyck language*. The Dyck language over

$$\{x_1, \ldots, x_n, y_1, \ldots, y_n\}$$

consists of all words P which can be reduced to λ by successively deleting from P subwords of the form x_iy_i. For instance, let $n = 1$ and regard x_1 and y_1 as parentheses: $x_1 = ($, $y_1 =)$. Then the Dyck language $L(G_1)$ consists of all sequences of correctly nested parentheses. Thus, $( ) (( ) ( )) \in L(G_1)$ but $( )) (( ) \notin L(G_1)$.

EXAMPLE 5. Define a *well formed formula* (w.f.f.) of the *propositional calculus* recursively as follows:

   (i) Each variable alone is a w.f.f., where a variable means any member of the infinite sequence $x1, x11, x111, \ldots$.

   (ii) If α and β are w.f.f.'s, then so are $A\alpha\beta$, $K\alpha\beta$ and $N\alpha$.

   (iii) Nothing else is a w.f.f., unless its being so follows from a finite number of applications of (i) and (ii).

Then the following grammar generates the language consisting of all well formed formulas:

$$G = (\{X\}, \{x, 1, A, K, N\}, X, \{X \to X1, X \to x1, X \to AXX,$$
$$X \to KXX, X \to NX\}).$$

EXAMPLE 6. Regular expressions over the alphabet $I_r = \{x_1, \ldots, x_r\}$ are themselves words over the alphabet

$$I_T = I_r \cup \{+, {}^*, \phi, (,)\}.$$

The language consisting of regular expressions over I_r is generated by the grammar

$$G = (\{X\}, I_T, X, \{X \to x_1, \ldots, X \to x_r, X \to \phi, X \to (X+X),$$
$$X \to (XX), X \to X^*\}).$$

Some derivations may be illustrated by "generation trees". (Cf. Exercise 1.7.) In Fig. 20, the derivation of x^9 from X_0 according to the grammar (1.6) is given. The word x^9 is obtained by catenating the words in the top nodes: $x^2x^2x^2\lambda x^3 = x^9$.

In the following definition, grammars are classified by imposing certain restrictions on the set of productions.

DEFINITION. For $i = 0, 1, 2, 3$, a grammar $G = (I_N, I_T, X_0, F)$ is of the *type i* iff the restrictions (i) on F, as given below, are satisfied.

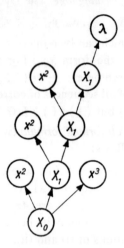

FIG. 20.

(0) No restrictions.

(1) Each production in F is either of the form $Q_1 X Q_2 \to Q_1 P Q_2$, where Q_1 and Q_2 are (possibly empty) words over the alphabet $I_N \cup I_T$, $X \in I_N$ and P is a *non-empty* word over $I_N \cup I_T$, or of the form $X \to \lambda$, where $X \in I_N$ does not occur on the right side of any production in F.

(2) Each production in F is of the form $X \to P$, where $X \in I_N$ and P is a (possibly empty) word over $I_N \cup I_T$.

(3) Each production in F is either of the form $X \to PY$ or of the form $X \to P$, where $X, Y \in I_N$ and P is a word over I_T.

For $i = 0, 1, 2, 3$, a *language* is of the *type i* iff it is generated by a grammar of the type i. The family of all languages of the type i is denoted by $\mathcal{L}_i$.

Thus, according to grammars of the type 1, a single non-terminal X may be replaced by a word P, but only in the context $Q_1 X Q_2$. Therefore, the type 1 languages are called *context-sensitive languages*. According to grammars of the type 2, a non-terminal X may be replaced by a word P, no matter what the letters adjacent to X are, i.e. independently of the context. Therefore, the type 2 languages are called *context-free languages*. Sometimes also type 1 and type 2 grammars are called context-sensitive and context-free, respectively.

It is obvious by the definition that all grammars are of the type 0 and, furthermore, that every grammar of the type 3 is also of the type 2. Consequently, the family $\mathscr{L}_0$ includes the families $\mathscr{L}_1$, $\mathscr{L}_2$, $\mathscr{L}_3$, and the family $\mathscr{L}_2$ includes the family $\mathscr{L}_3$. It will be seen that

$$\mathscr{L}_0 \supset \mathscr{L}_1 \supset \mathscr{L}_2 \supset \mathscr{L}_3,$$

where every inclusion is proper.

Although a language is generated by a grammar of the type i, it may still be also of a type $j > i$, because there may be an equivalent grammar of the type j. For instance, consider the language L generated by the grammar (1.6). Although (1.6) is of the type 2, L is of the type 3 because it is also generated by the following type 3 grammar:

$$(\{X_0, X_1\}, \{x\}, X_0, \{X_0 \to \lambda, X_0 \to x^3, X_0 \to x^5X_1, X_1 \to \lambda, X_1 \to x^2X_1\}).$$

In the next theorem, some common closure properties of the families $\mathscr{L}_i$ will be presented.

THEOREM 1.1. *Each of the families $\mathscr{L}_i$, $i = 0, 1, 2, 3$, contains all finite languages and is closed under the operations sum, catenation and catenation closure.*

Proof. The first part of the theorem follows because any non-empty finite language is generated by the grammar of Example 2 (which is of any type) and the empty language L_ϕ is generated, for instance, by a grammar with no terminals on the right sides of the productions.

Let i be arbitrary, $0 \leq i \leq 3$, and let L_1 and L_2 be languages generated by the grammars

$$G_1 = (I_{N_1}, I_{T_1}, X_1, F_1) \quad \text{and} \quad G_2 = (I_{N_2}, I_{T_2}, X_2, F_2)$$

of the type i. Without loss of generality, we may assume that the alphabets I_{N_1} and I_{N_2} are disjoint (because this situation can always be reached by renaming the non-terminals of G_2). We may also assume that if $i = 1$ then neither F_1 nor F_2 contains productions of the form $X \to \lambda$. For if this is originally the case then we remove these productions and, whenever necessary, add a new initial symbol Y_0 and the production $Y_0 \to \lambda$ to the final grammar.

The language $L_1 + L_2$ is generated by the type i grammar

$$(I_N, I_{T_1} \cup I_{T_2}, Y, F_1 \cup F_2 \cup \{Y \to X_1, Y \to X_2\}),$$

where

$$I_N = I_{N_1} \cup I_{N_2} \cup \{Y\} \text{ and } Y \notin I_{N_1} \cup I_{N_2}. \tag{1.7}$$

Therefore, the family $\mathcal{L}_i$ is closed under sum.

In the remaining part of the proof, we shall consider different values of i separately.

Assume first that $i = 2$. Then the language $L_1 L_2$ is generated by the type 2 grammar

$$(I_N, I_{T_1} \cup I_{T_2}, Y, F_1 \cup F_2 \cup \{Y \to X_1 X_2\}) \tag{1.8}$$

such that (1.7) is satisfied. The language L_1^* is generated by the type 2 grammar

$$(I_{N_1} \cup \{Y\}, I_{T_1}, Y, F_1 \cup \{Y \to \lambda, Y \to Y X_1\}),$$

where $Y \notin I_{N_1}$.

Assume next that $i = 3$. Replace in F_1 each production of the form

$$X \to P \, (X \in I_{N_1}, P \in W(I_{T_1})) \tag{1.9}$$

by the production $X \to PX_2$. Denote the resulting set of productions by F'. Then the type 3 grammar

$$(I_{N_1} \cup I_{N_2}, I_{T_1} \cup I_{T_2}, X_1, F_2 \cup F')$$

generates the language $L_1 L_2$. Replace in F_1 each production of the form (1.9) by the production $X \to PX_1$, and denote the resulting set by F''. The type 3 grammar

$$(I_{N_1} \cup \{Y\}, I_{T_1}, Y, \{Y \to \lambda, Y \to X_1\} \cup F_1 \cup F''),$$

where $Y \notin I_{N_1}$, generates the language L_1^*. Hence, we have shown that the families $\mathcal{L}_2$ and $\mathcal{L}_3$ are closed under catenation and catenation closure.

Finally, assume that $i = 0$ or $i = 1$. In this case, we modify the proof given for the case $i = 2$ in order to avoid "illegitimate" contexts, where the productions in F_1 or F_2 could be applied. We introduce four grammars

$$G_\mu^{(v)} = \left(I_{N_\mu}^{(v)}, I_{T_\mu}^{(v)}, X_\mu^{(v)}, F_\mu^{(v)}\right) \qquad (\mu, v = 1, 2),$$

where $I_{N_\mu}^{(v)}$ $\left(I_{T_\mu}^{(v)}\right)$ is obtained from $I_{N_\mu}(I_{T_\mu})$ by replacing each letter ξ by the letter $\xi^{(v)}$, and $F_\mu^{(v)}$ is obtained from F_μ by replacing each letter $\xi \in I_{N_\mu} \cup I_{T_\mu}$ appearing in some production by the letter $\xi^{(v)}$. It is easy to verify that the language $L_1 L_2$ is generated by the type i grammar

$$\left(\bar{I}_N, I_{T_1} \cup I_{T_2}, Y, F_1^{(1)} \cup F_2^{(2)} \cup \{Y \to X_1^{(1)} X_2^{(2)}\} \cup F^{(1)}\right),$$

where

$$\bar{I}_N = I_{N_1}^{(1)} \cup I_{N_2}^{(2)} \cup I_{T_1}^{(1)} \cup I_{T_2}^{(2)} \cup \{Y\},$$

and $F^{(1)}$ consists of all productions of the form $x^{(1)} \to x$ and $x^{(2)} \to x$, for $x \in I_{T_1} \cup I_{T_2}$. The language L_1^* is generated by the type i grammar

$$\left(\bar{\bar{I}}_N, I_{T_1}, Y, F_1^{(1)} \cup F_1^{(2)} \cup F^{(1)} \cup F^{(2)}\right),$$

where

$$\bar{\bar{I}}_N = I_{N_1}^{(1)} \cup I_{N_1}^{(2)} \cup I_{T_1}^{(1)} \cup I_{T_1}^{(2)} \cup \{Y, Y_1\}$$

and $F^{(2)}$ consists of the productions

$$Y \to \lambda, \; Y \to X_1^{(1)}, \; Y \to Y_1, \; Y_1 \to X_1^{(1)} X_1^{(2)}, \; Y \to Y_1 X_1^{(1)}, \; Y \to Y_1 X_1^{(1)} X_1^{(2)}.$$

(Considering L_1^*, we restrict $F^{(1)}$ to the terminals in I_{T_1} and assume, by Exercise 1.3, that $\lambda \notin L_1$ if $i=0$.) This implies that the families $\mathcal{L}_0$ and $\mathcal{L}_1$ are closed under catenation and catenation closure. □

We shall now establish a result concerning type 1 languages which is not true of type 0 languages.

THEOREM 1.2. *There is an algorithm of deciding whether or not a word P belongs to the language $L(G)$ generated by a grammar $G = (I_N, I_T, X_0, F)$ of the type* 1.

Proof. By the definition of type 1 grammars, it is obvious that $\lambda \in L(G)$ iff the production $X_0 \to \lambda$ belongs to F. Thus, we may assume that $P \neq \lambda$ and $P \in W(I_T)$. Consider sequences of the form

$$P_0 = X_0, P_1, \ldots, P_{n-1}, P_n = P, \tag{1.10}$$

where $n \geqq 1$, P_i are distinct words over $I_N \cup I_T$ and, for $0 \leqq i \leqq n-1$, $\lg(P_i) \leqq \lg(P_{i+1})$. Clearly, the number of such sequences is finite. It is also obvious that $P \in L(G)$ iff, for some sequence (1.10),

$$X_0 = P_0 \Rightarrow P_1 \Rightarrow \ldots \Rightarrow P_{n-1} \Rightarrow P_n = P. \qquad (1.11)$$

Thus it suffices to check, for each of the finitely many sequences (1.10), whether or not (1.11) is satisfied. $\square$

The essential point in the proof is that, for type 1 grammars, we may assume that the derivation (1.11) satisfies the condition $\lg(P_i) \leqq \lg(P_{i+1})$, $i = 0, \ldots, n-1$.

EXERCISE 1.1. Construct a type 3 grammar generating the language $W(I)$, where I is a given finite alphabet.

EXERCISE 1.2. Prove that if $P_i \overset{*}{\Rightarrow} Q_i$ ($i = 1, \ldots, n$), then $P_1 \ldots P_n \overset{*}{\Rightarrow} Q_1 \ldots Q_n$.

EXERCISE 1.3. Given a type 0 grammar G, construct a type 0 grammar generating the language $L(G) - \{\lambda\}$.

EXERCISE 1.4 (Jones, 1967, 1). A word P over the alphabet

$$I(n) = \{x_1, \ldots, x_n, y_1, \ldots, y_n\}$$

is termed *balanced* iff, for $i = 1, \ldots, n$, the number of occurrences of x_i in P equals the number of occurrences of y_i in P. Prove that a word P over $I(n)$ belongs to the Dyck language over $I(n)$ iff each of the following conditions is satisfied:

(i) P is balanced.
(ii) If $P = Q_1 x_i Q_2$, $1 \leqq i \leqq n$, then there is a balanced initial subword of $x_i Q_2$.
(iii) If $P = Q_1 y_i Q_2$, $1 \leqq i \leqq n$, then there is a balanced final subword of $Q_1 y_i$.

EXERCISE 1.5. Construct an algorithm for deciding whether or not the empty word belongs to a given context-free language.

EXERCISE 1.6. Prove that the family of type 3 languages remains unaltered if the definition of type 3 grammars is modified in such a way that productions of the form $X \rightarrow YP$ are allowed instead of productions of the form $X \rightarrow PY$.

EXERCISE 1.7. Give a formal definition of the notion of a generation tree for a context-free grammar.

EXERCISE 1.8. Show by an example that the grammar (1.8) does not always generate the language $L_1 L_2$ if L_1 and L_2 are context-sensitive languages. (This is the reason why a modified approach was needed for the cases $i = 0$ and $i = 1$ in the proof of Theorem 1.1.)

EXERCISE 1.9. (For those familiar with logic.) Construct a grammar generating the language consisting of all (i) well-formed formulas, (ii) theorems in a given formal system. (Begin with some simple example.) What can you say of the type of the grammar in the general case?

EXERCISE 1.10. Let L be the language over the alphabet

$$I_r \cup \{+, *, \phi, (,), = \}$$

consisting of all valid equations between regular expressions over the alphabet I_r. Construct a grammar generating L. (Consider first the easier case, where ϕ is removed. Cf. Exercise III.7.4.)

EXERCISE 1.11. Determine the types of the languages considered in Examples 4–6 above.

§ 2. Type 3 languages

We shall now study properties of the different families $\mathcal{L}_i$. It turns out that the family $\mathcal{L}_3$ consists of all regular languages.

THEOREM 2.1. *A language is of the type 3 iff it is regular.*

Proof. By Theorem 1.1, if a language is regular, then it is of the type 3. Conversely, assume that $G = (I_N, I_T, X_0, F)$ is a type 3 grammar, where $I_N = \{X_0, \ldots, X_m\}$. Consider productions of the form

$$X_i \to P X_j \quad (0 \leq i, j \leq m), \quad P \in W(I_T),$$

occurring in F. Let $P_1, \ldots, P_n$ be all the words over I_T (including the empty word) which occur in these productions. Define a finite non-deterministic automaton $\mathbf{NA} = (I_N, \{X_0\}, f)$ over the alphabet $\{P_1, \ldots, P_n\}$ by the condition: $f(X_i, P_k)$ equals the set of those X_j's for which there is a production $X_i \to P_k X_j$ in F (where $0 \leq i, j \leq m$ and $1 \leq k \leq n$). Then

$$L(\mathbf{NA}, \{X_i\}) = \{P \mid X_0 \overset{*}{\underset{G}{\Rightarrow}} P X_i\}, \quad 0 \leq i \leq m. \tag{2.1}$$

Furthermore,

$$L(G) = \sum L(\mathbf{NA}, \{X_i\}) \, Q_j, \qquad (2.2)$$

where the sum is taken over all the (finitely many) pairs (i, j) such that the production $X_i \rightarrow Q_j$, $Q_j \in W(I_T)$, is in F. By Theorems II.1.1 and I.2.4, each of the languages (2.1) is regular over the alphabet $\{P_1, \ldots, P_n\}$. Because $P_1, \ldots, P_n$ are words over I_T, we conclude that the languages (2.1) are regular over I_T. Hence, by (2.2), $L(G)$ is regular. $\square$

The following theorem is an immediate corollary of Theorems 2.1 and I.2.6.

THEOREM 2.2. *The intersection of two type 3 languages is of the type 3. The complement of a type 3 language is of the type 3. Hence, the type 3 languages over a given alphabet form a Boolean algebra of sets.*

Because, by Theorems II.1.1 and I.2.2, a regular expression denoting the language (2.2) can be constructed, we obtain the following results (using Theorems I.2.5 and I.2.6, and the constructions of Theorem 1.1).

THEOREM 2.3. *There is an algorithm of deciding whether or not the languages generated by two type 3 grammars are equal. There is an algorithm of constructing a grammar which generates the intersection of the languages generated by two type 3 grammars, and also an algorithm of constructing a grammar which generates the complement of the language generated by a type 3 grammar.*

Finally, note that a language L_1 is contained in a language L_2 iff $L_1 + L_2 = L_2$. Furthermore, a grammar generating the union of two given languages can be constructed as in the proof of Theorem 1.1. This yields the following

THEOREM 2.4. *There is an algorithm of deciding whether or not a type 3 language is contained in another type 3 language.*

We shall now introduce another operation for languages.

DEFINITION. Let $L(x_1, \ldots, x_r)$, $L_1(x_1, \ldots, x_r)$, $\ldots$, $L_r(x_1, \ldots, x_r)$ be languages over the alphabet $I_r = \{x_1, \ldots, x_r\}$. Define a mapping φ of the set $W(I_r)$ into the set of subsets of $W(I_r)$ as follows:

$$\varphi(\lambda) = \{\lambda\},$$
$$\varphi(x_i) = L_i, \quad i = 1, \ldots, r,$$
$$\varphi(PQ) = \varphi(P)\varphi(Q), \quad \text{for} \quad P, Q \in W(I_r).$$

Then the language

$$\varphi(L) = \{Q \mid Q \in \varphi(P),\ P \in L\}$$

is obtained from the languages $L, L_1, \ldots, L_r$ by *substitution*. We denote

$$\varphi(L) = L(L_1, \ldots, L_r).$$

Thus, substitution is an $(r+1)$-ary operation for the languages over the alphabet I_r. If $L, L_1, \ldots, L_r$ are languages over I_r denoted by the regular expressions $\alpha, \alpha_1, \ldots, \alpha_r$, respectively, then $\varphi(L)$ is denoted by the regular expression obtained from α by replacing each letter x_i by the regular expression α_i. Hence, we have established the subsequent result.

THEOREM 2.5. *The family $\mathcal{L}_3$ of type 3 languages is closed under substitution.*

We shall now derive another characterization of type 3 languages.

DEFINITION. A type 2 grammar $G = (I_N, I_T, X_0, F)$ is *self-embedding* iff $X \overset{*}{\Rightarrow} PXQ$, for some $X \in I_N$ and *non-empty* P, $Q \in W(I_N \cup I_T)$. A type 2 language L is *self-embedding* iff all type 2 grammars generating L are self-embedding.

Thus, no type 3 grammar is self-embedding.

THEOREM 2.6. *A type 2 language is of the type 3 iff it is not self-embedding.*

Proof. By the remark preceding the theorem, if a language L is self-embedding, then it is not of the type 3. Conversely, assume that $L(G)$ is the language generated by a non-self-embedding type 2 grammar $G = (I_N, I_T, X_0, F)$. Without loss of generality, we may assume that, for each $X \in I_N$, there are P, $Q \in W(I_N \cup I_T)$ (possibly empty) such that $X_0 \overset{*}{\Rightarrow} PXQ$ (because, otherwise, X and all productions involving X can be removed without altering $L(G)$).

Suppose first that each non-terminal generates a word containing the initial symbol. Every production in F containing non-terminals on the right side is of one of the forms (i) $X \to PYQ$, (ii) $X \to PY$, (iii) $X \to YQ$, (iv) $X \to Y$, where $X, Y \in I_N$ and P and Q are non-empty words over $I_N \cup I_T$. If F contains a production of the form (i), we obtain a derivation of the form

$$X \Rightarrow PYQ \overset{*}{\Rightarrow} PP_1 X_0 Q_1 Q \overset{*}{\Rightarrow} PP_1 P_2 X Q_2 Q_1 Q.$$

If F contains both a production $X \to PY$ of the form (ii) and a production $X' \to Y'Q$ of the form (iii), we obtain a derivation of the form

$$X \Rightarrow PY \overset{*}{\Rightarrow} PP_1X_0Q_1 \overset{*}{\Rightarrow} PP_1P_2X'Q_2Q_1 \Rightarrow PP_1P_2Y'QQ_2Q_1$$
$$\overset{*}{\Rightarrow} PP_1P_2P_3X_0Q_3QQ_2Q_1 \overset{*}{\Rightarrow} PP_1P_2P_3P_4XQ_4Q_3QQ_2Q_1.$$

In both cases, G is self-embedding, which is impossible. Therefore, if F contains a production of the form (ii), then in all productions of the form (ii) contained in F the word P is over I_T (because, otherwise, F would contain also a production of the form (i) or (iii)). Hence, by definition, $L(G)$ is of the type 3. The same conclusion holds true if F contains a production of the form (iii). (Cf. Exercises 1.6 or 2.1.) Clearly, $L(G)$ is of the type 3 if F contains no productions of the forms (i)–(iii).

Suppose secondly that there is a non-terminal $X_1 \in I_N$ generating no word containing the initial symbol, i.e. for no P and Q, $X_1 \overset{*}{\Rightarrow} PX_0Q$. The proof of $L(G)$ being of the type 3 is in this case by induction on the number n of non-terminals. For $n = 1$, the assertion is vacuous because always $X_0 \overset{*}{\Rightarrow} X_0$. Assume that the assertion holds true for $n = k$. Let the number of non-terminals in I_N be $k+1$. Consider the grammar

$$G_1 = (I_N - \{X_0\}, I_T, X_1, F'),$$

where F' is obtained from F by removing all productions containing X_0, and the grammar

$$G_2 = (I_N - \{X_1\}, I_T \cup \{X_1\}, X_0, F''),$$

where F'' is obtained from F by removing all productions with X_1 on the left side. (Hence, G_2 is obtained from G by considering X_1 as a terminal.) Both of the languages $L(G_1)$ and $L(G_2)$ are of the type 3, either by the inductive hypothesis or by the first part of the proof. Clearly,

$$L(G) = L' + (L(G_2) \cap W(I_T)),$$

where L' is the result of substituting X_1 in $L(G_2)$ by $L(G_1)$. Hence, by Theorems 2.5, 2.2 and 1.1, $L(G)$ is of the type 3. (Clearly, $W(I_T)$ is of the type 3; cf. Exercise 1.1 or Theorem 2.1.) This implies that our assertion holds true for $n = k+1$, which completes the induction. □

Summarizing the results in Theorems 2.1, 2.6, I.2.4, I.4.1 and I.4.2, we obtain the following:

THEOREM 2.7. *For a language L over a finite alphabet I, the following eight conditions are equivalent:*

(i) *L is of the type* 3;
(ii) *L is of the type* 2 *and not self-embedding;*
(iii) *L is regular;*
(iv) *L is f.a.r.;*
(v) *L is the union of some equivalence classes of a right invariant equivalence relation (over W(I)) of finite index;*
(vi) *the equivalence relation induced by L is of finite index;*
(vii) *L is the union of some equivalence classes of a congruence (over W(I)) of finite index;*
(viii) *the congruence induced by L is of finite index.*

EXERCISE 2.1. Prove that the mirror image of a type 3 language (cf. Exercise I.1.2) is of the type 3. Can you do this without using Theorem 2.1?

EXERCISE 2.2. Prove that a type 3 language is regular (i) by a direct application of the analysis method of Theorem I.2.2 and (ii) using Theorems III.2.1 and III.2.5. (Note that in (ii) the definition of type 3 languages given in Exercise 1.6 or the result proved in Exercise 2.1 has to be used.)

EXERCISE 2.3. Assume that in the definition of substitution the languages $L, L_1, \ldots, L_r$ are allowed to be languages over different alphabets. Does this lead to a more general notion than the one defined in the text?

EXERCISE 2.4. Prove that there is an algorithm of deciding whether or not a given grammar is self-embedding.

EXERCISE 2.5. Prove that the language (1.1) is self-embedding.

§ 3. Context-free languages

Properties of the family $\mathcal{L}_2$ will be discussed in this section. We shall first derive another characterization of context-free languages.

DEFINITION. Let

$$H_0(X_0, X_1, \ldots, X_n), H_1(X_0, X_1, \ldots, X_n), \ldots, H_n(X_0, X_1, \ldots, X_n)$$

$$(3.1)$$

be languages over the alphabet $\{X_0, X_1, \ldots, X_n\} \cup I_T$, where I_T is a finite alphabet which does not contain any of the letters X_i. By the *recursion*

$$
\begin{aligned}
L &:: = H_0(L, L_1, \ldots, L_n), \\
L_1 &:: = H_1(L, L_1, \ldots, L_n), \\
&\cdots \\
L_n &:: = H_n(L, L_1, \ldots, L_n)
\end{aligned}
\tag{3.2}
$$

we mean the $(n+1)$-ary operation which associates with the languages $H_0, H_1, \ldots, H_n$ the following language $L = L_0$ over the alphabet I_T:

$$
L = L_0 = \sum_{i=1}^{\infty} H_0^{(i)}(L_\phi, L_\phi, \ldots, L_\phi),
\tag{3.3}
$$

where

$$
H_j^{(i+1)} = H_j(H_0^{(i)}, H_1^{(i)}, \ldots, H_n^{(i)}), \; H_j^{(1)} = H_j \quad (0 \leqq j \leqq n; i \geqq 1).
$$

Thus, for $n = 0$, we obtain a unary operation which associates with a language $H_0(X_0)$ over the alphabet $\{X_0\} \cup I_T$ the language

$$
L_0 = \sum_{i=1}^{\infty} H_0^{(i)}(L_\phi) = H_0(L_\phi) + H_0(H_0(L_\phi)) + H_0(H_0(H_0(L_\phi))) + \ldots
$$

over the alphabet I_T. For instance, if $I_T = \{x, y\}$ and H_0 is the finite language consisting of the words $X_0 xy$ and xyy, then

$$
\begin{aligned}
L_0 &= \{xyy\} + (\{xyy\} + \{xyyxy\}) + (\{xyy\} + \{xyyxy\} + \{xyyxyxy\}) + \ldots \\
&= | xyy(xy)^* |,
\end{aligned}
$$

the result being obvious in view of Theorem III.2.2. In general, it can be shown that the result (3.3) of the recursion (3.2) equals the first component of a solution of (3.2), when (3.2) is viewed as a system of equations and solution is defined as in Section III.2. (Cf. Exercise 3.1.) Note that we have studied in Section III.2 a special type of recursion, where the result can be expressed in a "closed" form. Note also that substitutions are performed in the languages (3.1) only for the letters $X_0, X_1, \ldots, X_n$.

DEFINITION. A language L over an alphabet I_T is *ALGOL-like* iff there is a non-negative integer n and finite languages $H_0, H_1, \ldots, H_n$ over the alphabet $\{X_0, X_1, \ldots, X_n\} \cup I_T$ such that L is obtained by recursion from the languages $H_0, H_1, \ldots, H_n$.

It is immediate that every regular language over I_T is ALGOL-like, because it is the result of a recursion of the form (III.2.1), where the coefficients are letters over the alphabet I_T. Another example is obtained by choosing $I_T = \{x, y\}$, $n = 0$ and $H_0 = \{xX_0y, xy\}$. Then the recursion yields the language (1.1) which, therefore, is ALGOL-like. We shall now establish a more general result.

THEOREM 3.1. *A language is ALGOL-like iff it is context-free.*

Proof. Assume that L_0 is the result (3.3) of a recursion (3.2), where each of the languages (3.1) is finite. Consider the grammar $G = (I_N, I_T, X_0, F)$, where $I_N = \{X_0, X_1, \ldots, X_n\}$ and F consists of all productions $X_i \rightarrow P$, where P is a word in the language H_i and i runs through the numbers $0, 1, \ldots, n$. By the assumption, F is finite. Clearly, G is of the type 2. To prove the theorem, it suffices to show that

$$L_0 = L(G). \tag{3.4}$$

The equation (3.4) proves, namely, that every ALGOL-like language is context-free. But it establishes also the converse statement because, given a context-free grammar with non-terminals $X_0, X_1, \ldots, X_n$, we can form finite languages H_i consisting of all words P such that $X_i \rightarrow P$ is a production and obtain, thus, a recursion (3.2).

To establish (3.4), we show first that $L_0 \subset L(G)$ by applying induction on i to prove that, for all $j = 0, \ldots, n$, if

$$P \in H_j^{(i)}(L_\phi, L_\phi, \ldots, L_\phi),$$

then there exists a derivation of P from X_j. (This proves that if $P \in L_0$, then $P \in L(G)$.) The basis of the induction is clear: for each $j = 0, \ldots, n$, if

$$P \in H_j^{(1)}(L_\phi, L_\phi, \ldots, L_\phi) = H_j(L_\phi, L_\phi, \ldots, L_\phi),$$

then $X_j \Rightarrow P$. We make the following inductive hypothesis: for each $j = 0, \ldots, n$, if

$$P \in H_j^{(k)}(L_\phi, L_\phi, \ldots, L_\phi),$$

then $X_j \overset{*}{\Rightarrow} P$. Assume that

$$P \in H_j^{(k+1)}(L_\phi, L_\phi, \ldots, L_\phi)$$
$$= H_j(H_0^{(k)}(L_\phi, L_\phi, \ldots, L^\phi), \ldots, H_n^{(k)}(L_\phi, L_\phi, \ldots, L_\phi)).$$

Hence, there is a production $X_j \rightarrow \xi_P$ such that P is obtained from ξ_P by substituting for each non-terminal X_ν some word P' in the language $H_\nu^{(k)}(L_\phi, L_\phi, \ldots, L_\phi)$. By the inductive hypothesis, for each such non-terminal X_ν and word P', $X_\nu \overset{*}{\Rightarrow} P'$. Hence, $X_j \overset{*}{\Rightarrow} P$, which completes the induction.

Finally, we shall prove that $L(G) \subset L_0$, which together with the already established result $L_0 \subset L(G)$ implies the equation (3.4). Together with L_0, we consider also the languages

$$L_j = \sum_{i=1}^{\infty} H_j^{(i)}(L_\phi, L_\phi, \ldots, L_\phi), \quad 1 \leqq j \leqq n.$$

For a word P over $I_N \cup I_T$, we denote by $L(P)$ the language obtained when, for each non-terminal X_j occurring in P, is substituted the language L_j $(j = 0, \ldots, n)$. It suffices to prove that whenever $P_1 \overset{*}{\Rightarrow} P_2$, then $L(P_1) \supset L(P_2)$. (If this is true, then the relation $X_0 \overset{*}{\Rightarrow} P$, where $P \in W(I_T)$, implies the inclusion $L(X_0) \supset L(P)$, which means that $P \in L_0$.) Assume first that $P_1 \Rightarrow P_2$. Hence, for some Q_1, Q_2, X_j and P', $P_1 = Q_1 X_j Q_2$, $P_2 = Q_1 P' Q_2$ and $X_j \rightarrow P'$ is in F. By the definition of L_j, it follows that $L(X_j) \supset L(P')$. From this it is immediate that $L(P_1) \supset L(P_2)$. Assume next that $P_1 \overset{*}{\Rightarrow} P_2$ where $P_1 \neq P_2$. Hence, for some $P_1', \ldots, P_k'$,

$$P_1 \Rightarrow P_1' \Rightarrow \ldots \Rightarrow P_k' \Rightarrow P_2.$$

By applying our earlier result, we obtain

$$L(P_1) \supset L(P_1') \supset \ldots \supset L(P_k') \supset L(P_2),$$

which shows that $L(P_1) \supset L(P_2)$. $\square$

Our next theorem is a useful lemma for proofs concerning context-free languages.

THEOREM 3.2. *Let $G = (I_N, I_T, X_0, F)$ be a context-free grammar. Then there is a context-free grammar G_1, with no productions of the form $X \rightarrow \lambda$, such that $L(G_1) = L(G) - \{\lambda\}$. If $\lambda \in L(G)$, there is a context-free grammar $G_2 = (I_N', I_T, X_0', F')$ such that $L(G_2) = L(G)$, the only production in G_2 involving λ is $X_0' \rightarrow \lambda$, and X_0' does not appear on the right side of any production of G_2.*

Proof. The grammar $G_1 = (I_N, I_T, X_0, F_1)$ is constructed as follows.

Define

$$U_1 = \{X \mid X \to \lambda \text{ in } F\},$$

$$U_{i+1} = U_i \cup \{X \mid X \to P \text{ in } F, P \in W(U_i)\} \quad (i \geq 1).$$

There is a natural number k such that $U_k = U_{k+1}$. For this k, $U_k = U_{k+v}$, $v = 1, 2, \ldots$, and furthermore,

$$X \overset{*}{\underset{G}{\Rightarrow}} \lambda \quad \text{iff} \quad X \in U_k. \tag{3.5}$$

We now let $X \to P_1$ be a production in F_1 iff $P_1 \neq \lambda$ and there is a production $X \to P$ in F such that P_1 is obtained from P by deleting 0 or more occurrences of elements of U_k. Then $L(G_1) = L(G) - \{\lambda\}$. In fact, the inclusion $L(G_1) \subset L(G) - \{\lambda\}$ is obvious by (3.5). The reverse inclusion is established by considering the grammar $G_3 = (I_N, I_T, X_0, F \cup F_1)$. Clearly, $L(G) \subset L(G_3)$. If $P \in L(G_3)$ and $P \neq \lambda$ then $P \in L(G_1)$ because all applications of productions $X \to \lambda$ can be replaced by some applications of productions in F_1. Hence, the first part of the theorem follows.

Assume that $\lambda \in L(G)$. Construct first the grammar G_1 as above. Let

$$G_2 = (I_N \cup \{X_0'\}, I_T, X_0', F_1 \cup \{X_0' \to \lambda, X_0' \to X_0\}).$$

Then $L(G_2) = L(G_1) + \{\lambda\} = L(G)$. Furthermore, the required conditions concerning productions of G_2 are satisfied. $\square$

The proof of Theorem 3.2 gives an algorithm to construct the grammars G_1 and G_2, because there is an algorithm to decide whether or not $\lambda \in L(G)$ (cf. Exercise 1.5).

THEOREM 3.3. *The family $\mathcal{L}_2$ of context-free languages is closed under substitution.*

Proof. Let $L_i(x_1, \ldots, x_r)$, $i = 0, \ldots, r$, be languages over the alphabet $I_r = \{x_1, \ldots, x_r\}$ generated by the type 2 grammars

$$G_i = (I_N^{(i)}, I_r, X_0^{(i)}, F^{(i)}) \quad (i = 0, \ldots, r),$$

and let

$$L = L_0(L_1, \ldots, L_r). \tag{3.6}$$

Without loss of generality, we may assume that the sets $I_N^{(i)}$, $i = 0, \ldots,$ r, are pairwise disjoint. Consider the grammar

$$G = (I_N^{(0)} \cup \ldots \cup I_N^{(r)}, I_r, X_0^{(0)}, F), \qquad (3.7)$$

where

$$F = F_1^{(0)} \cup F^{(1)} \cup \ldots \cup F^{(r)}$$

and $F_1^{(0)}$ is obtained from $F^{(0)}$ by replacing in each production every letter x_i, $1 \le i \le r$, by the letter $X_0^{(i)}$. It is immediately verified that the grammar (3.7) generates the language (3.6). $\square$

We shall now prove that the results of Theorem 2.2 do not carry over to context-free languages.

THEOREM 3.4. *The family $\mathscr{L}_2$ is not closed under intersection and complementation, i.e. there are context-free languages L_1 and L_2 such that $L_1 \cap L_2$ is not a context-free language, and there is a context-free language L such that $\sim L$ is not context-free.*

Proof. Consider two grammars of the type 2

$$G_1 = (\{X_0, X_1\}, \{x, y, z\}, X_0, \{X_0 \to X_0 z, X_0 \to X_1 z, X_1 \to xy, X_1 \to x X_1 y\})$$

and

$$G_2 = (\{X_0, X_1\}, \{x, y, z\}, X_0, \{X_0 \to x X_0, X_0 \to x X_1, X_1 \to yz, X_1 \to y X_1 z\}).$$

Clearly,

$$L(G_1) = \{x^n y^n z^m \mid n, m \ge 1\} \qquad (3.8)$$

and

$$L(G_2) = \{x^m y^n z^n \mid n, m \ge 1\}. \qquad (3.9)$$

Hence,

$$L(G_1) \cap L(G_2) = \{x^n y^n z^n \mid n \ge 1\}. \qquad (3.10)$$

We shall prove that (3.10) is not a context-free language.

Assume the contrary: (3.10) is generated by a type 2 grammar $G = (I_N, \{x, y, z\}, X_0, F)$. Let $X \ne X_0$ be a non-terminal generating at least one terminal word. If X generates exactly one terminal word P, then we remove X from I_N, remove all productions of the form $X \to Q$ from F and replace every occurrence of X on the right sides of the productions of F by P. Clearly, the language generated by G remains unaltered. Thus, we may assume that no non-terminal $X \ne X_0$ generates exactly one terminal word. This holds obviously true also with respect to X_0.

Let k be the length of the longest word appearing on the right side of some production in F. By the assumption,

$$x^{k+1}y^{k+1}z^{k+1} \in L(G).$$

Let

$$X_0 \Rightarrow \ldots \Rightarrow P_1 X P_2 \Rightarrow P_1 Q P_2 = x^{k+1}y^{k+1}z^{k+1}$$

be one of its derivations. Thus, $X \to Q$ is a production in F, $\lg(Q) \le k$ and there is also a terminal word $Q' \ne Q$ such that $X \overset{*}{\Rightarrow} Q'$. Hence, we have obtained the following result: there is a subword Q of the word $x^{k+1}y^{k+1}z^{k+1}$ with $\lg(Q) \le k$ and a word $Q' \ne Q$ such that when Q is replaced by Q' in the word $x^{k+1}y^{k+1}z^{k+1}$, then the resulting word belongs to the language (3.10). But this is immediately seen to be impossible. Therefore, the language (3.10) cannot be generated by a type 2 grammar. This shows that the family $\mathcal{L}_2$ is not closed under intersection.

Consequently, $\mathcal{L}_2$ is not closed under complementation. For if it were closed under complementation, then the equation

$$L(G_1) \cap L(G_2) = \sim (\sim L(G_1) + (\sim L(G_2)))$$

would imply, by Theorem 1.1, that the language (3.10) is context-free, which is impossible. □

The next theorem shows that a partial result concerning closure under intersection can be obtained.

THEOREM 3.5. *The intersection of a context-free language L_1 and a regular language L_2 is a context-free language.*

Proof. Without loss of generality, we may assume that L_1 and L are languages over the same alphabet I_T. Let $G_1 = (I_N, I_T, X_0, F)$ b a type 2 grammar which generates the language L_1. Let $\mathbf{A} = (S, s_0, f)$ be a finite deterministic automaton over the alphabet I_T such that L_2 is represented by the set $S_1 \subset S$ in $\mathbf{A}$. We assume first that $\lambda \notin L_1$ and $\lambda \notin L_2$. By Theorem 3.2, we may assume that none of the productions in F is of the form $X \to \lambda$. Let $S_1 = \{s^{(1)}, \ldots, s^{(h)}\}$ and let L_2^i be the language represented by the set $\{s^{(i)}\}$ in $\mathbf{A}$, for $i = 1, \ldots, h$. Clearly,

$$L_1 \cap L_2 = (L_1 \cap L_2^{(1)}) + \ldots + (L_1 \cap L_2^{(h)}). \qquad 3.11)$$

Consider a fixed i, $1 \leqq i \leqq h$. The language $L_1 \cap L_2^{(i)}$ is generated by the grammar

$$((I_N \cup I_T) \times S \times S, \ I_T, \ (X_0, s_0, s^{(i)}), \ F'), \qquad (3.12)$$

where F' consists of all productions having one of the following forms:

(i) $(X, s, s') \rightarrow (Y_1, s, s_1)(Y_2, s_1, s_2) \ldots (Y_n, s_{n-1}, s')$, where s, s' and each s_j belong to S and the production $X \rightarrow Y_1 Y_2 \ldots Y_n$, $Y_j \in I_N \cup I_T$, belongs to F;

(ii) $(x, s, s') \rightarrow x$, where $x \in I_T$ and $f(s, x) = s'$.

Thus, non-terminals are triples whose first component belongs to $I_N \cup I_T$ and the other two components belong to S. All derivations according to G_1 are preserved by the first components of the productions (i), whereas the other two components give an arbitrary sequence of states. By (ii) and the choice of the initial symbol, the triples can be eliminated iff the terminal word formed by the first components causes a state transition from s_0 to $s^{(i)}$ in A. Thus, $L_1 \cap L_2^{(i)}$ is the language generated by (3.12).

Because (3.12) is of the type 2, we conclude that $L_1 \cap L_2^{(i)}$ is context-free. Hence, by (3.11) and Theorem 1.1, $L_1 \cap L_2$ is context-free.

If one of the languages L_1 and L_2 contains the empty word, then we construct first a type 2 grammar with the initial symbol X_0 generating the language

$$(L_1 - \{\lambda\}) \cap (L_2 - \{\lambda\})$$

and then, if $\lambda \in L_1$ and $\lambda \in L_2$, add a new initial symbol X_0' and the productions $X_0' \rightarrow \lambda$ and $X_0' \rightarrow X_0$. $\square$

It is an immediate consequence of Theorems 3.5 and 2.2 that if L_1 is context-free and L_2 is regular, then the difference $L_1 - L_2$ is context-free.

One of the main differences between regular and context-free languages is the non-existence of algorithms for the latter in several such cases, where we have constructed corresponding algorithms for regular languages. Since problems concerning undecidability lie beyond the scope of this book, we shall only briefly mention some of these negative results. There is no algorithm for deciding whether or not two context-free languages are equal and no algorithm for deciding if a context-free language is contained in another. There is no algorithm for deciding if the complement of a context-free language is empty, finite, regular or context-free. Analogous results hold true for the intersection of two context-free languages. However, for languages over a one-letter alphabet, algorithms for these decision problems can be given. (Cf. Exercise 4.1.) There is also an algorithm to decide whether or not two given *parenthesis grammars* (i.e. all productions are of the form $X \to (P)$, where P contains no parentheses) are equivalent. For this, cf. McNaughton (1967).

Finally, we shall briefly mention some results concerning the ambiguity of type 2 grammars and languages. A type 2 grammar $G = (I_N, I_T, X_0, F)$ is said to be *ambiguous* iff there is a word in $L(G)$ possessing two distinct *leftmost* derivations from X_0. Hereby, a derivation

$$X_0 = P_0 \Rightarrow P_1 \Rightarrow P_2 \Rightarrow \ldots \Rightarrow P_k$$

is *leftmost* iff, for each $i = 0, \ldots, k-1$, whenever $P_i = \xi_i X^{(i)} \eta_i$, $P_{i+1} = \xi_i \zeta_i \eta_i$ and the production $X^{(i)} \to \zeta_i$ is in F, then ξ_i contains no non-terminals.

Thus, the existence of two distinct derivations of the same word does not imply that the grammar is ambiguous. As regards generation trees, a grammar is ambiguous iff there is a word possessing two distinct generation trees. For instance, the grammar

$$(\{X_0, X_1\}, \{x, y\}, X_0, \{X_0 \to xy, X_0 \to xX_0y, X_0 \to xX_1, X_1 \to xX_0y^2\})$$

$$(3.13)$$

is ambiguous because the word x^3y^3 possesses two leftmost derivations:

$$X_0 \Rightarrow xX_0y \Rightarrow x^2X_0y^2 \Rightarrow x^3y^3,$$
$$X_0 \Rightarrow xX_1 \Rightarrow x^2X_0y^2 \Rightarrow x^3y^3.$$

The corresponding generation trees are given in Fig. 21.

It frequently happens that the same language is generated both by an ambiguous and an unambiguous grammar. Thus, it is easy to see that the language generated by the grammar (3.13) (which, in fact, equals the language (1.1)) can be generated also by an unambiguous grammar. A language L is *inherently ambiguous* iff all type 2 grammars generating L are ambiguous. (Otherwise, L is *unambiguous*.)

Some results are now mentioned without proofs. A reader interested in these questions, as well as in the decidability problems mentioned above, is referred to Ginsburg (1966). The sum of the languages (3.8) and (3.9) is an inherently ambiguous language. There is no algorithm for deciding whether or not a grammar is ambiguous. There is no algorithm for deciding whether or not a language is inherently ambiguous.

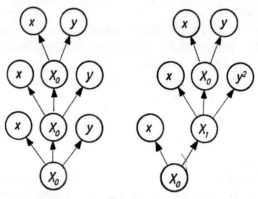

FIG. 21.

EXERCISE 3.1. Prove that the language (3.3) defined by the recursion (3.2) is the first component L' of a solution

$$(L', L_1', \ldots, L_n')$$

of the system of equations (3.2). Prove also that the solution in question is minimal in the sense that, for any solution $(L, L_1, \ldots, L_n)$ of the system (3.2),

$$L' \subset L, L_1' \subset L_1, \ldots, L_n' \subset L_n.$$

(Cf. also Ginsburg and Rice, 1962.) Verify the latter result for the special type of recursion studied in Section III.2, where all solutions of the system (3.2) can be given.

EXERCISE 3.2 (Redko, 1965). Let $H(y)$ be a language over the alphabet $\{y\} \cup I_T$, where I_T is a finite alphabet. Consider the equation

$$y = H(y). \tag{1}$$

Prove that if $H(y)$ does not contain any non-empty word over the alphabet $\{y\}$, then the language L defined by the recursion

$$L :: = H(L)$$

is the unique solution of (1). Prove that if $y \in H(y)$ then, for every language H_1 over I_T, the language L defined by the recursion

$$L :: = H_1 + H(L)$$

is a solution of (1) and that all solutions are obtained in this way. Prove that if $y \notin H(y)$ but $y^k \in H(y)$, $k > 1$, then, for every language H_2 over I_T which either is empty or contains the empty word, the language L defined by the recursion

$$L :: = H_2 + H(L)$$

is a solution of (1) and that all solutions are obtained in this way. Conclude that Theorems III.2.2 and III.2.4 are special cases of these results.

EXERCISE 3.3 (Redko, 1965). Let

$$H_1(y_1, \ldots, y_n), \ldots, H_n(y_1, \ldots, y_n)$$

be languages over the alphabet $\{y_1, \ldots, y_n\} \cup I_T$, where I_T is a finite alphabet, such that none of the languages H_i contains a non-empty word over the alphabet $\{y_1, \ldots, y_n\}$. Prove that the system of equations

$$y_1 = H_1(y_1, \ldots, y_n)$$
$$\ldots$$
$$y_n = H_n(y_1, \ldots, y_n)$$

possesses a unique solution. Define the solution by recursion.

EXERCISE 3.4. Give another proof of the fact that the family $\mathcal{L}_2$ is closed under the operations sum, catenation and catenation closure, using Theorem 3.3.

EXERCISE 3.5 (Ginsburg and Rice, 1962). A language L is *sequentially definable* iff it is the result of a recursion of the form

$$L_n :: = H_n(L_n),$$
$$L_{n-1} :: = H_{n-1}(L_{n-1}, L_n),$$
$$\ldots$$
$$L_1 :: = H_1(L_1, \ldots, L_n),$$
$$L :: = H_0(L, L_1, \ldots, L_n),$$

where H_i are finite languages. (An equivalent condition is that L is generated by a type 2 grammar $G = (I_N, I_T, X_0, F)$, where

$$I_N = \{X_0, X_1, \ldots, X_n\}$$

and whenever $X_i \to P$ is in F, then

$$P \in W(I_T \cup \{X_j \mid i \leq j \leq n\}).)$$

Prove that every regular language is sequentially definable. Prove that there is a sequentially definable language which is not regular, and a context-free language which is not sequentially definable. Prove that the family of sequentially definable languages is not closed under intersection. Is it closed under substitution?

EXERCISE 3.6. Prove that a language is context-free if it is almost equal (cf. Section I.8) to a context-free language.

EXERCISE 3.7 (Bar-Hillel, Perles and Shamir, 1961). A type 2 grammar $G = (I_N, I_T, X_0, F)$ is *reduced* iff, for each non-terminal $X \neq X_0$, (i) X_0 generates a word containing X and (ii) X generates some terminal word. Prove that, for each type 2 grammar, there is an equivalent reduced grammar.

EXERCISE 3.8 (Ginsburg, 1966). In the proof of Theorem 3.4 it was seen that a non-terminal $X \neq X_0$ generating only one terminal word can be removed from a context-free grammar. Extend this result to the case, where X generates only finitely many terminal words.

EXERCISE 3.9. Prove that, for any $P \in L(G)$, where G is a type 2 grammar, there is a leftmost derivation of P according to G. Define the notion of a *rightmost* derivation, and prove the same result for rightmost derivations.

EXERCISE 3.10. Construct two context-free languages L_1 and L_2 such that the difference $L_1 - L_2$ is not context-free.

EXERCISE 3.11 (Chomsky, 1959). A type 2 grammar (I_N, I_T, X_0, F) is *normal* iff F contains only productions of the forms $X \to x$, $X \to \lambda$ or $X \to Y_1 Y_2$, where $X, Y_1, Y_2 \in I_N$, $Y_1 \neq Y_2$ and $x \in I_T$. (Thus, a generation tree has no more than two branches from each node.) Prove that, for any type 2 grammar, there is an equivalent normal grammar.

EXERCISE 3.12 (Chomsky and Schützenberger, 1963). A production is *linear* iff it is of the form $X \to P$ or $X \to PYQ$, where P and Q are words over the terminal alphabet. A grammar is *linear* iff each of its productions is linear. A language is *linear* iff it is generated by some linear grammar. Show that regular languages form a proper subfamily of linear languages.

EXERCISE 3.13 (Amar and Putzolu, 1964). A linear grammar is *even linear* iff, for all productions of the form $X \to PYQ$, $\lg(P) = \lg(Q)$. A language is *even linear* iff it is generated by some even linear grammar. Show that regular languages form a proper subfamily of even linear languages.

EXERCISE 3.14 (Gross, 1964). A grammar $(\{X_0\}, I_T, X_0, F)$ is *minimal linear* iff there is exactly one letter $x \in I_T$ such that $X_0 \to x$ is in F and all other productions are of the form $X_0 \to PX_0Q$, where $P, Q \in W(I_T - \{x\})$. Prove that the language

$$L = \{x^m y x^n \mid m \geqq n \geqq 0\}$$

is generated by a minimal linear grammar and that all minimal linear grammars generating L are ambiguous. Prove that L is generated by an unambiguous linear grammar. Cf. Haines (1964) for an example of a language L' generated by a minimal linear grammar such that the complement of L' is not context-free.

EXERCISE 3.15 (Bar-Hillel, Perles and Shamir, 1961). Prove that, for each type 2 grammar G, there exist integers m and n such that each word P in $L(G)$, where $\lg(P) > m$, is of the form

$$P = P_1Q_1P_2Q_2P_3,$$

where

$$Q_1Q_2 \neq \lambda, \quad \lg(Q_1P_2Q_2) \leqq n \quad \text{and} \quad P_1Q_1^kP_2Q_2^kP_3 \in L(G),$$

for all $k \geqq 1$. Use this result to obtain a new proof of the fact that the language (3.10) is not context-free. What is the corresponding result for regular languages?

EXERCISE 3.16. Prove that there is an algorithm to decide whether or not a context-free language is (i) empty, (ii) infinite.

EXERCISE 3.17. Prove that every regular language is unambiguous by constructing a grammar where the non-terminals are the states of the corresponding finite deterministic automaton. In this fashion, you also obtain another proof of the fact that every regular language is of the type 3.

§ 4. Inclusion relations

A suitable position has now been reached to compare the families $\mathscr{L}_i$, $i = 0, 1, 2, 3$.

THEOREM 4.1. $\mathscr{L}_1 \supset \mathscr{L}_2 \supset \mathscr{L}_3$, where each inclusion is proper.

Proof. The inclusion

$$\mathscr{L}_2 \supset \mathscr{L}_3 \tag{4.1}$$

follows, by the definition of type 2 and type 3 grammars. The inclusion

$$\mathscr{L}_1 \supset \mathscr{L}_2 \tag{4.2}$$

is a consequence of Theorem 3.2 which shows that, for each context-free grammar, there is an equivalent context-sensitive grammar. The inclusion (4.1) is proper because the language (1.1) generated by the type 2 grammar (1.4) is obviously not f.a.r. and hence, by Theorem 2.7, it is not of the type 3. The inclusion (4.2) is proper because the type 1 grammar

$$G = (\{X_0, X_1, Y, Y_1, Y_2, Z, Z_1, Z_2, Z_3\}, \quad \{x, y, z\}, X_0, F),$$

where F consists of the productions

$$X_0 \to X_0 Z_1, \quad X_0 \to X_1 Z_1, \quad X_1 \to xY_1, \quad X_1 \to xX_1 Y_1,$$
$$Y_1 Z_1 \to Y_1 Z_3, \quad Y_1 Z_3 \to YZ_3, \quad YZ_3 \to YZ,$$
$$Y_1 Y \to Y_1 Y_2, \quad Y_1 Y_2 \to YY_2, \quad YY_2 \to YY_1,$$
$$ZZ_1 \to Z_2 Z_1, \quad Z_2 Z_1 \to Z_2 Z, \quad Z_2 Z \to Z_1 Z,$$
$$Y \to y, \quad Z \to z,$$

generates the language (3.10) which was shown to be not of the type 2. This follows because the first four productions generate from X_0 all words of the form $x^n Y_1^n Z_1^m$, where $m, n \geqq 1$. Using the remaining productions, the non-terminals Y_1 and Z_1 can be eliminated from these words iff $m = n$. $\square$

(By Theorem 6.1, G could be replaced, for instance, by the grammar

$$(\{X_0, X_1, X_2, X_3\}, \{x, y, z\}, X_0, F_1),$$

where F_1 consists of the six productions

$$X_0 \to xX_1X_2, \quad xX_1 \to xxX_1y, \quad X_1y \to yX_1X_3,$$
$$X_3y \to yX_3, \quad X_3X_2 \to X_2z, \quad X_1X_2 \to yz.)$$

It is a consequence of the definition of type 0 and type 1 languages that $\mathcal{L}_0 \supset \mathcal{L}_1$. The type 1 languages are decidable in the sense of Theorem 1.2. It follows from the theory of recursively enumerable sets, which lies beyond the scope of this book, that this is not true of type 0 languages. (Cf. Davis, 1958, p. 93.) Hence, also the inclusion $\mathcal{L}_0 \supset \mathcal{L}_1$ is proper. Combining these results, we obtain

$$\mathcal{L}_0 \supset \mathcal{L}_1 \supset \mathcal{L}_2 \supset \mathcal{L}_3, \tag{4.3}$$

where every inclusion is proper. The different types of grammars introduced in Section 1 yield, thus, a proper hierarchy of languages.

We have shown in Theorem 2.7 that the family $\mathcal{L}_3$ consisting of all type 3 languages is exactly the family of languages representable in finite deterministic automata. In the following sections we shall present, for each of the families $\mathcal{L}_2$, $\mathcal{L}_1$ and $\mathcal{L}_0$, a class of automata such that exactly the languages in the family are representable by automata in this class. This leads to a hierarchy of automata corresponding to (4.3).

EXERCISE 4.1. Prove that a language over the alphabet $\{x\}$ is context-free iff it is regular. Conclude the existence of algorithms in this special case for problems discussed at the end of Section 3.

EXERCISE 4.2. Prove that there exists a language over the alphabet $\{x\}$ which is context-sensitive but not context-free.

EXERCISE 4.3. Study inclusion relations between $\mathcal{L}_2$, $\mathcal{L}_3$ and the families of languages introduced in Exercises 3.5, 3.12–3.14.

PROBLEM 4.1. Study the position of the family of stochastic languages in the hierarchy introduced in Section 1. (It seems likely that all context-free languages are not stochastic because the counting of the exact number of occurrences of a given letter is difficult for a finite probabilistic automaton. However, some non-regular context-free languages are stochastic, for instance, the language (II.4.6).)

§ 5. Pushdown automata

In this section, we shall introduce a class of recognition devices which bear the same relation to context-free languages as finite deterministic automata do to regular languages. We shall first give an intuitive description of these devices, called *pushdown automata*.

Like a finite automaton, a pushdown automaton reads input words from left to right and is capable of a finite number of internal states.

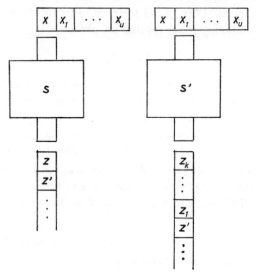

Fig. 22.

But, in addition, it has an auxiliary memory called the *pushdown store*, which is potentially infinite. A pushdown automaton scans the letters of an input word, one at a time. After scanning a letter x in a state s and with z as the topmost letter in the pushdown store, the automaton (i) erases z and inserts a word $z_1 \ldots z_k$ (possibly empty) to the pushdown store, (ii) goes to another state s' and (iii) starts scanning the next letter x_1 of the input word (cf. Fig. 22). At each moment, the behavior of the automaton depends only on (i) the scanned input letter, (ii) the state and (iii) the topmost letter in the pushdown store. Thus, the information in the pushdown store must be used in the order reverse to the one in which it is inserted into the store, i.e. first in—last out.

At the beginning, a pushdown automaton is in a specified initial state and has a specified non-empty start letter in the pushdown store. If the pushdown store is empty when the whole input word has been scanned, then the automaton *accepts* the word. Thus, a word is accepted iff it, through some sequence of moves, empties the pushdown store.

These notions will be formalized in the following definitions. The automaton introduced will be *non-deterministic*: at each moment, there may be several choices for the next move. It is also possible to scan the empty word from the input tape and, thus, leave the position of the input tape unchanged. (A deterministic pushdown automaton is introduced in Exercise 5.2. For deterministic devices, the corresponding family of languages is a proper subfamily of $\mathcal{L}_2$. It is an open problem how to characterize this family in terms of grammars.)

DEFINITION. A *pushdown automaton* is an ordered sixtuple

$$\textbf{PDA} = (I, Z, S, z_0, s_0, f),$$

where I and Z are finite alphabets (referred to as the *input* and *pushdown alphabet*), S is a non-empty finite set (the set of *internal states*), $z_0 \in Z$ (the *start symbol*), $s_0 \in S$ (the *initial* state), and f is a function mapping the set $S \times (I \cup \{\lambda\}) \times Z$ into the set of all finite subsets of $S \times W(Z)$ (the *move function*).

The behavior of a pushdown automaton will be formalized in the next definition.

DEFINITION. Let $\textbf{PDA} = (I, Z, S, z_0, s_0, f)$ be a pushdown automaton. An *instantaneous description* is an ordered triple (s, P, Q), where $s \in S$, $P \in W(I)$ and $Q \in W(Z)$. The instantaneous description (s, xP, Qy), where $x \in I \cup \{\lambda\}$ and $y \in Z$, *directly yields* the instantaneous description (s', P, QQ_1), in symbols,

$$(s, xP, Qy) \vdash (s', P, QQ_1) \tag{5.1}$$

iff $f(s, x, y)$ contains the pair (s', Q_1). The instantaneous description U *yields* the instantaneous description U', in symbols $U \vdash^* U'$, iff there is a finite sequence of instantaneous descriptions

$$U_0, U_1, \ldots, U_k \qquad (k \geq 0)$$

such that $U = U_0$, $U' = U_k$ and, for all $i = 0, \ldots, k-1$, U_i directly yields U_{i+1}. The sequence is referred to as a *computation* and denoted by

$$U = U_0 \vdash U_1 \vdash \ldots \vdash U_k = U'.$$

Thus, the instantaneous description (s, P, Q) represents the fact that the automaton is in the state s, P is the unscanned part of the input word and Q is the word in the pushdown store, with rightmost letter on the top. Relation (5.1) indicates that if (i) the automaton is in the state s, (ii) y is the topmost letter in the pushdown store and (iii) either x is the leftmost unscanned letter of the input word or $x = \lambda$, then one possible behavior is to (i) go to the state s', (ii) replace y by Q_1 and (iii) expend x. The relation

$$(s, x_1 \ldots x_k P, Q) \overset{*}{\vdash} (s', P, Q') \tag{5.2}$$

indicates that if (i) the automaton is in the state s, (ii) Q is the word in the pushdown store and (iii) $x_1 \ldots x_k P$ is the unscanned part of the input word, then there is a sequence of moves after which (i) the automaton is in the state s', (ii) Q' is the word in the pushdown store and (iii) P is the unscanned part of the input word. If the automaton **PDA** is not understood from the context, then in (5.1) and in (5.2) the symbols $\vdash$ and $\overset{*}{\vdash}$ may be replaced by the symbols $\vdash$ **PDA** and $\overset{*}{\vdash}$ **PDA**.

DEFINITION. Let **PDA** $= (I, Z, S, z_0, s_0, f)$ be a pushdown automaton. Then the language $L(\textbf{PDA})$ *represented* (or *accepted*) by **PDA** is defined by

$$L(\textbf{PDA}) = \{P \,|\, (s_0, P, z_0) \overset{*}{\vdash} (s, \lambda, \lambda), s \in S\}.$$

Note that an instantaneous description of the form (s, P, λ) yields no other instantaneous descriptions. This is the reason why the start symbol is in the pushdown store at the beginning.

As an example, we consider the pushdown automaton

$$\textbf{PDA} = (\{x, y\}, \{x, y, z_0\}, \{s_0\}, z_0, s_0, f),$$

where

$$f(s_0, \lambda, z_0) = \{(s_0, yz_0x), (s_0, yx)\},$$
$$f(s_0, x, x) = \{(s_0, \lambda)\},$$
$$f(s_0, y, y) = \{(s_0, \lambda)\},$$
$$f(s_0, P, Q) = \phi, \text{ otherwise.}$$

(Thus, if the argument of f differs from the arguments on the three first lines of the definition, then there is no possible move for **PDA**.) Consider the word x^3y^3. We obtain the following sequence of instantaneous descriptions, each of which directly yields the next one:

$$(s_0, x^3y^3, z_0) \vdash (s_0, x^3y^3, yz_0x) \vdash (s_0, x^2y^3, yz_0)$$
$$\vdash (s_0, x^2y^3, yyz_0x) \vdash (s_0, xy^3, y^2z_0) \vdash (s_0, xy^3, y^3x)$$
$$\vdash (s_0, y^3, y^3) \vdash (s_0, y^2, y^2) \vdash (s_0, y, y) \vdash (s_0, \lambda, \lambda). \quad (5.3)$$

Beginning with the same word, we obtain also the sequence

$$(s_0, x^3y^3, z_0) \vdash (s_0, x^3y^3, yx) \vdash (s_0, x^2y^3, y), \quad (5.4)$$

where there is no possible next move from the last instantaneous description and, hence, the pushdown store will not be emptied. We obtain also the sequence

$$(s_0, x^3y^3, z_0) \overset{*}{\vdash} (s_0, xy^3, y^2z_0) \vdash (s_0, xy^3, y^3z_0x)$$
$$\vdash (s_0, y^3, y^3z_0) \vdash (s_0, y^3, y^4x) \quad (5.5)$$

with the same property. However, the existence of the sequence (5.3) shows that

$$(s_0, x^3y^3, z_0) \overset{*}{\vdash} (s_0, \lambda, \lambda)$$

and, hence, $x^3y^3 \in L(\mathbf{PDA})$. It is obvious that similarly, for all $n \geq 1$,

$$(s_0, x^ny^n, z_0) \overset{*}{\vdash} (s_0, \lambda, \lambda).$$

(In order to find a sequence leading to (s_0, λ, λ), the automaton has to "guess" when to insert the word yx, instead of yz_0x, into the pushdown store. This has to be done when the unscanned portion of the input word is xy^n. In sequence (5.4) it was done too early, in sequence (5.5) too late. However, the automaton has no way of knowing when the unscanned part contains only one x.)

It is also easy to see that no word other than the words x^ny^n, $n \geq 1$, can empty the pushdown store. Thus, $L(\mathbf{PDA})$ is the language (1.1). This result will be obtained also as a special case of the proof of Theorem 5.1.

We shall now prove that every context-free language can be represented in a pushdown automaton with one state, and conversely. Thus, the family $\mathcal{L}_2$ equals the family of languages of the form $L(\mathbf{PDA})$, where **PDA** possesses only one state. The converse part of this result can be strengthened to include all pushdown automata, the proof being the same in principle but more complicated notationally. (Cf. Exercise 5.4.) Hence, the family $\mathcal{L}_2$ equals the family of languages representable in pushdown automata.

In the proofs of Theorems 5.1 and 5.2, the internal state will be omitted from instantaneous descriptions (because it is always the same).

THEOREM 5.1. *For every context-free language L, there is a pushdown automaton* **PDA** *with one state such that $L = L(\text{PDA})$.*

Proof. Let L be generated by the type 2 grammar

$$G = (I_N, I_T, X_0, F).$$

As in Section II.4, we denote by mi (P) the mirror image of a word P. Consider the pushdown automaton

$$\text{PDA} = (I_T, I_N \cup I_T, \{s_0\}, X_0, s_0, f),$$

where

$$f(s_0, \lambda, X) = \{(s_0, \text{mi}(\xi)) \mid X \to \xi \text{ in } F\}, \text{ for } X \in I_N, \qquad (5.6)$$

$$f(s_0, x, x) = \{(s_0, \lambda)\}, \text{ for } x \in I_T, \qquad (5.7)$$

$$f(s_0, P, Q) = \phi, \text{ otherwise.}$$

Denote $L_1 = L(\text{PDA})$. We shall prove that $L_1 = L$.

Assume that $P \in L$. This implies (cf. Exercise 3.9) that there is a derivation of P of the form

$$X_0 \Rightarrow P_1 X_1 V_1 \Rightarrow P_1 P_2 X_2 V_2 \Rightarrow \ldots \Rightarrow P_1 P_2 \ldots P_{k-1} X_{k-1} V_{k-1}$$
$$\Rightarrow P_1 P_2 \ldots P_k = P,$$

where $P_i \in W(I_T)$ and $X_i \in I_N$, for $i = 1, \ldots, k$. Note that $P_k = P'_k V_{k-1}$, for some P'_k. By (5.6) and (5.7),

$$(P_1 P_2 \ldots P_k, X_0) \vdash (P_1 P_2 \ldots P_k, \text{mi}(V_1) X_1 \text{mi}(P_1))$$

$$\overset{*}{\vdash} (P_2 \ldots P_k, \text{mi}(V_1)X_1) \vdash (P_2 \ldots P_k, \text{mi}(V_2)X_2 \text{mi}(P_2))$$

$$\overset{*}{\vdash} (P_3 \ldots P_k, \text{mi}(V_2)X_2) \overset{*}{\vdash} (P_{k-1}P_k, \text{mi}(V_{k-1})X_{k-1} \text{mi}(P_{k-1}))$$

$$\overset{*}{\vdash} (P_k, \text{mi}(V_{k-1})X_{k-1}) \vdash (P_k, \text{mi}(P_k)) \overset{*}{\vdash} (\lambda, \lambda).$$

Therefore, $P \in L_1$. We have shown that

$$L \subset L_1. \qquad (5.8)$$

Conversely, assume that $Q \in L_1$. Hence, there exists a computation

$$(Q, X_0) = (Q_0 Q_1 \ldots Q_{n-1} Q_n, \xi_0) \vdash (Q_1 \ldots Q_{n-1} Q_n, \xi_1)$$
$$\vdash \ldots \vdash (Q_{n-1} Q_n, \xi_{n-1}) \vdash (Q_n, \xi_n),$$

where $Q_n = \xi_n = \lambda$, each $\xi_i \in W(I_N \cup I_T)$ and each $Q_i \in I_T \cup \{\lambda\}$. We shall prove that, for $0 \leqq i \leqq n$,

$$\mathrm{mi}\,(\xi_i) \overset{*}{\Rightarrow} Q_i \ldots Q_n. \tag{5.9}$$

Because $\mathrm{mi}\,(\xi_0) = \xi_0 = X_0$, this implies that $X_0 \overset{*}{\Rightarrow} Q$. Hence, $Q \in L$ and, therefore, $L_1 \subset L$. Combining this with (5.8), we obtain the final result $L_1 = L$.

The proof of (5.9) is by descending induction on i. For $i = n$, (5.9) is obvious. Assume that (5.9) holds for a fixed value of i, $1 \leqq i \leqq n$. We shall prove that

$$\mathrm{mi}\,(\xi_{i-1}) \overset{*}{\Rightarrow} Q_{i-1} Q_i \ldots Q_n, \tag{5.10}$$

using the relation

$$(Q_{i-1} Q_i \ldots Q_n, \xi_{i-1}) \vdash (Q_i \ldots Q_n, \xi_i). \tag{5.11}$$

Assume first that $Q_{i-1} \in I_T$. Then $\xi_{i-1} = \xi_i Q_{i-1}$, and (5.11) is the result of an application of (5.7). By (5.9),

$$\mathrm{mi}\,(\xi_{i-1}) = Q_{i-1}\,\mathrm{mi}\,(\xi_i) \overset{*}{\Rightarrow} Q_{i-1} Q_i \ldots Q_n.$$

Assume next that $Q_{i-1} = \lambda$. In this case (5.11) is the result of an application of (5.6). Thus, $\xi_{i-1} = \xi'_{i-1} X$, where $X \in I_N$, $\xi_i = \xi'_{i-1}\,\mathrm{mi}\,(\eta)$ and $X \rightarrow \eta$ is in F. Hence,

$$\mathrm{mi}\,(\xi_{i-1}) = X\,\mathrm{mi}\,(\xi'_{i-1}) \Rightarrow \eta\,\mathrm{mi}\,(\xi'_{i-1}) = \mathrm{mi}\,(\xi_i).$$

Therefore, by (5.9),

$$\mathrm{mi}\,(\xi_{i-1}) \overset{*}{\Rightarrow} Q_i \ldots Q_n = Q_{i-1} Q_i \ldots Q_n,$$

which proves that (5.10) holds true also in this case. $\square$

THEOREM 5.2. *For every pushdown automaton* **PDA** *with only one state, there is a type 2 grammar* G *such that* $L(G) = L(\mathbf{PDA})$.

Proof. Given a pushdown automaton

$$\mathbf{PDA} = (I, Z, \{s_0\}, z_0, s_0, f),$$

we consider the type 2 grammar $G = (Z', I, z'_0, F)$, where $Z' = \{z' \,|\, z \in Z\}$ (Z' and I are assumed to be disjoint) and F consists of all productions obtained as follows: whenever $(s_0, P) \in f(s_0, x, z)$, where $x \in I \cup \{\lambda\}$, $z \in Z$ and $P \in W(Z)$, then the production $z' \to x \operatorname{mi}(P')$ is in F. (Here P' is obtained from P by replacing every letter $z \in Z$ by the letter $z' \in Z'$. By definition, $\lambda' = \lambda$.) We shall prove that $L(G) = L(\mathbf{PDA})$.

Assume first that $P \in L(\mathbf{PDA})$. This implies that there is a computation of **PDA**

$$(P, z_0) = (P_0 P_1 \ldots P_{n-1} P_n, \xi_0) \vdash (P_1 \ldots P_{n-1} P_n, \xi_1)$$
$$\vdash \ldots \vdash (P_{n-1} P_n, \xi_{n-1}) \vdash (P_n, \xi_n),$$

where each $P_i \in I \cup \{\lambda\}$, and $P_n = \xi_n = \lambda$. We shall show that, for $i = 0, \ldots, n$,

$$\operatorname{mi}(\xi_i') \overset{*}{\Rightarrow} P_i \ldots P_n. \tag{5.12}$$

For $i = n$, (5.12) is obvious. Assume that (5.12) holds for a fixed value $i, 1 \leq i \leq n$. Consider the relation

$$(P_{i-1} P_i \ldots P_n, \xi_{i-1}) \vdash (P_i \ldots P_n, \xi_i). \tag{5.13}$$

Let $\xi_{i-1} = \eta z$, where $z \in Z$ and $\eta \in W(Z)$. Assume that $f(s_0, P_{i-1}, z)$ contains the pair (s_0, ζ), where ζ is a word over Z, and that (5.13) is the resulting relation, i.e. $\xi_i = \eta \zeta$. By the definition, F contains the production $z' \to P_{i-1} \operatorname{mi}(\zeta')$. Hence, by (5.12),

$$\operatorname{mi}(\xi_{i-1}') = z' \operatorname{mi}(\eta') \Rightarrow P_{i-1} \operatorname{mi}(\zeta') \operatorname{mi}(\eta') = P_{i-1} \operatorname{mi}(\xi_i')$$
$$\overset{*}{\Rightarrow} P_{i-1} P_i \ldots P_n.$$

By descending induction, we conclude that

$$\operatorname{mi}(\xi_0') = z_0' \overset{*}{\Rightarrow} P_0 \ldots P_n = P.$$

Therefore, $P \in L(G)$. We have established the inclusion

$$L(\mathbf{PDA}) \subset L(G). \tag{5.14}$$

Conversely, assume that $Q \in L(G)$. Then there is a derivation of Q of the form

$$z_0' \Rightarrow Q_0 z_1' \zeta_1' \Rightarrow Q_0 Q_1 z_2' \zeta_2' \Rightarrow \ldots \Rightarrow Q_0 Q_1 \ldots Q_{k-1} z_k' \zeta_k'$$
$$\Rightarrow Q_0 Q_1 \ldots Q_{k-1} Q_k = Q,$$

where each $z_i' \in Z'$, each $Q_i \in W(I)$ and each $\zeta_i' \in W(Z' \cup I)$. Furthermore, by the definition of F, it follows that, for each $i = 0, \ldots, k$, $Q_i = \lambda$ or $Q_i \in I$, and $\zeta_i' \in W(Z')$. In particular, this implies that $\zeta_k' = \lambda$

and $z'_k \rightarrow Q_k$ is a production in F. It is another consequence of the definition of F that whenever $z' \Rightarrow xR'$, where $x \in I \cup \{\lambda\}$ and $R' \in W(Z')$, then, for any $R_1 \in W(I)$ and $R_2 \in W(Z)$,

$$(xR_1, R_2 z) \vdash (R_1, R_2 \text{ mi } (R)).$$

This implies that there exists the following computation of **PDA**:

$$(Q_0 Q_1 \ldots Q_{k-1} Q_k, z_0) \vdash (Q_1 \ldots Q_{k-1} Q_k, \text{mi } (\zeta_1) z_1)$$
$$\vdash (Q_2 \ldots Q_{k-1} Q_k, \text{mi } (\zeta_2) z_2) \vdash \ldots \vdash (Q_k, \text{mi } (\zeta_k) z_k) \vdash (\lambda, \lambda).$$

Consequently, $Q \in L(\textbf{PDA})$ and, hence, $L(G) \subset L(\textbf{PDA})$. By (5.14), we obtain the result $L(\textbf{PDA}) = L(G)$. $\square$

As an example, consider the pushdown automaton

$$\textbf{PDA} = (\{x, y\}, \{z_0, z_1, z_2\}, \{s_0\}, z_0, s_0, f),$$

where

$$f(s_0, \lambda, z_0) = \{(s_0, \lambda), (s_0, z_1 z_0 z_1), (s_0, z_2 z_0 z_2)\},$$
$$f(s_0, x, z_1) = \{(s_0, \lambda)\},$$
$$f(s_0, y, z_2) = \{(s_0, \lambda)\},$$
$$f(s_0, P, Q) = \phi, \text{ otherwise.}$$

The corresponding grammar is

$$G = (\{z'_0, z'_1, z'_2\}, \{x, y\}, z'_0, \{z'_0 \rightarrow \lambda, z'_0 \rightarrow z'_1 z'_0 z'_1,$$
$$z'_0 \rightarrow z'_2 z'_0 z'_2, z'_1 \rightarrow x, z'_2 \rightarrow y\}).$$

By Theorem 5.2, $L(G) = L(\textbf{PDA})$. It is easy to see that

$$L(G) = \{P \text{ mi } (P) \,|\, P \in W(\{x, y\})\}.$$

EXERCISE 5.1 (Ginsburg, 1966). How can a pushdown automaton be viewed as a generalization of a non-deterministic finite automaton with one initial state?

EXERCISE 5.2 (Schützenberger, 1963; Ginsburg, 1966). A pushdown automaton $\textbf{PDA} = (I, Z, S, z_0, s_0, f)$ is *deterministic* iff, for each $s \in S$ and $z \in Z$, either (i) $f(s, \lambda, z)$ contains at most one element and $f(s, x, z)$ is empty for all $x \in I$, or (ii) $f(s, \lambda, z)$ is empty and $f(s, x, z)$ contains at most one element for all $x \in I$. A language L is *deterministic* iff $L = L(\textbf{PDA})$, for some deterministic pushdown automaton **PDA**.

Prove that all regular languages are deterministic. Give an example of a non-regular deterministic language. (It is known that deterministic languages form a proper subfamily of $\mathcal{L}_2$, which is closed under complementation. Furthermore, every deterministic language is unambiguous.)

Exercise 5.3. Assume that $\mathbf{PDA} = (I, Z, S, z_0, s_0, f)$ and P is a word over I such that $P \notin L(\mathbf{PDA})$. Give examples of the various ways in which $\mathbf{PDA}$ can "reject" P, i. e. characterize various types of sequences of instantaneous descriptions beginning with (s_0, P, z_0).

Exercise 5.4.   Generalize Theorem 5.2 to concern all pushdown automata. (Cf. Ginsburg, 1966, Lemma 2.5.3.)

Exercise 5.5.   Construct, by Theorem 5.1, a pushdown automaton $\mathbf{PDA}$ representing the language generated by the grammar

$$G = (\{X_0, X_1\}, \{x, y\}, X_0, \{X_0 \to X_0 X_1, \; X_1 \to x X_1 y, \; X_0 \to y, \; X_1 \to y\}).$$

Use then Theorem 5.2 to obtain a grammar G_1 such that $L(G_1) = L$ $(\mathbf{PDA})$, and compare G_1 with G. Perform a similar "double translation", beginning with some given pushdown automaton.

Exercise 5.6   (Ginsburg, 1966). A *generalized* pushdown automaton is an ordered sixtuple (I, Z, S, z_0, s_0, H), where I, Z, S, z_0, s_0 are as in a pushdown automaton and H is a finite subset of the set

$$S \times W(I) \times W(Z) \times S \times W(Z).$$

For $s, s' \in S$; $P_1, P_2 \in W(I)$ and $Q_1, Q_2, Q_3 \in W(Z)$, write

$$(s, P_1 P_2, Q_1 Q_2) \vdash (s', P_2, Q_1 Q_3)$$

iff $(s, P_1, Q_2, s', Q_3) \in H$. Define the notions of a computation and the language represented by a generalized pushdown automaton. Prove that if L is represented by some generalized pushdown automaton, then L is represented also by some pushdown automaton.

§ 6. Context-sensitive languages and linear bounded automata

We shall now study properties of context-sensitive languages and introduce a class of automata corresponding to the family $\mathcal{L}_1$.

Definition. A grammar $G = (I_N, I_T, X_0, F)$ is *length-increasing* iff, for each production $P \to Q$ in F, either $\lg(P) \leq \lg(Q)$; or $Q = \lambda$, $P \in I_N$ and P does not occur on the right side of any production in F.

Clearly, every type 1 grammar is length-increasing. The following theorem shows that also the converse holds true, as far as the generated languages are concerned.

THEOREM 6.1. *For every length-increasing grammar, there is an equivalent type* 1 *grammar.*

Proof. We may assume (cf. the proof of Theorem 1.1) that the grammars considered do not contain productions of the form $X \rightarrow \lambda$. Consider a type 1 grammar $G = (I_N, I_T, X_0, F)$, and let P and Q be words over $I_N \cup I_T$ such that P contains at least one letter of I_N and $\lg(P) \leq \lg(Q)$. We shall prove that, for the grammar

$$G_1 = (I_N, I_T, X_0, F \cup \{P \rightarrow Q\}),$$

there is an equivalent type 1 grammar. If $P = \xi_1 \xi_2 \ldots \xi_m$ and $Q = \eta_1 \eta_2 \ldots \eta_n$, where each $\xi_i \in I_N$ and each $\eta_i \in I_N$, then we add to I_N new non-terminals $Y_1, \ldots, Y_m$ and add to F the productions

$$\xi_1 \xi_2 \ldots \xi_m \rightarrow Y_1 \xi_2 \ldots \xi_m,$$
$$Y_1 \xi_2 \ldots \xi_m \rightarrow Y_1 Y_2 \xi_3 \ldots \xi_m,$$
$$\ldots$$
$$Y_1 Y_2 \ldots Y_{m-1} \xi_m \rightarrow Y_1 \ldots Y_{m-1} Y_m \eta_{m+1} \ldots \eta_n,$$
$$Y_1 Y_2 \ldots Y_m \eta_{m+1} \ldots \eta_n \rightarrow \eta_1 Y_2 \ldots Y_m \eta_{m+1} \ldots \eta_n,$$
$$\ldots$$
$$\eta_1 \ldots \eta_{m-1} Y_m \eta_{m+1} \ldots \eta_n \rightarrow \eta_1 \eta_2 \ldots \eta_n.$$

Clearly, the resulting grammar is of the type 1 and equivalent to G_1. Almost the same procedure is applicable if P or Q contains some letters of I_T. In this case, for each such letter x, a new non-terminal x' is added to I_N, and x is replaced by x' in all productions in the set $F \cup \{P \rightarrow Q\}$. This enables us to apply the procedure considered above. Finally, all productions of the form $x' \rightarrow x$ are added.

Assume that $G_2 = (I_N, I_T, X_0, F_2)$ is a length-increasing grammar. Then

$$F_2 = F_2' \cup \{f_1, \ldots, f_u\},$$

where F_2' contains all such productions of F_2 which satisfy the restriction on type 1 grammars, and f_i is of the form $P_i \rightarrow Q_i$, where $\lg(P_i) \leq$

$\leqq \lg (Q_i), i = 1, \ldots, u$. If F_2' is empty, then also the language $L(G_2)$ is empty. In this case, there clearly exists an equivalent type 1 grammar. If F_2' is not empty then, by what was shown above, the language generated by the grammar $(I_N, I_T, X_0, F_2' \cup \{f_1\})$ is of the type 1. From this it follows that the language generated by the grammar

$$(I_N, I_T, X_0, F_2' \cup \{f_1, f_2\})$$

is of the type 1. By an obvious inductive argument, we see that the language generated by G_2 is of the type 1. $\square$

DEFINITION. A *grammar* with the *end marker* # is a grammar

$$G_\# = (I_N \cup \{\#\}, I_T, X_0, F)$$

such that $\# \notin I_N \cup I_T$ and every production in F is of one of the forms

$$P \to Q, \quad \# P \to \# Q, P \# \to Q \#, \tag{6.1}$$

where P and Q are words over $I_N \cup I_T$ and P contains at least one letter of I_N. The grammar $G_\#$ with the end marker # is of the *type* 1 iff the productions obtained from (6.1) by leaving out the end marker satisfy the restriction on length-increasing grammars. The language $L(G, \#)$ *generated* by the grammar $G_\#$ is defined by

$$L(G, \#) = \{P \mid P \in W(I_T), \ \# X_0 \# \overset{*}{\Rightarrow} \# P \#\}.$$

The notion of the equivalence of grammars is extended to concern also grammars with end markers. (Thereby, languages $L(G, \#)$ rather than $L(G_\#)$ are considered.) Clearly, for every type 1 grammar, there is an equivalent type 1 grammar with an end marker. Our following theorem shows that also the converse holds true. The theorem gives a useful tool for several constructions dealing with type 1 grammars.

THEOREM 6.2. *For every type 1 grammar with an end marker, there is an equivalent type 1 grammar.*

Proof. Let $G_\# = (I_N \cup \{\#\}, I_T, X_0, F)$ be a type 1 grammar with the end marker #. We may again assume that no production of the form $P \to \lambda$ is in the set obtained from F by leaving out the end marker. For each letter $X \in I_N \cup I_T = I$, we introduce three letters ${}^\# X$, $X^\#$ and ${}^\# X^\#$ (each of which is, thus, viewed as a single letter) and denote

$$ {}^\# I = \{{}^\# X \mid X \in I\}, \quad I^\# = \{X^\# \mid X \in I\}, \quad {}^\# I^\# = \{{}^\# X^\# \mid X \in I\}.$$

For $P = \xi_1\xi_2 \ldots \xi_{n-1}\xi_n$, where $n \geqq 1$ and $\xi_i \in I$, we denote

$$^\#P = (^\#\xi_1)\,\xi_2 \ldots \xi_{n-1}\xi_n, \quad P^\# = \xi_1\xi_2 \ldots \xi_{n-1}(\xi_n^\#),$$

$$^\#P^\# = \begin{cases} (^\#\xi_1)\,\xi_2 \ldots \xi_{n-1}(\xi_n^\#) & \text{for } n > 1, \\ ^\#\xi_1^\# & \text{for } n = 1. \end{cases}$$

Consider the grammar

$$G_1 = (I_N \cup {}^\#I \cup I^\# \cup {}^\#I^\#, I_T, {}^\#X_0^\#, F_1),$$

where F_1 consists of all productions obtained as follows. (In (i)−(iv), P and Q are non-empty words over I and $\xi \in I$.)

(i) If $P \to Q$ is in F, then $P \to Q$, $^\#P \to {}^\#Q$, $P^\# \to Q^\#$ and $^\#P^\# \to {}^\#Q^\#$ are in F_1.

(ii) If $\#P \to \#Q$ is in F, then $^\#P \to {}^\#Q$ and $^\#P^\# \to {}^\#Q^\#$ are in F_1.

(iii) If $P\# \to Q\#$ is in F, then $P^\# \to Q^\#$ and $^\#P^\# \to {}^\#Q^\#$ are in F_1.

(iv) $^\#\xi \to \xi$, $\xi^\# \to \xi$ and $^\#\xi^\# \to \xi$ are in F_1.

It is easily verified that $L(G_1) = L(G, \#)$. In fact, the derivation of any word P according to G_1 is converted to a derivation of P according to $G_\#$, and vice versa. (Hereby, $\# P$, $P \#$ and $\# P \#$ correspond to $^\#P$, $P^\#$ and $^\#P^\#$, respectively.) It is also obvious that G_1 is length-increasing and hence, by Theorem 6.1, there is a type 1 grammar equivalent to $G_\#$. □

THEOREM 6.3. *For every length-increasing (type 1) grammar G, there is an equivalent length-increasing (type 1) grammar G' such that every production of G' which involves non-empty terminal letters is of the form $X \to x$, where X is a non-terminal and x a terminal.*

Proof. To obtain G', we replace every non-empty terminal letter y in the productions of G by a new non-terminal Y (in such a way that distinct Y's correspond to distinct y's and none of the Y's is among the non-terminals of G) and add the productions $Y \to y$. (In fact, the same argument was used already in the proof of Theorem 6.1.) □

DEFINITION. A grammar G is of *order n, $n \geqq 1$*, iff for all productions $P \to Q$ of G, $\lg(P) \leqq n$ and $\lg(Q) \leqq n$.

THEOREM 6.4. *For every length-increasing grammar, there exists an equivalent length-increasing grammar of order 2.*

Proof. It suffices to prove that, for a length-increasing grammar G of order $n \geqq 3$, there is an equivalent length-increasing grammar G' of order $n-1$. By Theorem 6.3, we may assume that no terminal letter appears in any production of G, unless the production is of the form $X \to x$, where X is a non-terminal and x is a terminal. The grammar G' is constructed as follows.

Let $P \to Q$ be a production of G. If $\lg(Q) \leqq 2$, then we let $P \to Q$ be a production of G'. (Clearly, in this case also $\lg(P) \leqq 2$.) Otherwise, there exist non-terminals X_1, X_2, X_3, X_4 such that $P = X_1 P'$ and $Q = X_2 X_3 X_4 Q'$, for some (possibly empty) words P' and Q'. If $P' = \lambda$, then we introduce two new non-terminals Y_1 and Y_2, and let

$$X_1 \to Y_1 Y_2, \quad Y_1 \to X_2 \quad \text{and} \quad Y_2 \to X_3 X_4 Q'$$

be productions of G'. If $P = X_1 X_5 P''$, for some non-terminal X_5 and a word P'', then we introduce two new non-terminals Y_3 and Y_4, and let

$$X_1 X_5 \to Y_3 Y_4, \quad Y_3 \to X_2 \quad \text{and} \quad Y_4 P'' \to X_3 X_4 Q'$$

be productions of G'. This procedure is repeated for each production $P \to Q$ of G. Clearly, $L(G') = L(G)$. Furthermore, G' has also the property that no terminal letter appears in any production of G', unless the production is of the form $X \to x$, where X is a non-terminal and x is a terminal. $\square$

DEFINITION. A grammar $G = (I_N, I_T, X_0, F)$ is *linear bounded* iff every production is of one of the forms $X_0 \to X_0 X$, $X_1 X_2 \to Y_1 Y_2$ and $X_1 \to \xi$, where $\xi \in I_N \cup I_T$; $X, X_1, X_2, Y_1, Y_2 \in I_N$ and $X_0 \neq \xi, Y_1, Y_2, X$.

THEOREM 6.5. *For every type 1 grammar G, there is a linear bounded grammar G' which either is equivalent to G or generates the language $L(G) - \{\lambda\}$.*

Proof. By Theorems 6.3 and 6.4, we may assume that $G = (I_N, I_T, X_0, F)$, where every production in F is of one of the following forms (i)–(iv).

  (i) $X_0 \to \lambda$.
  (ii) $X \to \xi$, where $X \in I_N$ and $\xi \in I_N \cup I_T$.
  (iii) $X \to Y_1 Y_2$, where $X, Y_1, Y_2 \in I_N$.
  (iv) $X_1 X_2 \to Y_1 Y_2$, where $X_1, X_2, Y_1, Y_2 \in I_N$.

Consider the grammar $G' = (I_N \cup \{X'_0, X'_1\}, I_T, X'_0, F')$, where X'_0, $X'_1 \notin I_N$ and F' consists of productions (ii) and (iv) of F and of the following productions:

$$X'_0 \to X'_0 X'_1, \quad X'_0 \to X_0,$$
$$X'_1 \xi \to \xi X'_1, \quad \xi X'_1 \to X'_1 \xi, \quad \text{for} \quad \xi \in I_N,$$
$$XX'_1 \to Y_1 Y_2, \text{ for each production (iii) in } F.$$

Clearly, G' is linear bounded. Let G_0 be the grammar obtained from G by removing the production (i). Whenever

$$X'_0 \underset{G'}{\overset{*}{\Rightarrow}} P \quad \text{and} \quad P \in W(I_T), \quad \text{then} \quad X_0 \underset{G_0}{\overset{*}{\Rightarrow}} P,$$

where the latter derivation is obtained by removing all occurrences of X'_1. Conversely, if

$$X_0 \underset{G_0}{\overset{*}{\Rightarrow}} P, \quad \text{then} \quad X_0 (X'_1)^n \underset{G'}{\overset{*}{\Rightarrow}} P,$$

for some $n \geqq 0$, and hence,

$$X'_0 \underset{G'}{\overset{*}{\Rightarrow}} P.$$

This proves that $L(G') = L(G_0)$. □

We shall now introduce a class of recognition devices which bear the same relation to context-sensitive languages as pushdown automata do to context-free languages and as finite deterministic automata do to regular languages. Again, we shall first give an intuitive description of these devices, called *linear bounded automata*.

A linear bounded automaton possesses the capability of finite deterministic two-way automata to move in both directions when scanning the input word. Furthermore, it is able to replace the scanned letter by another letter. However, while doing this it may use as much space only as is occupied by the input word. This is the distinction between linear bounded automata and Turing machines. (The latter will be discussed in the next section.)

A linear bounded automaton is capable of a finite number of internal states. Like in connection with all of the recognition devices we have considered, the actions of a linear bounded automaton at any moment depend only on its internal state and the scanned letter. The actions are specified by a list of instructions, each of the form

$$(s', y, k) \in f(s, x), \tag{6.2}$$

where s and s' are states, x and y letters and $k = 0, 1, -1$. The instruction (6.2) means that if x is scanned in the state s, then one possible behavior is as follows: (i) replace x by y, (ii) move scanning position one step to the right (left) if $k = 1$ ($k = -1$), or do not move if $k = 0$, and (iii) go to the state s'. The instruction (6.2) with $k = -1$ is illustrated in Fig. 23. Linear bounded automata are non-deterministic:

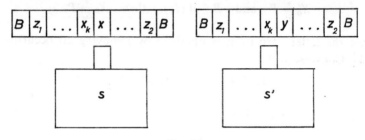

Fig. 23.

there may be several instructions for each pair (s, x). If the automaton scans x in the state s and there are no instructions of the form (6.2), then it halts.

The input words are given between two boundary markers B. (The boundary markers are introduced only to simplify constructions. In fact, they are dispensable.) The automaton can neither replace B by another letter nor other letters by B. In addition to a specified initial state, the automaton has also a *designated set of final states*. Given an input word between boundary markers, the automaton starts scanning the left boundary marker in the initial state. If there is a sequence of moves such that the automaton goes off the right end of the tape in one of the designated final states, then the input word is accepted by the automaton. As in connection with non-deterministic devices in general, the existence of one such sequence of moves implies that the input is accepted, no matter whether or not the same input causes other sequences of moves during which, for instance, the automaton halts with-

out going off the right end of the tape or does the latter in a non-desig-
nated state or goes into a loop, i.e. enters a never-ending computation.
All accepted input words constitute the language represented by the
linear bounded automaton. It will be shown that the family of languages
represented by linear bounded automata equals the family $\mathcal{L}_1$.
These notions will now be formalized.

DEFINITION. A *linear bounded automaton* is an ordered sixtuple
$\mathbf{LBA} = (I, S, B, s_0, S_1, f)$, where I is a finite alphabet, S is a finite non-
empty set (the set of *internal states*), $B \in I$ (the *boundary marker*), $s_0 \in S$
(the *initial state*), $S_1 \subset S$ (the set of *final* states) and f is a mapping of
the set $S \times I$ into the set of all subsets of $S \times I \times \{1, 0, -1\}$ such that
whenever $(s', y, k) \in f(s, B)$ then $y = B$, and whenever $(s', B, k) \in$
$f(s, x)$ then $x = B$ (the *move* function).

An *instantaneous description* is a word of the form $R = PsQ$, where
$s \in S$ and $P, Q \in W(I)$. The instantaneous description R_1 *directly
yields* the instantaneous description R_2, in symbols, $R_1 \vdash_{\mathbf{LBA}} R_2$ or
shortly $R_1 \vdash R_2$ iff one of the following conditions (i)–(iii) is satisfied, where $s, s' \in S$, $x, y, z \in I$ and $P, Q \in W(I)$.

  (i) $R_1 = PsxQ$, $R_2 = Ps'yQ$ and $(s', y, 0) \in f(s, x)$.
 (ii) $R_1 = PsxQ$, $R_2 = Pys'Q$ and $(s', y, 1) \in f(s, x)$.
(iii) $R_1 = PzsxQ$, $R_2 = Ps'zyQ$ and $(s', y, -1) \in f(s, x)$.

The instantaneous description R *yields* the instantaneous description
R', in symbols, $R \vdash^{*}_{\mathbf{LBA}} R'$ or shortly $R \vdash^{*} R'$ iff there is a finite
sequence of instantaneous descriptions, referred to as a *computation*,

$$R_0, R_1, \ldots, R_k \qquad (k \geqq 0)$$

such that $R_0 = R$, $R_k = R'$ and, for all $i = 0, \ldots, k-1$, R_i directly
yields R_{i+1}. A word P over $I - \{B\}$ is *accepted* by $\mathbf{LBA}$ iff there is a
word Q over I and a state $s_1 \in S_1$ such that the instantaneous description $s_0 BPB$ yields the instantaneous description Qs_1, i.e.

$$s_0 BPB \vdash^{*} Qs_1.$$

The language $L(\mathbf{LBA}, I_1)$ over an alphabet $I_1 \subset I - \{B\}$ *represented*
(or *accepted*) by $\mathbf{LBA}$ consists of all words over I_1 accepted by $\mathbf{LBA}$,
i.e.

$$L(\mathbf{LBA}, I_1) = \{P | P \in W(I_1), s_0 BPB \vdash^{*} Qs_1, s_1 \in S_1, Q \in W(I)\}.$$

Note that all instantaneous descriptions appearing in a computation are words of the same length. As an example, consider the linear bounded automaton

$$\textbf{LBA} = (\{X, Y, x, y, B\}, \{s_0, s', s_1, s_2, s_3, s_4\}, B, s_0, \{s'\}, f), \quad (6.3)$$

where

$$f(s_0, B) = \{(s_1, B, 1)\}, \qquad f(s_1, B) = \{(s', B, 1)\},$$
$$f(s_1, x) = \{(s_2, X, 1)\}, \qquad f(s_1, Y) = \{(s_1, Y, 1)\},$$
$$f(s_2, x) = \{(s_2, x, 1)\}, \qquad f(s_2, y) = \{(s_2, y, 1)\},$$
$$f(s_2, Y) = \{(s_3, Y, -1)\}, \qquad f(s_2, B) = \{(s_3, B, -1)\},$$
$$f(s_3, y) = \{(s_4, Y, -1)\}, \qquad f(s_4, x) = \{(s_4, x, -1)\},$$
$$f(s_4, y) = \{(s_4, y, -1)\}, \qquad f(s_4, X) = \{(s_1, X, 1)\},$$
$$f(s, \xi) = \phi, \text{ for all other arguments } (s, \xi).$$

Note that **LBA** is *deterministic* in the sense that, given a state s and a letter ξ, there is at most one possible move for **LBA**. (Cf. Exercise 6.5.) Consider the following two computations of (6.3):

$$s_0BxxyyB \vdash Bs_1xxyyB \vdash BXs_2xyyB \overset{*}{\vdash} BXxyys_2B \vdash BXxys_3yB$$

$$\vdash BXxs_4yYB \overset{*}{\vdash} Bs_4XxyYB \vdash BXs_1xyYB \vdash BXXs_2yYB \vdash BXXys_2YB$$

$$\vdash BXXs_3yYB \vdash BXs_4XYYB \vdash BXXs_1YYB \overset{*}{\vdash} BXXYYBs'$$

and $\qquad\qquad s_0BxB \vdash Bs_1xB \vdash BXs_2B \vdash Bs_3XB. \qquad\qquad (6.4)$

The first computation shows that the word $xxyy$ is accepted by (6.3). Because there is no computation of (6.3) beginning with s_0BxB other than (6.4), we conclude that the word x is not accepted by **LBA**. It is easy to see that the language $L(\textbf{LBA}, \{x, y\})$ over the alphabet $\{x, y\}$ represented by (6.3) equals the language $\{x^ny^n \mid n \geqq 0\}$. Thus, all words of the form x^ny^n, $n \geqq 0$, are accepted by **LBA**, whereas no other word *over the alphabet* $\{x, y\}$ is accepted by **LBA**.

In the next two theorems it will be shown that a language is context-sensitive iff it is represented by some linear bounded automaton.

THEOREM 6.6. *For any context-sensitive language L, there exists a linear bounded automaton* **LBA** *such that L is represented by* **LBA**.

Proof. By Theorem 6.5, we may assume that $L - \{\lambda\}$ is generated by a grammar $G = (I_N, I_T, X_0, F)$ such that every production is of one of the following forms (6.5)–(6.7).

$$X \to \xi \quad (X \in I_N, \xi \in I_N \cup I_T, \xi \neq X_0), \qquad (6.5)$$
$$X_0 \to X_0 X_1 \quad (X_1 \in I_N, X_1 \neq X_0), \qquad (6.6)$$
$$X_1 X_2 \to Y_1 Y_2 \quad (X_1, X_2, Y_1, Y_2 \in I_N, Y_1, Y_2 \neq X_0). \qquad (6.7)$$

Furthermore, $\lambda \in L$ iff in the grammar generating L there is the production $Y_0 \to \lambda$, where Y_0 is the initial symbol.

We define a linear bounded automaton

$$\mathbf{LBA} = (I_N \cup I_T \cup \{A, B\}, S, B, s_0, \{s_3\}, f)$$

(where $A, B \notin I_N \cup I_T$) as follows. The set S contains the states s_0, s_1, s_2, s_3, s_4 and, furthermore, a state s_{X_1} for each X_1 such that there is a production (6.7) in F. In defining the move function f, we use the notation

$$(s, \xi) \vdash (s', \xi', k)$$

to mean that $(s', \xi', k) \in f(s, \xi)$. For each s and ξ, $f(s, \xi)$ consists of exactly the triples given below. (If, for some s and ξ, there is no triple (s', ξ', k) such that $(s, \xi) \vdash (s', \xi', k)$, then $f(s, \xi) = \phi$.)

$$
\begin{aligned}
&(s_0, B) \vdash (s_0, B, 1), \\
&(s_0, B) \vdash (s_4, B, 1) \quad \text{if} \quad \lambda \in L;
\end{aligned}
\qquad (6.8)
$$

$$
\left.
\begin{aligned}
&(s_0, \eta) \vdash (s_0, \eta, 1) \\
&(s_0, \eta) \vdash (s_0, \eta, -1)
\end{aligned}
\right\} \text{ for all } \eta \in I_N \cup I_T;
\qquad (6.9)
$$

$$(s_0, \xi) \vdash (s_0, X, 0) \quad \text{whenever (6.5) is in } F; \qquad (6.10)$$

$$
\left.
\begin{aligned}
&(s_0, Y_1) \vdash (s_{X_1}, X_1, 1) \\
&(s_{X_1}, Y_2) \vdash (s_0, X_2, 0)
\end{aligned}
\right\} \text{ whenever (6.7) is in } F;
\qquad (6.11)
$$

$$(s_0, X_0) \vdash (s_1, X_0, -1), \qquad (6.12)$$

$$
\begin{aligned}
&(s_1, B) \vdash (s_2, B, 1), \\
&(s_1, A) \vdash (s_2, A, 1), \\
&(s_2, X_0) \vdash (s_3, A, 1), \\
&(s_3, X_1) \vdash (s_0, X_0, 0) \quad \text{whenever (6.6) is in } F, \\
&(s_3, B) \vdash (s_3, B, 1), \quad (s_4, B) \vdash (s_3, B, 1).
\end{aligned}
$$

Obviously, (6.8) begins the computation and checks whether $\lambda \in L$. Instruction (6.9) allows **LBA** to move back and forth while looking for a suitable position to continue the computation. Instructions (6.10) and (6.11) mimic the productions (6.5) and (6.7), respectively, backwards. Instructions beginning with (6.12) do the same for productions (6.6) in the case where $X_0 X_1$ is in the position $BA^n X_0 X_1$, for some $n \geqq 0$. In this case $BA^n X_0 X_1$ is replaced by $BA^{n+1} X_0$. Finally, instructions beginning with (6.12) also check whether or not X_0 is in the position $BA^n X_0 B$, for some $n \geqq 0$. If it is, then **LBA** goes off the right end in the designated final state. The only other case (for words over I_T), where this can happen, is that $\lambda \in L$ and the computation begins with the instantaneous description $s_0 BB$.

Hence, **LBA** accepts only such words over I_T which are generated by G. On the other hand, **LBA** can simulate any derivation according to G backwards. Thus,

$$L(\mathbf{LBA}, I_T) = L. \quad \square \qquad (6.13)$$

THEOREM 6.7. *For any linear bounded automaton* $\mathbf{LBA} = (I, S, B, s_0, S_1, f)$ *and any alphabet* $I_1 \subset I - \{B\}$, *the language* $L(\mathbf{LBA}, I_1)$ *is context-sensitive.*

Proof. We denote by S_1' the set of all states s_1' such that, for some sequence of states $s_1', \ldots, s_k'$ $(k \geqq 1)$, $f(s_i', B)$ contains the element $(s_{i+1}', B, 0)$ (where $i = 1, \ldots, k-1$) and $f(s_k', B)$ contains the element $(s_1, B, 1)$, where $s_1 \in S_1$.

Consider the grammar $G = (I_N, I_1, X_0, F)$, where I_N and F are defined as follows. The set I_N contains

(i) for each $s \in S$ and $x \in I - \{B\}$, the elements X_{sx}, $^B X_{sx}$, X_{sx}^B and $^B X_{sx}^B$;

(ii) for each $x \in I - \{B\}$, the elements $^B x$ and x^B;

(iii) all elements of $I - I_1 - \{B\}$;

(iv) the letters X_0 and X_1 (which are assumed not to belong to I).

The set F consists of the following productions (i)−(x).

(i) $X_1 \to {}^B X$, $X_1 \to X_1 x$, for all $x \in I - \{B\}$.

(ii) $X_0 \to {}^B X_{sx}^B$, $X_0 \to X_1 X_{sx}^B$, provided $f(s, x)$ contains, for some $y \in I - \{B\}$, the element $(s_1', y, 1)$, where $s_1' \in S_1'$.

(iii) $X_{s'z} y \to z X_{sx}$, $^B X_{s'z} y \to {}^B z X_{sx}$, $X_{s'z} y^B \to z X_{sx}^B$, $^B X_{s'z} y^B \to {}^B z X_{sx}^B$, provided $f(s, x)$ contains the element $(s', y, -1)$ and $z \in I - \{B\}$.

(iv) $yX_{s'z} \to X_{sx}z$, $^By X_{s'z} \to {}^B X_{sx}z$, $yX^B_{s'z} \to X_{sx}z^B$, $^B y X^B_{s'z} \to {}^B X_{sx}z^B$, provided $f(s, x)$ contains the element $(s', y, 1)$ and $z \in I - \{B\}$.

(v) $X_{s'y} \to X_{sx}$, $^B X_{s'y} \to {}^B X_{sx}$, $X^B_{s'y} \to X^B_{sx}$, $^B X^B_{s'y} \to {}^B X^B_{sx}$, provided $f(s, x)$ contains the element $(s', y, 0)$.

(vi) $X^B_{s'y} \to X^B_{sx}$, $^B X^B_{s'y} \to {}^B X^B_{sx}$, provided for some $s''_1, \ldots, s''_k \in S$ $(k \geqq 1)$, $f(s, x)$ contains the element $(s''_1, y, 1)$, $f(s''_i, B)$ contains the element $(s''_{i+1}, B, 0)$, where $i = 1, \ldots, k-1$, and $f(s''_k, B)$ contains the element $(s', B, -1)$.

(vii) $^B X_{s'y} \to {}^B X_{sx}$, $^B X^B_{s'y} \to {}^B X^B_{sx}$, provided for some $s''_1, \ldots, s''_k \in S$ $(k \geqq 1)$, $f(s, x)$ contains the element $(s''_1, y, -1)$, $f(s''_i, B)$ contains the element $(s''_{i+1}, B, 0)$, where $i = 1, \ldots, k-1$, and $f(s''_k, B)$ contains the element $(s', B, 1)$.

(viii) $x^B \to x$, for all $x \in I - \{B\}$.

(ix) $^B X_{sx} \to x$, $^B X^B_{sx} \to x$, provided $f(s_0, B)$ contains the element $(s, B, 1)$. (Without loss of generality, we assume that $f(s_0, B)$ contains only elements of the form $(s', B, 1)$.)

(x) $X_0 \to \lambda$, provided $\lambda \in L(\textbf{LBA}, I_1)$.

By Theorem 6.1, $L(G)$ is context-sensitive.

Consider all such words P which contain neither X_0 nor X_1 and can be derived from X_0 using productions (i)–(vii). Clearly, every such word P contains exactly one letter X_{sx} (possibly with one or two superscripts B), the first (last) letter of P is marked by a left (right) superscript B, and all letters between the first and last one are without superscripts B. To each such word P, we associate the instantaneous description $\varphi(P)$ by replacing X_{sx} by sx and the superscript B by the letter B. (For instance, if $P = {}^B X^B_{sx}$, then $\varphi(P) = BsxB$.)

If P_1 and P_2 are words of the considered form, then $P_1 \overset{*}{\Rightarrow} P_2$ iff $\varphi(P_2) \overset{*}{\vdash} \varphi(P_1)$. (In fact, by (iii)–(vii), for each step in the computation, there corresponds a step in the derivation, and vice versa. Hereby,

$$QsxB \vdash Qys''_1 B \vdash \ldots \vdash Qys''_k B \vdash Qs'yB$$

is counted as one step in the computation. The same convention is made with respect to the left boundary marker.) By (i) and (ii), exactly all words P such that $\varphi(P) = BQsxB$, where $Q \in W(I - \{B\})$ and

$$sxB \vdash ys'_1 B \vdash ys'_2 B \vdash \ldots \vdash ys'_k B \vdash yBs_1, \quad s_1 \in S_1,$$

can be derived from X_0. On the other hand, the only way to eliminate the non-terminals X_{sx} (possibly with superscripts) is to use some production (ix), and x^B can be eliminated by (viii). Hence, we conclude that, for a non-empty word P over $I-\{B\}$, $X_0 \overset{*}{\Rightarrow} P$ iff $s_0 BPB \overset{*}{\vdash} BP'Bs_1$, where $P' \in W(I-\{B\})$ and $s_1 \in S_1$. By (x), the same conclusion holds true also if $P = \lambda$. Therefore, by the choice of the terminal alphabet of G,

$$L(G) = L(\mathbf{LBA}, I_1). \quad \square$$

The proof of Theorem 6.7 is much easier in the absence of boundary markers for linear bounded automata. (Cf. Exercises 6.9 and 6.11.) As a corollary of Theorems 6.6 and 6.7, we obtain the following

THEOREM 6.8. *The intersection of two context-sensitive languages* L' *and* L'' *is context-sensitive.*

Proof. By Theorem 6.6, there exist linear bounded automata

$$\mathbf{LBA}' = (I', S', B, s_0', S_1', f') \text{ and } \mathbf{LBA}'' = (I'', S'', B, s_0'', S_1'', f'')$$

such that

$$L' = L(\mathbf{LBA}', I_1') \text{ and } L'' = L(\mathbf{LBA}'', I_1'').$$

Denote $I = I_1' \cap I_1''$. We may assume that S' and S'' are disjoint.

We now construct a linear bounded automaton $\mathbf{LBA}$ which acts as follows. The alphabet of $\mathbf{LBA}$ includes all pairs (x, y), where $x \in I'$ and $y \in I''$. Given a word P (over I) between the boundary markers, $\mathbf{LBA}$ first replaces every letter x in P by the letter (x, x). It then goes back to the left boundary marker and simulates the computation of $\mathbf{LBA}'$ on the first members of the pairs. If $\mathbf{LBA}'$ accepts P, then $\mathbf{LBA}$ starts the computation again from the left boundary marker, this time simulating $\mathbf{LBA}''$ on the second members of the pairs. If $\mathbf{LBA}''$ accepts P, then $\mathbf{LBA}$ goes off the right end in a designated final state and, thus, accepts P. Furthermore, this is the only possibility for $\mathbf{LBA}$ to go off the right end in a designated final state. Hence, $L(\mathbf{LBA}, I) = L' \cap L''$. By Theorem 6.7, $L' \cap L''$ is context-sensitive.

The formal definition of $\mathbf{LBA}$ is now given.

$$\mathbf{LBA} = (I \cup I' \times I'', S' \cup S'' \cup \{s_0, s_1, s_2, s_3\}, (B, B), s_0, S_1'', f),$$

where f is defined below. In the definition of f, we use the same notation as in the proof of Theorem 6.6, whereby $\vdash$, $\vdash'$ and $\vdash''$ refer to f, f' and f'', respectively.

$(s_0, (B, B)) \vdash (s_1, (B, B), 1),$

$(s_1, x) \vdash (s_1, (x, x), 1),$ for all $x \in I,$

$(s_1, (B, B)) \vdash (s_2, (B, B), -1),$

$(s_2, (x, x)) \vdash (s_2, (x, x), -1),$ for all $x \in I,$

$(s_2, (B, B)) \vdash (s_0', (B, B), 0),$

$(s', (x, y)) \vdash (\bar{s}', (\bar{x}, y), k)$ whenever $(s', x) \vdash' (\bar{s}', \bar{x}, k)$ and $y \in I'',$

$(s', (B, B)) \vdash (s_3, (B, B), -1)$ whenever $(s', B) \vdash' (s_1', B, 1)$ and $s_1' \in S_1',$

$(s_3, (x, y)) \vdash (s_3, (x, y), -1),$ for all $(x, y) \in I' \times I'',$

$(s_3, (B, B)) \vdash (s_0'', (B, B), 0),$

$(s'', (x, y)) \vdash (\bar{s}'', (x, \bar{y}), k)$ whenever $(s'', y) \vdash'' (\bar{s}'', \bar{y}, k)$ and $x \in I'.$ $\square$

EXERCISE 6.1. Show in detail that $L(G_1) = L(G, \#)$ in the proof of Theorem 6.2. Can you establish Theorem 6.2 also for type 0 grammars? (Note that in this case you have to pay special attention to the productions $P \to \lambda$.)

EXERCISE 6.2. Is Theorem 6.3 valid for type 0 (type 2, type 3) grammars?

EXERCISE 6.3. Give another proof of Theorem 6.1 using Theorems 6.3 and 6.4.

EXERCISE 6.4. In what way can a pushdown automaton be viewed as a linear bounded automaton?

EXERCISE 6.5. A linear bounded automaton $\mathbf{LBA} = (I, S, B, s_0, S_1, f)$ is *deterministic* iff, for all $s \in S$ and $x \in I$, the set $f(s, x)$ contains at most one element. Thus, (6.3) is deterministic. What are the languages represented by (6.3) over different subalphabets of the alphabet $\{X, Y, x, y\}$?

EXERCISE 6.6 (Kuroda, 1964). Prove that every context-free language is represented by a deterministic linear bounded automaton. Use Exercise 3.11 to conclude that pushdown automata can be simulated by deterministic linear bounded automata. Conclude that the complement of a context-free language is context-sensitive.

EXERCISE 6.7. Give a detailed proof of (6.13).

EXERCISE 6.8 (due to M. Soittola). Prove that the deterministic $\mathbf{LBA} = (\{B, X, Y, x\}, \{s_0, s_1, s_2, t_0, t_1, t_2, t_3, r_0, r_1, u_0, u_1\}, B, s_0, \{s_2\}, f),$ where f is defined below, accepts over $\{x\}$ the language consisting of all words of prime length.

$(s_0, B) \vdash$ $(s_0, B, 1)$, $(s_0, x) \vdash (s_1, x, 1)$; $(s_1, x) \vdash (s_2, X, 1)$;
$(s_2, B) \vdash$ $(s_2, B, 1)$, $(s_2, x) \vdash (t_0, Y, -1)$; $(t_0, x) \vdash (t_0, x, -1)$,
$(t_0, X) \vdash$ $(t_0, X, -1)$, $(t_0, Y) \vdash (t_1, x, 1)$, $(t_0, B) \vdash (t_1, B, 1)$;
$(t_1, x) \vdash$ $(t_2, Y, 1)$, $(t_1, X) \vdash (r_0, X, 1)$; $(t_2, x) \vdash (t_2, x, 1)$,
$(t_2, X) \vdash$ $(t_2, X, 1)$, $(t_2, Y) \vdash (t_3, x, 1)$; $(t_3, x) \vdash (t_0, Y, -1)$,
$(t_3, B) \vdash$ $(u_0, B, -1)$; $(r_0, x) \vdash (r_0, x, 1)$, $(r_0, Y) \vdash (r_1, x, 1)$;
$(r_1, x) \vdash$ $(t_0, Y, -1)$; $(u_0, x) \vdash (u_0, x, -1)$, $(u_0, X) \vdash (u_0, X, -1)$,
$(u_0, Y) \vdash$ $(u_1, x, 1)$; $(u_1, x) \vdash (u_1, x, 1)$, $(u_1, X) \vdash (s_1, x, 1)$.

EXERCISE 6.9. Prove the following simplified version of Theorem 6.7: for any language $L_1 = L(\mathbf{LBA}, I_1)$, there is a type 1 grammar G such that
$$L(G) = \{BPB \mid P \in L_1\}.$$

EXERCISE 6.10. Modify the definition of a linear bounded automaton in such a way that there is only the right boundary marker. Prove Theorem 6.6 for this modified notion. After that remove also the right boundary marker and prove Theorem 6.6. (The latter task will be much more involved than the former.)

EXERCISE 6.11. Use Theorem 6.2 to establish Theorem 6.7 for linear bounded automata without boundary markers.

EXERCISE 6.12 (Landweber, 1963). Prove Theorem 6.8 by constructing directly the grammar which generates the intersection, i.e. without using Theorems 6.6 and 6.7.

EXERCISE 6.13. Prove that $\mathcal{L}_0$ and the subfamily of $\mathcal{L}_1$ consisting of languages not containing λ are closed under substitution.

EXERCISE 6.14. For two languages K and L, define the *left derivative* of L with respect to K by
$$\partial_K L = \{P \mid \exists Q \in K, QP \in L\}.$$

Define similarly the *right derivative* of L with respect to K. (Cf. also Exercise III.7.6.) Prove that if K and L are regular, then the left (right) derivative of L with respect to K is regular. Study the same problem for the case where K and L are context-free.

PROBLEM 6.1. Is the complement of a context-sensitive language context-sensitive?

§ 7. Type 0 languages and Turing machines

In this section, we shall discuss type 0 languages and the corresponding recognition devices, namely, Turing machines. Most of the proofs concerning type 0 languages, including the proof of the equality of the family $\mathscr{L}_0$ and the family of languages accepted by Turing machines, require tools which lie beyond the scope of this book. (In fact, a language is of the type 0 iff it is recursively enumerable. For recursively enumerable sets, the reader is referred to Davis (1958).) Many results in this section are given without proofs.

We shall first establish a result corresponding to Theorems 2.2, 3.4 and 6.8.

THEOREM 7.1. *The intersection of two type* 0 *languages is a type* 0 *language.*

Proof. Assume that $L' = L(G')$ and $L'' = L(G'')$, where

$$G' = (I'_N, I'_T, X'_0, F'), \quad G'' = (I''_N, I''_T, X''_0, F'').$$

Without loss of generality, we assume that the sets I'_N and I''_N are disjoint. Consider the grammar

$$G = (I'_N \cup I''_N \cup I_N, \quad I'_T \cup I''_T, X_0, F' \cup F'' \cup F),$$

where I_N contains, for every $x \in I'_T \cup I''_T$, an element X_x and, furthermore, four additional elements X_0, X_1, X_2, X_3, and where F consists of the following productions:

$$X_0 \rightarrow X_1 X'_0 X_2 X_3 X''_0 X_1, \tag{7.1}$$

$$X_2 X_3 x \rightarrow X_x X_3, \qquad \text{for all } x \in I'_T \cup I''_T, \tag{7.2}$$

$$y X_x \rightarrow X_x y, \qquad \text{for all } x, y \in I'_T \cup I''_T, \tag{7.3}$$

$$X_1 X_x x \rightarrow x X_1 X_2, \qquad \text{for all } x \in I'_T \cup I''_T, \tag{7.4}$$

$$X_2 x \rightarrow x X_2, \qquad \text{for all } x \in I'_T \cup I''_T, \tag{7.5}$$

$$X_1 X_2 X_3 X_1 \rightarrow \lambda. \tag{7.6}$$

Using (7.1) and the productions in $F' \cup F''$, all words of the form

$$X_1 P' X_2 X_3 P'' X_1 \qquad (P' \in L', P'' \in L''), \tag{7.7}$$

can be derived from X_0. By (7.2)–(7.5), the word

$$P' X_1 X_2 X_3 X_1 \tag{7.8}$$

can be derived from (7.7) iff $P' = P''$. By (7.6), the word P' can be derived from (7.8). Because this is the only case where a derivation leads from X_0 to a terminal word, we conclude that $L(G) = L' \cap L''$. $\square$

It can be shown that there is a type 0 language whose complement is not of the type 0, i.e. is not generated by any grammar. The following table summarizes the discussed closure properties of the families $\mathcal{L}_i$. Thereby "yes" ("no") indicates that the family is (is not) closed under the operation.

	Substitution	Catenation	Catenation closure	Sum	Intersection	Complementation
$\mathcal{L}_0$	yes	yes	yes	yes	yes	no
$\mathcal{L}_1$	no	yes	yes	yes	yes	?
$\mathcal{L}_2$	yes	yes	yes	yes	no	no
$\mathcal{L}_3$	yes	yes	yes	yes	yes	yes

We shall now introduce the notion of a Turing machine. A Turing machine acts in the same way as a linear bounded automaton. The essential difference is that the former is capable of "extending the tape", i.e. a Turing machine can replace the boundary marker by some other letter and after that add another boundary marker. Another difference is that a Turing machine is deterministic, i.e. at each moment there is at most one possible next move. One can introduce also a non-deterministic Turing machine. However, this is not the customary formulation because of the following reason. As regards linear bounded automata, it is not known whether or not there is an essential difference between deterministic and non-deterministic automata in the sense that the family of languages represented in the former is smaller. This difference does not exist as regards Turing machines.

DEFINITION. A *Turing machine* is an ordered sixtuple $\mathbf{TM} = (I,$ $S, B, s_0, S_1, f)$, where I is a finite alphabet, S is a finite non-empty set (the set of *internal states*), $B \in I$ (the *boundary marker*), $s_0 \in S$ (the *initial state*), $S_1 \subset S$ (the set of *final states*) and f is a function mapping some subset of $S \times I$ into the set $S \times I \times \{1, 0, -1\}$ (the *move function*).

An *instantaneous description* is a word of the form $R = PsQ$, where $s \in S$ and $P, Q \in W(I)$. The instantaneous description R_1 *directly yields* the instantaneous description R_2, in symbols $R_1 \vdash_{\mathbf{TM}} R_2$ or shortly $R_1 \vdash R_2$, iff one of the following conditions (i)–(v) is satisfied, where $s, s' \in S$; $x, y, z \in I$ and $P, Q \in W(I)$.

(i) $R_1 = PsxQ$, $R_2 = Ps'yQ$ and $f(s, x) = (s', y, 0)$.

(ii) $R_1 = PsxQ$, $Q \neq \lambda$, $R_2 = Pys'Q$ and $f(s, x) = (s', y, 1)$.

(iii) $R_1 = PsB$, $R_2 = Pys'B$ and $f(s, B) = (s', y, 1)$.

(iv) $R_1 = PzsxQ$, $R_2 = Ps'zyQ$ and $f(s, x) = (s', y, -1)$.

(v) $R_1 = sBQ$, $R_2 = s'ByQ$ and $f(s, B) = (s', y, -1)$.

The instantaneous description R *yields* the instantaneous description R', in symbols, $R \vdash^*_{\mathbf{TM}} R'$ or shortly $R \vdash^* R'$ iff there is a finite sequence of instantaneous descriptions

$$R_0, R_1, \ldots, R_k \quad (k \geqq 0),$$

referred to as a *computation* such that $R_0 = R$, $R_k = R'$ and, for all $i = 0, \ldots, k-1$, R_i directly yields R_{i+1}. The instantaneous description R is *final* iff R yields no instantaneous description $R' \neq R$. $\mathbf{TM}$ *halts* with R iff R is final.

A word P is *accepted* by $\mathbf{TM}$ iff the instantaneous description s_0BPB yields some final instantaneous description which contains a final state, i.e. iff

$$s_0BPB \vdash^* Q_1s_1Q_2,$$

for some $Q_1, Q_2 \in W(I)$ and $s_1 \in S_1$ such that $Q_1s_1Q_2$ is final. The language $L(\mathbf{TM}, I_1)$ over an alphabet $I_1 \subset I - \{B\}$ *represented* (or *accepted*) by the Turing machine $\mathbf{TM}$ consists of all words over I_1 accepted by $\mathbf{TM}$.

The proof of the following theorem, being analogous to the proof of Theorem 6.7, is left to the reader.

THEOREM 7.2. *For any Turing machine* **TM** $= (I, S, B, s_0, S_1, f)$ *and any alphabet* $I_1 \subset I - \{B\}$, *there is a type* 0 *grammar G such that*

$$L(G) = L(\text{TM}, I_1).$$

Also the converse of Theorem 7.2 holds true: for any type 0 language, one can construct a Turing machine representing it. The proof of this fact requires a more elaborate theory of Turing machines. However, it can be proved for non-deterministic Turing machines in the same way as Theorem 6.6. (Cf. Exercise 7.2.)

We shall mention another difference between Turing machines and linear bounded automata. The family of languages represented by Turing machines is not affected if the "auxiliary symbols" are not permitted, i.e. for any Turing machine **TM** $= (I, S, B, s_0, S_1, f)$, only the language $L(\text{TM}, I - \{B\})$ is considered. However, the absence of auxiliary symbols properly diminishes the family of languages represented by linear bounded automata.

We have seen that the same formal language families can be obtained using two different methods, namely, by the hierarchy of grammar types and by various kinds of automata. These methods can be described as definition by *generation* and *recognition*, respectively. There is still another method, namely, to construct formulas denoting a given language. This definition by *construction* has been illustrated by regular expressions which denote type 3 languages. (References to other formulas denoting type 3 languages are given in Problem I.2.1.) A general procedure to construct formulas denoting languages is to specify a basis and some operations (such as those of the propositional calculus and bounded or unbounded quantifiers). A very fruitful approach, due originally to Smullyan (1960), has been to consider the catenation relation $PQ = R$ as a basis and to apply so-called *rudimentary* operations (conjunction, disjunction, negation, bounded quantification, introduction and identification of variables, substitution of a variable by a constant). To see how this leads to a simple characterization of type 0 and type 1 languages, the reader is referred to the work of Jones (1967, 1, 2).

EXERCISE 7.1. Prove Theorem 7.2. Discuss why the resulting grammar is not (in general) of the type 1.

EXERCISE 7.2. Introduce the notion of a non-deterministic Turing machine and, for this notion, prove the converse of Theorem 7.2. (Cf. Theorem 6.6.)

EXERCISE 7.3. (For those familiar with Turing machines.) Prove the converse of Theorem 7.2.

EXERCISE 7.4. (Jones, 1966; for those familiar with Turing machines.) Without loss of generality, we may assume that, for any type 0 grammar $G = (I_N, I_T, X_0, F)$,

$$I_N \subset \{X_0, X_2, X_4, \ldots\}, \quad I_T \subset \{X_1, X_3, X_5, \ldots\}.$$

Denote $I_X = \{X_0, X_1, X_2, \ldots\}$. For $X_i \in I_X$, we define $g(X_i) = x1^i$. For $P = Y_1 \ldots Y_k \in W(I_X)$, define $g(P) = g(Y_1) \ldots g(Y_k)$. Finally, define $g(\lambda) = \lambda$. Thus, for any word P over any alphabet, we have a unique word $g(P)$, referred to as the *Gödel word* of P, over the alphabet $\{x, 1\}$. For a type 0 grammar $G = (I_N, I_T, X_0, F)$, where F consists of the productions $\xi_i \to \eta_i, i = 1, \ldots, n$, we define a *basis* of G to be the word

$$G^b = \# g(\xi_1) Y g(\eta_1) \# \ldots \# g(\xi_n) Y g(\eta_n) \#$$

over the alphabet $\{x, 1, \#, Y\}$. (Note that other bases are obtained by permuting the productions in F.) The language

$$U_0 = \sum_G \{G^b g(P) \mid P \in L(G)\},$$

where G ranges over all type 0 grammars, is termed the *universal type 0 language*. Thus, U_0 is a language over the alphabet $\{x, 1, \#, Y\}$ and, for any type 0 language $L = L(G)$,

$$L = \{P \mid G^b g(P) \in U_0\}.$$

Prove that U_0 is of the type 0. Conclude by diagonalization argument that $\mathcal{L}_0$ is not closed under complementation.

EXERCISE 7.5 (Jones, 1966). Let $G = (I_N, I_T, X_0, F)$ be a type 0 grammar. For a derivation D of a word $P \in L(G)$, define the *workspace of P by the derivation D*, in symbols ws (P, D), to be the length of the longest word in D. By definition, the *workspace* ws (P) of P equals min $\{ws (P, D)\}$, where D ranges over all derivations of P.

Prove that if there is a natural number n such that

$$\mathrm{ws}\,(P) \le n \lg (P),$$

for all $P \in L(G)$, then $L(G)$ is of the type 1. Use this result to obtain another proof of Theorem 6.8. (In fact, the proof of Theorem 7.1 becomes applicable.)

PROBLEM 7.1. Under what regularity preserving operations studied in Chapters I and III is $\mathscr{L}_i$, $i = 0, 1, 2$, closed? (Cf. Exercise III.8.5.)

§ 8. Infinite-state machines

A natural way to generalize the various types of automata considered is to relax the condition that the sets involved have to be finite. It is easy to see that such a generalization of the finite deterministic automaton, which is given in the next definition, is able to represent any languages. However, there is no way to regard the processes involved as effectively executable.

DEFINITION. A *deterministic automaton* over the alphabet I is an ordered triple $\mathbf{A} = (S, s_0, f)$, where S is a non-empty set (the set of *internal states*), $s_0 \in S$ (the *initial state*) and f is a function mapping the set $S \times I$ into the set S (the *transition function*).

The domain of the function f is extended from $S \times I$ to $S \times W(I)$ in the same way as for finite deterministic automata. (Cf. equations (I.2.1) and (I.2.1)'.) For $S_1 \subset S$, the language

$$L(\mathbf{A}, S_1) = \{P \,|\, f(s_0, P) \in S_1\}$$

over the alphabet I is referred to as the language *represented* by the set S_1 in $\mathbf{A}$. The automaton $\mathbf{A}$ is *free* iff, for all $P_1, P_2 \in W(I)$ such that $P_1 \ne P_2$, $f(s_0, P_1) \ne f(s_0, P_2)$.

THEOREM 8.1. *For any family $\mathscr{L}$ of languages over an alphabet I, there is a free deterministic automaton $\mathbf{A}$ over I such that every language belonging to $\mathscr{L}$ is represented in $\mathbf{A}$.*

Proof. Consider the automaton $\mathbf{A} = (W(I), \lambda, f)$ over I, where f is defined by the equation

$$f(P, x) = Px, \quad P \in W(I), \quad x \in I. \tag{8.1}$$

Clearly, **A** is free. Because (8.1) implies that

$$f(\lambda, P) = P,$$

for all $P \in W(I)$, we conclude that any language $L \in \mathscr{L}$ is represented in **A** by the set $S_L = L$.

A generalization of the finite sequential Mealy machine will now be introduced. (A further generalization is introduced in Exercise 8.3.)

DEFINITION. A *sequential Mealy machine* is an ordered quintuple **ME** $= (I, O, S, f, \varphi)$, where I and O are alphabets (*input* and *output alphabet*), S is a non-empty set (the set of *internal states*) and f and φ are functions mapping the set $S \times I$ into S and O, respectively (*transition* and *output* function). The *response* function resp_s induced by a state $s \in S$ is defined exactly as for finite sequential Mealy machines (cf. (I.5.1)). A function ψ mapping the set $W(I)$ into the set $W(O)$ is *realized* by **ME** iff, for some $s \in S$, $\psi = \mathrm{resp}_s$.

Clearly, a necessary condition for a function ψ to be realized by a sequential Mealy machine is that ψ is both length and initial subwords preserving. (For these notions, cf. Section I.7.) The following theorem shows that these conditions are also sufficient.

THEOREM 8.2. *Let F be a set of length and initial subwords preserving functions mapping $W(I)$ into $W(O)$, where I and O are fixed alphabets. Then there exists a sequential Mealy machine* **ME** $= (I, O, S, f, \varphi)$ *such that every function in F is realized by* **ME**.

Proof. We consider F as an alphabet and choose $S = FW(I)$. (Thus, S consists of elements of the form $\psi_i P$, where $\psi_i \in F$ and $P \in W(I)$.) The function f is defined by

$$f(\psi_i P, x) = \psi_i P x \qquad (\psi_i \in F, \quad P \in W(I), \quad x \in I).$$

The value $\varphi(\psi_i P, x)$ is defined to be the last letter of the word $\psi_i(Px)$. Then, for all $\psi_i \in F$,

$$\psi_i = \mathrm{resp}_{\psi_i \lambda}.$$

In fact, let $P = x_1 x_2 \ldots x_k \in W(I)$ be arbitrary and assume that

$$\psi_i(P) = y_1 y_2 \ldots y_k.$$

If **ME** is in the state $\psi_i\lambda$ and receives the input P, then it enters the states

$$\psi_i\lambda, \psi_i x_1, \psi_i x_1 x_2, \ldots, \psi_i x_1 x_2 \ldots x_k$$

and gives the output $y_1 y_2 \ldots y_k$. $\square$

The sequential Mealy machine constructed in the proof of Theorem 8.2 is not economical as regards the number of states. The smallest number of states needed to realize a given function is presented in the following theorem. The proof of the theorem, being almost the same as that of Theorem I.7.2, is left to the reader.

THEOREM 8.3. *Let c be the cardinal of the set of derivatives of a length and initial subwords preserving function ψ mapping $W(I)$ into $W(O)$, where I and O are alphabets. Then ψ is realized by a sequential Mealy machine* **ME** $= (I, O, S, f, \varphi)$, *where the cardinal of S equals c. Furthermore, ψ is realized by no sequential Mealy machine* **ME**$' = (I, O, S', f', \varphi')$, *where the cardinal of S' is less than c.*

EXERCISE 8.1. Introduce the notion of a sequential Moore machine. State and prove the result corresponding to Theorem I.5.1.

EXERCISE 8.2. Extend Theorem I.6.4 to (infinite-state) sequential Mealy machines.

EXERCISE 8.3. (Ginsburg, 1962; for those familiar with the basic notions concerning semigroups.) A *quasimachine* is an ordered quintuple **Q** $= (I, O, S, f, \varphi)$, where I and O are non-empty semigroups (the input and output semigroup), S is a non-empty set (states), f is a mapping of $S \times I$ into S such that

$$f(s, xy) = f(f(s, x), y),$$

for all $s \in S$ and $x, y \in I$, and φ is a mapping of $S \times I$ into O such that

$$\varphi(s, xy) = \varphi(s, x)\,\varphi(f(s, x), y),$$

for $s \in S$ and $x, y \in I$. (Note that according to this definition dependencies may exist among the inputs and also among the outputs.) An *abstract machine* is a quasimachine in which the output semigroup satisfies the left cancellation law. Give examples of abstract machines and examples of quasimachines which are not abstract machines.

Two states s and s' (either in the same quasimachine or in two distinct quasimachines $\mathbf{Q} = (I, O, S, f, \varphi)$ and $\mathbf{Q}' = (I, O', S', f', \varphi')$) are *equivalent* iff $\varphi(s, x) = \varphi'(s', x)$, for all $x \in I$. Two quasimachines $\mathbf{Q}_1$ and $\mathbf{Q}_2$ are *equivalent* iff, for each state in $\mathbf{Q}_1$, there is an equivalent state in $\mathbf{Q}_2$, and vice versa. A quasimachine is *reduced* iff no two states in it are equivalent. Prove that for each abstract machine $\mathbf{Q}$ there corresponds a unique (up to isomorphism) reduced abstract machine which is equivalent to $\mathbf{Q}$. Prove that there is a quasimachine for which there is no equivalent reduced quasimachine.

EXERCISE 8.4 (Salomaa, 1964, 2). A non-empty language L over an alphabet I is termed *reducible* iff there is a deterministic automaton $\mathbf{A}$ over I, where L is represented by a set S_1 of states such that the cardinal of S_1 is smaller than the cardinal of L. Prove that any language almost equal to an infinite reducible language is reducible. Prove that if I consists of one letter only, then L is reducible iff L is regular and infinite.

A word Q is an *ending* in a language L iff, for some word P, both P and PQ belong to L. Prove that an infinite language possessing only a finite number of endings is reducible.

EXERCISE 8.5. Introduce the notions of a probabilistic automaton and sequential machine without assuming that the set of states is finite. Study interconnections between various types of these infinite-state devices. (Cf. Bukharaev, 1964.) In particular, show that the result corresponding to Theorem II.5.6 is not valid.

EXERCISE 8.6 (Agasandjan, 1967). Consider finite deterministic automata with a *variable structure*: instead of a transition function f, there is an infinite sequence of functions $f_i (i = 1, 2, \ldots)$ and, instead of a designated set S_1 of final states, there is an infinite sequence of subsets S_i of S. (Note that the number of distinct functions f_i is finite because each function f_i maps $S \times I$ into S.) At the time instant $t = i$, the function f_i and the set S_i are considered. A word of length n is accepted iff it causes a sequence of state transitions from the initial state into a state in S_n. A language is *f.v.a.r.* iff it is represented in some finite deterministic automaton with a variable structure. Define formally all of these notions.

For a language L over a finite alphabet I and a natural number n, let $k(L, n)$ be the number of equivalence classes induced by $\mathcal{E}_L$ on words of length n. Prove that L is f.v.a.r. iff there is a finite upper bound for the numbers $k(L, n), n = 1, 2, \ldots$. Conclude that the family of f.v.a.r. languages is closed under Boolean operations.

Prove that the family of f.v.a.r. languages is non-denumerable. Prove that if L_1 is f.v.a.r. and L_2 is regular, then L_1L_2 is f.v.a.r. Show by an example that, under these assumptions, L_2L_1 is not necessarily f.v.a.r. Prove that if L_2 is finite and L_1 is f.v.a.r., then L_2L_1 is f.v.a.r.

Study also the case, where both of the sequences f_i and S_i are almost periodic.

§ 9. Abstract pushdown automata

We shall consider in this section a simple subclass of (infinite-state) deterministic automata over a finite alphabet. The automata in this class are termed *abstract pushdown automata* because they resemble the devices considered in Section 5, both with respect to the pushdown store and to the corresponding languages: the family of languages represented by abstract pushdown automata equals the family $\mathcal{L}_2$ of context-free languages. Thus, we obtain a class of *deterministic* recognition devices corresponding to the family of context-free languages.

DEFINITION. Let I be a finite alphabet and $\mathcal{L}$ a family of languages over I. $\mathcal{L}$ is an *sc-algebra* iff it is closed under sum and catenation, i.e. for $L_1, L_2 \in \mathcal{L}$, also $L_1+L_2, L_1L_2 \in \mathcal{L}$. An sc-algebra $\mathcal{L}$ is *generated* by a subfamily $\mathcal{L}'$ of $\mathcal{L}$ iff every language in $\mathcal{L}$ is obtained from the languages in $\mathcal{L}'$ by finitely many applications of the operations sum and catenation. $\mathcal{L}'$ is referred to as a *set of generators* of $\mathcal{L}$. $\mathcal{L}$ is *finitely generated* iff it possesses a finite set of generators. An sc-algebra $\mathcal{L}$ is *automatonic* iff, for every $L \in \mathcal{L}$ and $x \in I$, $\partial_x(L) \in \mathcal{L}$.

Clearly, for $x \in I$, left derivatives satisfy the following equations:

$$\partial_x(L_1 + L_2) = \partial_x(L_1) + \partial_x(L_2), \tag{9.1}$$

$$\partial_x(L_1L_2) = (\partial_x(L_1))L_2, \text{ for } \lambda \notin L_1. \tag{9.2}$$

If an sc-algebra $\mathcal{L}$ is automatonic, then every language $L_0 \in \mathcal{L}$ is represented in the automaton $(\mathscr{L}, L_0, f)$ by the set $\mathscr{L}(\lambda)$ of states which contain the empty word, provided f is defined by the equation

$$f(L, x) = \partial_x(L), \quad L \in \mathscr{L}, \ x \in I.$$

DEFINITION. An *abstract pushdown automaton* is an ordered quadruple $\mathbf{APA} = (I, Z, s_0, f)$, where I and Z are finite alphabets (*input* and *internal alphabet*), s_0 is a finite language over Z (the *initial state*) and f is a mapping of $\mathscr{F\!L}(Z) \times I$, where $\mathscr{F\!L}(Z)$ denotes the set of all finite languages over Z, into $\mathscr{F\!L}(Z)$ such that the following conditions are satisfied:

$$f(L_\phi, x) = f(\{\lambda\}, x) = L_\phi, \quad \text{for} \ \ x \in I, \tag{9.3}$$

$$f(zP, x) = f(z, x)P, \quad \text{for} \ \ x \in I, \ z \in Z \text{ and } P \in W(Z), \tag{9.4}$$

$$f(L_1 + L_2, x) = f(L_1, x) + f(L_2, x), \quad \text{for} \ \ x \in I \ \text{ and } \ L_1, L_2 \in \mathscr{F\!L}(Z). \tag{9.5}$$

Clearly, an abstract pushdown automaton $\mathbf{APA} = (I, Z, s_0, f)$ can be considered as a deterministic automaton $\mathbf{A} = (\mathscr{F\!L}(Z), s_0, f)$ over the alphabet I. Furthermore, it suffices to specify s_0 and the finitely many values

$$f(z, x), \quad z \in Z, \ x \in I.$$

Then f will be uniquely determined by the conditions (9.3)–(9.5).

For $L_1 \in \mathscr{F\!L}(Z)$ and $x \in I$, consider the value $f(L_1, x)$. By (9.4) and (9.5), this value is computed by using the first letters of the words in L_1 and catenating the result with the remaining letters. Thus, all letters except the first one are left untouched in the "pushdown store". In this sense, $\mathbf{APA}$ resembles a pushdown automaton.

As an example, consider the abstract pushdown automaton

$$\mathbf{APA} = (\{x, y\}, \{z_0, z_1, z_2\}, \{z_0\}, f), \tag{9.6}$$

where f is defined by the following table:

f	z_0	z_1	z_2
x	z_1	$z_1 z_2$	ϕ
y	ϕ	λ	λ

(In this table as well as in Fig. 24, languages over $\{z_0, z_1, z_2\}$ are denoted by regular expressions.) All values of f are determined by this table and (9.3)–(9.5). A part of the graph of **APA** is given in Fig. 24, where only arrows leading to states other than ϕ are shown.

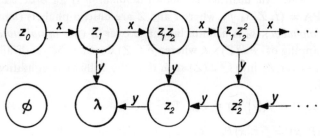

FIG. 24.

DEFINITION. Let $\mathbf{APA} = (I, Z, s_0, f)$ be an abstract pushdown automaton. The domain of the function f is extended from $\mathcal{FL}(Z) \times I$ to $\mathcal{FL}(Z) \times W(I)$ by the equations

$$f(L, \lambda) = L, \quad \text{for} \quad L \in \mathcal{FL}(Z),$$
$$f(L, Px) = f(f(L, P), x), \quad \text{for} \quad L \in \mathcal{FL}(Z), P \in W(I) \quad \text{and} \quad x \in I.$$

Denote by $\mathcal{FL}_\lambda(Z)$ the family of all such finite languages over Z which contain the empty word. The language $L(\mathbf{APA})$ *represented* (or *accepted*) by **APA** consists of all such words over I which lead from the initial state s_0 to some state marked by a language containing the empty word, i.e.

$$L(\mathbf{APA}) = \{P \mid f(s_0, P) \in \mathcal{FL}_\lambda(Z)\}.$$

We shall prove that the family of languages represented by abstract pushdown automata equals the family of context-free languages. We shall first derive another characterization of context-free languages.

THEOREM 9.1. *A language is context-free iff it is an element of a finitely generated automatonic sc-algebra.*

Proof. Assume first that $L \in \mathcal{L}$, where $\mathcal{L}$ is an automatonic sc-algebra over an alphabet $I_r = \{x_1, \ldots, x_r\}$ generated by a family

$$\{L_1, \ldots, L_n\} \subset \mathcal{L}.$$

By the definition of left derivatives,

$$L_i = \sum_{j=1}^{r} x_j \partial_{x_j}(L_i) + \delta(L_i) \qquad (i = 1, \dots, n), \qquad (9.7)$$

where $\delta(L_i)$ is either the empty language or the language consisting of the empty word. Because $\mathscr{L}$ is automatonic and generated by the family $\{L_1, \dots, L_n\}$, we may write (9.7) in the form

$$L_i = \sum_{j=1}^{r} x_j H_{ij}(L_1, \dots, L_n) + \delta(L_i) \qquad (i = 1, \dots, n), \qquad (9.8)$$

where each $H_{ij}(L_1, \dots, L_n)$ is a language obtained by substitution from a finite language $H_{ij}(y_1, \dots, y_n)$. It is easy to prove (cf. Exercise 3.3) that the system of equations (9.8) uniquely determines the languages $L_1, \dots, L_n$. On the other hand, (9.8) can be considered as a recursion. This implies that the languages $L_1, \dots, L_n$ are ALGOL-like and therefore, by Theorem 3.1, context-free. Because L is generated by the family $\{L_1, \dots, L_n\}$, we have

$$L = H(L_1^\circ, \dots, L_n^t),$$

where the right side is obtained by substitution from a finite language $H(y_1, \dots, y_n)$. Hence we conclude, by Theorem 3.3 or 1.1, that L is context-free.

Conversely, assume that L is a context-free language over an alphabet $I_r = \{x_1, \dots, x_r\}$. It suffices to consider the case where $\lambda \notin L$. For if $\lambda \in L$ and $L-\{\lambda\}$ is an element of a finitely generated automatonic sc-algebra $\mathscr{L}$, then also L is an element of a finitely generated automatonic sc-algebra $\mathscr{L}'$. $\mathscr{L}'$ is obtained from $\mathscr{L}$ by adding the languages $\{\lambda\}$ and L_ϕ to the set of generators of $\mathscr{L}$.

Thus, assume that $\lambda \notin L$. By Theorem 3.2, L is generated by a grammar with no productions of the form $X \to \lambda$. This implies, by Theorem 3.1, that L satisfies the equation (3.3), for some finite languages H_0, $H_1, \dots, H_n$ over the alphabet

$$\{X_0, X_1, \dots, X_n\} \cup I_r, \qquad (9.9)$$

where none of the languages H contains the empty word. By (3.3), we denote $L = L_0$. We use also the notations

$$L_j = \sum_{i=1}^{\infty} H_j^{(i)}(L_\phi, L_\phi, \ldots, L_\phi) \qquad (j = 1, \ldots, n).$$

Hence, we obtain

$$H_i = \sum_{j=1}^{r} x_j H_{ij} + \sum_{j=0}^{n} X_j K_{ij} \qquad (i = 0, \ldots, n), \qquad (9.10)$$

for some finite (possibly empty) languages H_{ij} and K_{ij} over (9.9). Thus,

$$H_{ij} = \partial_{x_j}(H_i), \quad K_{ij} = \partial_{X_j}(H_i).$$

Consider the system

$$Y_i = \sum_{j=1}^{r} x_j H_{ij} + \sum_{j=0}^{n} Y_j K_{ij} \qquad (i = 0, \ldots, n) \qquad (9.11)$$

of $n+1$ equations in $n+1$ unknowns Y_i. By Theorem III.2.5, (9.11) possesses a solution

$$(U_0, U_1, \ldots, U_n), \qquad (9.12)$$

where U_i are regular languages over the alphabet (9.9). Furthermore, (9.12) is minimal in the sense that, for any solution

$$(U_0', U_1', \ldots, U_n')$$

of (9.11), $U_i \subset U_i'$, $i = 0, \ldots, n$.

For any language $H(x_1, \ldots, x_r, X_0, X_1, \ldots, X_n)$ over the alphabet (9.9), we denote

$$\bar{H}(x_1, \ldots, x_r, X_0, X_1, \ldots, X_n) = H(x_1, \ldots, x_r, L_0, L_1, \ldots, L_n).$$

Thus, $\bar{H}$ is obtained from H by substituting the "auxiliary letters" X_i by the languages L_i and, hence, $\bar{H}$ is a language over the alphabet I_r.

Regarding the right sides of (9.11) as languages over the union of the alphabets (9.9) and $\{Y_0, Y_1, \ldots, Y_n\}$, we obtain

$$U_j = \sum_{i=1}^{\infty} H_j^{(i)}(X_0, \ldots, X_n, L_\phi, \ldots, L_\phi) \qquad (j = 0, \ldots, n) \quad (9.13)$$

and

$$L_j = \sum_{i=1}^{\infty} H_j^{(i)}(L_\phi, \ldots, L_\phi, L_\phi, \ldots, L_\phi) \qquad (j = 0, \ldots, n). \quad (9.14)$$

We shall now prove that

$$\overline{U}_j = L_j \qquad (j = 0, \ldots, n). \qquad (9.15)$$

In fact, the inclusion $L_j \subset \overline{U}_j$ is immediate, by (9.13) and (9.14), because we have

$$\overline{U}_j = \sum_{i=1}^{\infty} H_j^{(i)}(L_0, \ldots, L_n, L_\phi, \ldots, L_\phi). \qquad (9.16)$$

Note that the languages H are finite and, hence, "monotonic": if for all $i = 0, \ldots, n$, $\alpha_i \subset \beta_i$ and $\gamma_i \subset \delta_i$ then

$$H(\alpha_0, \ldots, \alpha_n, \gamma_0, \ldots, \gamma_n) \subset H(\beta_0, \ldots, \beta_n, \delta_0, \ldots, \delta_n).$$

Furthermore, (9.16) implies that

$$\overline{U}_j \subset \sum_{i=1}^{\infty} H_j^{(i)}(L_0, \ldots, L_n, L_0, \ldots, L_n). \qquad (9.17)$$

Because $L_\nu = H_\nu(L_0, \ldots, L_n, L_0, \ldots, L_n)$, for $\nu = 0, \ldots, n$, we obtain by an obvious inductive argument the result that the right side of (9.17) equals L_j. Hence, $\overline{U}_j \subset L_j$ and the equation (9.15) follows.

By Theorem I.2.3, there is a finite deterministic automaton $\mathbf{A} = (S, s_0, f)$ over the alphabet (9.9) and subsets $S_0, S_1, \ldots, S_n$ of S such that U_i is represented by S_i in $\mathbf{A}$, for $i = 0, \ldots, n$. Consider the languages

$$L(s, S_i) = \{P \mid P \neq \lambda, f(s, P) \in S_i\} \qquad (s \in S, \quad i = 0, \ldots, n). \quad (9.18)$$

It is obvious by (9.11) that all words in the language U_i, $i = 0, \ldots, n$, begin with a letter of I_r and, thus, $\lambda \notin U_i$. Hence, by (9.15),

$$L_j = \overline{U}_j = \overline{L}(s_0, S_j) \qquad (j = 0, \ldots, n). \qquad (9.19)$$

Denote by $\mathcal{L}(\mathbf{A})$ the sc-algebra with a finite set of generators consisting of L_ϕ, $\{\lambda\}$ and of all of the languages $\overline{L}(s, S_i)$, where $s \in S$ and $i = 0, \ldots, n$. Clearly, the languages in $\mathcal{L}(\mathbf{A})$ are over the alphabet I_r. Because, by (9.19), $L = L_0 = \overline{L}(s_0, S_0)$, it suffices to prove that $\mathcal{L}(\mathbf{A})$

is automatonic. By the definition (9.18), for $s \in S$ and $i = 0, \ldots, n$,

$$L(s, S_i) = \sum_{j=1}^{r} x_j(L(f(s, x_j), S_i) + \delta(f(s, x_j), S_i))$$

$$+ \sum_{j=0}^{n} X_j(L(f(s, X_j), S_i) + \delta(f(s, X_j), S_i)), \qquad (9.20)$$

where

$$\delta(s', S_i) = \begin{cases} \{\lambda\}, & \text{if } s' \in S_i, \\ L_\phi, & \text{if } s' \notin S_i. \end{cases}$$

Because all words in the language U_i, $i = 0, \ldots, n$, begin with a letter of I_r we obtain, for all i and j,

$$L(f(s_0, X_j), S_i) = \delta(f(s_0, X_j), S_i) = L_\phi.$$

Hence by (9.20), for $i = 0, \ldots, n$,

$$L(s_0, S_i) = \sum_{j=1}^{r} x_j(L(f(s_0, x_j), S_i) + \delta(f(s_0, x_j), S_i)). \qquad (9.21)$$

Since $\overline{X}_j = L_j = \overline{U}_j = \overline{L}(s_0, S_j)$, we obtain by (9.20) and (9.21):

$$\overline{L}(s, S_i) = \sum_{j=1}^{r} x_j(\overline{L}(f(s, x_j), S_i) + \delta(f(s, x_j), S_i))$$

$$+ \sum_{j=0}^{n} \left(\sum_{\nu=1}^{r} x_\nu(\overline{L}(f(s_0, x_\nu), S_j) + \delta(f(s_0, x_\nu), S_j))(\overline{L}(f(s, X_j), S_i) \right.$$

$$\left. + \delta(f(s, X_j), S_i)) \right).$$

Hence, for $s \in S$, $l = 1, \ldots, r$ and $i = 0, \ldots, n$,

$$\partial_{x_l}(\overline{L}(s, S_i)) = \overline{L}(f(s, x_l), S_i) + \delta(f(s, x_l), S_i)$$

$$+ \sum_{j=0}^{n} (\overline{L}(f(s_0, x_l), S_j) + \delta(f(s_0, x_l), S_j)) (\overline{L}(f(s, X_j), S_i) + \delta(f(s, X_j), S_i)).$$

$$(9.22)$$

Clearly, (9.22) is a language over the alphabet I_r. By (9.1), (9.2) and (9.22), the left derivative of any language in $\mathcal{L}(\mathbf{A})$ with respect to any letter of I_r belongs to $\mathcal{L}(\mathbf{A})$. Hence, $\mathcal{L}(\mathbf{A})$ is automatonic. □

THEOREM 9.2. *A language is context-free iff it is represented by an abstract pushdown automaton.*

Proof. Let L be a context-free language over the alphabet I_r. We assume first that $\lambda \notin L$ and consider the automatonic sc-algebra $\mathcal{L}(\mathbf{A})$

constructed in the proof of Theorem 9.1. To each of the languages $\bar{L}(s, S_i)$, $s \in S$, $i = 0, \ldots, n$, we associate a letter $z(s, S_i)$ and denote by Z the (finite) alphabet consisting of all these letters. Consider the abstract pushdown automaton

$$\mathbf{APA}_L = (I_r, Z, \{z(s_0, S_0)\}, \varphi)$$

where φ is defined by the equation

$$\varphi(z(s, S_i), x_l) = z(f(s, x_l), S_i) + \delta(f(s, x_l), S_i)$$
$$+ \sum_{j=0}^{n} (z(f(s_0, x_l), S_j) + \delta(f(s_0, x_l), S_j))(z(f(s, X_j), S_i) + \delta(f(s, X_j), S_i)).$$
$$(9.23)$$

Equation (9.23) defines $\varphi(z, x)$ for all arguments $(z, x) \in Z \times I_r$, and the value is always a finite language over Z. By comparing (9.22) and (9.23), it is seen that, for $P \in W(I_r)$ such that $P \neq \lambda$, $\varphi(z(s_0, S_0), P)$ contains the empty word iff

$$\lambda \in \partial_P(\bar{L}(s_0, S_0)) = \partial_P(L). \qquad (9.24)$$

(Note that none of the languages $\bar{L}(s, S_i)$ contains the empty word.) On the other hand, (9.24) is satisfied iff $P \in L$. This implies that L is represented by $\mathbf{APA}_L$.

If $\lambda \in L$ the procedure remains exactly the same except that the initial state of $\mathbf{APA}_L$ is chosen to be the language $\{z(s_0, S_0), \lambda\}$. Because of (9.3) and (9.5), the state transitions will remain unaltered.

Conversely, consider a language $L' = L(\mathbf{APA})$, where $\mathbf{APA} = (I, Z, s_0, f)$ is an abstract pushdown automaton. For any finite language U over Z, we denote

$$L_\lambda(U) = \{P \mid \lambda \in f(U, P)\}. \qquad (9.25)$$

Thus, $L_\lambda(U)$ consists of those words P which lead from the state marked by U to a state marked by a language containing the empty word. Clearly,

$$L_\lambda(s_0) = L'. \qquad (9.26)$$

It is an immediate consequence of (9.5) that

$$L_\lambda(U_1 + U_2) = L_\lambda(U_1) + L_\lambda(U_2), \qquad (9.27)$$

for any U_1 and U_2. We shall prove that also

$$L_\lambda(U_1 U_2) = L_\lambda(U_1) L_\lambda(U_2), \qquad (9.28)$$

for any U_1 and U_2. Thus (assuming (9.28)), the sc-algebra $\mathscr{L}'$ generated by the (finitely many) languages L_ϕ, $\{\lambda\}$ and $L_\lambda(z)$, $z \in Z$, contains all of the languages $L_\lambda(U)$. By (9.26), $\mathscr{L}'$ contains L'. Furthermore, $\mathscr{L}'$ is automatonic because

$$L_\lambda(f(U, x)) = \{Q \mid \lambda \in f(f(U, x), Q)\} = \{Q \mid \lambda \in f(U, xQ)\},$$

for $x \in I$, and hence, by (9.25),

$$\partial_x(L_\lambda(U)) = L_\lambda(f(U, x)).$$

Therefore, L' is an element of a finitely generated automatonic sc-algebra. By Theorem 9.1, L' is context-free.

To complete the proof, we shall now show that (9.28) is valid. By (9.3), (9.28) is valid in the case where U_1 or U_2 is one of the languages L_ϕ or $\{\lambda\}$. Furthermore, by (9.27) and the distributivity of catenation over sum, it suffices to consider the case where $U_1 = \{z\}$, $z \in Z$, and $U_2 = \{Q\}$, $Q \in W(Z)$, $Q \neq \lambda$, i.e. it suffices to prove that

$$L_\lambda(zQ) = L_\lambda(z) L_\lambda(Q). \tag{9.29}$$

It is immediately verified that both sides of (9.29) contain the same words of length less than 2. Assume that

$$P = x_1 x_2 \ldots x_k \in L_\lambda(zQ) \qquad (k \geqq 2). \tag{9.30}$$

Hence,

$$\lambda \in f(zQ, x_1 x_2 \ldots x_k). \tag{9.31}$$

By (9.4),

$$f(zQ, x_1 x_2 \ldots x_k) = f(f(zQ, x_1), x_2 \ldots x_k) = f(f(z, x_1) Q, x_2 \ldots x_k).$$

Assuming that $\lambda \notin f(z, x_1)$, we obtain, by (9.4) and (9.5),

$$f(f(z, x_1)Q, x_2 \ldots x_k) = f(f(f(z, x_1) Q, x_2), x_3 \ldots x_k)$$
$$= f(f(f(z, x_1), x_2) Q, x_3 \ldots x_k) = f(f(z, x_1 x_2) Q, x_3 \ldots x_k).$$

Similarly, if

$$\lambda \notin f(z, x_1), \ \lambda \notin f(z, x_1 x_2), \ \ldots, \ \lambda \notin f(z, x_1 \ldots x_i),$$

where $1 \leqq i < k$, then

$$f(zQ, x_1 x_2 \ldots x_k) = f(f(z, x_1 \ldots x_i) Q, x_{i+1} \ldots x_k).$$

This implies that, for some i,

$$\lambda \in f(z, x_1 \ldots x_i), \quad 1 \leqq i < k, \tag{9.32}$$

because, otherwise,

$$f(zQ, x_1x_2 \ldots x_k) = f(f(z, x_1 \ldots x_{k-1})Q, x_k) = f(z, x_1x_2 \ldots x_k)Q,$$

which contradicts (9.31). We choose the smallest number i such that (9.32) is satisfied. Let

$$f(z, x_1 \ldots x_i) = \{\lambda\} + V,$$

for some language V which may be empty but does not contain λ. Hence,

$$f(zQ, x_1x_2 \ldots x_k) = f(f(z, x_1 \ldots x_i)Q, x_{i+1} \ldots x_k)$$
$$= f(Q, x_{i+1} \ldots x_k) + f(VQ, x_{i+1} \ldots x_k).$$

If $\lambda \in f(Q, x_{i+1} \ldots x_k)$ then, by (9.32),

$$P = x_1x_2 \ldots x_k \in L_\lambda(z) L_\lambda(Q). \tag{9.33}$$

Otherwise, by (9.31), $\lambda \in f(VQ, x_{i+1} \ldots x_k)$. In this case, the same procedure is repeated, and the validity of (9.33) is established by an obvious inductive argument.

Conversely, assume (9.33). Hence, $P = P_1P_2$, where $P_1 \in L_\lambda(z)$ and $P_2 \in L_\lambda(Q)$. If $P_1 = x_1 \ldots x_i$ is the shortest initial subword of P which satisfies (9.32), then

$$f(zQ, P_1P_2) = f(Q, P_2) + f(V'Q, P_2),$$

for some V'. Because $\lambda \in f(Q, P_2)$ we conclude that $\lambda \in f(zQ, P_1 P_2)$, which proves (9.30). Otherwise,

$$f(zQ, P_1P_2) = f(f(z, P_1')Q, P_1''P_2), \quad \lambda \in f(z, P_1'),$$

for some words P_1' and P_1'' such that $P_1 = P_1' P_1''$. By (9.3), the result (9.30) is obtained also in this case. Hence, (9.30) and (9.33) are equivalent, which proves the equations (9.29) and (9.28). $\square$

As an example, consider the language generated by the type 2 grammar

$$G = (\{X_0\}, \{x, y\}, X_0, \{X_0 \to xy, X_0 \to xX_0y\}).$$

$L_0 = L(G)$ is defined by the recursion

$$L_0 :: = xy + xL_0y.$$

The system of equations (9.11) is in this case ($n = 0$)

$$Y_0 = x(y + X_0y)$$

which, in fact, gives the solution U_0 for Y_0 over the alphabet $\{x, y, X_0\}$. U_0 is represented by the set $S_0 = \{s_3\}$ in the automaton defined by Fig. 25. (Only transitions leading to states other than s_4 have been marked.) The internal alphabet of the automaton $\mathbf{APA}_{L_0}$ representing L_0 (cf. the proof of Theorem 9.2) consists of the letters

$$z_0 = z(s_0, S_0), \quad z_1 = z(s_1, S_0), \quad z_2 = z(s_2, S_0),$$
$$z_3 = z(s_3, S_0), \quad z_4 = z(s_4, S_0).$$

The input alphabet is $\{x, y\}$, initial state $\{z_0\}$, and the transition function φ is defined according to (9.23):

φ	z_0	z_1	z_2	z_3	z_4
x	$z_1 + z_1 z_4$	$z_4 + z_1 z_2$	$z_4 + z_1 z_4$	$z_4 + z_1 z_4$	$z_4 + z_1 z_4$
y	$z_4 + z_4 z_4$	$z_3 + \lambda + z_4 z_2$	$z_3 + \lambda + z_4 z_4$	$z_4 + z_4 z_4$	$z_4 + z_4 z_4$

As far as the represented language is concerned, $\mathbf{APA}_{L_0}$ coincides with the abstract pushdown automaton of Fig. 24.

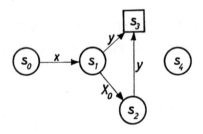

Fig. 25.

EXERCISE 9.1. Prove that Theorem 9.2 remains valid if the following condition is added to the definition of an abstract pushdown automaton: for all $x \in I$ and $z \in Z$, every word in the language $f(z, x)$ is of length ≤ 2.

EXERCISE 9.2. Give a direct proof of the fact that every regular language is an element of a finitely generated automatonic sc-algebra.

PROBLEM 9.1. Construct classes of deterministic (infinite-state) automata which represent some of the language families considered in this chapter, such as the subfamilies of $\mathcal{L}_2$ considered in Section 3. In particular, find a family of deterministic automata which bear the same relation to context-sensitive languages as abstract pushdown automata do to context-free languages.

§ 10. Regular canonical systems

The family $\mathcal{L}_0$ of languages generated by type 0 grammars is also generated by the so-called *Post canonical systems*. Rather than introducing this notion in its full generality (cf. Exercise 10.1), we shall now study a special case. It turns out that in this fashion we obtain still another characterization of regular languages.

DEFINITION. A *regular canonical system* is an ordered triple $C = (I, I_T, F)$, where I and I_T are finite alphabets such that $I_T \subset I$ and F is a finite set of ordered pairs (P, Q) of words over I. I_T is referred to as the *terminal* alphabet, $I - I_T$ as the *non-terminal* or *auxiliary* alphabet and F as the set of *productions*. A production (P, Q) in F is denoted by

$$PX \to QX. \tag{10.1}$$

A word P_1 over I *directly generates* (according to C) a word P_2 over I, in symbols,

$$P_1 \underset{C}{\rightrightarrows} P_2$$

or shortly $P_1 \Rightarrow P_2$ iff there is a word P' over I such that $P_1 = PP'$ and $P_2 = QP'$, for some production (10.1) in F. A word R over I *generates* a word R' over I, in symbols,

$$R \underset{C}{\overset{*}{\Rightarrow}} R'$$

or shortly $R \overset{*}{\Rightarrow} R'$ iff there is a finite sequence

$$R_0, R_1, \ldots, R_k \qquad (k \geq 0)$$

of words over I such that $R_0 = R$, $R_k = R'$ and R_i directly generates R_{i+1}, for $i = 0, \ldots, k-1$.

For a regular canonical system $C = (I, I_T, F)$ and two finite sets U and V of words over I, the language

$$L_g(C, U, V) = \{P \mid P \in W(I_T), P_u \overset{*}{\Rightarrow} P_v P, P_u \in U, P_v \in V\} \tag{10.2}$$

is termed the language *generated* by the triple (C, U, V) and the language

$$L_a(C, U, V) = \{P \mid P \in W(I_T),\ P_u P \overset{*}{\Rightarrow} P_v,\ P_u \in U,\ P_v \in V\} \quad (10.3)$$

is termed the language *accepted* by the triple (C, U, V).

Thus, the language generated (accepted) by the triple (C, U, V) consists of the terminal words P such that the word $P_v P$ (P_v) is generated by the word P_u ($P_u P$), for some $P_u \in U$ and $P_v \in V$.

DEFINITION. A regular canonical system $C = (I, I_T, F)$ is *pure* iff $I_T = I$. C is *reduced* iff every production in F is of one of the forms

$$Y_1 x X \rightarrow Y_2 X,\quad x \in I_T,\quad Y_1, Y_2 \in I - I_T, \quad (10.4)$$

$$Y_1 X \rightarrow Y_2 X,\quad Y_1, Y_2 \in I - I_T, \quad (10.5)$$

$$Y_1 X \rightarrow Y_2 x X,\quad x \in I_T,\quad Y_1, Y_2 \in I - I_T. \quad (10.6)$$

Productions of the forms (10.4)–(10.6) are referred to, respectively, as *contractions, neutrations* and *expansions*.

We shall now establish a sequence of theorems to the effect that a language is regular iff it is of the form (10.2) or (10.3).

THEOREM 10.1. *If $L = L_g(C, U, V)$, where C is a (pure, reduced) regular canonical system, then $L = L_a(C_1, V, U)$, where C_1 is a (pure, reduced) regular canonical system, and conversely.*

Proof. Assume that $L = L_g(C, U, V)$, for some regular canonical system $C = (I, I_T, F)$ and finite sets U and V of words over I. Consider the regular canonical system $C_1 = (I, I_T, F_1)$, where a production $PX \rightarrow QX$ belongs to F_1 iff the production $QX \rightarrow PX$ belongs to F. Then $L = L_a(C_1, V, U)$. If C is pure (reduced), then also C_1 is pure (reduced). The converse part of the theorem is obtained similarly. □

THEOREM 10.2. *For every pure regular canonical system $C = (I_T, I_T, F)$ and every finite set $U \subset W(I_T)$, there is a reduced regular canonical system $C_1 = (I, I_T, F_1)$ and subsets U_1 and V_1 of $I - I_T$ such that*

$$L_g(C, U, \{\lambda\}) = L_g(C_1, U_1, V_1). \quad (10.7)$$

Proof. Consider a sequence $Y_1, Y_2, \ldots$ of letters not contained in I_T. Let

$$C^1 = (I_T \cup \{Y_1\}, I_T, F^1),$$

where F^1 consists of all productions $Y_1PX \to Y_1QX$ such that $PX \to QX$ belongs to F. Denote

$$U^1 = \{Y_1P \,|\, P \in U\}.$$

Then $L_g(C, U, \{\lambda\}) = L_g(C^1, U^1, \{Y_1\})$.

Having defined the pair (C^i, U^i), $i \geqq 1$, we define the pair (C^{i+1}, U^{i+1}) if one of the following rules (i)–(iii) is applicable.

(i) If $Y_jxP \in U^i$, where $x \in I_T$, choose a letter Y_v which does not occur in C^i. C^{i+1} is obtained from C^i by adding the auxiliary letter Y_v and the production $Y_vX \to Y_jxX$. U^{i+1} is obtained from U^i by removing Y_jxP and adding Y_vP.

(ii) If the production $Y_jxPX \to QX$, which is not a contraction and where $x \in I_T$, is one of the productions of C^i, then choose a letter Y_v which does not occur in C^i. C^{i+1} is obtained by adding the auxiliary letter Y_v and the productions $Y_vPX \to QX$ and $Y_jxX \to Y_vX$. $U^{i+1} = U^i$ in this case.

(iii) If the production $QX \to Y_jxPX$, which is not an expansion and where $x \in I_T$, is one of the productions of C^i, then choose a letter Y_v which does not occur in C^i. C^{i+1} is obtained by adding the auxiliary letter Y_v and the productions $QX \to Y_vPX$ and $Y_vX \to Y_jxX$. Also in this case $U^{i+1} = U^i$.

It is obvious that there is a natural number m such that in the pair (C^m, U^m) C^m is reduced and U^m consists of the letters Y. Furthermore,

$$L_g(C^i, U^i, \{Y_1\}) = L_g(C^{i+1}, U^{i+1}, \{Y_1\}) \qquad (i = 1, \ldots, m-1).$$

By choosing $C_1 = C^m$, $U_1 = U^m$ and $V_1 = \{Y_1\}$, we see that (10.7) is satisfied. □

THEOREM 10.3. *For every reduced regular canonical system $C = (I, I_T, F)$ and subsets U and V of the set $I - I_T$, there is a reduced regular canonical system $C_1 = (I, I_T, F_1)$ such that F_1 does not contain expansions and*

$$L_a(C, U, V) = L_a(C_1, U, V). \qquad (10.8)$$

Proof. We define a reduced regular canonical system $C_1 = (I, I_T, F_1)$ such that F_1 does not contain any expansions as follows. For $x \in I_T$ and $Y_1, Y_2 \in I - I_T$, the contraction

$$Y_1xX \to Y_2X$$

belongs to F_1 iff $Y_1 x \underset{\sigma}{\overset{*}{\Rightarrow}} Y_2$. For Y_1, $Y_2 \in I - I_T$, the neutration

$$Y_1 X \rightarrow Y_2 X \tag{10.9}$$

belongs to F_1 iff $Y_1 \underset{\sigma}{\overset{*}{\Rightarrow}} Y_2$. We shall establish the equation (10.8).

It is obvious by the definition of F_1 that

$$L_a(C_1, U, V) \subset L_a(C, U, V). \tag{10.10}$$

Conversely, assume that $P \in L_a(C, U, V)$. If $P = \lambda$ then, for some $Y_1 \in U$ and $Y_2 \in V$, $Y_1 \underset{\sigma}{\overset{*}{\Rightarrow}} Y_2$. Consequently, (10.9) belongs to F_1 and $P \in L_a$ (C_1, U, V). Let $P = x_1 \ldots x_k$, $k \geq 1$, $x_i \in I_T$. Hence, for some $Y_1 \in U$ and $Y_2 \in V$,

$$Y_1 x_1 \ldots x_k \underset{\sigma}{\overset{*}{\Rightarrow}} Y_2. \tag{10.11}$$

The derivation (10.11) is of the form

$$Y_1 x_1 \ldots x_k \underset{\sigma}{\overset{*}{\Rightarrow}} Q_1 x_1 \ldots x_k \underset{\sigma}{\overset{*}{\Rightarrow}} Y_1^{(1)} x_2 \ldots x_k \underset{\sigma}{\overset{*}{\Rightarrow}} Q_2 x_2 \ldots x_k$$
$$\underset{\sigma}{\overset{*}{\Rightarrow}} Y_1^{(2)} x_3 \ldots x_k \underset{\sigma}{\overset{*}{\Rightarrow}} Q_k x_k \underset{\sigma}{\overset{*}{\Rightarrow}} Y_1^{(k)} \underset{\sigma}{\overset{*}{\Rightarrow}} Y_2,$$

where $Q_i \in W(I)$ and $Y_1^{(i)} \in I - I_T$, for $i = 1, \ldots, k$.

Consequently,

$$Y_1 x_1 \underset{\sigma}{\overset{*}{\Rightarrow}} Y_1^{(1)}, \ Y_1^{(1)} x_2 \underset{\sigma}{\overset{*}{\Rightarrow}} Y_1^{(2)}, \ \ldots, \ Y_1^{(k-1)} x_k \underset{\sigma}{\overset{*}{\Rightarrow}} Y_1^{(k)},$$

$$Y_1^{(k)} \underset{\sigma}{\overset{*}{\Rightarrow}} Y_2.$$

This implies that the productions

$$Y_1 x_1 X \rightarrow Y_1^{(1)} X, \ Y_1^{(1)} x_2 X \rightarrow Y_1^{(2)} X, \ \ldots, \ Y_1^{(k-1)} x_k X \rightarrow Y_1^{(k)} X, \ Y_1^{(k)} X \rightarrow Y_2 X$$

are in F_1. Therefore,

$$Y_1 x_1 \ldots x_k \underset{\sigma_1}{\overset{*}{\Rightarrow}} Y_2.$$

Because P was arbitrary, we conclude that

$$L_a(C, U, V) \subset L_a(C_1, U, V),$$

which together with (10.10) proves (10.8). □

THEOREM 10.4. *For every reduced regular canonical system* $C = (I, I_T, F)$ *such that F does not contain expansions and for all subsets U and V of* $I-I_T$, *the language* $L_a(C, U, V)$ *is f.a.r.*

Proof. Consider the finite non-deterministic automaton

$$\mathbf{NA} = (I - I_T, U, f)$$

over the alphabet I_T, where f is defined as follows. For $Y \in I - I_T$ and $x \in I_T$, $f(Y, x)$ equals the set of those elements Y' of $I - I_T$ which satisfy the condition $Yx \overset{*}{\underset{\sigma}{\Rightarrow}} Y'$. Clearly,

$$L_a(C, U, V) = L(\mathbf{NA}, V) \text{ or } L_a(C, U, V) = L(\mathbf{NA}, V) + \{\lambda\}.$$

Thus, by Theorem II.1.1, $L_a(C, U, V)$ is f.a.r. □

THEOREM 10.5. *For every regular canonical system* $C = (I, I_T, F)$ *and all finite subsets U and V of the set* $W(I)$, *the languages* (10.2) *and* (10.3) *are f.a.r. and, thus, regular.*

Proof. By Theorem 10.1, it suffices to prove that the language (10.2) is f.a.r. We assume first that $C = (I_T, I_T, F)$ is pure. In this case, because

$$L_g(C, U, V) = \sum_{P \in V} \partial_P(L_g(C, U, \{\lambda\}))$$

and because all derivatives of a regular language are regular (cf. Exercise II.3.6), it suffices to prove that the language

$$L_g(C, U, \{\lambda\}) \tag{10.12}$$

is regular. By Theorem 10.2, the language (10.12) equals the language

$$L_g(C_1, U_1, V_1), \tag{10.13}$$

where $C_1 = (I_1, I_T, F_1)$ is reduced and U_1 and V_1 are subsets of $I_1 - I_T$. By Theorem 10.1, the language (10.13) equals the language

$$L_a(C_2, V_1, U_1), \tag{10.14}$$

where $C_2 = (I_1, I_T, F_2)$ is reduced. The language (10.14) is f.a.r., by Theorems 10.3 and 10.4.

Thus, we have shown that the language (10.2) is regular if C is pure. Let $C = (I, I_T, F)$ be an arbitrary regular canonical system.

Consider the pure regular canonical system $C' = (I, I, F)$. Clearly,

$$L_g(C, U, V) = L_g(C', U, V) \cap W(I_T),$$

where the right side is regular, by Theorem I.2.6. $\square$

THEOREM 10.6. *For every regular language L over an alphabet I_T, there is a pure regular canonical system $C = (I_T, I_T, F)$ and a finite subset U of $W(I_T)$ such that*

$$L = L_g(C, U, \{\lambda\}). \tag{10.15}$$

Proof. Let the language L be represented in the finite deterministic automaton $A = (S, s_0, f)$ over I_T, where card $(S) = n$. For a word $P = x_1 x_2 \ldots x_n \in W(I_T)$ of length n, we consider the sequence of states

$$s_0 \lambda, s_0 x_1, s_0 x_1 x_2, \ldots, s_0 x_1 x_2 \ldots x_n. \tag{10.16}$$

The states (10.16) are not all distinct because the total number of states equals n. Let (i, j), where $0 \leq i < j \leq n$, be the first pair such that

$$s_0 x_1 \ldots x_i = s_0 x_1 \ldots x_i \ldots x_j.$$

We associate with the word P the production

$$x_1 \ldots x_i X \rightarrow x_1 \ldots x_i \ldots x_j X.$$

The same procedure is repeated for each word over I_T which is of length n. Let F be the set of productions thus obtained and let $C = (I_T, I_T, F)$ be the corresponding pure regular canonical system. Let U consist of those words of L which are of length less than or equal to n. We claim that (10.15) is satisfied.

To establish (10.15), we show by induction on k that both sides contain the same words of length k. For $k \leq n$, this follows by the definition of U and by the fact that the productions in F increase the length of words. Assume that both sides of (10.15) contain the same words of length less than or equal to m, where $m \geq n$. Let

$$P_1 = y_1 \ldots y_m y_{m+1}$$

be an arbitrary word over I_T of length $m+1$.

Assume first that $P_1 \in L$. Consider the initial subword of P_1 of length n and the pair (i, j) as in the definition of F. Then

$$s_0 P_1 = s_0 P_2, \tag{10.17}$$

where

$$P_2 = y_1 \ldots y_i y_{j+1} \ldots y_m y_{m+1}$$

is of length less than or equal to m. By (10.17), $P_2 \in L$ and thus, by our inductive hypothesis, $P_2 \in L_g(C, U, \{\lambda\})$. Because the production

$$y_1 \ldots y_i X \to y_1 \ldots y_i \ldots y_j X$$

is in F, this implies that

$$P_1 \in L_g(C, U, \{\lambda\}). \tag{10.18}$$

Assume next (10.18). This implies that there is a word P_3 such that $P_3 \underset{\overline{C}}{\Rightarrow} P_1$ and

$$P_3 \in L_g(C, U, \{\lambda\}). \tag{10.19}$$

Furthermore, $\lg(P_3) \le m$ because the productions in F increase the length of words. By (10.19) and our inductive hypothesis, $P_3 \in L$. On the other hand, by the definition of F, $s_0 P_3 = s_0 P_1$. Therefore, $P_1 \in L$.

We have shown that both sides of (10.15) contain the same words of length $m+1$, which completes the induction. $\square$

Our last theorem is an immediate corollary of Theorems 10.5 and 10.6.

THEOREM 10.7. *A language over an alphabet I_T is regular iff it is of the form* (10.2) *or* (10.3), *for some regular canonical system $C = (I, I_T, F)$ and finite subsets U and V of the set $W(I)$.*

EXERCISE 10.1. *A Post canonical system* is defined as a regular canonical system except that, instead of (10.1), the productions are allowed to be of the following general form:

$$P_{11} X_{11} P_{12} \ldots P_{1m_1} X_{1m_1} P_{1(m_1+1)}, \tag{1}$$

$$\cdots$$

$$P_{k1} X_{k1} P_{k2} \ldots P_{km_k} X_{km_k} P_{k(m_k+1)} \tag{k}$$

produce

$$P_1 X_1 P_2 \ldots P_u X_u P_{u+1}. \tag{k+1}$$

(It is assumed that each of the premises $(1)-(k)$ has to be satisfied before the conclusion $(k+1)$ can be made. Hereby, P's are words over the alphabet I and X's operational variables in the same sense as in

(10.1). Furthermore, each of the X's in the conclusion $(k+1)$ appears in some of the premises $(1)-(k)$.)

Define formally the languages generated and accepted by a Post canonical system. Cf. Post (1943) for a proof of the fact that a general Post canonical system can be reduced to a system, where every production is in the *normal form*

$$PX \to XQ.$$

EXERCISE 10.2. Prove that there is an algorithm of constructing the system C_1 in the proof of Theorem 10.3 and the automaton NA in the proof of Theorem 10.4. Prove that there is an algorithm of constructing, for a given regular language, the corresponding regular canonical system, and vice versa.

EXERCISE 10.3 (Kratko, 1966). How can one obtain directly from a regular expression the corresponding regular canonical system?

EXERCISE 10.4 (Kratko, 1966; Greibach, 1967). Prove that the language (10.2) is regular also if U and V are infinite regular languages over I.

EXERCISE 10.5 (Kratko, 1966). Prove that (as far as the generated languages are concerned) every Post canonical system can be reduced to a system, where every production is of one of the following two forms:

$$P_1X, P_2X \to QX,$$

$$XP_1', XP_2' \to XQ'.$$

EXERCISE 10.6 (Kratko, 1966). Prove that if the productions of a Post canonical system are of one of the following two forms

$$P_1X, P_2X, \ldots, P_kX \to QX$$

$$XP' \to XQ',$$

then the generated languages are regular. (Note that the regularity of (10.2) is obtained as a special case, where there are no productions of the latter form and where in all productions of the former form $k = 1$.)

HISTORICAL AND BIBLIOGRAPHICAL REMARKS

THE notion of a regular language (for which also the names "regular event" and "regular set" are used), as well as original versions of Theorems I.2.2 and I.2.3, are due to Kleene (1956). Ideas of McNaughton and Yamada (1960) and Glushkov (1961) are used in our proofs of these theorems. For other proofs, the reader is referred to Copi, Elgot and Wright (1958), Medvedev (1956) and Ott and Feinstein (1961). Characteristic equations are due to Brzozowski (1964), Bodnarchuk (1963) and Spivak (1965, 1, 2). The material in Section I.4 is drawn from Rabin and Scott (1959), Theorems I.4.1 and I.4.2 being due to Nerode (1958) and Myhill (1957). Mealy and Moore machines are introduced in Mealy (1955) and Moore (1956). Of the many existing proofs of Theorem I.5.1 we mention Ibarra (1967). The minimization methods of Section I.6 are due to Moore (1956). For a more recent approach, cf. Starke (1967) and for corresponding asymptotic estimates, cf. Barzdin' and Korshunov (1967). Theorem I.7.2 is due to Raney (1958) and Theorem I.7.3 to Gray and Harrison (1966). For a more advanced discussion on sequential functions, the reader is referred to Elgot (1961) and Elgot and Mezei (1963, 1965). The material on definite languages in Section I.8 is due to Perles, Rabin and Shamir (1963) and that on non-initial automata to Starke (1963) and Steinby (1967). Another approach is due to Brzozowski (1963). The material in Section I.9 is drawn from Salomaa (1964, 2), where also more detailed proofs are given. Theorem I.10.1 is due to Rabin, cf. Rabin and Scott (1959), and Shepherdson (1959).

Comprehensive discussions on finite deterministic automata are contained in Glushkov (1961), Gill (1962), Ginsburg (1962), Ajzerman, Gusev, Rozonoer, Smirnova and Tal' (1963) and Harrison (1965). For an approach based on predicate calculus, the reader is referred to the work of Trakhtenbrot, in Kobrinskij and Trakhtenbrot (1962), and Büchi (1960). For various algebraic approaches (differing also with respect to the subject matter), cf. Hartmanis and Stearns (1966), Krohn and Rhodes (1963) and Eilenberg and Wright (1967). For the theory of incompletely specified sequential machines (i.e. the functions f and φ of Section I.5 are not defined for all arguments), the reader is referred to Ginsburg (1962).

The material in Section II.1 is from Rabin and Scott (1959). Of the various early works on probabilistic automata we mention von Neumann (1956), although the approach is entirely different from that of Chapter II. The notions of probabilistic automata and sequential machines as generalizations of the corresponding deterministic devices were introduced by Bukharaev (1964), Carlyle (1963) and Rabin (1963). Representation with cut-point is due to Rabin (1963). Theorems II.3.1–II.3.3 are due to Bukharaev (1967), except the part of Theorem II.3.1 concerning values $\eta > \eta'$ due to Turakainen (1967), Theorem II.3.4 is new, Theorem II.3.5 is due to Rabin (1963) and Theorems II.3.6–II.3.8 are due to Turakainen (1967). The basic idea of Theorems II.4.1 and II.4.2 is in Rabin (1963), credited to Moore. Our presentation follows Even (1964) and Salomaa (1967). For an extension of Theorem II.4.2, cf. Hartmanis and Stearns (1967). A direct proof of Theorem II.4.3 which uses an example similar to the one given in Fig. 19 has been given by Starke (1966, 3). The material of Section II.5 is from Salomaa (1966, 1) except Theorem II.5.9 due to Carlyle (1963). Similar problems are considered also in Bukharaev (1964) and Starke (1965, 1966, 1, 2). Theorem II.6.2 is from Salomaa (1966, 1) and Theorem II.6.3 from Paz (1967).

The notion of star height has been introduced by Eggan (1963). The second sentence of Theorem III.1.1 is due to Eggan (1963) and McNaughton (1964). Our proof uses the method of Dejean and Schützenberger (1966). The material in Section III.2 is due to Bodnarchuk (1963). Theorems III.3.1, III.4.1 and several lemmas in the proofs of Theorems III.4.2 and III.5.1 are new. Theorems III.3.2 and III.5.1 are due to Redko (1964, 2, 1) and Theorem III.4.2 to Janov (1962). Theorems III.6.2 and III.6.3 are implicit (although not stated in this form) in the work of Redko (1964, 1, 2). The material in Section III.7 is drawn from Salomaa (1964, 1; 1966, 2). The completeness of an axiom system almost identical to $\mathcal{F}_2$ was established independently by Aanderaa (1965). Cf. also Ginzburg (1967). The material in Section III.8 is new.

The notion of a grammar as well as the hierarchy of languages was introduced by Chomsky (1956, 1957, 1959). The theory of type 3 languages (which are often called also finite state languages) is due to Bar-Hillel and Shamir (1960), Bar-Hillel, Perles and Shamir (1961), Chomsky and Miller (1958) and Chomsky (1959). The paper by Chomsky (1959) contains also the inclusion relations of Section IV.4, as well as Theorems IV.2.6 and IV.6.1. The fact that (IV.3.10) is not context-free is due to Scheinberg (1960). The Boolean properties of context-free languages are discussed first in Bar-Hillel, Perles and Shamir (1961) and Scheinberg (1960). The notion of an ALGOL-like language and Theorem IV.3.1 are due to Ginsburg and Rice (1962). Theorems IV.3.2 (in a slightly different form), IV.3.3 and IV.3.5 are in Bar-Hillel, Perles and Shamir (1961). The notion of inherent ambiguity was first discussed by Parikh (1961). For decidability and ambiguity problems of context-free languages, the reader is referred to Ginsburg (1966), Bar-Hillel, Perles and Shamir (1961), Greibach (1963), Ginsburg and Rose (1963) and Hibbard and Ullian (1966). The formal notion of a pushdown automaton and Theorems IV.5.1 and IV.5.2 are due to Chomsky (1962) and Evey (1963). A more powerful device (stack automaton) which is capable of reading but not rewriting the interior part of the pushdown store is introduced in Ginsburg, Greibach and Harrison (1967). Linear bounded automata were introduced in Myhill (1960), where also the expression "linear bounded" is explained by referring to the memory space available. Theorems IV.6.2, IV.6.7 and IV.6.8 are due to Landweber (1963) and Theorems IV.6.6, IV.6.4 and IV.6.5 (the last two being lemmas) to Kuroda (1964). Turing machines were introduced by Turing (1936). For a detailed discussion, the reader is referred to Davis (1958). A comprehensive theory of infinite-state machines and related devices is presented in Ginsburg (1962) and Glushkov (1961). Cf. also the survey by McNaughton (1961), for various other types of automata. The notion of an abstract pushdown automaton (in a slightly different form) and Theorems IV.9.1 and IV.9.2

are due to Letichevskij (1965). The material in Section IV.10 is due to Büchi (1964).

For a comprehensive exposition on context-free languages, the reader is referred to Ginsburg (1966). The book by Marcus (1964) deals almost exclusively with regular languages. Chomsky (1963) is a detailed survey article on the hierarchy of languages and automata. Our proofs of Theorems IV.1.1, IV.2.6, IV.3.4 and IV.7.1 apply ideas from Jones (1966), which is an introduction to the Chomsky hierarchy.

The subsequent list of references contains only works referred to in this book and, thus, it is not intended to be a bibliography on automata theory. The reader is referred to the bibliographies in Moore (1964), Marcus (1964), Ajzerman, Gusev, Rozonoer, Smirnova and Tal' (1963). McNaughton (1961), Harrison (1965) and Chomsky (1963). Reviews of recent papers can be found in the following journals (among others):

ACM Computing Reviews,
Journal of Symbolic Logic,
Mathematical Reviews,
Referativnyi Zhurnal Matematika.

Supplement added in proof. Recently there has been an increasing amount of research done on changing the manner in which the grammar is allowed to generate words. In addition to restrictions on the form of the productions, one has imposed restrictions on the use of them. For instance, an application of some production determines which productions are applicable on the next step (this is called a programmed grammar), or some productions can never be applied if some others are applicable (an ordered grammar), or the string of productions corresponding to a derivation must belong to a set of strings previously specified (a grammar with a control set). Of the various kinds of automata recently introduced we mention several types of stack automata and generalizations of pushdown automata. For some of these recent developments, the reader is referred to the article "The Theory of Languages" by A. V. Aho and J. D. Ullman in *Mathematical Systems Theory* **2** (1968), 97–125.

REFERENCES

AANDERAA, S. (1965) On the algebra of regular expressions, *Appl. Math.*, Harvard Univ.

AGASANDJAN, G. A. (1967) Avtomaty s peremennoj strukturoj, *Dokl. Akad. Nauk SSSR* **174**, 529–30.

AJZERMAN, M., GUSEV, L., ROZONOER, L., SMIRNOVA, I. and TAL', A. (1963) *Logika, avtomaty, algoritmy*, Gosud. izd. Fiz.-Mat. Lit., Moscow.

AMAR, V. and PUTZOLU, G. (1964) On a family of linear grammars, *Information and Control* **7**, 283–91.

BAR-HILLEL, Y., PERLES, M. and SHAMIR, E. (1961) On formal properties of simple phrase structure grammars, *Z. Phonetik Sprachwiss. Kommunikat.* **14**, 143–172; also appears in Y. BAR-HILLEL, *Language and Information*, Addison–Wesley, 1964.

BAR-HILLEL, Y. and SHAMIR, E. (1960) Finite-state languages: Formal representations and adequacy problems, *Bull. Res. Council Israel* 8F, 155–66; also appears in Y. BAR-HILLEL, *Language and Information*, Addison–Wesley, 1964.

BARZDIN', JA. M. and KORSHUNOV, A. D. (1967) O diametre privedennykh avtomatov, *Diskret. Analiz* **9**, 3–45.

BLOKH, A. (1960) O zadachakh, reshaemykh posledovatelnostnymi mashinami, *Problemy Kibernet.* **3**, 81–88.

BODNARCHUK, V. (1963) Sistemy uravnenij v algebre sobytij, *Zh. Vychisl. Mat. i Mat. Fiz.* **3**, 1077–88.

BRZOZOWSKI, J. A. (1963) Canonical regular expressions and minimal state graphs for definite events, *Proc. Symp. Math. Theory Automata*, Polytechnic Press.

BRZOZOWSKI, J. A. (1964) Derivatives of regular expressions, *J. Assoc. Comput. Mach.* **11**, 481–94.

BRZOZOWSKI, J. A. (1967) Roots of star events, *J. Assoc. Comput. Mach.* **14**, 466–77.

BÜCHI, J. R. (1960) Weak second-order arithmetic and finite automata, *Z. Math Logik Grundlagen Math.* **6**, 66–92.

BÜCHI, J. R. (1964) Regular canonical systems, *Arch. Math. Logik Grundlagenforsch* **6**, 91–111.

BUKHARAEV, R. (1964) Nekotorye ekvivalentnosti v teorii verojatnostnykh avtomatov, *Kazan. Gos. Univ. Uchen. Zap.* **124**, 45–65.

BUKHARAEV, R. (1965) Kriterij predstavimosti sobytij v konechnykh verojatnostnykh avtomatakh, *Dokl. Akad. Nauk SSSR* **164**, 289–91.

BUKHARAEV, R. (1967) Kriterij predstavimosti sobytij v konechnykh verojatnostnykh avtomatakh, manuscript to be published.

CARLYLE, J. W. (1963) Reduced forms for stochastic sequential machines, *J. Math. Anal. Appl.* **7**, 167–75.

CHOMSKY, N. (1956) Three models for the description of language, *IRE Trans. Information Theory* IT-2, 113–24.

CHOMSKY, N. (1957) *Syntactic Structures*, Mouton & Company, Gravenhage.

CHOMSKY, N. (1959) On certain formal properties of grammars, *Information and Control* **2**, 137–67.

CHOMSKY, N. (1962) Context-free grammars and pushdown storage, *M.I.T. Res. Lab. Electron. Quart. Prog. Rept.* 65.

CHOMSKY, N. (1963) Formal properties of grammars, in D. LUCE, R. BUSH and E. GALANTER (eds.), *Handbook of Mathematical Psychology*, vol. 2, Wiley.

CHOMSKY, N. and MILLER, G. A. (1958) Finite state languages, *Information and Control* **1**, 91–112.

CHOMSKY, N. and SCHÜTZENBERGER, M. P. (1963) The algebraic theory of context-free languages, in P. BRAFFORT and D. HIRSCHBERG (eds.) *Computer Programming and Formal Systems*, North Holland Publishing Company.

COPI, I. M., ELGOT, C. C. and WRIGHT, J. B. (1958) Realization of events by logical nets, *J. Assoc. Comput. Mach.* **5**, 181–96.

DAVIS, M. (1958) *Computability and Unsolvability*, McGraw-Hill.

DEJEAN, F. and SCHÜTZENBERGER, M. P. (1966) On a question of Eggan, *Information and Control* **9**, 23–25.

EGGAN, L. C. (1963) Transition graphs and the star-height of regular events, *Michigan Math. J.* **10**, 385–97.

EILENBERG, S. and WRIGHT, J. B. (1967) Automata in general algebras, distributed in conjunction with the Colloquium Lectures given at Toronto, August 29–September 1, 1967.

ELGOT, C. C. (1961) Decision problems of finite automata design and related arithmetics, *Trans. Amer. Math. Soc.* **98**, 21–51.

ELGOT, C. C. and MEZEI, J. (1963) Two-sided finite transductions, *IBM Research Paper* RC–1017.

ELGOT, C. C. and MEZEI, J. (1965) On relations defined by generalized finite automata, *IBM J. Res. Develop.* **9**, 47–68.

EVEN, S. (1964) Rational numbers and regular events, *IEEE Trans. Electronic Computers* EC-13, 740–741.

EVEY, R. J. (1963) The theory and application of pushdown store machines. *Mathematical Linguistics and Automatic Translation*, Harvard Univ. Computation Lab. Rept. NSF-IO.

FREY, T. (1964) Über die Konstruktion endlicher Automaten, *Acta Math. Acad. Sci. Hungar.* **15**, 383–98.

GILL, A. (1962) *Introduction to the Theory of Finite-State Machines*, McGraw-Hill.

GILL, A. (1966) Realization of input-output relations by sequential machines, *J. Assoc. Comput. Mach.* **13**, 33–42.

GINSBURG, S. (1962) *An Introduction to Mathematical Machine Theory*, Addison-Wesley.

GINSBURG, S. (1966) *The Mathematical Theory of Context-Free Languages*, McGraw-Hill.

GINSBURG, S., GREIBACH, S. A. and HARRISON, M. A. (1967) Stack automata and compiling, *J. Assoc. Comput. Mach.* **14**, 172–201.

GINSBURG, S. and RICE, H. G. (1962) Two families of languages related to ALGOL, *J. Assoc. Comput. Mach.* **9**, 350–71.

GINSBURG, S. and ROSE, G. F. (1963) Some recursively unsolvable problems in ALGOL-like languages, *J. Assoc. Comput. Mach.* **10**, 29–47.

GINSBURG, S. and ROSE, G. F. (1966) A characterization of machine mappings, *Canad. J. Math.* **18**, 381–8.

GINSBURG, S. and SPANIER, E. H. (1966) Semigroups, Presburger formulas and languages, *Pacific J. Math.* **16**, 285–96.

GINZBURG, A. (1966) About some properties of definite, reverse-definite and related automata, *IEEE Trans. Electronic Computers* EC-15, 806–10.

GINZBURG, A. (1967) A procedure for checking the equality of regular expressions, *J. Assoc. Comput. Mach.* **14**, 355–62.

GLUSHKOV, V. M. (1961) Abstraktnaja teorija avtomatov, *Uspehi Mat. Nauk* **16**, 3–62; appears also in German translation *Theorie der abstrakten Automaten*, VEB Deutscher Verlag der Wissenschaften, 1963.

GRAY, J. N. and HARRISON, M. A. (1966) The theory of sequential relations, *Information and Control* **9**, 435–68.

GREIBACH, S. A. (1963) Undecidability of the ambiguity problem for minimal linear grammars, *Information and Control* **6**, 119–25.

GREIBACH, S. A. (1967) A note on pushdown store automata and regular systems *Proc. Amer. Math. Soc.* **18**, 263–8.

GROSS, M. (1964) Inherent ambiguity of minimal linear grammars, *Information and Control* **7**, 366–8.

HAINES, L. H. (1964) Note on the complement of a (minimal) linear language, *Information and Control* **7**, 307–14.

HARRISON, M. A. (1965) *Introduction to Switching and Automata Theory*, McGraw-Hill.

HARTMANIS, J. and STEARNS, R. E. (1963) Regularity preserving modifications of regular expressions, *Information and Control* **6**, 55–69.

HARTMANIS, J. and STEARNS, R. E. (1966) *Algebraic Structure Theory of Sequential Machines*, Prentice-Hall.

HARTMANIS, J. and STEARNS, R. E. (1967) Sets of numbers defined by finite automata, *Amer. Math. Monthly* **74**, 539–42.

HEDETNIEMI, S. T. (1966) Homomorphisms of graphs and automata, *Univ. of Michigan Technical Report*, ORA Projects 03105 and 07363.

HIBBARD, T. N. and ULLIAN, J. (1966) The independence of inherent ambiguity from complementedness among context-free languages, *J. Assoc. Comput. Mach.* **13**, 588–93.

HUZINO, S. (1966) On some properties of derivative-mappings, structural diagrams and structural equations: Part I, *Mem. Fac. Sci. Kyushu Univ. Ser.* A 20, 179–265.

HUZINO, S. (1967) *Ibid.*: Part II, *Mem. Fac. Sci. Kyushu Univ. Ser.* A 21, 1–103.

IBARRA, O. (1967) On the equivalence of finite-state sequential machine models, *IEEE Trans. Electronic Computers* EC-16, 88–90.

JANOV, JU. I. (1962) O tozhdestvennykh preobrazovanijakh reguljarnykh vyrazhenij, *Dokl. Akad. Nauk SSSR* **147**, 327–30.

JANOV, JU. I. (1964) Ob invariantnykh operacijakh nad sobytijami, *Problemy Kibernet.* **12**, 253–8.

JANOV, JU. I. (1966) O nekotorykh podalgebrakh sobytij, ne imejushchikh konechnykh polnykh sistem tozhdestv, *Problemy Kibernet.* **17**, 255–8.

JONES, N. D. (1966) A survey of formal language theory, *Univ. of Western Ontario, Computer Science Department Technical Report* No. 3.

JONES, N. D. (1967, 1) Formal languages and rudimentary attributes, Dissertation, Univ. of Western Ontario.

JONES, N. D. (1967, 2) Formal languages and rudimentary attributes, *Information and Control*, to appear.

KARP, R. M. (1967) Some bounds on the storage requirements of sequential machines and Turing machines, *J. Assoc. Comput. Mach.* **14**, 478–89.

KLEENE, S. C. (1956) Representation of events in nerve nets and finite automata, in *Automata Studies*, Princeton Univ. Press.

KOBRINSKIJ, N. E. and TRAKHTENBROT, B. A. (1962) *Vvedenie b teoriju konechnykh avtomatov*, Gosud. izd. Fiz.-Mat. Lit., Moscow; also in English translation *Introduction to the Theory of Finite Automata*, North Holland Publishing Company, 1965.

KRATKO, M. I. (1966) Formalnye ischislenija Posta i konechnye avtomaty, *Problemy Kibernet.* **17**, 41–65.

KROHN, K. B. and RHODES, J. L. (1963) Algebraic theory of machines, *Proc. Symp. Math. Theory Automata*, Polytechnic Press.

KURODA, S.-Y. (1964) Classes of languages and linear-bounded automata, *Information and Control* **7**, 207–23.

LANDWEBER, P. S. (1963) Three theorems on phrase structure grammars of type 1, *Information and Control* **6**, 131–6.

LETICHEVSKIJ, A. A. (1965) The representation of context-free languages in automata with a push-down type store, translation to be found in *Cybernetics* of the original which appeared in *Kibernetika* **1**, No. 2, 80–84.

MARCUS, S. (1964) *Gramatici si automate finite*, Editura Academiei Republicii Populare Romine.

McNAUGHTON, R. (1961) The theory of automata, a survey; in *Advances in Computers*, vol. 2, Academic Press.

McNAUGHTON, R. (1964) Star height and order, M.I.T. Skeletal Lecture Notes.

McNAUGHTON, R. (1965) Techniques for manipulating regular expressions, *M.I.T. Machine Structures Group Memo* No. 10.

McNAUGHTON, R. (1966) The loop complexity of regular events, *M.I.T. Machine Structures Group Memo* No. 18.

McNAUGHTON, R. (1967) Parenthesis grammars, *J. Assoc. Comput. Mach.* **14**, 172–201.

McNAUGHTON, R. and YAMADA, H. (1960) Regular expressions and state graphs for automata, *IRE Trans. Electronic Computers* EC-9, 39–47.

MEALY, G. H. (1955) A method for synthesizing sequential circuits, *Bell System Tech. J.* **34**, 1045–79.

MEDVEDEV, JU. T. (1956) O klasse sobytij, dopuskajushchikh predstavlenie v konechnom avtomate, in *Avtomaty*, Izd. Inostr. Lit. Moscow; English translation appears in Moore (1964).

MOORE, E. F. (1956) Gedanken experiments on sequential machines, in *Automata Studies*, Princeton Univ. Press.

MOORE, E. F. (1964) (ed.) *Sequential Machines; Selected Papers*, Addison-Wesley.

MURSKIJ, V. L. (1964) O preobrazovanijakh nekotorykh tipov skhem, svjazannykh s konechnymi avtomatami, *Dokl. Akad. Nauk SSSR* **156**, 510–12.

MYHILL, J. (1957) Finite automata and the representation of events, *WADC Tech. Rept.* 57–624.

MYHILL, J. (1960) Linear bounded automata, *WADD Tech. Note* 60–165.

NERODE, A. (1958) Linear automaton transformations, *Proc. Amer. Math. Soc.* **9**, 541–44.

NEUMANN, J. VON (1956) Probabilistic logics and the synthesis of reliable organisms from unreliable components, in *Automata Studies*, Princeton Univ. Press.

OTT, G. and FEINSTEIN, N. (1961) Design of sequential machines from their regular expressions, *J. Assoc. Comput. Mach.* **8**, 585–600.

PAGE, C. V. (1966) Equivalences between probabilistic and deterministic sequential machines, *Information and Control* **9**, 469–520.

PARIKH, R. J. (1961) Language generating devices, *M.I.T. Res. Lab. Electron. Quart. Prog. Rept.* **60**, 199–212; later version in *J. Assoc. Comput. Mach.* **13** (1966) 570–81.

PAZ, A. (1966) Some aspects of probabilistic automata, *Information and Control* **9**, 26–60.

PAZ, A. (1967) Fuzzy star functions, probabilistic automata and their approximation by nonprobabilistic automata, manuscript to be published.

PAZ, A. and PELEG, B. (1965, 1) On concatenative decompositions of regular events, *U.S. Office of Naval Res. Inf. Systems Branch Tech. Rept.* No. 20.

PAZ, A. and PELEG, B. (1965, 2) Ultimate-definite and symmetric-definite events and automata, *J. Assoc. Comput. Mach.* **12**, 399–410.

PERLES, M., RABIN, M. O. and SHAMIR, E. (1963) The theory of definite automata, *IEEE Trans. Electronic Computers* EC-12, 233–43.

POST, E. L. (1943) Formal reductions of the general combinatorial decision problem, *Amer. J. Math.* **65**, 197–215.

RABIN, M. O. (1963) Probabilistic automata, *Information and Control* **6**, 230–45.

RABIN, M. O. and SCOTT, D. (1959) Finite automata and their decision problems, *IBM J. Res. Develop.* **3**, 114–25.

RANEY, G. N. (1958) Sequential functions, *J. Assoc. Comput. Mach.* **5**, 177–80.

REDKO, V. N. (1964, 1) Ob algebre kommutativnykh sobytij, *Ukrain. Mat. Zh.* **16**, 185–95.

REDKO, V. N. (1964, 2) Ob opredeljajushchej sobokupnosti sootnoshenij algebry reguljarnykh sobytij, *Ukrain. Mat. Zh.* **16**, 120–6.

REDKO, V. N. (1965) Some aspects of the theory of languages, translation to be found in *Cybernetics* of the original which appeared in *Kibernetika*, **1**, No. 4, 12–21.

SALOMAA, A. (1964, 1) Axiom systems for regular expressions of finite automata, *Ann. Univ. Turku. Ser.* AI 75.

SALOMAA, A. (1964, 2) On the reducibility of events represented in automata, *Ann. Acad. Sci. Fenn. Ser.* AI 353.

SALOMAA, A. (1964, 3) Theorems on the representation of events in Moore-automata, *Ann. Univ. Turku. Ser.* AI 69.

SALOMAA, A. (1965) On probabilistic automata with one input letter, *Ann. Univ. Turku. Ser.* AI 85.

SALOMAA, A. (1966, 1) On events represented by probabilistic automata of different types, *Canad. J. Math.*, to appear.

SALOMAA, A. (1966, 2) Two complete axiom systems for the algebra of regular events, *J. Assoc. Comput. Mach.* **13**, 158–69.

SALOMAA, A. (1966, 3) Aksiomatizacija algebry sobytij, realizuemykh logicheskimi setjami, *Problemy Kibernet.* **17**, 237–46.

SALOMAA, A. (1967) On *m*-adic probabilistic automata, *Information and Control* **10**, 215–19.

SCHEINBERG, S. (1960) Note on the Boolean properties of context free languages, *Information and Control* **3**, 372–5.

SCHÜTZENBERGER, M. P. (1963) Context-free languages and pushdown automata, *Information and Control* **6**, 246–64.

SHEPHERDSON, J. C. (1959) The reduction of two-way automata to one-way automata, *IBM J. Res. Develop.* **3**, 198–200.

SMULLYAN, R. (1960) *Theory of Formal Systems*, Princeton Univ. Press.

SPIVAK, M. A. (1965, 1) Algoritm abstraktnogo sinteza avtomatov dlja rasshirennogo jazyka reguljarnykh vyrazhenij, *Izv. Akad. Nauk SSSR Tehn. Kibernet.* No. 1, 51–57.

SPIVAK, M. A. (1965, 2) Razlozhenie reguljarnogo vyrazhenija po bazisu i ego primenenija, *Dokl. Akad. Nauk SSSR* **162**, 520–2.

SPIVAK, M. A. (1965, 3) Representation of automatonic mappings by regular expressions, translation to be found in *Cybernetics* of the original which appeared in *Kibernetika* **1**, No. 6, 15–17.

STARKE, P. H. (1963) Über die Darstellbarkeit von Ereignissen in nichtinitialen Automaten, *Z. Math. Logik Grundlagen Math.* **9**, 315–19.

STARKE, P. H. (1965) Theorie stochastischer Automaten I and II, *Elektron. Informationsverarbeit. Kybernetik* **1**, 5–32 and 71–98.

STARKE, P. H. (1966, 1) Einige Bemerkungen über nicht-deterministische Automaten, *Elektron. Informationsverarbeit. Kybernetik* **2**, 61–82.

STARKE, P. H. (1966, 2) Stochastische Ereignisse und stochastische Operatoren, *Elektron. Informationsverarbeit. Kybernetik* **2**, 177–90.

STARKE, P. H. (1966, 3) Stochastische Ereignisse und Wortmengen, *Z. Math. Logik Grundlagen Math.* **12**, 61–68.

STARKE, P. H. (1967) Über Experimente an Automaten, *Z. Math. Logik Grundlagen Math.* **13**, 67–80.

STEINBY, P. M. (1967) On definite events, manuscript to be published.

THATCHER, J. W. and WRIGHT, J. B. (1966) Generalized finite automata theory with an application to a decision problem of second-order logic, *IBM Research Paper* RC-1713.

TIXIER, V. (1967) Recursive functions of regular expressions in language analysis, Dissertation, Stanford Univ.

TURAKAINEN, P. (1966) On non-regular events representable in probabilistic automata with one input letter, *Ann. Univ. Turku. Ser.* AI 90.

TURAKAINEN, P. (1967) On probabilistic automata, manuscript to be published.

TURING, A. M. (1936) On computable numbers, with an application to the Entscheidungsproblem, *Proc. London Math. Soc.* **42**, 230–65.

YOELI, M. and GINZBURG, A. (1964) On homomorphic images of transition graphs, *J. Franklin Inst.* **278**, 291–6.

SYMBOL INDEX

AUTHOR INDEX

255

SUBJECT INDEX

OTHER TITLES IN THE SERIES IN PURE
AND APPLIED MATHEMATICS